THE FRENCH FOREIGN OFFICE
AND THE ORIGINS OF THE
FIRST WORLD WAR
1898–1914

THE FRENCH FOREIGN OFFICE AND THE ORIGINS OF THE FIRST WORLD WAR
1898–1914

M. B. HAYNE

CLARENDON PRESS · OXFORD
1993

Oxford University Press, Walton Street, Oxford OX2 6DP
Oxford New York Toronto
Delhi Bombay Calcutta Madras Karachi
Petaling Jaya Singapore Hong Kong Tokyo
Nairobi Dar es Salaam Cape Town
Melbourne Auckland
and associated companies in
Berlin Ibadan

Oxford is a trade mark of Oxford University Press

Published in the United States
by Oxford University Press, New York

British Library Cataloguing in Publication Data
Data available

Library of Congress Cataloging-in-Publication Data
Hayne, M.B.
The French Foreign Office and the Origins of the First World War 1898-1914 / M.B. Hayne.
p.   cm.
Includes bibliographical references and index.
1. France—Foreign relations—1870-1940.   2. World War, 1914-1918—Causes.
3. France. Ministère des affaires étrangères—Officials and employees.
4. Foreign ministers—France—History—20th century.
I. Title.
DC369.H36   1993
mi7.44—dc20   92-21914
ISBN 0-19-820270-9

Typeset by BP Integraphics Ltd, Bath, Avon
Printed and bound in Great Britain by
Bookcraft Ltd, Midsomer Norton, Bath

To Grace, Leigh, Emma,
Ken, and Justin

ACKNOWLEDGEMENTS

This book had its origins in a doctoral thesis I undertook at the University of Sydney in the 1980s under the excellent supervision of Dr L. B. Fulton. I take this opportunity to acknowledge my great debt of gratitude to him. His role was not only supervisory. Later he encouraged me to revise and update the work in order to make it publishable. I must also thank Professor James Joll, Professor Richard Bosworth, Dr Keith Hamilton, and Associate Professor Robert Aldrich for comments and constructive criticism.

The University of New England provided me with the financial assistance to complete the work. I was fortunate to receive study leave in 1990 which allowed me much valuable time spent in European archives. I would also like to express my gratitude to those who helped prepare the manuscript for publication: Ms Kim Lawes, Ms Jean Jackson, and Ms Madeleine Hyson. Mr Michael Walkom and Mr Sam Levy read the manuscript and the former helped in compiling the index.

I wish to acknowledge permission to utilize in the book some of the material from previous articles: M. B. Hayne, 'The Quai d'Orsay and Influences on the Formulation of French Foreign Policy, 1898–1914', *French History* (OUP), 2/4 (1988), 427–52; and M. B. Hayne, 'Change and Continuity in the Structure and Practices of the Quai d'Orsay, 1871–1898', *The Australian Journal of Politics and History*, 37/1 (1991), 61–76.

Finally, I would like to express my sincere gratitude to Jacqueline Pritchard for her meticulous copy-editing of the text; and to Mr Anthony Morris, editor at Oxford University Press. His faith, interest, and encouragement in the project have sustained me immeasurably in the task. No author could ask for a better editor.

December 1991   M. B. H.

CONTENTS

ABBREVIATIONS

AE	Affaires étrangères
AN	Archives nationales
AP	Archives privées
BD	G. P. Gooch and H. V. Temperley (eds.), *British Documents on the Origins of the War, 1898–1914* (London, 1926–38)
BN	Bibliothèque nationale
DDF	Ministère des affaires étrangères (ed.), *Documents diplomatiques français, 1871–1914* (Paris, 1930–53)
FO	British Foreign Office
GP	J. Lepsius, A. Mendelssohn Bartholdy, and F. Thimme (eds.), *Die große Politik der europäischen Kabinette, 1871–1914* (Berlin, 1922–7)
Inst. de Fr.	Bibliothèque de l'Institut de France
JO	*Journal officiel*
JOC	*Journal officiel, Chambre*
JOS	*Journal officiel, Sénat*
LN	R. Marchand (ed.), *Un livre noir: Diplomatie d'avant guerre d'après les documents russes: Novembre 1910–juillet 1914*, 2 vols. (Paris, 1922–3)
NLS	National Library, Scotland
NS	New Series
PRO	Public Reference Office, Kew
SP	State Papers

ry—the Quai d'Orsay—
7 of the machinery, the
ation of foreign policy.
s period is undeniable.
possessed a vast colonial
ne to an end. The Quai
n office, was responsible
icy.
1898 marked the begin-
rious career as foreign
which was to alter the
the pre-war period but
1 1898 the Quai d'Orsay
t of war in August 1914
a of French diplomacy.
influence of the leading
with successive foreign
nd of officials, and their
aspects, I am mindful of
s on freedom of choice
lthough *revanchisme* was
not particularly important by the turn of the century, French defeat in
the Franco-Prussian war in 1871, the pervading influence of Léon Gambetta and the national ethos of the École libre des sciences politiques
were of prime importance. Quite simply, the Foreign Ministry held
anti-German sentiments, with the notable exception of Ambassador
Jules Cambon. Even he could not fully escape such sentiments. Maurice
Paléologue, ambassador to St Petersburg in 1914, epitomized the worst
aspects of Germanophobia, with disastrous consequences for French
foreign policy in the July crisis of 1914.

Fritz Fischer and his School created in the 1960s a methodological
revolution in the critical evaluation of foreign policy. They amply illus-
trated in the German case 'Der Primat der Innenpolitik'. Vested interest
groups and extra-governmental forces substantially influenced decision-

making processes. On the other hand, Zara Steiner, while utilizing Fischer's methodology, has shown that the 'Outside World' had a limited impact on the Foreign Office and British government. This was due mostly to a 'firmer constitutional governmental framework'.

However, while the Foreign Office had a considerable consultative voice, ultimate authority rested with the British foreign minister. Almost characteristically the French were positioned rather haphazardly in between. The Third Republic's endemic constitutional and political problems frequently did not allow governments full scope in the formulation of policy, let alone its implementation. Consequently, outside interests and individuals could contribute reasonably significantly to policy. At the same time, the Quai, clearly mindful of the vacuum, stepped in decisively, especially in the Moroccan crises of 1905–6 and 1911 and the July crisis of 1914. For the most part, the Foreign Ministry was sufficiently able to utilize external influences to shape policy predicated on the Rankean principle of 'Der Primat der Außenpolitik'.

Over the last few years considerable attention has been paid to the significant subject of foreign ministries in Europe. Zara Steiner's innovative work *The Foreign Office and Foreign Policy, 1898–1914* (1969) provided a balanced examination of the bureaucratic machinery, the personnel, and the role of the office in the determination and administration of foreign policy. In 1976 Cecil's meritorious *The German Diplomatic Service, 1871–1914* similarly explored the workings of the Wilhelmstrasse and its incumbents. However, it did not concentrate as much on foreign policy issues, understandable given that the Fischer–Geiss debate was producing a plethora of books on German foreign policy at the time.

On the other hand, the Quai d'Orsay has received relatively little treatment despite the obvious importance of the topic. Christopher Andrew's definitive piece *Théophile Delcassé and the Making of the Entente Cordiale* (1968) focused much needed attention on arguably the Third Republic's most famous foreign minister. J. F. V. Keiger's monograph *France and the Origins of the First World War* (1983) provides some very useful insights into the French Foreign Ministry but largely concentrates on the policies of Raymond Poincaré in the period immediately preceding the Great War. Particularly disappointing is the book of P. G. Lauren, *Diplomats and Bureaucrats: The First Institutional Responses to Twentieth Century Diplomacy in France and Germany* (1976). For the most part it is heavily based on official published documents and hardly delves into abundant private manuscript material. Moreover, the piece examines the period between 1871 and 1930. Consequently, the book is punctuated with rather sweeping generalizations. In developing the theme of modernization, it fails quite often to examine paper reforms in a systematic manner or to place them in their proper context. It underestimates resistance to reform from many quarters and somewhat uncritically accepts, on the basis of public papers, that what was officially decreed was actually put into effect. A significant amount of private papers clearly suggests otherwise.

Lauren's book, by examining only the machinery of the Foreign Ministry, misses an essential point. As Ambassador Paul Cambon so frequently remarked, it was because of the personalities and in spite of the machinery that the Quai d'Orsay worked. As Steiner points out, it is people in the long run who make the decisions. No thorough work on the Quai d'Orsay can fail to put emphasis on the individuals.

One of the themes throughout the book is the lack of substantial and structural reform in the Quai d'Orsay. This was to have significant ramifications right up to July 1914. Chapter 7 deals totally with the 1907 reforms. P. G. Lauren's argument that the reforms led to a very substantial change in the organisational structure, the overseas services, and the personnel services of the Quai d'Orsay is untenable. The 1907 reforms, to the contrary, failed to provide a satisfactory basis for the efficient administration of foreign policy between 1907 and 1914. Despite some improvements, the failure of the reforms to create or even envisage a powerful secretary-general with the necessary overall control and co-ordination was a serious structural defect. It allowed bureaucrats and diplomats to retain much, even excessive, independence. While this could often be beneficial in periods of political instability, it might also lead to disastrous consequences.

This book seeks to contribute to the historiography of and the controversy surrounding the origins of the First World War. The last chapter dealing with the July crisis is of particular importance. J. F. V. Keiger has already amply demolished the myth that President Poincaré was urging the Russians to war. Moreover, the visit to St Petersburg between 20 and 23 July by him, René Viviani, the premier, and Foreign Ministry officials was not an occasion for either a war council or an assurance of explicit French diplomatic support. Indeed, during the crisis the government and the Quai d'Orsay in general were decidedly desirous of peace. It is paradoxical then that war came at the very time when the majority of the French, the Quai d'Orsay under Ambassador Paul Cambon's moderating influence, and the French government under Poincaré were pacific. The paradox is explicable in the aggressive policies of Maurice Paléologue, French ambassador to St Petersburg. The chapter focuses on Paléologue and brings forth new evidence which implicates the Ambassador substantially in the responsibility for the onset of war. Because of the serious structural defects in the Quai d'Orsay, it allowed Paléologue such independence and initiative that an 'ambassadorial dictatorship' was established. Such a dictatorship was disastrous and was a highly significant contribution to the outbreak of war in August 1914.

I

The Foreign Ministry at the End of the Nineteenth Century: Its History, Structure, and Practice

Although France has had an important part in the development of modern bureaucracy and although the Quai d'Orsay has been universally recognized as a model of twentieth-century bureaucratic reform, the art of professional diplomacy in France is a relatively recent phenomenon.[1] The words *diplomate* and *diplomatique* were unknown in the seventeenth and eighteenth centuries. They were coined only during the French Revolution in reference to *diplômes* or to eminent written acts of monarchs.[2] Those involved in the conduct of foreign relations outside France were labelled *négociateurs*.

Continuity and specialization were slow to develop. Until the sixteenth century the fate of embassies depended largely on the life of a particular court and society. Embassy staff were appointed and paid until the mid-seventeenth century by the ambassador, and consequently represented him more than the reigning monarch.[3] In the central administration organization was just as irregular. Foreign affairs were discussed in plenum in the king's executive council until the beginning of the seventeenth century. The reading and the transmission of correspondence was divided among four *secrétaires de finances*, who were allowed into the council and who carried the title *secrétaire d'état* after 1557.[4]

During the period after Henri IV's accession in 1589, foreign affairs were placed in the hands of one official, Louis de Revol. The beginnings

[1] The Quai d'Orsay took its name from the building built by Lacornée in 1845 and was situated on the banks of the Seine at 37 Quai d'Orsay. As used here, it refers to the central administration and to the diplomatic and consular services.

[2] A. Outrey, *L'Administration française des affaires étrangères* (Paris, 1954) p. 12. The Quai d'Orsay, under the direction of Monsieur Jean Baillou, has written a collective work about itself from the *ancien régime* to 1980. See *Les Affaires étrangères et le corps diplomatique français* 2 vols. (Paris, 1984).

[3] France sent the first permanent envoys in the early 16th century (Vienna 1509, Florence 1511, Valladolid 1520, London 1521, Venice 1521, Swiss Cantons 1522).

[4] H. Griolet, *Le Ministère des affaires étrangères* (Paris, 1900) p. 6.

of a stable organization were apparent. Revol was made responsible for the Italian states, Piedmont, Savoy, Switzerland, Spain, the Levant, Poland, Sweden, Denmark, Great Britain, and the German states. To provide him with assistance, a *commis* and six clerks were made available and the former was paid 'à raison de quatre livres dix sols par peau de parchemin et de quinze sols par feuillet de papier'.[5]

Subsequent reigns witnessed further evolution. By 1599 the six clerks, previously *expéditionnaires*, now became *rédacteurs* with the rank of *commis*, and the original *commis* became the principal *commis*, the forerunner of the *directeur politique* and *secrétaire-général*. It was, however, during Cardinal Richelieu's period that the change became definitive. His desire for professional competency created widespread reform in most major administrative areas. This was reinforced by Jean-Baptiste Colbert, who, as controller-general of finances under Louis XIV, stressed competence and improved administrative organization and procedure. Records became orderly and registers, memoirs, and periodic accounts were standardized. From 1659 the principal *commis* was joined by two or three *premiers commis*, who directed specialized bureaux and had between three and six *commis* under them by the beginning of the eighteenth century. Two geographical divisions, one embracing Spain, Portugal, Great Britain, the German states, and the Papacy, and the other embracing Turkey, Italy, Poland, Denmark, Russia, Sweden, and Switzerland, were established. In the course of the eighteenth century the *cabinet du ministre*, the Service du chiffre, and the Bureau des fonds were permanently established.[6]

The extent of professionalism should not be exaggerated, however. Although payment on a casual basis was stopped and an annual salary introduced, the exigencies of impoverished royal coffers led to the increased sale of offices in the eighteenth century. As P. G. Lauren suggests, 'Men were more interested in who filled the positions rather than the job itself and jobs were more the result of convenience, opportunity or personal intrigue than a rational system of organization.'[7]

The Revolutionary period in the 1790s gave added impetus to the bureaucratization of foreign affairs. Despite some initial curtailing of

---

[5] AE 'Mémoires et documents', France 31, fo. 310; C. Piccioni, *Les Premiers Commis des affaires étrangères* (Paris, 1929) p. 14.

[6] P. G. Lauren, *Diplomats and Bureaucrats* (Stanford, Calif., 1976), pp. 7–8; Outrey, *L'Administration française*, pp. 17–28.

[7] Lauren, *Diplomats and Bureaucrats*, p. 8; T. Zeldin, *France, 1848–1945*, i (Oxford, 1973) p. 113.

bureaucratic power on the part of the Legislative Assembly, by the time of the Directory (1795–9) the powers of the Foreign Ministry had been restored. Indeed, despite the Revolutionaries' intense dislike of the Bourbon regime, most concurred on the efficacy of its foreign policy. Besides, the National Convention was largely dependent upon experts and was primarily concerned with internal issues. This concurrence and dependence led not only to a restoration of bureaucratic power but to its augmentation. By 1793 the Ministère des relations extérieures had assumed total control over French consular services and foreign commercial relations, a responsibility which had once belonged to the Ministère de la marine. Subsequent decrees and *arrêtés* by the Directory in 1799 and by Napoleon in 1810 ensured that all handling of external correspondence was carried out by the Foreign Ministry and its agents.[8] By 1825, under the leadership of Talleyrand, the foreign minister, the structure of the Foreign Ministry (which was largely to persist until the turn of the century) was well established: political and commercial divisions, chancellery and archives division, protocol, and the private ministerial cabinet.[9]

As well as centralizing foreign affairs within one department, the Revolution and the Napoleonic era had the effect of making 'bureaucracy', especially in the Foreign Ministry, an advantageous 'investment'. Though the great noble families of France bestrode the diplomatic scene, the Ministry also catered to the bourgeoisie. Already the original *commis* received wages considered substantial in the period. They married amongst themselves and hoped to pass their employment on to their children. Consequently, the Revolution led to the blossoming of bureaucracy. A new notion of the public official arose. There was an attempt to define rights concerning remuneration, advancement, discipline and retirement, and a community of grades was established between the central administration and the external services.[10]

The Foreign Ministry won more than its fair share of attention in the bureaucratic 'expansion' which ensued in the nineteenth century. Though numbers remained quite small, the Foreign Ministry attracted the ambitious and status-seeking official superior in education and upbringing to counterparts in other departments. Admittedly the sale of offices was ended by the Revolution, but attachment to office-holding

---

[8] AE 'Organisation et règlements du Ministère', 1547–1806, fo. 182ᵛ.
[9] Outrey, *L'Administration française*, pp. 36–8, 42–3.
[10] Ibid. pp. 25, 29, 30.

remained strong. The civil service was seen as a desirable alternative to industry or to the liberal professions, which were considered risky by many. Though there might be only a moderate return, the Ministry offered a relatively safe career, reasonably high wages for the most senior posts, and required a relatively small investment of capital. When other civil services diminished in status towards the end of the century, the Quai d'Orsay remained relatively unaffected. For the aristocracy, the Foreign Ministry remained one of the few avenues open to it. More importantly, diplomacy was considered one of the few careers worthy of an aristocrat's attention.[11]

That the Revolution or the establishment of the Third Republic in 1871 inherently led to equality of opportunity was a myth. Admittedly there was a long-standing tradition of bourgeois employment in the Foreign Ministry and there was a qualitative difference between it and the thoroughly aristocratic foreign offices of Germany or Britain. Nevertheless, the education necessary to enter the Foreign Ministry was expensive and available mostly to those with a high income. Until 1894 candidates had to have a private income of 6,000 francs. Finally, while merit was needed to enter, 'supposedly democratic competitions set up by the Revolution were generally decided by criteria of patronage and nepotism'.[12]

Until the Delcassian period after 1898 the aristocracy continued to dominate the higher positions. Even after 1871 there was remarkably little discussion over the removal of personnel of the Second Empire. Changes in the Foreign Ministry were due more to normal retirement or to resignation by diplomats refusing to serve than by a movement on the part of the government. Actual purges were directed more at the incompetents and loafers than against supporters of a political grouping. While ambassadors associated with the Second Empire resigned, they were replaced by other less compromised aristocrats. Of the eleven young men in the cabinet of the Marquis de Moustier (1866–8) only four retired, willingly or unwillingly. Laboulaye and Montebello ended up as ambassadors in St Petersburg. Despite a reaction against Bonapartism, Bonapartists such as Valfrey and Chaudordy were left virtually untouched in their positions unless they openly defied the government.

---

[11] E. Charton, *Guide pour le choix d'un état* (Paris, 1842) p. 261; D. Halévy, *La République des comités* (Paris, 1934), p. 42.

[12] Zeldin, *France*, i. 113–16. From the Foreign Ministry's inception, the *petit bourgeois* have provided many of the *commis* of the 17th and 18th centuries. See Outrey, *L'Administration Française*, pp. 12–20.

Both Desprez, *directeur politique*, and Fourand, *directeur commercial*, were called on to remain in their positions and to ensure continuity.[13]

The wish to preserve continuity was the prime reason that a significant cleaning out of the Augean stables did not result. Favre, the new Republic's first foreign minister, was at pains to ensure it. Remusat, his successor in August 1871, though very much against the Second Empire, defended his existing personnel, believing the Ministry to be 'assez bien organisé'. He considered that change would naturally evolve from the recruitment and education of a new breed. Thiers, the first Republican president, had doubts about retaining imperial officials but applied his reservations sparingly. He was much more concerned to satisfy the monarchist majority in Parliament and to choose aristocrats with good personal positions and wealth.[14]

Other factors were at work. The Republic, facing a considerable threat to its existence from left-wing elements and extremely unsure of its political and constitutional framework, was preoccupied with internal rather than external issues. Governmental instability, which became inherent in the Third Republic, allowed the Quai d'Orsay a substantial measure of autonomy. Moreover, many diplomats were able to retain their posts because they did not venture into the realm of politics and acted normally as departmental specialists. Some diplomats showed a capacity to adapt to the dominant opinion. Finally, change was unlikely when relatively unimportant or disagreeable posts, especially those outside Europe, were involved.[15]

Yet, despite many similarities with the Wilhelmstraße and the British Foreign Office, the Quai d'Orsay was evolving along more bourgeois lines. A definite transition period ensued between 1877 and 1880, when the monarchists lost their hold on power. The new Republican majority was resolved on far more than touching the tip of the diplomatic iceberg. They wanted the republicanization of the civil service. As a result de Gontaut·Biron, de Broglie, Banneville, Bourgoing, Baude, Chaudordy, Choiseul-Praslin, d'Harcourt, de Vogé, Le Flô, and Gabriac all left the service. Jules Herbette, *chef du cabinet* at the time, persecuted anti-

[13] G. Kreis, 'Frankreichs republikanische Großmachtpolitik, 1870–1914', Ph.D. thesis (Basle, University, 1980), pp. 32–4. La Valette (London), La Tour (Vienna), Fleury (St Petersburg), Sevard (Quirinal), La Guerronière (Constantinople), Mercier (Madrid), de Chateaurenard (Berne), and Treilnara (Washington) all resigned or were forced to leave, but their successors, such as de Broglie, Noailles, Choiseul-Praslin, de Bouille, de Gontaut Biron, de Vogüé, d'Harcourt, and Le Flô, were almost always aristocrats.

[14] Gabriac to Chaudordy, 4 Mar. 1871, AE Chaudordy MSS.

[15] Kreis, 'Frankreichs Großmachtpolitik', p. 36; B. Auffray, *Pierre de Margerie (1861–1942) et la vie diplomatique de son temps* (Paris, 1976), p. 28.

Republican elements with vigour. By 1880 a new élite based on a
common educational background was emerging, and measures were
enacted to ensure that wages would attract Republican candidates. By
1898 75 per cent of the diplomatic and consular services were not aristocratic. For all that, however, the nature and extent of the diplomatic
purges, so little described by contemporaries and lumped together with
other *épurations*, should not be exaggerated. As was often the case,
politicians, once their immediate wishes had been fulfilled, did little to
follow up systematically reforms which required time, patience, and
effort. Some aristocrats were eliminated and the Quai d'Orsay was
becoming gradually bourgeois, but change was effected haphazardly.
Aristocrats who showed a reasonable disposition towards the Republic
continued to fill many important posts after 1880.[16]

On the whole, the results were rather disappointing for most Republicans. In view of France's abysmal credit in foreign courts after the
defeat in 1871, French governments were prone to send aristocrats of
great standing to important posts. Moreover, even if a Republican represented the French government, he usually made a clear distinction
between internal and international politics. Though the Russians might
occasionally play the 'Marseillaise', republicanism was simply not an
export commodity. Like his aristocratic counterpart, the new Republican diplomat also found parliamentary politics thoroughly repugnant even if he accepted the Republic as the least harmful form of
government.[17]

Largely because of the unstable nature of politics in nineteenth-
century France, the structure of the Foreign Ministry by 1898 had
changed but little since Talleyrand's time. In essence, there was a *direction politique*, a *direction commerciale*, and a *cabinet du ministre*, as well as
protocol, archives, and accounts departments. The foreign minister
presided over these bodies. In the period prior to the Revolution he had

[16] AE de Billy MSS, carton 1, pp. 14–15, 101; G. Hanotaux, *Histoire de la France contemporaine* (Paris, 1898), iv. 445; speech by E. Spuller, budget report, Sénat, 6 Dec. 1877,
no.178, p. 11; budget report of 4 Nov. 1878 for 1879, no.850, p. 18; report of Antoine Proust, 14
June 1880, no.2736, p. 3; report of 20 June 1882, no.992, p. 17; L. Legrand, 20 June 1882 for
1883, no.992, p. 3.

[17] De Freycinet in the 1890s had tried to purge the nobility but a large number still
remained afterwards. See J. F. V. Keiger, 'Raymond Poincaré and French Foreign Policy,
1912–1914', Ph.D. thesis (Cambridge University, 1980), p. 37; Comte de Saint-Aulaire, *Confessions d'un vieux diplomate* (Paris, 1953), pp. 27, 30–1; J. Cambon to P. de Margerie, 1
Mar. 1906, AE J. Cambon MSS, 11; C. Charle has calculated that in 1886 75% of *titulaires*
of important posts were aristocratic. C. Charle, *Les Hauts Fonctionnaires en France au
xix* *siècle* (Paris, 1979), pp. 153–4; E. Weber, *The Nationalist Revival in France, 1905–1914*
(Los Angeles, 1968), p. 99.

involved himself as much with the administration of his department as with political affairs, but the rise of a theoretically responsible system largely put an end to the former role. Under the Third Republic he acted often as a spokesman for the department, trying to account to Parliament as best he could and handling the various commissions in existence. In this task he was usually successful. Normally, the foreign minister was a lawyer with journalistic experience, as well as a member of the Chamber of Deputies adept at presenting his advisers' case to his colleagues.

Officially his duties comprised the negotiation and implementation of political and commercial treaties in addition to correspondence with diplomatic and commercial agents, but often he did not participate in the formulation of diplomatic policy. Apart from the fact that his parliamentary duties severely restricted his time at the Quai d'Orsay, he rarely lasted long enough to comprehend his duties sufficiently, let alone set a clearly defined course. Governments often rose and fell in a matter of months. At any rate, there were many occasions when a foreign minister took little active interest in his department. As Saint-Aulaire, a pre-war diplomat, rather sarcastically and a touch exaggeratedly remarked, 'En ce temps-là, sauf une fois par an pour donner au rapporteur du budget l'illusion qu'il les connaissait, aucun ministre ne pénétrait jamais dans ses bureaux.'[18]

The official representative of the minister, and hence of the government, was the ambassador (or a minister plenipotentiary in the case of a legation). It was noticeable that the power of the French representative abroad was substantially greater than that of his British or German counterpart in the latter half of the nineteenth century. In the British case, constitutional and stable government made the chain of command clear and diplomatic representatives, while having a voice, were rarely of decisive importance. In Germany diplomats existed in an atmosphere of subservience to the chancellor and the emperor. French diplomats, in contrast, were imbued with a sense of their own importance, which was in part a legacy of former aristocratic days and in part a product of their

---

[18] Saint-Aulaire, *Confessions*, p. 29; P. Cambon, to J. Cambon 9 Nov. 1908, AE J. Cambon MSS, 25; F. L. Schuman, *War and Diplomacy in the French Republic* (New York, 1931), pp. 30–1; *Almanach impérial* 1805 (Paris, 1805), p. 120; AE *Annuaire diplomatique et consulaire* (1889). Schuman says that between 1871 and 1931 there were 37 different foreign ministers but more ministries (*War and Diplomacy*, 30). D. J. Miller states that between 1880 and 1914 there were 39 different ministries averaging 7½ months. (L. Abrams and D. J. Miller, 'Who were the French Colonialists: A Reassessment of the "Parti colonial", 1890–1914', *Historical Journal*, 19 (1976), p. 704.)

education. Primarily, however, it was derived from the instability of the new Republican regime, and the turnover of foreign ministers. This state of affairs encouraged the ambassador to assume a large measure of independence and to take personal initiatives to safeguard France's higher interests. He saw himself as owing allegiance to the state rather than to a government, often had contempt for inept and inexperienced foreign ministers, and believed that, in view of cabinet's incapacity to set policy strategies, it was he who should actually formulate and direct policy in important areas.[19]

The most important section of the Quai d'Orsay was the political division, raised to the status of division (along with the commercial division) during Talleyrand's period. It dealt with all political matters and personnel. In the 1880s, it suffered a considerable decline when matters of personnel were increasingly handled by the minister's private cabinet. This development led to a serious rivalry between the two, which remained strong down to the First World War. The division itself was badly organized. In many instances political directors were appointed on the basis of friendship rather than ability. Lower positions were often assigned with little regard for qualifications. Non-specialists lacked clear-cut instructions and adequate supervision from above, as well as proper dossiers, journals, and lists of precedents. Work was conducted in a leisurely manner, and rarely did officials in the division achieve a six-hour working day.[20]

The head of the division was the political director. In view of the rapid turnover of ministers, their inexperience, and their preoccupation with parliamentary matters, he came to assume the role of chief manager of foreign affairs. Officially, he was concerned with the administration of all political and legal matters which the minister did not directly deal with, but in reality he usually handled matters *in toto*. When the minister was absent he presided over the Comité des services extérieurs et administratifs and he took precedence over the other directors.

The significance of his position was more a function of specific circumstances than of official regulations. Indeed, his position was only vaguely defined. It was shaped by the attitude of the foreign minister, who was often moved by political considerations or by personal friendships. In no sense was it a permanent under-secretaryship in the

[19] J. Cambon to P. Cambon, 18 Dec. 1905, 15 Mar. 1906, J. Cambon to de Margerie, 1 Mar. 1906, AE J. Cambon MSS, 19, 11; Saint-Aulaire, *Confessions*, pp. 30–1.
[20] Raindre to Billot, 18 Dec. 1882, AE Billot MSS; Herbette to Ring, 1885, AE Ring MSS, 15; A. Bréal, *Philippe Berthelot* (Paris, 1937), p. 51.

British sense and it was dependent on changes of ministries and elections.

The political director was sometimes placed at a distinct disadvantage in relation to ambassadors. He was himself only a *ministre plénipotentiaire* and in many instances could find it difficult to get his instructions or those of his government put into effect by ambassadors. Normally his position was seen as transitory, a stepping-stone to an embassy. Unlike most other directors in more technical services, the political director was a relatively young man by no means at the end of his career.

Finally, a political director's relationship with his subordinates and his own ability for work were relevant factors in determining his prestige. Laziness or an inability to master the often intricate and confused diplomatic machinery were indicators of failure. In particular, a failure to control deputy directors, usually little departmental imperialists, could seriously impair his authority.[21]

The political division was subdivided into numerous subdivisions with deputy directors at their head. The most prestigious was the *Sous-direction du Nord*, which dealt with Britain, Russia, Austria-Hungary, Germany, and the Scandinavian states. The *Sous-direction du Midi* was responsible for all remaining affairs but was never considered 'la grande sous-direction, celle de la haute politique et ... un poste d'honneur' like the other. It not only had an inferior brand of tea, but, more seriously, suffered constant incursions into its territory by ambitious officials in the Nord.[22]

Two other subdivisions suffered even worse fates. The *sous-direction des colonies*, created in the 1890s as a result of increasing interest in overseas possessions, dealt with colonies and central and southern Africa. It had originally started in 1881 as the Bureau de la Tunisie but later Annam, Madagascar, Obok, the French Congo, and the West Coast of Africa were added. It had had an inauspicious beginning due mainly to the jealousies of the Nord and Midi, and to the creation of a Colonial Ministry. Its chief had little status, being a mere *sous-directeur adjoint*.[23]

The final subdivision, the *Sous-direction du contentieux*, had had a varied existence in the nineteenth century. At one time it was a *direction autonome* (1880), but eventually it became a subdivision in the political division. It

[21] Auffray, *De Margerie* pp. 227–8; F. Lytton (Paris), Conf. no. 151, 18 Mar. 1889, fo. 99/274, Lytton to Salisbury, 27 Jan., 30 Mar., 15 Oct., 1888, SP 57; Dufferin to Salisbury, 3 June 1892, SP 59; Lyons to Salisbury, 27 Nov. 1885, SP 37; Charle, *Fonctionnaires* p. 172.
[22] Jusserand to Nisard, 31 Mar., 20 June 1890, AE Jusserand MSS, 21.
[23] Rocco to Doulcet, 4 Dec. 1896, AE Doulcet MSS, 17; *Annuaire diplomatique* (1898–1905), ch. 1.

dealt basically with international law and was strictly a technical division. As international law became increasingly important at the turn of the century and international conflicts more widespread, it developed into a more active part of the division. In the years preceding the First World War it was the instrument of attacks directed against the aristocracy.[24]

The other major section of the Quai d'Orsay was the commercial division, often disparagingly labelled the grocery by those in the political division. It was concerned with commerce abroad and foreign trade in France; the preparation of commercial and navigation treaties, commercial tariffs, monetary conventions, patent tariffs, consular affairs, and agents in the consular service. When the Foreign Ministry assumed total control over French commercial service, the *chef du bureau* and his six employees were transferred from the Marine. By Talleyrand's time the commercial section had increased in status from bureau to division.[25]

This upgrading could not mask its marked inferiority to the political division. Diplomatic and consular cadres remained distinct in principle. Initially, those unfortunate enough not to gain sufficient marks in the *concours* or those who did not have sufficient patronage were exiled to the consular service, doomed to read endless reports on Brazilian coffee. This boring, mundane employment was eased, however, as a result of the new imperialism of the latter half of the nineteenth century. Though the political division remained thoroughly European in its orientation, Africa, Asia, and America became increasingly important to French business and to French foreign policy. Consequently, not only did the work of the commercial division radically increase, but its chiefs gained a more substantial voice in political matters in regions where commerce and politics were closely linked. By the first decade of the twentieth century French officials were clearly leading the way in actively promoting French financial and business interests. Their European counterparts, while supporting national business concerns when required, were not as eager to participate in the often aggressive economic salesmanship of the French. By the twentieth century the stigma of being in the consular corps was not as great. Officials such as Raindre,

---

[24] A. Outrey, 'L'Histoire et principes de l'administration française des affaires étrangères', *Revue française de science politique*, 3 (1953), pp. 714–15; See also AE Beaucaire MSS, 10.
[25] Outrey, *L'Administration française*, pp. 15–30.

Louis, Berthelot, and Jusserand, who had begun their careers in it, were able to establish themselves in the top echelons of the diplomatic corps.[26]

But the very fact that they transferred to the diplomatic corps clearly demonstrated that the consular corps had not achieved an equality of status. Furthermore, though France was a leader in the recognition of new twentieth-century economic and geographic areas, change was still slow in coming, and pre-war French diplomatic considerations still revolved around the traditional European conglomeration. The role defined for a consul also involved limitations. In no strict sense did a consul represent the national government before a foreign power. His duty was to establish a liaison with fellow nationals and to defend their pecuniary interests. Consuls frequently complained of having to act as a courier service for French products, and when they encroached upon the diplomat's ground they were severely rebuked.

Finally, agents in the consular corps were often sent to the most abysmal backwaters of the globe. The French consular corps, to its credit, established consulates in the remotest regions of Asia, Oceania, and Africa, where commercial relations were assuming increasing importance. However, its representatives suffered the most atrocious conditions: extreme temperatures, unsanitary conditions, pestilence, political anarchy, and strange, unfriendly cultures. Though Palmerston was certainly correct in labelling French consuls 'vain' and 'petulant', the consul's 'lot was not a happy one'.[27]

Apart from the two major divisions, there were specialist services. The Division des fonds et de la comptabilité dealt with wages, secret funds, diplomatic gifts, and the costs incurred in running the administration. In 1898, the Division appeared to have little organization. Wages were sometimes paid months, or even years, late. The most elementary public accounting rules were disregarded. While the division was nominally accountable to the Finance Minister and subject to scrutiny by the Cour

[26] French consuls in the Levant had been far more active than their British counterparts as a result of the alliance between Francis I and Suleiman the Magnificent. In 1606 the first capitulations were signed between Turkey and France granting official recognition and immunities to French consuls. France created a career consular corps in 1833. See D. Busk, *The Craft of Diplomacy* (London, 1967), p. 125; Walewski to Louis, 7 July 1882, 23 July 1884, AE Louis MSS, 1; Henry to Pichon, 28 July 1909, Inst. de Fr. Pichon MSS, 3. Blade to Jusserand, 9 Oct. 1903, AE Jusserand MSS, 22. Saint-Aulaire, *Confessions* p. 241; Louis to Pichon, 14 May 1904, Inst. de Fr. Pichon MSS, 3.

[27] Paléologue to Collin de Plancy, 19 Aug. 1886, AE Collin de Plancy MSS, 2; ibid., Cogordan to Plancy, 12 July, undated; Raindre to Valfrey, undated 1878, AE Valfrey MSS, 2; 'Souvenirs: Russie, ancien régime' pp. 30–1, 'Notes concernant le Quai d'Orsay' p. 4, AN de Robien MSS; F. V. Parsons, *The Origins of the Morocco Question, 1880–1900* (London, 1976), p. 564.

des comptes and legislative commissions, it was not until immediately before First World War that the management of funds was subject to regular procedures. Unscrupulous officials were able so often to arrange the books in order to make profits for themselves that by 1913 the Quai d'Orsay was on the verge of bankruptcy. Yet corruption did not fully account for the Quai d'Orsay's financial predicament. It always employed double the numbers of the British Foreign Office and, especially after the 1907 reforms, increasing sophistication and expansion required considerable money. During the years 1898-1914, however, the Foreign Ministry's budget was increased only twofold and suffered from inflation of the franc.[28]

The archives were no better organized. The Division des archives (in the political division since 1880 and a subdivision from 1882) dealt with the preservation, classification, and communication of documents. It was far more suited to catering for the needs of historians such as Hanotaux, Paléologue, and Beaucaire than to meeting the demands of late nineteenth-century diplomacy. Moreover, documents were distributed unevenly and to a select élite. Archivists were loath to open the Quai d'Orsay's treasures to the public or to publish documentary publications which might implicate the makers of French foreign policy.[29]

Another little-known but important bureau was the Bureau du protocole. In 1814, Talleyrand grouped the protocol, diplomatic presents, passports, and naturalization into a Direction des chancelleries, to which the archives were attached in 1825. By 1844 the Bureau du protocole had a separate existence. The bureau dealt with all ceremonies, voyages, and the accreditation of diplomats. In the 1880s, under the guidance of Armand Mollard, the bureau assumed an importance which it had never had before, and, in the period preceding the war those in or assuming the direction of the bureau were described as the 'Dynastie Mollard'. Undoubtedly French Republican governments wished to compensate for not having a ready-made monarch and court society by impressing neighbouring officials, and it was to be doubted, as one protocole official once remarked, whether the court under Louis XIV had been more 'formaliste'. Moreover, the *rédacteur au protocole* frequently drafted important speeches. By 1902, the one official previously employed by the bureau had been replaced by ten, six of whom

---

[28] Chevandrier de Valdrome to Fonds, 24 Aug. 1908, AE Chevandrier de Valdrome MSS; Lauren, *Diplomats and Bureaucrats*, pp. 13, 95; Schuman, *War and Diplomacy*, p. 39.
[29] Lauren, *Diplomats and Bureaucrats*, p. 13.

were honorary. Nor was work in the bureau a menial task. The chief often had the ear of the foreign minister or of the president of the Republic, and former heads such as Philippe Crozier, who became ambassador to Vienna, were able to advance their careers.[30]

The liaison between the foreign minister and the divisions was the private ministerial cabinet. This was a specially selected group of assistants brought in to handle correspondence, arrange meetings, and act as a distributing centre for the divisions. It was a personal office staff and supposedly non-consultative. Though a minister might introduce members from outside the service, he would normally rely on bringing in officials already in the Quai d'Orsay who would return to the divisions or to overseas service after the end of a ministry. As such, the private ministerial cabinet rarely brought fresh ideas into a new ministry. Its workings were hardly discernible apart from the registered date of arrival of a despatch, and it was generally noted more for frequent leakages and indiscretions than for its competence.

Nevertheless, though its work was hardly perceptible it came to have an increasingly substantial consultative role. First, a minister who was inexperienced and preoccupied with electoral or Parliamentary business might often rely on his *chef du cabinet*. If the minister survived a certain period, the *chef* could assume the role of *de facto* under-secretary of state. Secondly, the political division was losing ground to the cabinet in matters of personnel. Officially the political division was charged with 'l'examen du toutes les questions qui se rattachent au personnel', but foreign ministers, under pressure from Parliamentary colleagues hoping to finish their careers in overseas service or to place their protégés in good positions, eroded its power. Desprez, political director in the 1870s, had consulted Pontécoulant, the *chef du cabinet*, so that the ministers or their private cabinets were not entirely to blame, but in the 1880s the private ministerial cabinet was clearly challenging the political director for control of personnel matters.

There was considerable confusion over the attributions and power of the *chef du cabinet*. First, there was both a *chef du cabinet* and a *directeur du cabinet*, although usually both positions were filled by the same official. The director maintained control over two departments, the cabinet proper and the Personnel. In precedence he ranked after the political and commercial directors and the three *chefs* (Protocole, Archives,

[30] *JOC*; J. Serres, *Manuel pratique de protocole à l'usage des postes diplomatiques et consulaires de France à l'étranger* (Paris, 1950); R. Dollot, *Les Introducteurs des ambassadeurs, 1585–1900* (Paris, 1901), p. 80; Desprez to de Mouy, 10 Jan. 1877, AE de Mouy MSS.

Comptabilité). His power derived from the particular relationships he sustained with the foreign minister, the political and commercial directors, and the *chefs du personnel* (when the latter were not *chefs du cabinet et du personnel*). Often the foreign minister chose his *chef du cabinet* on the basis of compatibility and friendship. Chiefs who enjoyed the minister's favour could exercise substantial influence.[31]

Perhaps the most influential department within the private ministerial cabinet was the *cabinet noir*, a secret section of the Cipher Office which opened letters and deciphered telegrams. Its origins dated back to the time of Richelieu. Though the *cabinet noir* was abolished in June 1790 as an office unworthy of the new Revolutionary France, Napoleon resurrected it under the jurisdiction of the Foreign Ministry. During the Second Empire, Victor Hugo attached to his letters the plea 'affaires de famille, inutile de lire', but to no avail. Until the invention of the telegram, it was employed mostly for internal political purposes.[32]

Though initially abolished by the Third Republic, it was soon resurrected and expressly utilized by the Quai d'Orsay for the deciphering of telegrams and, to a lesser extent, for the opening of letters. The British statesmen Gladstone and Lansdowne were only two of the many foreign leaders who became its victims. By the turn of the century the codes of Italy, Britain, Turkey, and Germany were all being deciphered, and the Spanish code was broken by 1906 at the latest. Russia's and Austria-Hungary's remained intact, probably because both countries themselves possessed well-run *cabinets noirs*.[33]

Though the *cabinet noir* was employed before the 1900s, it was during this period that it rose to particular prominence as a result of a professional cryptologist, Étienne Bazeries, a former army commandant who had joined the Quai d'Orsay in 1899. Yet, if anything, it had a rather negative influence on the course of French diplomacy because of Bazeries's peculiar methods and personality. At the same time, foreign

[31] Parsons, *The Origins of the Morocco Question*, pp. 562, 615; Schuman, *War and Diplomacy*, p. 35; Auffray, *De Margerie*, p. 228; Billot to Hanotaux, 8 Oct. 1885, AE Hanotaux MSS, 17; Raindre to Billot, 18 Dec. 1882, AE Billot MSS; Herbette to Ring, 1885, AE Ring MSS, 15. P. Legendre, *Origines et histoire des cabinets de ministres en France* (Geneva, 1975), p. 77; on indiscretions, see Dumaine to Doulcet, 12 May 1892, AE Doulcet MSS, 15; J. Cambon to de Margerie, 30 Mar. 1914, AE de Margerie MSS.

[32] See E. Vaillé, *Le Cabinet noir* (Paris, 1950).

[33] Monson to Lansdowne, 21 Feb. 1902, PRO, FO 800/12 Lansdowne MSS; C. M. Andrew, 'Déchiffrement et diplomatie: Le Cabinet noir du Quai d'Orsay sous la Troisième République', *Relations internationales*, 5 (1976), pp. 38–64; E. Carton de Wiart, *Léopold II: Souvenirs des dernières années, 1901–1909* (Brussels, 1944), p. 196. According to Andrew, its 'apparent existence caused widespread shock in France', C. M. Andrew, *Théophile Delcassé and the Making of the Entente Cordiale* (London, 1968), p. 69.

ministers and agents seemed 'mesmerized' by it. During the Dreyfus affair it incorrectly deciphered important Italian telegrams relevant to Dreyfus and in the course of the pre-war years its errors were more numerous than its accomplishments.[34]

The other bureau was that of personnel. When the *chef du personnel* was not the *directeur du cabinet*, the director, in the name of the minister, retained the final voice. It was a particularly inept bureau, badly managed, disrupted by secretive personnel, and lacking an objective set of rules. In May 1882 *dossiers personnels* were introduced (including *notes du chef, promotions, références et recommendations, sections réservés,* and *divers*) in the forlorn hope of providing a rational system of advancement for and information about agents. These dossiers, unfortunately, were not kept completely up to date. At times, the bureau seemed at a loss to account for all its agents and was sometimes forced to take an unofficial census. Up until the twentieth century there was no foreign ministry union, the directors being authoritarian and skilled at using individual ambitions to prevent the formation of syndicates. There was no established procedure for promotion and the hostility of ministers, politicians, high officials, and *directeurs du cabinet* sufficed often to hinder the promotion of meritorious or senior agents. Patronage allowed men to further their careers in the Centrale. Though there was an avalanche of requests for the more influential foreign positions, applicants with sway usually succeeded in obtaining them.[35]

For those who were not in the top echelons of the Quai d'Orsay, work was generally unsatisfying. Those entering the service learned their trade copying *ad infinitum* letters largely irrelevant to the issues of the day. Agents slightly higher on the scale fared little better, organizing reports, copying a superior's work, and rarely being included in decision-making. Often, because of the antiquated structure of the divisions, there was duplication of effort.[36]

Service in the Quai d'Orsay was not the path to wealth, though the French salaried system compared favourably with the British Foreign

[34] R. Candela, *The Military Cipher of Commandant Bazeries* (New York, 1938), pp. 6–7; AN F7 12829; note by Bazeries, 11 June 1900, AN F7 12829; telegram by G. Louis, AE, NS 'Espagne', 41.

[35] Taigny to Beaucaire, 26 May 1905, AE Beaucaire MSS, 1; Berthelot to Collin de Plancy, 21 Aug. 1907, AE Collin de Plancy MSS; Auffray, *De Margerie*, p. 230; Rouvier to Louis, 15 Apr. 1906, AE Louis MSS, 17; Saint-Aulaire, *Confessions*, p. 33; Charle, *Fonctionnaires*, pp. 171, 181; note, AE *dossier personnel*, Bompard; Lauren, *Diplomats and Bureaucrats*, pp. 100, 103, 107, 108.

[36] Charle, *Fonctionnaires*, p. 159; Delavaud to Delcassé, 17 July 1903, AE Delcassé MSS, 4; J. Laroche, *Au Quai d'Orsay avec Briand et Poincaré* (Paris, 1957) pp. 10–11.

Office and the Wilhelmstraße. The civil service was considered an important area of employment in France. Furthermore, the Republic had attempted to upgrade salaries in the hope of attracting permanent officials of bourgeois Republican persuasion. Yet good intentions did not necessarily translate into adequate incomes. Those working in the Centrale flourished but those representing France abroad often found that income did not meet expenses. Housing and entertainment expenses were frequently met from diplomats' private purses. In fact, the costs in embassies such as St Petersburg, Vienna, and Constantinople were prohibitive. Only the wealthy such as Montebello could hope to advance to the most senior positions. Those with lesser fortunes were forced to reject advantageous posts.[37]

Even apart from the fact that wages often did not meet expenses, the mismanagement or lack of funds by Personnel and Comptabilité led to chaotic situations. Many agents complained of having to wait months, even years, to receive their 'traitement'. Others, like Gaston Raindre, political director during Delcassé's first period as foreign minister, had to be satisfied with receiving salaries below their official entitlement. Agents might be promoted to a higher level but, because there was a certain ceiling on each hierarchical grade, they could not advance until someone in their grade moved higher, resigned, or retired. Not a few officials regularly complained of abominably low wages awarded at spasmodic intervals.[38]

The Bureau du personnel could not safeguard career diplomats from the frequent entry into the service of prefects and politicians, a process which exacerbated the problems already resulting from unbridled patronage and intrigue. During the 1880s and 1890s there was a constant

[37] In 1898 there were 122 in the diplomatic corps and 427 in the consular corps. France had embassies in 10 countries and legations in 26. Ambassadors received 40,000 francs, heads of legations 24,000–30,000, the political director 20,000–25,000, deputy directors 10,000, and attachés 150–1,500 francs. Wages hardly advanced in the immediate pre-war period. Representation costs between 1904 and 1913 were held at existing levels: St Petersburg 170,000 francs; London 160,000; Vienna 120,000; Constantinople 110,000; Berlin 100,000; Rome 80,000; Madrid 70,000; Berne 20,000; Tokyo 90,000; Washington 120,000. Wages levelled off and representation costs were reviewed yearly, sometimes resulting in considerable reductions. See J. Cambon to Pichon, 7 Feb. 1910, AE J. Cambon MSS, 16; *Annuaires diplomatiques*, (*1898–1914*); J. Cambon to de Margerie, 6 Feb. 1914, AE de Margerie MSS; budget report, Sénat, 2 Nov. 1878 for 1879, no.850, p. 18; 14 June 1880, no.2736, p. 3; 20 June 1892, no.992, p. 17.

[38] Chevalley to de Billy, 21 Aug. 1905, AE de Billy MSS, 27; note by Raindre for Delcassé (undated), AE *dossier personnel*, Raindre; Herbette to Delavaud, undated, AE *dossier personnel*, Herbette; Berthelot to Collin de Plancy, 20 July 1907, AE Collin de Plancy MSS, 25.

influx of *intrus* into important embassies or legations. Of 199 men who were prefects between 1876 and 1918, thirteen became diplomats. Of the twenty men appointed as ambassadors between 1898 and 1914, ten (Bompard, Touchard, Delcassé, the Cambons, Constans, Bihourd, Revoil, Barrère, and Gérard) came from prefectoral, military, or political posts.[39]

This constant threat of an inundation of higher positions by politically motivated *intrus* had a deleterious effect upon the *esprit de corps* of the Quai d'Orsay and led to resentment and lack of initiative on the part of career diplomats. The politicians were particularly blameworthy. Though they excused 'intrusions' by the need to place in important posts men whose allegiance to the Republic was known, their own ambitions were generally the motivating factor. An embassy was the perfect conclusion to a political career and appealed to those who wished to combine a diplomatic with a parliamentary career.[40]

In the late nineteenth century nepotism, patronage, and political persuasion were more often the determinants at basic entry level than merit. These informal factors remained highly influential in the early decades of the twentieth century, but their importance was somewhat diminished by the introduction of a regular *concours*. In the eighteenth century, the *concours* had appeared in the *corps technique*. Surprisingly enough, though the Revolution emphasized the ideal of merit over those of wealth or family, it was only in 1825, under the Restoration, that the first rather crude *concours* took place in the Foreign Ministry. Even this procedure was not formalized until 1848. Not until the years 1872–4 was a serious attempt made at the establishment of formal examinations, and not until the turn of the century did these become regular occurrences.[41]

The exams were rigorous. They were dominated by European questions and demanded considerable rote-learning. The *concours* could be attempted annually in the first two weeks of April by those between 21

[39] G. Kreis is of the opinion that if an *intru* had been in the Quai d'Orsay longer than 10 years he should then be labelled a 'career' diplomat. Thus in 1880, 3 out of 10 were *intrus*; in 1890, 2 out of 10, and in 1900, 2 out of 10. In 1910 all were career diplomats. These figures do not clearly show, however, that proper career men in the period 1898–1914 could not occupy 50% of ambassadorial posts. See Kreis, Frankreichs 'Großmachtpolitik', Notes p. 100 n. 295; J. Siwek-Pouydesseau, *Le Corps préfectoral sous la Troisième et la Quatrième République* (Paris, 1969), p. 70.

[40] P. Cambon to H. Cambon, 24 Oct. 1899, 12 Mar. 1909, Louis Cambon MSS (in private hands); Beau to Barrère, Apr. 1896, AE Barrère MSS, 1; Constans to Pichon, 31 Jan. 1909, AE Constans MSS, 3.

[41] Outrey, *L'Administration française*, p. 43; Charle, *Fonctionnaires*, p. 40; 'Conditions d'admission dans les carrières diplomatiques et consulaires', 24 Apr. 1900, AE Beaucaire MSS, 10.

and 27 years old. By 1898, a degree in law, letters, or sciences or a *diplôme* from schools like the École des chartes, the École nationale des mines, the École normale supérieure, the École polytechnique or the École libre des sciences politiques was required as a prerequisite. Members of the jury were taken equally from outside and inside the Quai d'Orsay. Though there were some minor alterations in the years 1880-1914, the *concours* retained a basic pattern. A composition on diplomatic history, usually on Europe, was mandatory. Interviews and oral examinations complemented the written exams. A candidate had to know at least one, and usually two, European languages other than French, give speeches on matters such as international law, and be interrogated on economic geography, colonial expansion, and general principles of political economy.[42]

Despite its rigour, the *concours* had surprisingly little importance and was designed to screen out the undesirables rather than to test qualities of diplomacy. The foreign minister always retained the right to nominate at will, under pretext of defending the existing regime. He used this privilege to employ friends or the sons of political allies. Diplomats, too, were influential in having their sons, relatives, or friends appointed. Furthermore, after 1880 priority was given to creating a new Republican élite and guaranteeing the Republican fraternity. The simple *certificat d'honorabilité*, instituted at a time when the *concours* did not exist, counted at times more than the examination, and a concierge was often consulted to attest to a candidate's 'social position' and 'Republican persuasions'. The wealth required to obtain the education necessary to succeed in the *concours* paradoxically eliminated those for whom the *concours* was expressly designed, talented Republicans of moderate means. Finally, the exam results themselves were disregarded on many occasions by examiners. Saint-Aulaire, ambassador to London in the 1920s, was admitted because his examiner, Jusserand, liked the way he evaded a question.[43]

Having passed the *concours*, the successful candidate was made an

---

[42] AE Beaucaire MSS, 10; Lauren, *Diplomats and Bureaucrats*, p. 101; Charle, *Fonctionnaires*, pp. 40, 43. Slight changes were introduced in the decrees of 14 Oct. 1890, 20 Nov. 1894, 6 Dec. 1899, 6 May 1900, 10 July 1902, and 17 Jan. 1907.

[43] 'Oeuvre administrative de M. de Freycinet au Ministère des affaires étrangères en 1880-82', AE de Freycinet MSS, 1; St Vallier to Billot, 22 Oct. 1883, AE Billot MSS; des Michels to Hanotaux, 6 Mar. 1899, AE Hanotaux MSS, 21; P. Cambon to Ribot, 19 Oct. 1891, AE Ribot MSS, 1; Montholon to d'Ormesson, 5 Jan. 1894, AE d'Ormesson MSS; *JOC* (1888), p. 193; J. d'Aumale, *Souvenirs d'un diplomate* (Montreal, 1945), pp. 10-13; budget report of E. Spuller, 1880, no. 1509, p. 13; Auffray, *De Margerie*, p. 28; Cogordan to Collin de Plancy, 24 Dec. 1886, 21 Aug. 1887, 4 Dec. 1902, AE Collin de Plancy MSS, 2, 3; R. Aynard to Pichon, Feb. 1911, Inst. de Fr. Pichon MSS, 1.

élève-consul or *attaché d'ambassade.* In 1900 the usual practice was to spend six months in the Direction des consulats and six in an embassy or legation. It was here that the newcomer learned the ancient arts of copperplate calligraphy, copying despatches on to gold-edged paper, and binding sheets together with blue silk ribbon. Though the copying was undoubtedly monotonous, surprisingly most later ambassadors viewed the exercise as being relatively instructive. Sometimes, too, the boredom was relieved by attachés being employed as couriers to European posts. Many such young attachés relished the prospect of a long train trip to St Petersburg or Constantinople.

After a two-year probationary period and another exam, the attaché or *élève-consul* became *secrétaire d'ambassade troisième classe.* He then proceeded on a regular basis up the scale (*troisième, deuxième, première classe, ministre plénipotentiaire, deuxième et première classe, ambassadeur*), and in principle advanced after a minimum period in his level (normally three years). In reality merit and seniority gave way to other factors; the level of patronage accorded by the foreign minister, diplomats, and politicians and the ability to remain at the Centrale. Often Centrale agents low in the hierarchy were raised above more senior colleagues without having to do overseas service.

Agents at all levels felt that they had a certain amount in common. There was a particularly closed community in the Quai d'Orsay. In the eighteenth and nineteenth centuries aristocrats viewed the diplomatic service as a family affair created for the prolongation of family dynasties. The new Republican élite hardly changed this attitude. The Cambons, the Herbettes, the de Margeries, and the de Courcels were only some of these dynasties. Others such as Saint-René-Taillandier, Jusserand, Berthelot, and Dumaine all had relatives employed. Among the ambassadors there was a real sense of community and as late as 1919 Jusserand, in welcoming de Margerie to ambassadorial ranks, instructed him on the correct paper to employ. Present and former deputy directors were members of a club which met together on social and political occasions. Even those at the lower level were included during the *thé de cinq heures.* This ritual was an opportunity for permanent officials, agents abroad, and visiting foreign diplomats to gather for conversation. It gave department heads the opportunity 'not only to know the names but also the attitudes of all ... from the chief of missions to the last *attaché*'.[44] Its most

---

[44] Saint-Aulaire, *Confessions,* pp. 23–4, 31–7; O. Homberg, *Les Coulisses de l'histoire: Souvenirs, 1898–1928* (Paris, 1938), pp. 17–18; d'Aumale, *Souvenirs,* pp. 10–13; Auffray, *De Margerie,* p. 37; Charle, *Fonctionnaires* p. 159; J. J. Jusserand, *What Me Befell* (New York, 1933) p. 41.

important function, however, was to foster a common spirit, doctrine, and manners among French diplomats and bureaucrats.[45]

Though aristocrats were gradually being replaced, the legacy of the aristocracy remained strong. Diplomacy was conducted as an art rather than a science, and informal conversations over a dinner were considered more profitable than the more formal diplomatic meetings. Long personal letters which established intimate relationships were in vogue.[46] The salon as a forum of diplomacy had not yet been superseded by more formal and less personal gatherings like the conference. The salon transmitted the old graces idealized even by the new Republicans: tact, the art of knowing others on a personal level, finesse, precision, and patience. When not frequenting the salon, the diplomat or functionary worked at a slow, easy pace in his cosy office with a fire in winter, the finest cigars, a good book, and vintage port. In the late nineteenth century diplomacy was still something of a leisurely hobby and was related to literary pursuits, horse-riding, hunting, and the establishment of fine literary and musical studios.[47]

A certain social and pecuniary position remained an important factor. In foreign courts, especially St Petersburg, which Paris was at pains to impress, aristocratic envoys were at a premium. There was often hostile condescension shown to bourgeois diplomats. French Republican governments were prepared to send aristocratic envoys, though aristocrats were becoming less willing to serve. In any case, French diplomats were expected in the more senior posts to entertain their political and social connections with lavish dinners, balls, or soirées. Apart from being useful means of meeting influential people, soirées or dinners set a relaxed atmosphere where private talks between friendly diplomats could have important consequences. Jules Cambon, for example, discerned a change in German policy towards France when the Kaiser, having dined at the French Embassy, stayed until after midnight (a unique occurrence for a mere diplomat's dinner) and discussed everything from good French wines to the *Folies Bergère*.

This rather aristocratic outlook and community of views could not mask the underlying currents of ambition, jealousy, and rivalry. Agents

[45] Jusserand to de Margerie, 17 July 1919, AE de Margerie MSS; Lauren, *Diplomats and Bureaucrats*, p. 52; Barrère to Pichon, 20 Jan. 1911, AE Barrère MSS, 4; J. Cambon to Pichon, 6 Sept. 1910, AE J. Cambon MSS, 16; Louis to Doulcet, undated, AE Doulcet MSS, 14; C. Andrew, *Delcassé*, p. 77; Laroche, *Au Quai d'Orsay*, p. 12.

[46] Waddington to Raindre, undated, AE Valfrey MSS, 2; J. Cambon to Paléologue, 18 Mar. 1912, AE J. Cambon MSS, 15.

[47] B. d'Agreval, *Les Diplomates français sous Napoléon III* (Paris, 1872), pp. 4–5.

were sometimes shoddily treated when senior officials in search of advancement decided upon a general displacement of personnel. Instances of officials coveting superiors' positions were on the increase and tended to weaken the *esprit de corps*. Agents carefully reflected upon which division they would be in or which superior they would have if they accepted a post, since a discordant relationship could ruin a career. There was the added dilemma that, in passing up a difficult post, the agent himself might be left standing at the gate while other more ambitious colleagues had bolted.[48]

The Republican regime contributed to this hotbed of intrigue. Though patronage was not new, the opportunity for new political forces to interfere in favour of protégés created a certain type of official. There was a distinct preference for the central administration and a preoccupation with party politics rather than with doing a job properly. The practices of the minister's private cabinet advanced rather than hindered such intrigues. Moreover, the status associated with high public functions, along with its substantial remuneration, led to increased competition between permanent officials.[49]

Nevertheless, the new Republican diplomat was not all that different from his aristocratic counterpart. He was usually from the *moyenne* or *haute bourgeoisie* but possessed conservative tendencies and normally had considerable wealth. He was Catholic and hostile to Jews, Protestants, and the parliamentary system. In fact, though political power in the Republic tended to shift downwards to the *petite bourgeoisie*, the Quai d'Orsay continued to be run by the *moyenne* and *haute bourgeoisie*.[50] Conservative governments were regarded more favourably than Radical ones. In addition, the French diplomat viewed himself as an expert, sometimes rejecting any outside interference. This sense of self-importance often led to the remark that French diplomats were an overbearing, intransigent, and haughty lot, and it was certainly true that they frequently conducted personal diplomacy and disobeyed instructions. Indeed, Republican diplomats sometimes

[48] In 1886 75% of French representatives in countries deemed important were still aristocratic: *Annuaire diplomatique* (1886); Charle, *Fonctionnaires*, pp. 156–7; J. Cambon to de Margerie, 10 Apr. 1901, AE de Margerie MSS; L. Cecil, *The German Diplomatic Service, 1871–1914* (Princeton, NJ, 1976), p. 68.

[49] Arnavon to Doulcet, 24 June 1913, AE Doulcet MSS, 20; Gavarry to Reinach, 9 Dec. 1901, BN (NAF 13540), Reinach MSS.

[50] In 1871, 34% of Parliament consisted of nobility and the upper bourgeoisie. By 1919 these groups constituted only 10%. In the same period, the number of middle and lower bourgeois entering Parliament went from 27% to 50%. See G. Dupeux, *La Société française, 1789–1960* (Paris, 1964), p. 185.

displayed a *snobisme* which was more pronounced than that of the aristocrats.[51]

Most agents married, usually into the *moyenne bourgeoisie* but occasionally into the aristocracy. The wife of a diplomat was an important economic, social, and political asset. Though there was a relatively high percentage of bachelors and though foreign posts were often considered too demanding for a woman, a wife was always required for high diplomatic posts. Not that this requirement prevented a married man from having mistresses. Far from being a scandal, affairs seemed morally acceptable as long as the wife was not brutally confronted. Consequently, there was somewhat of a division between sexual life on the one hand and the role of mistress of the house on the other.[52]

A common attitude to the world pervaded the pre-war Quai d'Orsay. There was a distinct emphasis placed on European affairs, no doubt reinforced by the structure of the central administration, the nature and number of European posts, and the quality of diplomats. This Eurocentric outlook led many diplomats to view in rather patronizing fashion less technically advanced parts of the world, an attitude which fitted the imperialist and colonialist ethos of the time. There was no pro-German group such as that which existed in the British Foreign Office. Almost all French diplomats were thoroughly anti-German. In the 1880s and 1890s hostility to Britain (over Egypt and other colonial issues) was strong but tended to dissipate and be replaced by pro-British feelings after 1904, when the *Entente Cordiale* was signed, and when Germany began to pose a distinct threat. The alliance system with Russia was viewed as extemely important, the natural balance to German pretensions. The Mediterranean for its part was seen as a natural sphere of French activity, and the empire in Tunisia, Algeria, and later Morocco was constantly justified by the argument that security in the North African empire would prevent enemy attack on the soft underbelly of France.

The Balkans and the Near East were given lower priority. The Quai d'Orsay tended to champion national Balkan movements, but had to weigh the cost of each action against the dissolution of the Ottoman Empire, whose survival was linked to the maintenance of important French interests. America and Asia were the new horizons, but the old

[51] Cogordan to Hanotaux, 6 Apr. 1895, AE Hanotaux MSS, 18.
[52] M. Paléologue, *Au Quai d'Orsay à la veille de la tourmente: Journal 1913–1914* (Paris, 1947), p. 253. On the various mistresses of officials, see the memoirs of Louis de Robien, AN de Robien MSS; Auffray, *De Margerie*, pp. 250–3.

diplomats were rather slow to recognize their potential and loath to depart from their narrow fields of competence.[53]

At the close of the nineteenth century the response of French diplomats to both internal and external politics was beginning to be shaped by a common education. In the British Foreign Office personnel would continue to be linked by social class rather than by the substance of their education.[54] In the French Foreign Ministry the reverse would be true, and the École libre des sciences politiques, a private school funded by financial magnates, was to play an increasingly decisive role. While it was only in the aftermath of the Boer War that a general demand for administrative competence had arisen in Great Britain, the demand for such competence had come earlier in France because of her defeat in the Franco-Prussian war of 1870-1.

Fully established before the Republicans took over the Third Republic, in an atmosphere of intellectual and moral reform,[55] the Sciences-po proclaimed a programme whose goal was to create new leadership qualities. Its basis was a combination of patriotic disgust over the defeat of 1871, dislike of the Paris Commune, and belief in science and education as the remedy for society's problems. It was the defender of conservative liberalism, marked more by its nationalism and desire for *revanche* than by any regard for democracy. On the whole, it was suspicious not only of the parliamentary process, but of French parliamentarians, who were seen as proclaiming ideological abstractions on the one hand while involving themselves in intrigue on the other. The Sciences-po went so far as to reject the politicians' competence to govern. Its professors, influenced by late nineteenth-century positivism, argued that the ignorant masses required determined leadership. Such an opinion led to an emphasis on personal initiative.

Admittedly, before the purges of the 1870s and 1880s the recruitment procedure of the Quai d'Orsay was somewhat haphazard, and even afterwards it remained subject to the working of patronage and nepotism. Only about 5 per cent of the diplomatic and consular services were graduates of the École des sciences politiques in 1898, but there-

---

[53] Parsons, *The Origins of the Morocco Question*, pp. 538, 551, 564; J. Cambon to de Margerie, 10 Apr. 1901, AE de Margerie MSS; Lauren, *Diplomats and Bureaucrats*, p. 12; Jusserand to Pichon, 5 Feb. 1907, Inst. de Fr. Pichon MSS, 3; Keiger, 'Poincaré', p. 20.

[54] Even during the 19th century many Republican diplomats and politicians rubbed shoulders at a high school like Louis le Grand (e.g., the Cambons, Saint-René-Taillandier, Paléologue, Millerand, and Poincaré).

[55] The title of Renan's work of 1871 which attributed France's defeat to its intellectual retardation.

after newcomers tended to come from this institution rather than any other. In the period 1899 to 1936 249 of the 284 individuals who entered the diplomatic corps came from it. In 1890 Foreign Minister Ribot ruled that a Sciences-po degree had the same value as the *licence* as a prerequisite. Sciences-po directors sat on committees set up by the Foreign Ministry to examine the nature of the *concours*, and diplomats appointed after 1898 viewed Sciences-po training as an essential preparation.[56]

Another source of education, though one less prized, was the École de langues orientales vivantes. In 1898 it provided around 8 per cent of those in the diplomatic and consular service. Introduced by the Convention in March 1795, its main aim was to train interpreters for duty in the Levant. It taught Turkish, Persian, literary and spoken Arabic, and, later, Far Eastern languages. As interest in Asia increased, its graduates took on more important political roles in spite of the technical nature of their training.[57]

Consequently, though the aristocracy could still advance in the Foreign Ministry at the end of the nineteenth century, a new Republican bourgeois élite had emerged as a result of the political struggles of the late 1870s and was being joined by men who shared a similar background. For all that, however, the structure and functioning of the Quai d'Orsay were little different from what they had been in 1825. Patronage flourished as before; work was conducted in a leisurely atmosphere and often by 'amateurs'; diplomacy continued to be practised as an art by the bourgeoisie, and by aristocrats whose credit was high in foreign courts; and policy-makers were still much concerned with European problems. The Quai d'Orsay was to become a model to other foreign offices in the areas of professionalism and reform but, prior to 1898, very little had disturbed the tranquillity and traditionalism that were so much a part of its nineteenth-century heritage.

[56] See T. R. Osborne, 'The Recruitment of the Administrative Elite in the Third French Republic, 1870–1905', Ph.D. thesis (Connecticut University, 1974). See also the book by the same author *A Grande École for the Grands Corps* (Boulder, Col., 1983).

[57] Outrey, *L'Administration française*, p. 34.

2

The Quai D'Orsay and External Influences, 1898–1914

The Quai d'Orsay was of decisive importance in the making of French foreign policy during the years 1898–1914, but a clear distinction between it and the 'outside world' did not exist. Government instability and intimate relations between officials and the press, big business, and Parliament worked against the development of such a dichotomy. As a result, external individuals and groups were able at times to bring an effective pressure to bear on the Quai d'Orsay and to shape governmental policy.[1]

Presidents of the Republic were entitled by the 1875 constitution to an important say in foreign policy matters but Raymond Poincaré, president between 1913 and 1920, was the only one during the period to utilize his powers to the full. Under the Third Republic presidents were elected for seven years, and fears of a *coup d'état* along with the Seize mai crisis of 1877, which saw a clash between President MacMahon and the Parliament, ensured that they reigned but did not rule.[2] Nevertheless, the president selected the premier and, in the realm of foreign policy, he could at times exercise substantial influence. The constitutional laws of 1875 empowered the president to negotiate and even to ratify treaties. He was not obliged to inform the legislature if the interest and safety of the state dictated otherwise. Unlike the British monarch, the president presided over cabinet meetings where he could admonish, encourage, or oppose. Likewise, he could receive foreign envoys privately, since they were directly accredited to him. Though the Radicals became increasingly anxious to restrict the powers of the presidency, political instability enabled presidents to retain considerable freedom of action in the international arena.[3]

[1] Z. Steiner, *Great Britain and the Origins of the First World War* (London, 1977), p. 2. Steiner has shown that the British Foreign Office and the 'outside world' could be differentiated largely because of a firmer constitutional and governmental framework.

[2] H. Leyret, *Le Président de la République* (Paris, 1973), pp. 31–42, 109–22.

[3] F. L. Schuman, *War and Diplomacy in the French Republic* (New York, 1931), pp. 12, 13, 19; G. Wright, *Raymond Poincaré, and the French Presidency*, (Los Angeles, 1942), pp. 3–6; P. G. Lauren, *Diplomats and Bureaucrats*, (Stanford, Calif., 1976), p. 29; E. Monteil, *L'Administration de la République* (Paris, 1893), p. 6.

Raymond Poincaré was the only president to make full use of his powers, but others, like Félix Faure, president from 1895 until his death in 1899, were equally conscious of the importance of the president in foreign affairs. Faure, labelled a 'vain, mediocre man who loved popular applause',[4] nevertheless acted as a source of stability during the Dreyfus affair. As Paul Cambon stated, 'il avait aussi le sens du dehors, il savait au moins en gros ce que c'était la politique extérieure'.[5] He influenced Delcassé's decision to withdraw from Fashoda, and he wanted to meet regularly with other heads of state.

Emile Loubet, his successor between 1899 and 1906, appeared less willing to exercise presidential prerogative in matters of foreign policy. Elected by left-wing parties, he was sensitive to the limits which the Left wanted to place on the presidency. He allowed Delcassé to follow an independent course and even to compose a number of his speeches, something which Faure would not have accepted.[6] The Quai d'Orsay was generally contemptuous of him, Paul Cambon rather acidly referring to his presidency as something 'qui n'était plus qu'un décor et qui ne sert plus à rien'.[7] During the First Moroccan Crisis he refused to support Delcassé because, according to his secretary, he was fearful of stretching the constitution.[8]

Armand Fallières (1906–13) chose equally to be a figurehead, mindful, like Loubet, that he was the candidate of the left-wing factions. After his election, he promised the cabinet that no policy would be initiated by the Élysée. His influence at the Quai was minimal. He was rarely consulted by the Foreign Minister nor was he kept *au courant* at cabinet meetings. Later he was to level severe criticism at Poincaré, his successor, for leading France into a conflagration. War might have been avoided, he argued, had the President remained aloof from international politics, had he restricted himself to his ceremonial duties, and had he not given encouragement to jingoist elements in both France and Russia.[9]

[4] Wright, *Raymond Poincaré*, p. 10.

[5] P. Cambon to J. Cambon, 18 Feb. 1899, Louis Cambon MSS.

[6] Le Gall to Faure, 16 Jan. 1898, Faure MSS, Fonds Berge; ibid., Faure interview with Muraviev, 28 Jan. 1897; R. Poincaré, *Au service de la France* (Paris, 1926–33), iii. 34; S. C. Hause, 'Théophile Delcassé's First Years at the Quai d'Orsay: French Diplomacy between Britain and Germany, 1898–1901', Ph.D thesis (Washington University, 1969), p. 127. For the debate about whether or not Faure could visit other heads of state abroad, especially the Tsar, see *Le Matin*, 1 July 1899; *Le Figaro* and *L'Éclair*, 2 July 1899. See reports by Münster 3 and 9 July 1897, Bonn, F. 105/19, vol. 8, also 5 Jan. 1899, vol. 10.

[7] P. Cambon to J. Cambon 16, 18 Feb. 1899, Louis Cambon MSS.

[8] Comte de Saint-Aulaire, *Confessions d'un vieux diplomate* (Paris, 1953), p. 83.

[9] Wright, *Raymond Poincaré*, p. 10; M. Paléologue, *Au Quai d'Orsay à la veille de la tourmente* (Paris, 1947), 8 June 1914, p. 297.

Fallières's successor, Raymond Poincaré (1913–20), had not the slightest intention of being a mere ceremonial lackey. He recognized that a president could legitimately play an important role in the realm of foreign policy. He had acceded to power at a time of nationalist fervour and international tension, when a strong presidency seemed to many an essential requirement for French prestige. His authority was exceptional because he had moved directly from the position of premier to that of president of the Republic.

For a time he was able to dominate policy. Jonnart, foreign minister in 1913, was his personal choice, and Poincaré made a daily visit to the Foreign Minister's office, where he read draft decrees. Not only that, he received ambassadors in private and chose embassies for his friends. Briand, when premier, was stupefied to learn that he had even written dispatches. As *président de la République*, Poincaré presided over the cabinet, and, following a procedure which he had introduced while premier, he chaired meetings of the Conseil supérieur de la défense.[10]

Poincaré maintained his ascendancy during Pichon's period.[11] His influence waned when Doumergue became foreign minister. In December 1913 the Radicals were eager to diminish Poincaré's authority. Doumergue respected their wishes by making decisions before cabinet went into session and by concealing the content of important telegrams.[12] The decline in Poincaré's power was considerable. Nevertheless, during the July crisis of 1914 he was able to reassert his authority at the expense of a highly nervous Viviani.

Poincaré's influence, however, did not necessarily bring him into conflict with the Quai d'Orsay. As he settled into his new position, he came to be much more at ease with Foreign Ministry officials, and by 1914 he was supporting many of the Quai's policies. Paul Cambon was struck by the manner in which the President listened to his advice. Alienated from the Radicals, and increasingly aware of the limits of his presidential power, Poincaré was prepared to ally himself with the Quai d'Orsay for the purpose of retaining the essential elements of France's

---

[10] J. F. V. Keiger, *France and the Origins of the First World War* (London, 1983), ch. 3; J. Cambon to P. Cambon, 19 Jan. 1913; P. Cambon to J. Cambon, 10 Jan. 1914, Louis Cambon MSS; Ribot to Jusserand, 8 Jan. 1913, AE Jusserand MSS, 60; Paléologue to Jusserand, 28 Jan. 1914, AE Jusserand MSS, 37; P. Cambon to H. Cambon, 12 Jan. 1914, Louis Cambon MSS.

[11] Paul Cambon wrote to his son: 'Il a fallu pousser à Pichon l'épée dans les seins pour le déterminer à marcher', 7 Dec. 1913, Louis Cambon MSS.

[12] 'Notes Journalières', 16 Jan. 1914, BN (NAF 16026), Poincaré MSS.

military programme.[13] This meant the creation of the three-year military service law and the retention of a more offensively orientated war plan under General Joffre, military chief of staff since 1911.

In general, the participation of the president of the Republic in the making of French foreign policy was limited and sporadic, and, with some exceptions, that of the *président du conseil* was hardly more pronounced. The crisis of the 1870s had led to a constitutional weakness in his position, and he was rarely an effective head of government. He was the leader of a shifting coalition which afforded him little security. His situation was the more precarious in that his cabinet often contained prominent politicians who were prepared to overthrow him at an opportune moment.[14]

The premier's stamp on foreign affairs was rarely to be seen. Most shunned the portfolio of foreign affairs, and preferred to combine the premiership with the Ministry of the Interior. The Quai had a rather contemptuous attitude towards the *président du conseil*, whom it viewed as a transient figure subject to the unhealthy pressures of powerful politicians or political groups. It was a common occurrence for the Foreign Ministry to keep the premier in the dark.[15] Casimir Périer resigned because of Hanotaux's curt refusal to transmit documents. Rouvier was not told of Anglo-French military conversations instigated in 1906 at Ambassador Jules Cambon's request. The gist of the conversation between Albert, King of Belgium, and Wilhelm II in November 1913 was not conveyed to Premier Barthou.

It is unlikely that some French premiers, even if they had been more fully informed, would have involved themselves more actively in the making of foreign policy. Apart from questioning Delcassé's judgement over the international force employed during the Boxer Rebellion, Waldeck-Rousseau rarely intervened in matters of foreign policy.[16] Combes, consumed by his anti-clerical policies, left Delcassé with a large freedom of action. Rouvier, though he was primarily responsible for

[13] J. F. V. Keiger, 'Raymond Poincaré and French Foreign Policy' (Cambridge University, 1980), pp. 327–8; See G. Krumeich, *Armaments and Politics in France on the Eve of the First World War: The Introduction of the Three Year Conscription* (Leamington Spa, 1984), pp. 118–22.

[14] R. D. Anderson, *France, 1870–1914: Politics and Society* (London, 1977), p. 79.

[15] Paléologue, *Au Quai d'Orsay*, p. 239; Saint-Aulaire, *Confessions*, p. 169. In the period 1898–1914 only 5 of 13 premiers headed the Foreign Ministry and of these Poincaré lasted a year, Bourgeois 7 months, Rouvier 8 months, Viviani 2 months, and Doumergue 6 months.

[16] Inst. de Fr., Waldeck-Rousseau MSS, 4596.

replacing Delcassé in 1905, was content to take the advice of career officials.

Clemenceau, on the other hand, took an active interest in foreign policy and did much to reduce Franco-German friction during the Moroccan incidents of 1907–8. Undoubtedly Foreign Minister Pichon kept him *au courant*, though that did not necessarily imply that decisions were emanating from him. In the case of the Franco-German agreement of February 1909 Clemenceau appears to have been presented with something of a *fait accompli*.[17] Briand, his successor, was highly inexperienced in foreign affairs and preoccupied by domestic issues. Monis, who was premier during the Fez crisis of April 1911, was a nonentity 'dédaignant systématiquement les questions de politique extérieure'.[18]

Caillaux and Poincaré, even more than Clemenceau, were exceptions to the rule. Caillaux's role was decisive in bringing about the November 1911 treaty.[19] Poincaré set out, with some success, to bring the Quai d'Orsay under his personal authority. With Poincaré's departure, however, the role of French premiers declined anew. Briand left foreign affairs in the hands of Pichon and Berthelot. Barthou was in power for a brief period, and both Doumergue and Viviani relied heavily on career officials.

As a rule, the cabinet was even less important in determining policy. The constitution of 1875 mentioned its role only incidentally. Until 1875 ministries had existed under the wing of the *président de la République*, and thereafter the limited respect commanded by the constitution weakened cabinets still further.[20] In addition, cabinets were the product of coalitions, and their members were much concerned with the surveillance of their colleagues and with putting a brake on governmental action. To make matters worse, individuals not in full sympathy with the government's aims were sometimes given ministries because of their technical expertise. The breakdown of a cabinet, far from being viewed as the possible termination of an individual's ministerial career, was regarded instead as a stepping-stone to higher office. The 1906 Sarrien cabinet, for example, included such ambitious individuals as Clemenceau, Poincaré,

---

[17] See Ch. 8 on the relationship between Pichon and Clemenceau. Louis to Pichon, 24, 28 August 1909, Inst. de Fr., Pichon MSS, 3.

[18] Messimy, 'Mes souvenirs', in AN Messimy MSS; J. Caillaux, *Mes mémoires* (Paris, 1942–7), ii. 43, 65–6.

[19] J. C. Allain, *Agadir* (Paris, 1978), pp. 350, 352.

[20] A. Soulier, *L'Instabilité ministérielle sous la Troisième République* (Paris, 1959), pp. 565–70.

Briand, Bourgeois, and Barthou. The competition and rivalry between these men made collective decision-making exceedingly difficult.

In theory, the cabinet should have been consulted on matters which were of international importance or which demanded the voting of credits.[21] In practice, it received quite different treatment. Foreign ministers and permanent officials alike were decidedly reluctant to inform the cabinet because of their fear that the delicate business of international relations would be employed for domestic political purposes. The Quai became even more reticent when the Radicals came to power, since many career officials believed that Radical leaders wished to overturn traditional practices. In addition, many Radical policies were often viewed with hostility by the Foreign Ministry. Consequently, the cabinet was kept in relative ignorance of foreign affairs. Though Poincaré had earlier been a cabinet minister, he learned of the contents of the Franco-Russian alliance only when he became premier and foreign minister in 1912.[22] There is no suggestion in his memoirs that the rest of the cabinet was then supplied with the relevant information. The other pillar of French policy, the *Entente Cordiale*, was almost entirely Foreign Minister Delcassé's work, and the independence he enjoyed between 1898 and 1905 in formulating France's policy contrasted sharply with the restrictions placed on his British counterpart by cabinet discussions.[23] Similarly, the French cabinet knew very little of the 1907 Mediterranean agreements until endorsement was hastily called for.[24] As for the February 1909 Franco-German Moroccan agreement, it was almost entirely Jules Cambon's doing. Although Clemenceau and Fallières knew of the general development, not until 6 February did cabinet receive the agreement for their approval.[25] Even though Pichon provided more information than his predecessors, he was equally concerned about the damage which a well-informed cabinet might do to essential policies.

The decision to march on Fez in April 1911 seems to have been taken without cabinet knowledge or approval. Fallières, Delcassé, and Pams were in Tunisia, Caillaux in London. Ultimately, the decision was made

[21] Allain, *Agadir*, p. 275.   [22] Poincaré, *Au service*, i. 141.

[23] C. M. Andrew, *Théophile Delcassé and the Making of the Entente Cordiale* (London, 1968), p. 212; C. W. Porter, *The Career of Théophile Delcassé* (Philadelphia, 1936), p. 112.

[24] Bertie to Grey, 7 Apr. 1907, PRO, FO 800/179, Bertie MSS; Bertie to Grey, 15 Apr. 1908, FO 425/300, confidential print.

[25] P. Cambon to Pichon, 6 Feb. 1909, AE NS 'Maroc', 16; D. J. Miller, 'Stephen Pichon and the Making of French Foreign Policy', Ph.D thesis (Cambridge University, 1976), p. 211.

by Foreign Minister Cruppi and communicated to Premier Monis, who then approved it without discussion. When convened, the cabinet was presented with a *fait accompli* which it accepted unanimously.[26]

For a short period during Caillaux's and Poincaré's premierships, the cabinet was kept frequently informed. Caillaux, during his resignation speech, waved a piece of paper stating that no step had been taken in Franco-German negotiations without prior discussion and approval. In fact, this procedure explains in part the tortuous longevity of the negotiations. Poincaré, who was mindful of public opinion, sensitive to criticism, and concerned about the finer points of the constitution, regularly consulted cabinet to the chagrin of the Cambons. In addition to acting as reassurance for his rather insecure personality, this policy acted as a counterweight to the power of career officials.[27]

Such periods were the exception rather than the rule. During Pichon's second term as foreign minister, the cabinet was ignored and, remarkably, it was not informed of the Albert–Wilhelm conversations in November 1913. By 1914, much to Poincaré's ire, Premier Doumergue was bypassing cabinet and presenting it with *faits accomplis*. The ultimate irony was the state of ignorance in which Messimy, minister for war, found himself during the July crisis. He knew nothing of the November 1913 conversations nor of Jules Cambon's reports concerning German military preparations. The Quai d'Orsay guarded its information jealously and simply refused to communicate information to politicians it considered incompetent.[28]

As might be expected France's political parties held varying attitudes towards foreign policy. Right-wing factions, while hardly united, generally supported the existing system of alliances, increased armaments, and commercial and colonial expansion. They opposed any agreement with Berlin and shunned manifestations of pacifism.[29] The Radical party was never as united on such issues. Though less concerned than elements of the Right about German aggression, most Radicals accepted the Franco-Russian alliance and the *Entente Cordiale*. Like the Rightists,

[26] Allain, *Agadir*, p. 275; C. M. Andrew and A. S. Kanya-Forstner, 'The French "Colonial Party": Its Composition, Aims and Influence, 1885–1914', *Historical Journal*, 14 (1971), pp. 123–4.

[27] P. Cambon to Poincaré, 1 Dec. 1912, AE J. Cambon MSS, 25.

[28] J. Cambon to Pichon, 10, 24 Nov. 1913, AE J. Cambon MSS, 16; 'Notes journalières', 13 Jan., 21 Feb. 1914, BN (NAF 16026), Poincaré MSS.

[29] J. C. Cairns, 'Politics and Foreign Policy: The French Parliament, 1911–1914', *Canadian Historical Review*, 34, (1953), p. 247. See the speech of Denys Cochin in the Chamber on 16 Dec. 1911 (JOC 17 Dec. 1911).

Radicalism favoured colonial expansion, but unlike them it regarded the 1911 Moroccan agreement as a necessary, if painful, expedient.[30] The Socialists, too, held definite views, whose rather doctrinaire and ideological character offended those of more moderate political persuasion. Most Socialists advocated a rather ill-defined international community in which France would participate. They were hostile to the Franco-Russian alliance and viewed with abhorrence the authoritarian and oppressive tsarist regime.[31]

Nevertheless, there was something about each of these political groupings which prevented them from trying to use the parliamentary forum to determine foreign policy. Right-wing groups, for their part, reviled the Republican and parliamentary system. They tended to believe that a republic could not readily safeguard France's 'grands et durables intérêts' because of its sordid political squabbles.[32] The Radicals immersed themselves in domestic politics in an effort to subordinate the Church and the army to the Republic. As for the Socialists, they made little real attempt to understand international politics. Such propositions as the abolition of embassies, the dissolution of all alliance systems, and the common action of European workers were naïve and unworkable.[33]

At bottom, however, Parliament failed to assume an important part in the making of foreign policy because most parliamentarians and their constituents were interested primarily in domestic politics, a phenomenon reinforced with the triumph of the Radicals. To make matters worse, the number and complexity of problems before the chambers and the nature of parliamentary procedure worked against a fruitful discussion of foreign affairs. Politicians were far from being as naïve and stupid as career officials imagined, but the plethora of local issues left little time for meaningful discussion of external affairs. Furthermore, oratorical skills often proved more advantageous than carefully reasoned argument, and parliamentary debates, when they concerned questions of foreign policy, usually lacked profundity.[34]

There were other reasons why Parliament did little to challenge the

[30] See B. R. Leaman, 'The Influence of Domestic Policy on Foreign Affairs in France, 1898–1905', *Journal of Modern History*, 14 (1942), p. 450.

[31] Cairns, 'The French Parliament, 1911–14', p. 265.

[32] Duc de Broglie, 'Discours au banquet monarchique', in *Histoire et diplomatie* (Paris, 1888), p. 44.

[33] JOC 24 Nov. 1902; P. Lissagaray, *Histoire de la Commune de 1871*, (Paris, 1896) p. 237.

[34] Schuman, *War and Diplomacy*, p. 24; J. Howard, *Parliament and Foreign Policy in France* (London, 1948), pp. 62, 63.

Quai d'Orsay's authority. First, there was a general consensus that the Quai's power should not be drastically weakened in view of governmental instability. Secondly, many politicians were of the opinion that *interpellations* in the Chamber on foreign policy were unpatriotic. Since the war of 1870 silence on foreign policy had become something of a duty.[35] There were two oral questions in the Chamber in 1907, four in 1908, three in 1909, and four in 1912.[36] Thirdly, when deputies or senators asked questions, they usually did so to clarify past legislation rather than to seek information about current problems. It was criticism after the event, and inevitably the *faits accomplis* presented by the government were swallowed.[37] Finally, Parliament's right to challenge the foreign minister was restricted constitutionally. Oral questions could be asked on two days a week during sessions. The foreign minister could be required to answer only by a majority vote of the Chamber. Ultimately, he could claim immunity by invoking the public interest.[38] The introduction of written questions in the Chamber of Deputies in June 1909 and the Senate some two years later did little to improve the situation. Of the 5,000 presented yearly, about one half related to fiscal laws. Less than 1 per cent dealt with foreign policy, and these were often phrased in such a manner as to direct attention to the questioner. The foreign minister usually found it easy to dismiss them.[39]

The Quai added to the inactivity of Parliament by starving the chambers of information. Protests were occasionally forthcoming but rarely sustained. When one agitated deputy, Paul Bluysen, lamented the deplorable lack of communication between the Quai and Parliament and the infrequency of debates about European politics, Poincaré curtly informed him that *interpellations* were always open to those who cared to utilize them.[40] In the years 1898–1914, *livres jaunes* were often issued only at the express demand of Parliament and after needless months of delay during which the issues at stake slid further into the past. Under Berthelot's skilful hand they obscured more than they revealed and always put the Quai in a favourable light.[41]

Hopes of putting an end to this lack of information and of achieving greater control over the diplomatic machinery were disappointed even by the various committees that were established to act as watchdogs. The Chamber's Commission du budget and the Senate's Commission

[35] E. Vacherot, *La Politique extérieure de la République* (Paris, 1881), p. 5.

[36] J. Barthélemy, *Démocratie et politique Étrangère* (Paris, 1917), p. 135.

[37] Allain, *Agadir*, p. 422; Howard, *Parliament*, p. 63.

[38] Howerd, *Parliament*, p. 62; Lauren, *Diplomats and Bureaucrats*, p. 48.

[39] Ibid.   [40] Ibid.; *JOC* 14 June 1912.   [41] *JOC Rapport* 3318 (1913).

des finances were theoretically influential. In their annual preparation of reports on the expenditure of the Foreign Ministry they could become vehicles for direction, criticism, and supervision. The internal operations of the Quai were thrown wide open for investigation, and its staff were required by law to assist the Budget Commission. Yet the Commission's terms of reference were strictly limited to administrative and financial matters, and the main body of policy-making was left largely untouched. The Commission's rather hasty proceedings precluded any depth of analysis or criticism of general policy. Attempts to supervise the Quai's secret funds through a small parliamentary commission were easily rebuffed. Even after financial mismanagement became apparent in 1911, the Commission remained as unsuccessful as ever in acting as a check on the Quai's activities.[42]

The Commission des affaires extérieures, des protectorats, et des colonies, established in 1902, was a similar disappointment. Until 1902 no permanent standing commission had existed. Foreign affairs were dealt with by temporary committees which reviewed specific events. The Commission prepared reports on treaties and other external developments, kept in constant communication with the Quai through *rapporteurs d'information*, and interviewed officials. However, it was never able to establish the principle of parliamentary or democratic control. It had no power to request secret documents from the Quai d'Orsay, nor could it summon a permanent official without the foreign minister's consent. Rarely did noteworthy discussion between the Commission, the current minister, and career officials take place. The Commission took no part in parliamentary *interpellations*. Unlike the German parliamentary commissions, it did not sit between sessions of Parliament, and it held no general mandate for investigation. Foreign ministers were not bound to present themselves upon request. Indeed, they often showed a distinctly hostile attitude towards any infringement on their prerogatives.[43]

The Commission's impotence was reinforced by its size. After 1910 forty-four members were elected by proportional representation and this proved to be an unwieldy number. Decisions were not made until months or even a year had elapsed. Some members of the Commission held it in outright contempt. As one politician, Joseph Reinach, remarked to British Ambassador Bertie: 'Ses quarante-quatre membres

---

[42] Ibid.; Lauren, *Diplomats and Bureaucrats*, pp. 30, 48, 49; Howard, *Parliament*, pp. 83–5.

[43] Lauren, *Diplomats and Bureaucrats*, pp. 113, 114; Cairns, 'The French Parliament, 1911–14', p. 271; Paléologue, *Au Quai d'Orsay*, 24 Nov. 1913, pp. 261–2; Schuman, *War and Diplomacy*, p. 384.

bavardent beaucoup, ils racontent confidentiellement les choses à leurs femmes, à leurs maîtresses, à leurs amis intimes qui, eux aussi bavardent.'[44]

The Commission's influence was not increased by the membership of former foreign ministers largely because men like Pichon and Delcassé had private access to inside information and were reluctant to share it with outsiders. As former ministers, they wanted no diminution of ministerial privilege. As for Paul Deschanel, eminent parliamentarian and president of the Commission, he was accorded scant respect either by the Quai d'Orsay or by the insiders. In view of the longevity of his term, his influence should have been more considerable, but the Foreign Ministry was highly suspicious of him. His efforts to obtain information or a clarification of policies came up against a brick wall, and his requests for written documentation met with curt refusal.[45] Consequently, the foreign policy of French governments was rarely challenged by either Parliament or parliamentary commissions.

Delcassé's disinclination to involve the chambers in his work brought surprisingly little reaction. The Senate, during the years of Delcassé's term of office, did not issue a single serious pronouncement on foreign policy. The Chamber of Deputies, for its part, listened to Delcassé with 'quiet awe' and 'timid acquiescence' whenever he prepared his bits of 'diplomatic reticence and patriotic fervour'. Parliament, like cabinet, knew very little of the contents of the Franco-Russian alliance and the *Entente Cordiale*.[46] Admittedly, by the end of 1904 Delcassé's neglect of Parliament was taking its toll, and with his resignation in June 1905 there was some questioning of governmental policy. Nevertheless, Delcassé's overthrow owed much to Rouvier's personal animosity. The government itself did not fall and, after a short period, Rouvier was following the Quai d'Orsay's line. He eventually lost office in March 1906 because of his handling of Church–State relations rather than his foreign policy.[47]

The Second Moroccan Crisis of 1911 similarly reflected the inability of Parliament to challenge governmental decisions. Cruppi, foreign

[44] Reinach to Bertie, 13 Jan. 1916, Bertie to Drummond, 13 Jan. 1916, FO 800/60, Grey MSS.

[45] Deschanel to J. Cambon, 26 Oct. 1911, AE J. Cambon MSS, 14; Deschanel to Louis, 2 Aug. 1910; Taigny to Louis, 22 Sept. 1910, AE Louis MSS, 2. See also the uninformative replies given to Deschanel by ministers such as Poincaré, Pichon, and Delcassé in AN, 151 AP 46 Deschanel MSS, 35.

[46] Porter, *Delcassé*, pp. 112, 185; C. Barrère, 'La Chute de Delcassé', *La Revue des deux mondes* (Jan. 1933), p. 612; *JOC* 25 Mar. 1902; *Manchester Guardian* (23 Feb. 1923), p. 13.

[47] Leaman, 'The Influence of Domestic Policy', p. 451.

minister in one of the Republic's weakest governments, was able to evade direct questions concerning the march on Fez with hollow-sounding platitudes.[48] Though Senator Delahaye criticized this decision, the Senate as a whole took little interest in the affair. The Monis government, like Rouvier's, fell over a domestic issue.[49] During the critical early days of the Agadir crisis, Caillaux averted an *interpellation* with the feeble excuse that the Foreign Minister was absent. When de Selves returned from Holland, no debate ensued. For the remainder of the crisis Parliament played no part, though it might have shown greater interest had not the Socialist leader, Jean Jaurès, been travelling in South America. After the signing of the November treaty between Germany and France, Caillaux easily postponed parliamentary discussion by arguing that issues such as rising meat costs and tariffs were of more importance. He eventually lost office more because of the manner in which he had lied to the Senate Commission than because of his policy. The Franco-German treaty of November 1911 was duly ratified, and a motion attacking secret treaties was summarily defeated.[50]

The reaction of Parliament to the crisis of 1911 was therefore surprisingly mild and reflected the notion that there could be little alternative to the Quai d'Orsay's immense power while cabinet instability remained rife. Between 1911 and 1914 neither chamber was prepared to persist if a foreign minister showed a reluctance to answer questions. Schemes envisaging the use of chambers of commerce, professional associations, employers' associations, and workers' syndicates to increase democratic control never got off the ground. A right-wing proposal suggesting that Parliament should inform the government of its attitude before decisions were made was not seriously considered. A left-wing plan involving the creation of a council of former foreign ministers meeting in session with the current foreign minister was not taken up. By 1914 Parliament was no closer to democratic control of foreign policy than it had ever been, and the July crisis ran its course without any parliamentary intervention whatsoever.[51]

Neither the army nor the War Ministry posed any serious threat to the ascendancy of the Quai d'Orsay in the formulation of foreign policy. After the defeat of 1871 the military found itself in disarray. The high

[48] Cairns, 'The French Parliament, 1911–14', p. 269.   [49] *JOS* 14 June 1911.

[50] *JOC* 5 Dec. 1911. Cairns, 'The French Parliament, 1911–14', p. 270; *JOS* 26 Jan., 16 Mar. 1912.

[51] *JOC* 5 Feb., 8 Mar. 1912; *JOS* 29 Mar. 1913.

command had been decimated, and the new Republican regime viewed the largely aristocratic, anti-democratic remnants with considerable fear and distrust. Republican leaders were determined to deny the French army the kind of power which the German army possessed.[52]

In fact, the military showed little inclination to be disloyal towards the Republic. Between 1871 and 1895 an accommodation was reached between Republican governments and the military which, while certainly not based on mutual admiration, survived because of common goals: the restoration of French influence in Europe, the ending of diplomatic isolation, and revision of the Treaty of Frankfurt.[53] Despite mounting tensions during the Dreyfus affair, the Republican regime generally adopted a pragmatic approach, accepting a military build-up after 1870 and rarely interfering with the army's internal affairs.

The corollary was that the army did not question governmental authority and was content to seek independence in its own technical areas. Essentially, it did not question the right of the government to decide issues such as conscription, budget appropriations, or even military organization. Nor, in spite of political differences, did army leaders make any move against the government of the day.[54] In 1898 the Duc d'Orléans, who was seeking military support for a royalist restoration, sadly lamented the unwillingness of a single high-ranking officer to promote it.[55] Even when War Minister André undertook substantial measures to republicanize the military at the turn of the century, the army's leaders remained basically obedient to the government of the day.

Under the Third Republic the chief of staff was given considerable freedom in internal matters but hardly any voice in foreign policy issues. This lack of influence contrasted markedly with the authority of German military officials such as von Moltke. The chief advisory bodies of the French army had still less importance. The Conseil supérieur de la guerre, the mouthpiece of the army, met infrequently and discussed matters of limited political significance. The Conseil supérieur de la défense nationale, created by decree in April 1906, brought together members of the navy, army, and similar bodies. It met just as infrequently and dealt with the co-ordination of the armed forces in times of

---

[52] D. B. Ralston, *The Army of the Republic* (Cambridge, Mass., 1967), pp. 4, 372; A. Mitchell, 'A Situation of Inferiority: France's Military Organisation after the Defeat of 1870', *American Historical Review*, 86 (1981), pp. 49–63.

[53] Ralston, *Army*, pp. 222, 224, 372; M. Anderson, *Conservative Politics in France* (Oxford, 1974), p. 128; P. M. de la Gorce, *The French Army* (London, 1963), p. 2.

[54] Ralston, *Army*, p. 292.   [55] AN F712434, police report of 9 Dec. 1898.

war. As its inaugural meeting on 6 December 1906 made clear, it had no intention of disobeying the instructions of the government.[56]

The Ministry of War, for its part, posed little threat to the Quai d'Orsay's ascendancy. Indeed, it was often labelled contemptuously as a 'technical ministry' with hardly any voice in larger affairs. The portfolio was often filled by Republican generals such as André or Messimy, or by lesser political figures, all of whom were subservient to the government. The Quai d'Orsay made little effort to keep these men informed. Even after the 1907 reforms, when more military and naval attachés were appointed, the Quai jealously guarded its prerogatives. Attachés had direct access to the Ministry of War, but their reports were usually sent through the Quai d'Orsay. During the crises of 1911 and 1914 information was relayed in especially dilatory fashion. One war minister, Messimy, argued that the Quai d'Orsay had adopted this procedure in order to eliminate his department from the decision-making process.[57] Admittedly, the War Ministry was more influential than usual in 1912–13. Eugène Étienne, who headed it, was a powerful parliamentarian, and the Three Year Law was becoming a leading political issue. Nevertheless, Étienne's influence derived more from the strength of his personality than from the authority of his office. His successor, Messimy, was a politician of much less stature. As for the conscription issue, it was basically a response to the German military threat and thus reflected the primacy of foreign policy rather than the internal ambitions of the military. Indeed, Ambassador Jules Cambon contributed much to its enactment and Ambassador Paléologue was equally important in having it maintained.[58]

The Colonial Ministry, like the War Ministry, did not threaten the dominance of the Quai d'Orsay. In fact, during the early 1890s, the Foreign Ministry possessed a Sous-direction des colonies, and it proved abortive not so much because a Ministry of Colonies was established in 1894, but because other subdivisions encroached upon its territory.[59] In any case, the Colonial Ministry never controlled all of France's imperial interests. Algeria was the concern of the Ministry of the Interior. Mili-

---

[56] See dossiers, 1911–14, AN Messimy MSS, 2. These hitherto unused manuscripts provide valuable information about military bodies and their links with the Quai d'Orsay.

[57] Ibid., 'Les Semaines qui ont précédé la mobilisation', s. 2, carton 5, p. 10.

[58] Paléologue, appointed ambassador to St Petersburg in Jan. 1914, rushed back to Paris in June 1914. Fearful of the newly elected Socialist government's policies he argued persuasively that any modification of the Three Year Law would undermine his position in St Petersburg. See Paléologue, *Au Quai d'Orsay*, 6, 7 June 1914, pp. 293–4.

[59] See ch. 1 for a discussion of this subdivision.

tary territories in southern Algeria were administered by the Ministry of War. The Quai d'Orsay was primarily responsible for Moroccan, Tunisian, and Near Eastern affairs, and was always reluctant to give up its prerogatives.

As C. M. Andrew and A. S. Kanya-Forstner have noted, the Colonial Ministry always remained the 'Cinderella Ministry' at the bottom of the ministerial pecking order along with the Ministry of Public Works.[60] Civil servants who aspired to prestigious positions rarely opted for Colonies. Consequently, the general quality of officials was so abysmal that the organization of the Colonial Ministry was even worse than that of the Quai d'Orsay and its general influence decidedly limited. In 1911 four administrative services were added to the existing geographical services (Indo-China, the Indian Ocean, Black Africa, and Oceania). The results were thoroughly disastrous. There were repeated cases of 'three of four departments deal[ing] simultaneously with a question of principle whose settlement required a single executive decision'. It was not uncommon for them to arrive at different solutions.[61] On the whole, the Colonial Ministry was incapable of setting wider policy goals and of seriously challenging the Quai d'Orsay's authority.

In France, the links between the Foreign Ministry and the press were somewhat unique. In Britain, there was always a certain distance between the Foreign Office and the press. The Foreign Office did not go out of its way to establish newspaper links or to influence opinion. Similarly, the ability of a British journalist to influence Foreign Office decisions was limited.[62] So clear a separation did not exist in France. Because of a lack of constitutional guidelines and because of endemic ministerial instability, the press was able to impinge more markedly upon decision-making. The influence of newspapers in France was further strengthened by the fact that almost half of the Third Republic's foreign ministers had at one time pursued literary or journalistic careers.[63] Journalism was seen as the natural stepping-stone to politics, and even when journalists became parliamentarians many retained a pecuniary and literary interest in their newspapers. Professional diplomats constantly bemoaned the fact that foreign ministers appeared

---

[60] C. M. Andrew and A. S. Kanya-Forstner, *France Overseas* (London, 1981), p. 19.

[61] Quoted ibid., p. 21.

[62] See Z. Steiner, *The Foreign Office and Foreign Policy, 1898–1914* (Cambridge, 1969), chapter entitled 'The Outside World'.

[63] I. Halfond, 'Maurice Paléologue: The Diplomat, the Writer, the Man', Master's thesis (Temple University, 1974), p. 82.

more willing to express their attitudes to former colleagues in journalism than to their permanent officials. Moreover, even within the Quai d'Orsay there existed a considerable number of officials who had once been journalists. Often, therefore, the transition from journalism to the diplomatic service was made quite naturally.[64]

Though the lines of communication between foreign minister and the press were almost always open, it was sometimes difficult to discern in which direction they flowed. Undoubtedly the Quai d'Orsay in certain crises, like the First Moroccan Crisis or the July 1914 crisis, was able to guide most newspapers towards a supportive consensus. On the other hand, the 1911 crisis pointed to the fact that the press could go its own way or at least become factionalized. The Quai d'Orsay was never as successful as the Wilhelmstraβe in imparting a discipline to the press. In France the relationship reflected more of an alternating current whereby at times the Foreign Ministry could successfully win support for its point of view. At other times it was hopelessly incapable of controlling opinion or even of avoiding direct attack.

Several reasons explain the ability of French newspapers to avoid some type of domination or control by the Foreign Ministry. The press law of 29 July 1881, by granting freedom of speech, sometimes allowed the press to operate not only free of control but irresponsibly. The disappearance of earlier governmental restraints with the decay of the press bureau of the Ministry of the Interior led to an increasing disregard for men and governments. This process was intensified with the purchase of newspapers by differing political and business interests. Papers often reflected the whims of their owners, whether politicians like Dupuy or business concerns, and, apart from certain restrictions placed on the anarchists in 1895–6, governments lacked effective means of control and surveillance. Papers often became intimately linked with a particular party. If the government did not have sufficient backing, sustained press campaigns could seriously impair its work and contribute to its downfall.[65]

Other reasons were no less cogent. The extent of government direction depended on personal relations between the foreign minister and members of the press. It also depended on the issues of the day and on

[64] The Cambons, Jean Giradoux, Pichon, and Hanotaux were only a few examples of men who had had careers in journalism before entering the Quai d'Orsay. See Lauren, *Diplomats and Bureaucrats*, p. 82; P. Cambon to Pichon, 17 June 1913, Inst. de Fr., Pichon MSS, 2; P. Cambon to J. Cambon, 9 Nov. 1908, AE J. Cambon MSS, 25.

[65] P. Albert in C. Bellanger *et al.*, *Histoire générale de la presse française*, III (Paris, 1972), pp. 240–50.

the ability of the press bureau to act as a co-ordinating agency. If the Quai's secret funds could not satisfy the appetite of the press, newspapers might seek a subsidy from financial institutions or from foreign governments. The venality of the press was considerable, and during the Russo-Japanese and Balkan wars St Petersburg bribed French newspapers on a massive scale.[66]

There was no exact parallel in France to the *Norddeutsche allgemeine Zeitung*, which was considered the official Wilhelmstraße organ, but the *Agence Havas* usually received and published semi-official communications.[67] The most noted and notorious French newspaper, with influence rivalling the London *Times*, was *Le Temps*, run by the Hébrard brothers. Adrien Hébrard avoided enslavement to any policy, yet usually supported the government, was moderate in outlook, and hostile to the Radicals. *Le Temps* was a quality newspaper, 'serious almost to boredom'.[68] It discussed social questions at length, but excelled in the sphere of foreign affairs.

André Tardieu, successor to de Pressensé after 1905, was accurately described by German Chancellor von Bülow as the seventh Great Power of Europe. He had been in the Foreign Ministry prior to becoming a journalist.[69] Moreover, he remained in the secret service of the Ministry until Briand struck him off the Quai's secret funds list in 1911. What appeared in the *Bulletin de l'étranger* undoubtedly came from official ministry sources.[70] Tardieu was a daily visitor to the Foreign Ministry, and foreign emissaries frequently commented on his closeness to French diplomats. His friendships with officials such as de Billy, Berthelot, Revoil, Taigny, Dupeyrat, de Fleuriau, Louis, and de Margerie were matched only by his intimacy with foreign ministers such as Pichon and Poincaré, over whom he had an almost mesmeric hold.[71]

While his *Bulletin de l'étranger* was frequently inspired by the Quai d'Orsay, Tardieu often had a say in the making of decisions in the first place. The Foreign Ministry was very much aware of his standing in

[66] Ibid., p. 250; H. Feis, *Europe: The World's Banker, 1870–1914* (New Haven, Conn., 1930), p. 158.

[67] See E. M. Carroll, *French Public Opinion and Foreign Affairs 1870–1914* (New York, 1931), p. 12. According to Francis Delaise, the Quai d'Orsay was able to control the *Agence Havas. La Guerre qui vient* (Paris, 1911).

[68] Albert, in *Presse française*, pp. 352–6.

[69] Dossier AN, 324 AP 2 A. Tardieu MSS.

[70] Bertie to Grey, 3 Mar. 1913, PRO, FO 800/166, Bertie MSS.

[71] Dupeyrat to Tardieu, 25 Aug. 1910, AN, 324 AP 7 Tardieu MSS; ibid. AN 324 AP 14 Tardieu MSS; Revoil to Tardieu, 24 Mar. 1907.

the courts of Europe,[72] and his ideas were therefore well received by French policy-makers. Though critical of British laxity, he favoured Anglo-Russian *rapprochement* and a general tightening up of the Triple *Entente's* links so as to form some viable balance to Germany's might. He worked closely with de Billy and de Margerie at the Algeçiras Conference of 1906, where he fought hard (with the Quai's full consent and gratitude) to defend French interests against German demands. By 1908 he was advocating the formation of a Franco-British military alliance to supplement the *Entente Cordiale*.[73]

Tardieu, as closely linked as he was to the Foreign Ministry, always retained his independence. Until 1909 he had been extremely pro-Pichon, perhaps because, as Paul Cambon lamented, it was really Tardieu who directed the Minister: 'Le fait est que ce monsieur dont on se plaint est reçu quand il veut, comme il veut au Quai d'Orsay et chez Clemenceau et qu'on ne lui inflige jamais un démenti.'[74]

When Pichon chose not to support Tardieu's pursuit of a Homs–Baghdad railway concession, the journalist turned against him and attacked his handling of the Russo-German Potsdam talks and Franco-Russian relations in general. Pichon added to Tardieu's enmity by severing relations with him and by pointing out in a private letter that it was the minister who determined policy.[75]

Tardieu's attacks upon the Quai d'Orsay continued through 1911, and Poincaré came to power anxious to put an end to his antagonism.[76] Indeed, he particularly feared Tardieu and it was noted, especially during the Balkan crisis, that Tardieu's pro-Balkan activities influenced Poincaré to take a harsh line against the Porte and Vienna. Admittedly, there were times when Poincaré differed with Tardieu, notably over the future of Asian Turkey in 1914 and British policies in general. Ultimately, however, Tardieu was reconciled with the government, even patching up his quarrel with Pichon in May 1913. Throughout the immediate pre-war period he was always listened to, usually followed, and never ignored.[77]

[72] Dupeyrat to Tardieu, 25 Feb. 1910, AN, 324 AP 7 Tardieu MSS.

[73] Carroll, *French Public Opinion*, pp. 222–4, 231.

[74] Tardieu to de Billy, 25 Nov. 1903, AE de Billy MSS, 30; P. Cambon to J. Cambon, 28 Jan. 1908, AE J. Cambon MSS, 25.

[75] Bertie to Grey, 4 May 1911, FO 371/1118; Revoil to Pichon, 18 Jan. 1911, AE Revoil MSS, 5; Bompard to Pichon, 19 Jan. 1911, Inst. de Fr., Pichon MSS, 1.

[76] Berckheim to J. Cambon, 15 Mar. 1911, AE J. Cambon MSS, 14.

[77] P. Cambon to J. Cambon, 4, 5 Nov. 1912, AE J. Cambon MSS, 25; Keiger, *France and the Origins*, p. 65; Cartwright to Nicholson, 27 Nov. 1913, PRO, FO 800/360; Graham to Tyrell, 5 Dec. 1912, PRO, FO 800/53, Grey MSS.

Le Matin, the rival of *Le Temps*, lacked the official tone of its rival but was sometimes employed as a means of floating trial balloons. After a period under Alfred Edwards, the brother-in-law of politician Waldeck-Rousseau, it was sold to Henry Poidatz, a banker and stockbroker. Bunau-Varilla, a businessman, also had an important interest in it, while Stephen Lauzanne was editor-in-chief in 1901. *Le Matin* prided itself on being politically neutral and assigned its political column to a different writer each day. However, its claim to be neutral and a servant of the general interest masked its dislike for the Radicals and its support of Briand and Poincaré. Indeed, Caillaux was not far from the mark in labelling *Le Matin* 'un journal Poincariste'. Nevertheless, in domestic politics, it attacked almost all governments, with the Caillaux and the Clemenceau ministries receiving special attention. *Le Matin* provided considerable coverage of foreign issues. By 1905, it had turned against Delcassé and even tried to contact both German Chancellor von Bülow and Wilhelm II. Though it was known for its American sympathies, *Le Matin's* attachment to St Petersburg characterized it, and it received more than its share of Russian money.[78]

Le Figaro, too, had a considerable readership in political circles. Its rather aristocratic outlook and high-quality journalism ensured readership by the upper middle class and the aristocracy. By 1880, it had abandoned monarchism to rally to the Republic, though it later sympathized with the Boulanger movement. Initially it was pro-Dreyfus, but it gradually altered its line because of the protests of its readers. Generally it supported the cause of more conservative governments. Calmette, its editor, had links with Poincaré and Barthou, and may have been inspired by these two in his campaign against Caillaux and the Radicals in 1914.[79]

Even more influential was the *Journal des débats*. Though it reached fewer numbers, it was invariably read and listened to by the academic élite. These intellectuals appreciated its commentaries, even if the course it proposed was not adopted. Like *Le Figaro*, it eventually rallied to the Republic. It showed great enthusiasm for colonial policy and limited sympathy for Russia while supporting the territorial integrity of the Ottoman Empire. Next to *Le Temps*, the *Journal des débats* was the newspaper most frequently used by French governments as a mouthpiece, though it could be highly critical of Radical ministries.[80]

---

[78] Andrew, *Delcassé*, pp. 67–8; Albert, in *Presse française*, pp. 309–14.
[79] Albert, in *Presse française*, 347.
[80] Ibid., p. 351.

Though links between the press and the Foreign Ministry were consistently close during the Third Republic, they were particularly intimate during the period 1898–1914, largely because two long-serving foreign ministers, Delcassé and Pichon, had formerly been journalists. There can be no doubt that the closer ties which developed between the press and the Foreign Ministry at the turn of the century owed less to the creation of a press bureau than to Delcassé's determination to utilize French newspapers. He sometimes divulged much more to journalist friends than to his permanent officials.[81] Every night he summoned Robert de Billy, his press chief, to whom he dictated items which were to appear in various dailies, making sure that the writing suited the particular style of each paper.[82] *Le Temps* and the *Journal des débats* were Delcassé's favourite newspapers, though he made use of *Le Figaro* until he quarrelled with its editors in 1903. Eugène Lautier, editor of *Le Temps*, was a close personal friend and took pains to support Delcassé's policies.[83] Charles Laurent, who had been his boss on *Le Paris* and who had switched to *Le Matin*, supported him until 1905. Jezierski, from *La Dépêche de Toulouse*, was occasionally utilized by Delcassé to convey communications to Barrère.[84] Francis Charmes of *La Revue des deux mondes* was given Delcassé's instructions by Paléologue. Mevil, who was on the editorial staff of *L'Écho de Paris*, was another of the Foreign Minister's personal friends.[85]

Delcassé's downfall was all the more surprising in view of his press connections. However, his rather dictatorial manner and his narrow-mindedness in certain foreign policy areas alienated some influential newspapermen. If a paragraph displeased him, he was quick to have it struck out with blue pencil, or, if already published, to demand an apology. Despite his experience in journalism, he made the serious mistake of supposing that journalists would always agree with him.[86]

Pichon, who shared Delcassé's ideas about the utility of the press, formalized the relationship in 1907 by establishing an independent press bureau under the control of Maurice Herbette. Pichon was far more

---

[81] In Jan. 1902, for example, he stated to *Il giornale d'Italia* without Ambassador Barrère's knowledge that Russia would view favourably Italian expansion in Albania. In 1903 an interview in *Le Matin* annoyed St Petersburg so much that its publication in Russia was forbidden. See *Le Matin*, 18 Feb. 1903.

[82] Andrew, *Delcassé*, p. 67; de Margerie to de Billy, 24 Dec. 1904, 12 Aug. 1905, AE, de Billy MSS, 63.

[83] Lautier to Delcassé, 14 May, 14 June 1902, AE Delcassé MSS, 4.

[84] Hause, 'Delcassé', p. 131; Andrew, *Delcassé*, pp. 67–8.

[85] Andrew, *Delcassé*, 67–8; Porter, *Delcassé*, pp. 114–15.

[86] See L. Jerrold, *The Real France* (London, 1911).

concerned with influencing the press than with making a contribution
to democratic decision-making. Herbette was largely successful in
satisfying the Foreign Minister, although he was later powerless against
the onslaughts of Tardieu, who developed a distinct animosity towards
him.

Pichon emulated his predecessor Delcassé, by talking more extensively to journalists than was desirable. He was in constant communication with the likes of Lautier and, until 1911, Tardieu.[87] In 1913, when
Pichon wanted to express his opinion of Sir Edward Grey to a British
newspaper, Paul Cambon peremptorily restrained him, and reminded
him that such conversations, so normal in France, were considered
unsuitable in Britain.[88]

Poincaré, another foreign minister with a relatively long tenure, was
equally mindful of relations with the press. In fact, he was the accredited
legal representative of the Syndicat de la presse parisienne. Though he
told Parliament in February 1912 that he intended to conduct foreign
policy in accordance with public opinion, he gave little substance to this
statement.[89] He was far more concerned with making himself and his
policies stand out. On several occasions calculated leaks to the press
served him well.[90] He was directly connected with the distribution of
Russian money to various newspapers during the Balkan wars, money
which served in part to bolster his prestige.[91]

While Poincaré sought to enlist the press, he never tried to direct it as
Delcassé did. He had an almost unnatural fear of press criticism, and the
threat of an unfriendly article or attack upon himself, his wife, or his
policies stunned him. Journalists such as Judet and Tardieu were able to
gain a certain ascendancy over him, so much so that, by the end of his
period as foreign minister, Tardieu was able to enter his office freely.[92]

Quite apart from French foreign ministers, the permanent staff of the
Quai established a liaison with a large number of journalists and newspapers. Both bureaucrats and diplomats found the press a useful means
of applying pressure on recalcitrant foreign ministers.[93] The Parisian
press was frequently employed to extend feelers to foreign govern-

[87] P. Cambon to J. Cambon, 9 Nov. 1900, AE J. Cambon MSS, 25; Pichon to Barrère, 8
June 1908, 28 Jan. 1909, AE Barrère MSS, 4.

[88] P. Cambon to Pichon, 17 June 1913, Inst. de Fr. Pichon MSS, 2.

[89] Poincaré, *Au service*, i. 65.

[90] P. Cambon to Poincaré, 25 July 1912, AE NS 'Italie', 12.

[91] Carroll, *French Public Opinion*, p. 268.

[92] 'Notes journalières', Dec. 1912, Jan. 1913 (BN NAF 16024), Poincaré MSS; Millerand MSS.

[93] Bertie to Grey, 12 Mar. 1910, FO 425/335, confidential print.

ments.[94] Furthermore, the foreign press was sometimes bribed in an effort to influence foreign governments. Jules Cambon, for example, directed funds towards the Spanish press during the Algeçiras Conference.[95] French newspapers were, on occasion, employed to sabotage the policies of other powers. The Centrale, through constant leakage to the press during the Balkan wars, was able to provide the Balkan states with important advantages. The Centrale's policy so irritated some of the Great Powers that Paris was abandoned as a possible conference site.[96] Finally, individuals in the Centrale supplied material to the press in an attempt to further their careers.[97] Indeed, quite a number of permanent officials wrote press articles, and journalists such as Hansen and de Houx received regular subsidies from the Foreign Ministry.[98]

While the links between the press and the Quai d'Orsay were strong, those between the Foreign Ministry and big business were no less powerful. Eyre Crowe, a permanent official at the British Foreign Office, was extremely perceptive about the form these commercial ties sometimes took.

One of the most noteworthy features of the French policy is ... the permanent part played by French diplomatic and consular officials in obtaining from foreign governments orders and contracts for French commercial firms. It is not surprising that under this system the majority of French diplomatists and consuls acquire a direct pecuniary interest in the business schemes which they are pushing. It is unhappily well known that personal corruption so engendered pervades all French government circles, both at Paris and abroad.[99]

Crowe was not exaggerating. French permanent officials frequently derived direct pecuniary gain from their association with business ventures. What he failed to emphasize was that French financial and commercial concerns were often able to bring effective pressure to bear on governments of the Third Republic. In the pre-war Republic politicians and businessmen mixed easily together. Companies took care to employ

[94] For example, Hedeman, who was London correspondent of *Le Matin*, was in the Quai's confidence and was used as an intermediary between France and Germany (Lauren, *Diplomats and Bureaucrats*, p.182). Hedeman to de Billy, 25 Nov. 1908, AE de Billy MSS, 30; P. Cambon to Revoil, 1 Dec. 1905, AE Revoil MSS, 2; Daeschner to de Billy, 14 Jan. 1904, AE de Billy MSS, 27.

[95] J. Cambon to P. de Margerie, 1, 15 Feb. 1906, AE J. Cambon MSS, 11.

[96] Grahame to Tyrell, 15 Dec. 1912, PRO, FO 800/53, Grey MSS.

[97] J. Laroche, *Au Quai d'Orsay avec Briand et Poincaré* (Paris, 1957), p.15.

[98] Andrew, *Delcassé*, p.189. See accounts of Hanotaux's *fonds secrets*, 1898, AE Hanotaux MSS, 4.

[99] Marginal note by Crowe on Bertie to Grey, 24 Oct. 1908, F.O. 371/456.

influential politicians or retired ambassadors as members of their *conseils d'administration* in the hope of exercising greater influence over Republican ministries and the Quai d'Orsay.[100] Nor did Crowe recognize that while French governments sometimes yielded to business pressure they more often utilized financial and industrial enterprises to further France's political aims.[101]

The relationship between French governments and French businessmen followed neither the British nor the German models as depicted by historians such as Steiner and Cecil. In Britain the Foreign Office was rather loath to support British business interests unless they were of vital political concern. The two merely converged. In Turkey for example the British 'continued to put the maintenance of political equilibrium of Europe before the exigence of British finance'.[102] In Germany, big business was often successful in obtaining the support of the Wilhelmstraße, but competing concerns led to conflicting and chaotic policies. In France, on the other hand, business and politics were intertwined, but French economic concerns were almost always made subservient to broader foreign policy aims. France's external economic policies were given remarkable coherence by the efforts of the Foreign Ministry.

Though French financiers were important in the non-European and colonial spheres, French foreign investment there amounted to only one-tenth of overall foreign investment.[103] French capital was invested primarily in Europe and often served political purposes. It was of particular importance in cementing the Franco-Russian alliance. In negotiating this agreement, Ribot and de Freycinet were motivated not by financial concerns, but rather by strategic and political considerations.[104]

There was a clear limit to the influence which businessmen could exercise, and, with the aid of existing legislation, the Foreign Ministry could manoeuvre financiers in the interest of general policy. A decree of 1880 provided the Ministry of Finance with the power to veto the quotation of French loans on the Bourse, a power which was used increasingly

---

[100] Feis, *Europe: The World's Banker*, p. 158; Saint-Aulaire, *Confessions*, p. 231; Miller, 'Pichon', p. 109.

[101] Allain, *Agadir*, p. 422; R. Poidevin, *Les Relations économiques et financières entre la France et l'Allemagne de 1898 à 1914*, (Paris, 1969), p. 823.

[102] K. A. Hamilton, 'An Attempt to Form an Anglo-French "Industrial Entente"', *Middle Eastern Studies*, II (1975), p. 66.

[103] Feis, *Europe*: *The World's Banker*, pp. 5, 54, 119, 134.

[104] R. Girault, *Emprunts russes et investissements français en Russie, 1887–1914* (Paris, 1973), p. 581.

after 1900. French governments were thus able to prevent French banks from making loans to foreign powers whose policies were in disfavour with the Foreign Ministry. Official listing could be made conditional upon the receipt of pledges or compensations of a political nature as well as orders for French industry. Finally, governments could utilize their muscle so as to provide loans for friendly or dependent states. In some cases the government virtually promised a loan and then selected a particular financial institution to manage it. Banks, though often reluctant, usually co-operated when the national interest was invoked.

Quai d'Orsay officials were placed in international financial institutions. For example, arrangements were made for French diplomatic personnel to have seats on the Egyptian and Ottoman Debt Commissions. The 1907 reforms further strengthened this tradition. Consequently, agents such as Gaston Guiot, who was officially *en disponibilité* but never really outside the diplomatic corps, were appointed to the Moroccan Debt Commission and to the board of directors of the Moroccan State Bank.[105]

The Quai d'Orsay's determination to use finance as a foreign policy weapon was strongly reinforced by several foreign ministers. Delcassé was particularly adept at taking advantage of France's financial power. He attempted to arrest German expansion in Turkey by opposing the use of French capital in the Baghdad railway project. He encouraged a financial-political offensive in Italy and in some Balkan states. He tried to limit German participation in Russian loans. But, most importantly, he employed the financial weapon in Morocco as a means of *pénétration pacifique*. The activities of groups such as Schneider and the Banque de Paris et des Pays-Bas were closely supervised. During Delcassé's years in power the flow of capital became increasingly linked to orders for industry, but Delcassé made certain that he was not subjugated by financial and industrial representatives.[106]

Pichon was equally struck by the role of French financiers in French politics and diplomacy[107] and equally determined to control financial interests. It was under his administration that the commercial division and political division were joined and that other economic reforms were enacted to increase the efficacy of French diplomacy. He restrained the intrigues of financial and industrial concerns in Morocco, tried to

[105] Miller, 'Pichon', p. 109; Allain, *Agadir*, p. 424.
[106] Poidevin, *Les Relations économiques*, 811.
[107] Pichon to J. Cambon, 1 Aug. 1907, AE J. Cambon MSS, 16.

use economic links with Japan to win political friendship, and used France's economic might in Turkey to bolster French influence.

The Second Moroccan Crisis offers an example of general policy aims prevailing over economic interests. Until 1911 French and German financial institutions had co-operated in a number of ventures in Bulgaria, Romania, Serbia, and Turkey. Franco-German tension during 1911 ensured that such financial co-operation was largely reduced. Consequently French banks were urged to go beyond their existing zones of influence. In the course of the Agadir crisis Caillaux and Jules Cambon skilfully manoeuvred so as to employ French banking and commercial interests to tighten France's grip on Morocco.[108]

The 1911 crisis led French governments to take an even more active part in economic affairs. Despite their internationalist, pacific, and co-operative outlook French bankers were persuaded to sever links with their German counterparts and to compete in vital areas. The Austro-Hungarian loan which was proposed by Ambassador Crozier in November 1911 as a means of weakening the Triple Alliance was summarily rejected by Poincaré on political grounds. Struggles in the Balkans between French and German economic interests were severe, and the once intimate co-operation of the Banque ottomane and the Deutsche Bank broke down. The fight for political predominance in the Balkans and Turkey clearly outweighed individual economic interests.[109]

Despite the frequent chaos of Republican politics, the ability of pressure groups to influence weak governments was surprisingly limited. Outside Parliament there were few pressure groups. Economic and local interests were directly represented by deputies or senators. Even the chambers of commerce displayed a marked lack of enthusiasm. Many employer associations concerned themselves with price-fixing and strike-breaking rather than lobbying. The Comité Républicain du commerce et de l'industrie was not so much a pressure group as a conduit through which the Radical party obtained funds from business sympathizers.[110]

The Comité des forges was undoubtedly an important pressure group but one with a limited capacity to influence the Foreign Ministry. Formed in 1864 to represent the interests of the steel industry, it eventu-

---

[108] Allain, *Agadir*, pp. 7, 8, 35; Poidevin, *Les Relations économiques*, 812.
[109] Ibid.
[110] M. Rebérioux, *La République radicale: 1899–1914* (Paris, 1975), pp. 51, 59–60.

ally acted as the central organization for all French heavy industry. In the areas of labour legislation and tariff duties it was able to achieve considerable success, thanks largely to its close ties with Poincaré, Briand, and Millerand. After 1903 the Quai d'Orsay pleased it by increasingly linking foreign loans to orders for French industry. Berthelot was instructed to support the demands of the Comité des forges in the columns of *Le Matin*. Yet such assistance was usually provided in the interests of general policy. Le Creusot was more often supported against Krupp because of strategic, military, or political considerations than because of economic considerations. The government usually asserted its prerogative and was unwilling to jeopardize alliances or friendships merely to procure additional orders for heavy industry. As it was, French industrialists were divided and sometimes presented competing claims.[111]

Another pressure group of some significance was the Colonial party, whose adherents were to be found both inside and outside Parliament. As a parliamentary group its influence has been overrated. Nearly everyone with an interest in colonial policy affixed their name to this rather unwieldly, amorphous group, but having done this, they demonstrated little interest in its activities. The Colonial party was far from being a conspiratorial pressure group. By 1898, there was a general consensus in favour of colonial expansion, which meant that pressure did not usually have to be applied to French governments.[112] The influence of the Colonial party within the Quai d'Orsay has been similarly exaggerated. Just about all high-ranking officials, including de Margerie, Gout, Bapst, and Berthelot, joined as a matter of course. Even its critics, such as Jules Cambon and Pichon, belonged to one of the various committees.[113]

The Colonial Party probably needs some redefining. Even C. M. Andrew and A. S. Kanya-Forstner have recognized that it was totally within the realm of normality for permanent officials to defend the national interest abroad in their capacity as officials rather than in their

[111] See H. Lebovics, *The Alliance of Iron and Wheat in the Third French Republic, 1860–1914: Origins of the New Conservatism* (London, 1988); M. J. Rust, 'Business and Politics in the Third Republic: The Comité des forges and the French Steel Industry, 1896–1914', Ph.D. thesis (Princeton University, 1973), pp. 1–20. Also R. Girault, 'Pour un portrait nouveau de l'homme d' affaires français vers 1914', *Revue d'histoire moderne*, 16 (1969).

[112] Rebérioux, *La République radicale*, pp. 51, 59–60.

[113] L. Abrams and D. J. Miller, 'Who were the French Colonialists: A Reassessment of the "Parti Colonial", 1890–1914', *Historical Journal*, 19 (1976), pp. 703–5.

capacity as members of the Colonial party.[114] A clearer distinction should be made between those who defended imperial interests as a matter of professional obligation and those who were genuinely committed to the imperialist cause.

Usually the colonial committees provided information or support for French officials, whose views they often sought to popularize. Agents like Bompard, Berthelot, de Margerie, and Gout, while members of the Comité de l'Asie française, did not share the Comité's views about the fate of the Ottoman Empire. Ambassador Bompard, in particular, rejected the rather extreme views of Robert de Caix, who wrote for the organ of the Comité de l'Asie française. Delcassé, who was thought to be the choice of the Colonial party as foreign minister, made it clear from the outset that he would remain his own man. During the Boer War he rejected its demands for the Moroccan–Egyptian barter and a more aggressive policy in Morocco. He broke with Étienne, leader of the Colonial party, after disagreeing with him about France's policy in Siam. If, by 1903, Delcassé was encouraging a more forward policy in Morocco, it was because he feared an Anglo-German initiative. He was prepared to envisage the acquisition of Morocco only at the beginning of 1904 when negotiations with Britain were concluding and a British reaction was no longer to be feared. Despite their considerable influence he made it abundantly clear to Étienne and the Colonial party that he was the minister, that a gradual penetration of Morocco was the best policy, and that such a policy was to be scrupulously followed.[115]

In the end, Delcassé's foreign policy was largely in accord with the aims of the Colonial party, but it had not resulted from pressure applied by that group. The Colonial party, while it approved of the *Entente Cordiale*, had not been responsible for its achievement. It remained critical of the Siam and Newfoundland agreements, and did not thoroughly endorse the manner in which the Egyptian–Moroccan barter was carried out. Delcassé, for his part, opposed its pro-German proclivities.[116]

The Comité du Maroc, founded in 1904, was of limited significance. As J. C. Allain has observed, the French protectorate of 1912 was the product of a 'groupe dirigeant marocain': the Foreign Ministers Pichon

---

[114] Andrew and Kanya-Forstner, *France Overseas*, p. 27.

[115] Leaman, 'The Influence of Domestic Policy', p. 461; P. Guillen, *Les Emprunts marocains 1902–1904* (Paris, 1974), p. 158; Andrew, *Delcassé*, pp. 54, 107, 108.

[116] Andrew, *Delcassé*, pp. 54, 107, 108.

and Cruppi, diplomatic agents such as the Cambons, Regnault, and Saint-Aulaire, and influential business groups. The Comité had little impact on French decision-making. It occupied itself with publicizing government decisions and with acting as 'une officine de publicité et même d'information sérieuse sur le Maroc'.[117] It had nothing to do with the 1909 Franco-German agreement. Indeed, under the Cambons' influence, Pichon was extremely cautious in his dealings with it.[118] As to the decision to march on Fez, there is little evidence to suggest that the Comité inspired it.[119]

The power of the Comité du Maroc cannot be dismissed altogether. Undoubtedly its wishes were respected by the Tangier legation, and it was generally influential in Algeria. Yet Delcassé was determined to have policy decided in Paris and to subordinate both the Algerian military and the Governor-General of Algeria.

It would be a mistake, finally, to suppose that either the Colonial party or its various committees formed solid, unified blocks. There were as many disagreements as agreements, and all members were not necessarily involved in decision-making. What held the various committees together were a few enthusiasts such as Étienne, Bourde, Chailley-Bert, and de Caix, whose personal relations with French governments and the Quai d'Orsay do more to explain the influence of the Colonial party than any conspiratorial pressure group theory.

Eugène Étienne appears to have been a consistently powerful figure in French imperial expansion. He was in constant contact with Delcassé, apart from a short rift over Siam in 1902. Not only did agents like Regnault and Saint-Aulaire correspond directly with him, but Delcassé seems to have kept him *au courant* of most developments, even transmitting secret documents. Clearly Delcassé listened to Étienne, but the final decisions were usually his own. It should be remembered, moreover, that, though Étienne was a leading member of the Colonial party,

---

[117] Allain, *Agadir*, pp. 423–5.   [118] Miller, 'Pichon', p. 211.

[119] Andrew's evidence is based on a remark by Jules Cambon about a supposed *déjeuner* attended by Étienne and the Cambons. Cambon was at his least objective when referring to Étienne and the Algerian clique which had forced him out of Algeria. Louis's comments are hardly more impartial in view of the bitterness which he felt after his dismissal as ambassador to St Petersburg. Messimy and Caillaux were primarily concerned in their memoirs to defend their action in the crisis. Caillaux did not attribute the decision to march on Fez to any Colonial party dinner. See Andrew and Kanya-Forstner, 'Colonial Party', pp. 123–4. Raynard to J. Cambon, 26 July, AE J. Cambon MSS, 15; Saint-René-Taillandier to Étienne, 31 July 1903, Allenberg to Étienne, 28 Feb. 1908, BN (NAF 24237), Étienne MSS.

much of his activity can be explained by his Algerian business and political interests.[120]

Two other leaders of the Colonial party stand out during the pre-war period, Bourde and de Caix. Bourde, perhaps erroneously described by Saint-Aulaire as Delcassé's *éminence grise*, nevertheless possessed the Foreign Minister's confidence.[121] Delcassé employed him as an intermediary in his negotiations with Britain during 1902, and it was through Bourde, in the following year, that Governor Jonnart's Algerian expansionism was restrained.[122] In later years de Caix, who was associated with the *Journal des débats*, appears to have been influential at the Quai d'Orsay. A journalist-intellectual and large landowner, he worked closely with officials of the Foreign Ministry during the First Moroccan Crisis and later in a general way as an adviser on Asian affairs, about which he was thought highly knowledgeable by Berthelot and the Cambons.[123]

In the final analysis, the Quai d'Orsay was responsible for most of the foreign policy decisions made in the years 1898–1914. Perhaps the most remarkable feature of the decision-making process was the apathy, ignorance, and powerlessness of both the French cabinet and French Parliament. Involved with divisive internal issues which led to unstable government and sometimes to no government at all, French politicians hardly glanced at European or colonial maps. It was this internalized, chaotic political system which at times allowed outside forces like the press, banks, and heavy industry to shape the thinking of the Quai d'Orsay. Individuals such as Tardieu and Poincaré, as *président de la République*, were temporarily able to achieve exceptional influence. In general, however, the Foreign Ministry was able to utilize outside forces for purposes of general policy while avoiding subjugation to special interests.

---

[120] Andrew, *Delcassé*, p. 107. For an extremely illuminating view of the Étienne–Delcassé relationship, see the exchange of letters in 1904 in BN (NAF 24237), Étienne MSS. See also Saint-Aulaire to Étienne, 8 Oct. 1904, Revoil to Étienne, 13 Aug. 1904, BN (NAF 24237), Étienne MSS.

[121] Saint-Aulaire, *Confessions*, p. 49.

[122] Jonnart to Delcassé, 17 June 1903, AE Delcassé MSS, 4; *La Quinzaine coloniale*, 25 March 1990.

[123] Berthelot to Gérard, undated, AN 329 AP 26 Gérard MSS: J. Cambon to de Margerie, 15 January 1906, AE J. Cambon MSS, ii.

3

Delcassé and the Centrale, 1898–1904

The emergence of Théophile Delcassé as foreign minister in June 1898 ushered in a new period in foreign policy and in the administration of the Quai d'Orsay. Delcassé not only completed the work of his predecessors relating to the Franco-Russian alliance, but he was also involved in creating the new political alignments inherent in the Franco-Italian and Franco-British *rapprochements*. Moreover, he seriously curtailed the power of the central administration because of his desire to control policy formulation. Nevertheless, if Delcassé ignored his permanent officials in Paris, the corollary was not necessarily that the Quai d'Orsay's influence declined. On the contrary, the emergence at this time of an ambassadorial élite in the form of Barrère, the Cambon brothers, Constans, and Jusserand ensured that the diplomats' voices remained powerful and indeed instrumental in the determination of policy-making.

Théophile Delcassé, foreign minister between 1898 and 1905, was competent but not brilliant. A short man of 5′4″ (he was sometimes acidly referred to by his critics as 'the hallucinated lilliputian' and the 'gnome of Fashoda'), emotional, shy, tenacious, and a workaholic, he had a lucid brain but one with rather limited imagination. He had formulated three or four relatively fixed ideas and in this sense he was a minister of clear vision. His tenacious will, however, sometimes made him inflexible. Consequently, he was often slower than many to realize the impracticalities of his notions. His obsession with certain grand designs, combined with his suspicion of other great powers, sometimes led him to misinterpret the policies of other governments.

This is not to suggest that he was a second-rate minister. He was deeply imbued with cultural and emotional nationalism. When he was a young man, the Franco-Prussian war appears to have had a powerful impact upon him. Consequently his entire life was devoted to the resurrection of France as a major continental, colonial, and global force.[1]

---

[1] *Le National*, 3 August 1892; C. M. Andrew, *Théophile Delcassé and the Making of the Entente Cordiale* (London, 1968), p. 90; E. Blanc, *La Jeunesse de Delcassé* (Paris, 1934), pp. 51–2.

Delcassé's outlook owed much to Gambetta, who, as unpublished manuscript sources make clear, had a powerful influence not only on Delcassé but on other French statesmen of the period. Though he differed with Gambetta about Russia, Delcassé concurred with his mentor's belief that a Franco-German *rapprochement* was impossible and that it was necessary to arrive at *ententes* with Britain and Italy. National resurrection through colonial expansion was also seen as imperative.[2]

While Delcassé classified himself as a Radical in politics and entered Parliament in the 1880s as a member of the Gauche radicale, a small group consisting mainly of Gambetta's old supporters, he appears to have moderated his earlier left-wing ideas by the time he became foreign minister and to have involved himself only minutely with internal politics. As Andrew suggests, his 'radical sympathies were less a leaning towards radical policies than an emotional attachment to the revolutionary tradition and to the ideal of a united republican movement'. He was not convinced by others of the urgency of the socialist threat and viewed the Right rather than the Left as the main enemy of the Republic. Even here he proved himself moderate, non-doctrinaire, and essentially practical. While being anti-clerical himself and supportive of labour reforms, he was unwilling to immerse himself in the political struggle. Like Gambetta he believed that anti-clericalism was not for export.[3]

Delcassé's style and his relations with his staff in Paris clearly reflected his desire to dominate. The efficiency of the central administration in this period was the result of his ability to supervise the most mundane diplomatic activities and to co-ordinate the policies of his ambassadors. Though normally arriving each day at the Quai d'Orsay at 9 a.m., he was sometimes at work before dawn and did not leave until midnight.[4] All important dispatches were brought to his attention and it was he, rather than the political director, who

---

[2] Manuscrit, 'La Chute de Delcassé', in Barrère's writing (AE Barrère MSS, 5) carries more explicit reference to the influence of Gambetta on Delcassé than the published version.

[3] AE Delcassé MSS, 1, pp. 27f; S. C. Hause, 'Théophile Delcassé's First Years at the Quai d'Orsay: French Diplomacy between Britain and Germany, 1898–1901', Ph.D. thesis (Washington University, 1969), p. 9; Andrew, *Delcassé*, pp. 55–7; M. Paléologue, *Three Critical Years, 1904–1906* (New York, 1957), pp. 153–5; C. W. Porter, *The Career of Théophile Delcassé* (Philadelphia, 1936), p. 18.

[4] Delcassé to Barrère, 17 January 1900, AE Barrère MSS, 3.

drafted dispatches to various missions.[5] His own description of himself as working 'comme un boeuf' was in no way exaggerated. Indeed, on several occasions Paul Cambon admonished him severely, advising him to delegate more responsibility to his permanent officials.[6] Such advice went unheeded. He went less frequently than before to the Comédie-Française and the Opéra, refused many dinner invitations, disliked the long summer holidays and worked through them.[7]

Secrecy was equally a trademark of Delcassé's style. By keeping work in his own hands (or in the hands of those he had carefully chosen) he sought to retain overall control. He feared that, unless matters were restricted to a few trustworthy personnel, his policies could fail. Indiscretion in Parliament and the central administration was rife, and his own knowledge of the workings of the *cabinet noir* made him realize the ease with which foreign powers could intercept French messages.[8]

Because of this obsession with secrecy Delcassé wrote the most important dispatches himself. He preferred either to call in his ambassadors for confidential talks when they were passing through Paris or to send a secret envoy with oral instructions. It was usually Paléologue who would inform ambassadors of Delcassé's orders and bring back their reactions.[9] Delcassé encouraged ambassadors to write letters which would bypass central officials and reach him personally. He was constantly devising new ciphers.[10]

Generally Delcassé did not mingle in internal politics and he was largely immune from parliamentary crises. According to Saint-Aulaire, he considered most politicians as cretins and abhorred the manner in which their petty squabbles demeaned France.[11] Although his ear was closer to the ground than is generally supposed, and although he firmly believed in Parliament's ultimate control, he wanted a strong executive

[5] Andrew, *Delcassé*, pp. 66, 76.

[6] P. Cambon to Delcassé, 11 December 1901, AE Delcassé MSS, 3.

[7] Andrew, *Delcassé*, pp. 66, 76; Porter, *Delcassé*, p. 116.

[8] P. J. V. Rolo, *Entente Cordiale* (London, 1969), p. 83; B. R. Leaman, 'The Influence of Domestic Policy on Foreign Affairs in France 1898–1905', *Journal of Modern History*, 14 (1942), p. 450; Porter, *Delcassé*, pp. 113, 144; Lord Newton, *Lord Lansdowne* (London, 1929), p. 209.

[9] Bompard to Madame Nogues, 29 October 1931, Saint-René-Taillandier to Madame Nogues, 30 October 1931, AE Delcassé MSS, 1.

[10] Porter, interview with J. Cambon in Porter, *Delcassé*, p. 113; I. Halfond, 'Maurice Paléologue' (Temple University, 1974), p. 54.

[11] Cited in J. F. Macdonald, 'Camille Barrère and the Conduct of Delcassian Diplomacy, 1898–1902' (University of California, 1969), p. 57.

divorced from Parliament.[12] In his case he preferred personal control of foreign policy to cabinet control, especially after the resignation of the Waldeck-Rousseau ministry in June 1902. Premier Combes's anti-clerical and anti-military policies were repugnant. Consequently, on many occasions neither Parliament nor cabinet was sufficiently informed and in later years this obsession with secrecy extended to Combes's successor Maurice Rouvier. If Delcassé was able through his secrecy to 'immunize' his office, the other side of the coin was that such tactics gave him little authority in Parliament or in the cabinet when premiers chose to confront him.

The Quai d'Orsay underwent transition from nineteenth- to twentieth-century diplomacy only slowly, and change in this Delcassian period remained haphazard. In all, there were 122 in the diplomatic corps and 427 in the consular corps.[13] Although an *arrêté* in 1891 had limited numbers to 137 excluding unpaid attachés, this decree had been disregarded and had even been exceeded by having officials placed *hors cadres*. As a result, there had been an explosion in numbers, especially in the consular corps, and the Quai had double the numbers of the British Foreign Office.[14] Most in the diplomatic corps knew each other personally and continued to hold deep-seated biases against the mass of consular officials. Though the 'purges' begun in the 1890s ensured that the majority of officials were Republican, many of the major posts continued to be filled by aristocrats or by ultra-conservative Catholic Republicans.

Primarily, Delcassé's horror of administrative change explains why reform was often piecemeal.[15] His response was simply to handle as much as possible himself and to ignore the intricate workings of the diplomatic machinery. Paul Beau, his *chef du cabinet* from 1898 to 1901, worked intimately with him but acted more as a personal secretary than as a *chef* concerned with the administration of the Quai d'Orsay. Beau's successor Delavaud submitted numerous proposals to Delcassé but none was acted on. Delavaud, in turn, quickly fell out of favour with the Foreign Minister while Mollard, *chef du protocole*, and Jullemier, *chef du personnel*, were able to exercise influence only by circumventing him.[16]

[12] Andrew, *Delcassé*, pp. 300–6.
[13] *Annuaire diplomatique et consulaire* (1898). See also F. V. Parsons, *The Origins of the Morocco Question, 1880–1900* (London, 1976), p. 563.
[14] Parsons, *Origins of the Morocco Question*, 563.
[15] J. Cambon to de Margerie, 22 August 1902, 16 January, 2 April 1903, AE de Margerie MSS.
[16] Ibid. 18 December 1902, 9 January 1903, 24 March, 11 May 1905.

This was not the only reason, however, for the lack of administrative change under Delcassé. The longevity of the Dreyfus affair in the 1890s and 1900s and the intensity of the Church–State struggle concentrated attention on domestic politics. Only with the victory of the Radicals was more attention paid to the Quai d'Orsay. Finally, the habitual intrigues and lack of definitive rules relating to essential areas such as the private ministerial cabinet, Personnel, and political division contributed to a highly unstable situation.

There were minor changes effected during the period, but these were hardly systematic enough to be considered valid responses to the twentieth century. American and Far Eastern affairs, which had been shared by the Midi and Nord subdivisions, were now transferred to the Nord. This arrangement simply underlined the slowness of the Quai d'Orsay to recognize the importance of extra-European affairs. Admittedly, a third, less important Sous-direction des colonies had been created under a Sous-direction adjoint. But its beginning was inauspicious and its development unstable. In a period where colonial affairs were intimately linked with European questions, it could not resist the frequent encroachment of the Nord and the Midi.[17]

Some change, though largely unplanned, was occurring in other areas. For example, the use of propaganda as a weapon appears to have begun during Delcassé's period. Delcassé himself systematically prepared articles for selected newspapers. This achievement had little to do with general foresight on the part of the Quai d'Orsay. Delcassé was a former journalist who enjoyed good relations with the press and was personally convinced of its usefulness. The *service de la presse* remained in the hands of a few individuals in the private ministerial cabinet, notably Robert de Billy, and a proper bureau was not established until after 1907.

Matters relating to personnel also reflected a non-systematic and uneven approach to change. A decree of May 1891 stated that agents working in the Centrale were temporarily *hors cadres* but kept the grade of their external career. This measure ensured that an agent in Paris would not be disadvantaged with respect to men in external posts. A decree of 15 March 1904 abolished any such technical distinction and treated all equally in their respective grades.[18] Yet major problems relating to political interference, patronage, and the workings of important bureaux were usually ignored. It was significant that one dossier presented to Delcassé in 1900 covering a whole range of reforms simply had

---

[17] *Annuaire diplomatique* (1898), ch. 1.
[18] Note by Gavarry, undated, AE *dossier personnel*, Gavarry.

the word 'rejeté' scribbled on its front cover.[19] As Lauren suggests, political, financial, and personal factors were formidable barriers to change.[20]

Matters relating to work conditions were hardly decided in an objective, professional manner. Despite decrees of July 1882, January 1891, and May 1891 fixing levels of payment, the Foreign Ministry was living from day to day, with funds disbursed at random.[21] It was noticeable during this period that the overlapping responsibilities of the Ministries of Finance, Commerce, and the Quai d'Orsay made it difficult to decide which department should pay an agent. Payment to those working secretly for the French government was difficult to justify at a time when the accounting department was coming under increased parliamentary scrutiny. Count Beaucaire, Maurice Herbette, and Pierre de Margerie, all agents of the Foreign Ministry, were only some who complained of the haphazard system. Often an agent waited years before receiving remuneration commensurate with his grade.[22] Furthermore, the handling of personnel was shoddy, unsystematic, and highly biased. Ambassador Jules Cambon waged a battle with the Bureau du personnel for no less than one and a half years to have de Margerie transferred with him from Washington to Madrid.[23] Cambon's brother Paul fought an even more intense battle when Delavaud, *chef du cabinet* from 1902 to 1906, decided to promote some of his friends over Manneville, Cambon's subordinate in London, who had greater seniority.[24]

Later, Delavaud himself was to complain of the same prejudicial treatment. In 1904 Doumergue, former colonial minister, attempted to obtain a good post for a protégé.[25] At no time before 1914 was a *statut de la carrière* or objective criteria established. The foreign minister, usually in the form of his politically motivated *chef du cabinet*, retained and made frequent use of the right to nominate officials irrespective of grade. In the end frustrated ambassadors like the Cambons, who were in the forefront in attacking personnel problems, gave up their idealism and

[19] 'Projet de la réorganisation de l'administration centrale, 1899–1900', AE Direction du personnel, carton 28.

[20] P. G. Lauren, *Diplomats and Bureaucrats* (Stanford, Calif., 1976), p. 31.

[21] 1901 budget report; Berthelot to Collin de Plancy, 20 July 1902, AE Collin de Plancy MSS, 25.

[22] AE *dossiers personnels*, Herbette, Beaucaire, de Margerie.

[23] J. Cambon to de Margerie, 22 August 1902, 16 January, 2 April 1903, AE de Margerie MSS.

[24] P. Cambon to H. Cambon, 16, 17 March, 20 April, 12 May, 9, 29 November 1904, 26 April 1905, Louis Cambon MSS.

[25] Delavaud to Delcassé, 17 December 1904, AE Delcassé MSS, 4.

played the game by placing their protégés Thiebaut, Daeschner, and de Margerie at the head of the private ministerial cabinet.

Quite apart from the patronage of the foreign minister and powerful diplomats, French politicians continued to view an embassy as a means of advancing or concluding their political careers.[26] Admittedly, during the years 1898–1904 there was a diminution in the number of *intrus* who filled senior positions. Delcassé himself was mindful of the deleterious effects of this practice on the service. Yet former *intrus* already occupied nearly 50 per cent of French embassies, and the power of the government to name whom it wished remained unfettered. Such politicians as Bourgeois, Pichon, and Hanotaux seriously threatened, from time to time, to take a vacant embassy.[27]

It is hardly surprising, given limited guidelines, political interference, and patronage, that the efficiency of the Quai d'Orsay suffered. In practice, in Delcassé's period, most officials failed to work a five-hour day. An example was the Division des fonds, where employees were supposed to work from midday to 6 p.m. Delavaud wrote Delcassé a memorandum which explained that this theory simply did not apply: 'Hier j'ai constaté qu'à midi ½, 6 agents seulement étaient présents sur 14; 3 sont arrivés entre midi et 1 heure, 4 entre 1 heure et 1 heure ½. Un est arrivé à 2 heures. Celui-ci était d'ailleurs parti à 5 heures ayant donné au département 3 heures au plus au lieu de 6.'[28]

In the political division, the custom until 1891 was for most *rédacteurs* and attachés to work only in the afternoon (except for the Bureau d'ordre, which began at 9.30 a.m.). Ribot then imposed five hours on all agents, and some from each of the Sous-directions worked in the morning from 10 to 12 and then returned in the afternoon. This system had functioned reasonably well during the 1890s, but Delcassé's desire to do everything himself and his dislike of strict routine often allowed agents to stay away during the morning, to arrive after an extended lunch, and to leave well before 5 p.m. While the commercial division and the private ministerial cabinet, because of Bompard's and Delavaud's efficiency, began to work at 9 a.m., most officials were in the political division. Raindre, political director between 1898 and 1901, lamented the general laziness. It is inter-

---

[26] Some of the more notable *intrus* were Barrère, Bihourd, Bompard, Revoil, the Cambons, Constans, Touchard, Pichon, and Delcassé himself.

[27] P. Cambon to H. Cambon, 15 April 1905, 20 July, 21 September 1906, Louis Cambon MSS; Delcassé had initially rejected Jules Cambon as a replacement for Patenôtre by arguing that his appointment would discourage the service and take away all security (ibid., P. Cambon to J. Cambon, 14 April 1899).

[28] Delavaud note to Delcassé, 17 July 1903, AE Delcassé MSS, 4.

esting to note that one high-ranking official, Paléologue, could employ his time at the Quai day-dreaming and writing 'romantic' novels, be severely taken to task by his superior, and then be promoted by the Foreign Minister.[29]

Delcassé's determination to do as much as possible in the privacy of his office led to a considerable reliance on information provided by the *cabinet noir*. However, the results were often mixed, and Delcassé was sometimes led astray, notably over the incorrect deciphering of an Italian telegram during the Fashoda crisis. By 1903, the number of errors had been substantially reduced by the employment of Octave Homberg, who ensured that the deciphering was exact before transmission to the Minister.[30] Thus, when the Japanese code was deciphered during the Russo-Japanese war, Delcassé was able to assess his mediatory efforts.[31] More importantly, he had at his fingertips the correspondence of Premier Rouvier and the Germans, when the former began to work for his dismissal in 1905.[32]

Under Delcassé, the power of the political division and especially the director was substantially diminished as a result of his determination to control the machinery of the Quai d'Orsay. This trend was reinforced by the authority of Ambassadors Paul and Jules Cambon and Camille Barrère. Because of ministerial instability after 1870 the political director had been an almost *de facto* foreign minister and during Hanotaux's period before Declassé the political division had become even more in-fluential. Delcassé changed all that. He quickly relieved Nisard of his major duties as political director by delegating him to minor adminis-trative tasks, and eventually forced him to accept the Vatican Embassy. Despite Nisard's advocacy of Jusserand as his successor, Delcassé placed the latter in Copenhagen, clearly fearing that he would be a challenge to his own power. Cogordan and Aubigny were also thought of as Nisard's replacement, but Delcassé wanted to keep the former in Cairo during the Anglo-French conflict over Fashoda. Finally, to the surprise of everyone and without consulting anyone, Delcassé chose Gaston Raindre.[33]

Little is known about Delcassé's first political director. He was born

---

[29] Note by Raindre 1902, AE *dossier personnel*, Paléologue.

[30] O. Homberg, *Les Coulisses de l'histoire* (Paris, 1938), pp. 38–9.

[31] AN F7 12829 and 12930.

[32] 'Notes journalières', BN (NAF 16026), Poincaré MSS; G. Louis, *Les Carnets de George Louis* (Paris, 1926), pp. 18–19.

[33] Note on change of political director, 1898, by Jusserand (undated), Nisard to Jusser-and, 27 September, 14 October 1898, d'Aubigny to Jusserand, 30 September 1898, Paléologue to Jusserand, 27, 30 September 1898, AE Jusserand MSS, 21, 22.

in January 1848 at Montmedy-Meuse to bourgeois parents. He was an
intelligent man who had obtained a degree in law and could speak
German fluently. His superiors were decidedly taken with his 'intelligence, goût des affaires, esprit prudent ... habileté, et esprit de décision'.[34] He was married and believed that the secret of success in the
diplomatic career was application and a restricted social life. He was
critical of subordinates who spent too much time in the salons or who
treated the diplomatic life as a pastime rather than as a full-time occupation.[35]

Raindre had decided at an early age to work outside the Centrale. As
de Courcel wrote to Jules Herbette in 1886, 'la vie d'ambassade lui parais-
sait plus facile, plus commode'. However, it was also more lucrative, an
important point for a diplomat of limited financial means.[36] In the 1870s
he had been to Baghdad, Aleppo, and Antananarivo, working in the
consular corps. But boredom, terrible posts, and slender financial compensation had persuaded him to change to the diplomatic corps. In
Egypt in 1878 he had fought hard against British influence. With his
knowledge of German he had been an extremely helpful aide in Berlin
during most of the 1880s and the early 1890s. Had de Freycinet remained
as foreign minister in 1886 he would have put Raindre at the head of
his soon-to-be-created Sous-direction des protectorats.[37] Eventually
Raindre had gone to Luxembourg, only to be shifted in 1893 because of
claims by high-ranking officials there that he was too pro-German.[38] In
the years 1893–95, prior to becoming minister in Copenhagen, he had
held the post of deputy director of the political division.

Though he preferred foreign posts to the central administration,
Raindre was equally conscious of the advancement possible in the latter,
especially if the Minister's confidence was won.[39] Undoubtedly this
realization encouraged him to take up Delcassé's offer. Nevertheless,
though he was not a nonentity as political director, nor was he a powerful
figure. He found his task a little frightening. During the difficult period
that France was passing through he preferred to have Delcassé shoulder
the burden of responsibility. More importantly, his strong sense of devo-

[34] Notes by J. Herbette, 8 December 1887, 25 November 1890, by de Courcel, 9
August 1886, and Le Myre le Vilers, undated, AE *dossier personnel*, Raindre.

[35] Undated conversation between Doulcet and Paléologue, AE Doulcet MSS, 23.

[36] De Courcel to J. Herbette, 5 January 1886, AE *dossier personnel*, Raindre; DDF (4) iv.
544, 554, 559, 566, 579, 580, 596, 601, 604, 608.

[37] De Freycinet to de Courcel, 2 January 1886, AE *dossier personnel*, Raindre.

[38] Ibid., Baron de Stockhausen, to the Quai d'Orsay, 30 July 1891; Raindre to Valfrey,
30 September 1878, 5 September 1879, AE Valfrey MSS, 2.

[39] AE *dossier personnel*, Raindre, de Courcel to J. Herbette, 5 January 1886.

tion meant that his *esprit de décision* yielded to the Minister's authority and goals. Writing to Rouvier in December 1905, he clearly outlined the nature of his relationship with Delcassé when he spoke of 'm'incliner devant sa décision, dans l'esprit qui a guidé ma longue carrière'.[40] Consequently, though he was a skilful administrator, he was a rather servile official.

On occasion, however, Raindre undoubtedly exercised considerable influence. He seems to have contributed to Delcassé's Italian and German policies. Initially he was opposed to an agreement with Italy over Tripolitania. When this objection failed, he suggested that Morocco be grafted on to any Franco-Italian agreement. Similarly, he appears to have been important in shaping the relatively cordial attitude adopted by Delcassé towards Germany until 1900, one which envisaged co-operation with Germany against Britain in the Boer War as well as military and economic collaboration in China. Finally, he staunchly supported the French religious protectorate in the Ottoman Empire and strengthened Delcassé's resolve to maintain it.[41]

By the summer of 1902 the Egyptian question required someone with specialized knowledge, and Raindre made way for Georges Cogordan. Cogordan proved more influential. Born in 1849, he had entered the service as an unpaid attaché in 1874. He filled various posts abroad and at the Centrale in the next twenty years. However, his most important task in a period of tense relations with Britain was being consul-general in Cairo from April 1894.

Cogordan was a highly intelligent man, full of talent and charm, and a hard worker. He had a degree in letters and a doctorate in law. Although he had a 'caractère droit et sûr' he was also flexible. This trait was to be extremely helpful during the Anglo-French negotiations which eventually led to the *Entente Cordiale*.[42] Another great ability was his capacity to handle colleagues and to run his department efficiently. He was well liked by the Cambons, Nisard, and Jusserand, and was a close friend of Paléologue. In 1885 he specifically requested that the latter accompany him to China.[43] Throughout 1903, a crucial year in negotiations for the

[40] Ibid., Raindre to Rouvier, 5 December 1905.

[41] *DDF* (1) xiv. 74, 79; P. Guillen, *L'Allemagne et le Maroc, 1870-1905* (Paris, 1969), p. 823.

[42] AE *dossier personnel*, G. Cogordan; P. Cambon to H. Cambon, 25 March 1904; *Paul Cambon: Correspondance: 1870-1924*, ed. H. Cambon (Paris, 1940-6), ii. 130; Cogordan to Hanotaux, 26 October 1895, AE Hanotaux MSS, 18.

[43] Paléologue to Collin de Plancy, January 1886, AE Collin de Plancy MSS, 4; Quai d'Orsay to Cogordan, 1 July 1885, AE *dossier personnel*, Cogordan.

Anglo-French *Entente Cordiale*, he arrived before 7 a.m. at the Centrale. His untimely death in March 1904 from an acute attack of appendicitis could be attributed in part to the time he put into his work.

Cogordan was thoroughly Republican in outlook and background. He married Marie Duclerc, the daughter of a Republican senator, in 1884, and became the president of the Conseil général des Basses-Alpes. While minister to Cairo in 1895, he sought election to the French Senate.[44] Though he took this step primarily to increase his authority in Cairo (a measure not unusual for diplomats of the Third Republic) he was genuinely interested in Republican politics. Even so, like most diplomats he was contemptuous of politicians who entered the realm of diplomacy, and he fought bitterly against a visit to Egypt in 1885 by a politician, Deloncle.[45]

Cogordan was happy to exchange Cairo's intemperate climate and difficult political situation for a powerful position in Paris. Delcassé named him political director before he had made up his mind to concede Egypt to Britain. Cogordan therefore thought that in his new position he could strengthen the French government's hostility to Britain's occupation of Egypt. While Delcassé certainly had a high esteem for his director, it is to be doubted that Cogordan altered his views.[46] His desire to expel Britain from Egypt, which persisted until 1903, required no prompting from the political director. In 1903, Cogordan dutifully facilitated Anglo-French talks as much as possible, but he was by nature anti-British, highly suspicious of Britain's activity in Egypt, and thus hardly the man to persuade Delcassé to come speedily to terms with her.[47]

Apart from Raindre and Cogordan, the other important director during Delcassé's first ministry was Maurice Bompard, head of the commercial division between 1895 and 1902. Maurice Bompard's career was representative of those bourgeois civil servants who entered the Foreign Ministry after the purges of the late 1870s and who had a prefectoral background. He was born in 1854 in Metz and received a thoroughly Catholic education. After studying law, he rose though the administration of the Ministry of the Interior to become Paul Cambon's *chef du cabinet* at a time when Cambon was prefect of the Nord. Thus

[44] Cogordan to Hanotaux, 19 May, 3 July 1895, AE *dossier personnel*, Cogordan.

[45] Cogordan to Hanotaux, 6 April 1895, AE Hanotaux MSS, 18.

[46] Dumaine to Jusserand, 30 August 1902, AE Jusserand, MSS, 60; Jusserand to Delcassé, 18 July 1902, AE Delcassé MSS, 4. Delcassé had first asked Jusserand, who rejected the post as too physically demanding.

[47] P. Cambon to H. Cambon, 25 March 1904, *Correspondance*, ii. 130.

began a lifelong collaboration. Bompard befriended, admired, and was strongly influenced by Paul Cambon, whom he freely acknowledged as his mentor.[48]

Cambon, for his part, held Bompard's technical expertise in high esteem, and employed him as his principal subordinate in the organization of the Tunisian protectorate after 1882. Bompard's organizational ability, his success in combining firmness with flexibility, and his sympathy towards the natives won him high praise. On returning to the Centrale, he became the chief of the African bureau of the Quai d'Orsay. In this capacity he was made responsible in 1889 for the establishment of the protectorate in Madagascar. Shortly after he was sent to Montenegro as resident minister, but his financial expertise and his administrative competence were soon needed in Paris. Commercial affairs were assuming more importance, and in 1895 he became commercial director.[49]

Bompard was an almost perfect administrator. Apart from his intelligence, his tremendous financial and legal knowledge, and his capacity for work, he was an extremely skilful organizer, clear-minded and rational. He instilled in his subordinates a high degree of professional expertise.[50] He prescribed regular hours of work for the commercial division, and even Delavaud, so critical of the hours and quality of work of most officials, could lay no complaint. None the less, Bompard was open to criticism as commercial director. Not only did his mechanical efficiency and cold logical approach make him 'un peu distant' to his colleagues, but his high level of technical skill prevented him from deriving general concepts from philosophical rather than technical ideas. Some colleagues even considered him rather narrow-minded and rigid.[51]

During his eight years as commercial director, Bompard believed that the Quai d'Orsay had little appreciation of the importance of economic questions. Not only was he instrumental in making the commercial division important in political decisions but he was one of the first bureaucrats who saw the great political advantages which could accrue

[48] AE *dossier personnel*, Bompard; M. Bompard, *Mon ambassade en Russie* (Paris, 1937), pp. 291, 304, 305.

[49] P. Cambon, notes, 1 July 1886, AE *dossier personnel*, Bompard.

[50] D. Phelps, 'La France et la Crise Liman von Sanders', *Revue d'histoire de la Guerre mondiale* (January 1937), p. 24; P. Cambon to Pichon, 3 February 1908, Inst. de Fr. Pichon MSS, 2; Delavaud to Delcassé, note, 17 July 1903, AE Delcassé MSS, 4.

[51] Douclet's conversation with Paléologue, August 1914, AE Doulcet MSS; J. Cambon to P. Cambon, 30 January, 4 March 1911, AE J. Cambon MSS, 19; Bompard to Hanotaux, 28, 29, 31 December 1894, AE Hanotaux MSS, 18: J. J. Jusserand, *What Me Befell* (New York, 1933), p. 66.

from commercial concessions. He was the principal negotiator of treaties of commerce, agreements concluded with foreign powers, and international conventions of a technical nature. He completed his work in Tunisia by giving the territory a statute which largely liberated it from engagements undertaken to other countries prior to the protectorate. Finally, he participated in the foundation of the Office national du commerce extérieur in 1898, an establishment which acted as a co-ordinating centre for the Ministries of Foreign Affairs, Finance and Commerce, and various business groups.[52]

He was able to shape policy when economic questions were involved. Delcassé thought him highly professional, and worked closely with him. Bompard helped prepare the 1898 Franco-Italian commercial accord, believing it would unlock the door to political *rapprochement*. He contributed to Delcassé's cautious response to a proposal to divide China into spheres of influence before the Russians, Americans, and British became deeply entrenched. To the chagrin of Ernest Constans, French ambassador to Constantinople, he frequently concerned himself with France's Turkish policy, which was as much economic as political.[53]

Under Delcassé the evolution of the central administration of the Quai d'Orsay contrasted noticeably with that of the British Foreign Office between 1898 and 1905. In the early twentieth century the Foreign Office was beginning to flex its muscle and to become more involved in decision-making at a high level. In France the Sous-direction du Nord and the Sous-direction du Midi had been consistently powerful bureaux before 1898, but their power had owed much to personal relations with the foreign minister and to government instability. Their legal status remained ill defined, their attributions often hazy. Delcassé brought stability and jealously guarded his ministerial prerogatives. Those officials, notably Saint-René-Taillandier, Beau, and Paléologue, who were influential with him generally confirmed his wider reading of international relations.

Though the Sous-direction du Midi was not as important in this period as the Sous-direction du Nord, it had considerable influence in Mediterranean questions. Its chief between 1895 and 1901, Georges Saint-René-Taillandier, had a substantial voice in the Moroccan question, which came to figure prominently in French foreign policy under Delcassé.

[52] Bompard, *Mon ambassade*, pp. 315, 335.
[53] Pichon to Delcassé, 29 August 1898, Bompard to Mme Nogues, 29 October 1931, Constans to Delcassé, 10 September 1902, AE Delcassé MSS; Bompard to Constans, 12 February 1901, AE Constans MSS, 3.

Saint-René-Taillandier was born at Montpellier in September 1852. His father was a professor of poetry at the Sorbonne, and he entered the Quai d'Orsay in August 1876 as attaché to the political division. After successive posts in Rome, Egypt, Munich, The Hague, and Beirut, where as consul-general he was under Paul Cambon's supervision, an important point to note, he became *sous-directeur du Midi*.[54]

As *sous-directeur du Midi*, a position which demanded a grasp of oriental and Moroccan affairs, he was a highly competent administrator. He was noted for his 'autorité', 'assiduité du travail', and his 'jugement'. He rarely spared himself and demanded punctuality, hard work, and competence from his colleagues. He could, as well, be intransigent and narrow-minded, and these characteristics undoubtedly created enemies eager to prevent him from obtaining an embassy.[55]

Saint-René-Taillandier's main problem was the Moroccan question, and Delcassé appears to have leaned on him heavily for advice. He was an ardent nationalist and approached his mission in Morocco with a kind of religious zeal. Despite being an agnostic he was committed to the French religious protectorate. Though Delcassé had planned to delay a forward policy in Morocco until the international conjuncture became more favourable, he gradually succumbed to his adviser's aggressive outlook. Saint-René frequently drafted many of the instructions he carried out. He was clearly worried about British involvement in Morocco and was instrumental, with Paul Cambon, in initiating measures which would lead to Britain's withdrawal.[56]

Saint-René's career was shrouded with controversy, perhaps because much of it was associated with the Mediterranean region. As consul-general in Beirut, he was violently attacked in February 1895 by the then *rapporteur du budget*, Doumer, for not taking care of French economic interests in Syria. Later, in April 1909, a deputy, Dubief, attacked him for his careless protection of French nationals in Morocco, especially Dr Mauchamp, a French doctor, whose assassination contributed to the Casablanca incidents. The press also assailed him for his supposed timidity as minister in Morocco. The press outcry was so strong at one

[54] AE *dossier personnel*, G. Saint-René-Taillandier. It was the fall of Delcassé and the failure of his mission which led to the decline of Saint-René's career and his exile to Lisbon.

[55] Ibid.; Comte de Saint-Aulaire, *Confessions d'un vieux diplomate* (Paris, 1953), pp. 61, 72; J. Cambon to P. Cambon, 24 February 1907, AE J. Cambon MSS, 19; Regnault to Revoil, 28 March 1905, AE Revoil MSS, 2; letters from Saint-René in 1899 to Doulcet, AE Doulcet MSS, 14.

[56] Delcassé to Étienne, 16 August 1904; Saint-René-Taillandier to Étienne, 31 July 1903, BN (NAF 24237), Étienne MSS; Nicolson to FO, 20 January 1902, FO 99/394, confidential print; Rolo, *Entente Cordiale*, pp. 133–4.

stage that his wife, an author of great note, asked the eminent journalist Tardieu to her Parisian apartment to explain her husband's policies. It was to no avail.[57] He continued to be attacked, and Foreign Minister Jonnart made him retire in 1913. There appears to have been something personal in this forced retirement, since Jonnart had been governor-general of Algeria during Saint-René's ministry in Morocco and had criticized him for timidity.

Saint-René-Taillandier's successor as *sous-directeur du Midi*, Comte Charles Prosper Maurice Horric de Beaucaire, did not have the same influence, though he achieved a considerable say in specific areas. He was born in May 1854 in Nantes to aristocratic Catholic parents. He hailed from a long line of nobles who had served the state and who had family links with the highest Austrian nobility. Like many diplomats, he viewed government service as a family business and his cousin du Halgouet was also employed by the Foreign Ministry. In 1889 he cemented his links with the aristocracy by marrying Yvonne le Goilldec de Traissan.

Beaucaire's career had been spent mainly in dealing with *questions méridionales et orientales*. In 1876 he had been attached to Berlin, where he attended the Congress of Berlin in 1878 and the Conférence africaine in 1886. He had also spent time in Serbia and Egypt, where he replaced Saint-René-Taillandier. He returned to the Centrale in May 1888 and was made *sous-directeur adjoint* in 1895 and *sous-directeur du Midi* in 1901.[58]

Beaucaire carried on superbly the traditions of the *ancienne carrière*. He was a particularly gifted *littérateur*. He had acquired degrees in law, literature, and science and knew English, Italian, Danish, Norwegian, Russian, Arabic, and German, the last of which he spoke like a mother tongue. Apart from these remarkable linguistic qualities, he was a prolific writer of histories and most notably had written a superb history on Serbian nationalism under the influence of Michel Obrenovitch III.[59]

Beaucaire was an extremely able administrator who was liked by most of his colleagues. He worked closely with Nisard, former political director and ambassador to the Vatican from 1899. The two were intimately involved in the formulation of France's religious policy in the Levant.[60] His friendship with Raindre was even closer. They had worked together

[57] Mme Saint-René-Taillandier to Tardieu, dated 1910, AN 324 AP 15 Tardieu MSS.

[58] AE *dossier personnel*, Beaucaire; J. Cambon to Pichon, 24 June 1909, AE J. Cambon MSS, 16.

[59] J. Cambon to Pichon, 24 June 1909, AE J. Cambon MSS, 16; 'La Serbie contemporaine' (in manuscript form), AE Beaucaire MSS, 13.

[60] Nisard to Beaucaire, 10 July 1901, AE Beaucaire MSS, 1.

as attachés in Berlin in the 1870s, at the Congress of Berlin in 1878, and at the Conférence africaine in Berlin in 1886.[61] Beaucaire was on less amicable terms with Louis, who became political director in 1904 and whom he later blamed for his subsequent demise after 1909 and his failure to obtain the St Petersburg Embassy.[62]

As *sous-directeur du Midi* Beaucaire adopted a professional approach. Though he rarely wrote notes or annotations on particular issues, his historical works show that he had a profound knowledge of the East. As Raindre explained, he showed 'un souci constant de connaîotre les origines et les diverses phases des questions'. Besides this intellectual curiosity, colleagues noted his taste for 'méthode et précision', his 'sûreté', and his 'remarquable puissance de travail'.[63] Yet despite his valuable work, which Delcassé himself noted, he does not seem to have been especially important in the formulation of France's Italian policy or in deciding the Moroccan and Egyptian questions. Basically he was concerned with the Levant, especially the Macedonian question and the issue of the religious protectorate, and it was in these areas that he made his mark.

Beaucaire's role, then, was limited in scope. He was a good technical adviser with a sound knowledge of the Orient. Yet Delcassé appears to have consulted him only on highly specialized questions: incidents in the holy places, the Macedonian question, and legal aspects of the Tunisian protectorate. However, this role was largely inevitable since, in Delcassé's period, the government was unwilling to upset the status quo in the Balkans or to consider a dissolution of the Ottoman Empire. Finally, the Macedonian question defied analysis and solution. Temporary expedients such as calling for reforms from Turkey appeared to be the only answer in a situation which was highly explosive.[64]

The role of Alfred Chilhaud-Dumaine, *sous-directeur du Nord* from 1899 to 1904, is hard to discern despite his long career. Born in 1852, he took a degree in law, as well as completing studies in archives and palaeography.[65] In later years he was considered to be a conservative clerical and was ostracized by Clemenceau and some of the Radicals. Nevertheless, he was protected by Poincaré when the latter came to power.[66] He was something of an intriguer, acting as a source for overseas agents about the

[61] Ibid., Raindre to Beaucaire, 26 December 1898.
[62] Ibid. 10, Beaucaire to unknown, 29 January 1909.
[63] Notes by Raindre, 26 February 1901, d'Aunay, 27 June 1886, de Freycinet, 2 July 1885, AE *dossier personnel*, Beaucaire.
[64] Manuscript of work on Serbia, AE Beaucaire MSS, 13, 14.
[65] *Annuaire diplomatique* (1909), pp. 173–4.
[66] *Notes journalières*, 31 January 1914, BN (NAF 16026), Poincaré MSS.

Centrale's 'potins des couloirs' and successfully manoeuvring Jusserand out of the Sous-direction du Nord in 1899.[67]

His entrance into the Quai d'Orsay in 1877 resulted from the intervention of his father, a career diplomat. After minor posts in the Contentieux (1877), Constantinople (1878), the private ministerial cabinet (1880), and the political division in the 1880s, he served in Berlin (1887–91), and Brussels (1892–96). When recalled to the Centrale, he was put in charge of the Sous-direction du contentieux, but felt the job to be thankless and of limited importance.[68] These sentiments in part explain why he pushed for Jusserand's removal. Delcassé named him deputy director in January 1899, a position he retained until becoming chargé d'affaires in Munich in September 1904.

Surprisingly little is known about his role during the years 1899–1904. The manner in which Delcassé included him in the general reshuffling of personnel suggests that the Foreign Minister believed him to be a faithful follower who would act according to instructions.[69] He did not play an important part in any major negotiations. Nevertheless, prior to 1903 he may have helped to shape the Quai d'Orsay's attitude towards Britain. He was thoroughly anti-British, knew no English, and was disgusted with British customs and public life. Furthermore he had refused a position in London in 1895 under de Courcel.[70] He pressed Delcassé to defend French interests (in Egypt and elsewhere) against Britain and he seems to have been totally ignored after Delcassé decided to seek an *Entente Cordiale.*

Dumaine had a more balanced approach to Germany. Whether this developed after he became chargé d'affaires in Munich or before is uncertain. He discounted theories that Germany would provoke a war, and, during the Moroccan crisis of 1905, tended to see France rather than Germany in the role of aggressor. He was appalled by talk on the French side in favour of a war, seeing such a conflict as an 'effroyable aventure'. He thought that political instability in France, the weakness of the French officer corps, and the strength of the German army precluded any such aggression on France's part.[71]

Such an attitude would not have met with Delcassé's approval, and it was clear that the deputy director's usefulness in the Centrale was at an

[67] Note by Jusserand, AE Jusserand MSS, 21; Dumaine to Doulcet, 12 May 1892, AE Doulcet MSS, 15.
[68] Dumaine to Doulcet, undated, AE Doulcet MSS, 17.
[69] Dumaine to Delcassé, 30 April 1904, AE Delcassé MSS, 4.
[70] Dumaine to Doulcet, 22 May 1895, AE Doulcet MSS, 17.
[71] Ibid. 15, Dumaine to Doulcet, 24 January 1906.

end. Nevertheless Delcassé continued to look favourably on him, even
granting a request relating to one of Dumaine's subordinates, Le
Marchand.[72] In the Centrale itself he seems to have got on well with most
colleagues, Paléologue being his 'ami spirituel'.[73] He had a good working
relationship with Jules Cambon, then ambassador to Washington. He
was impressed by the latter's observations on America, and usually
supported Cambon's views in the Centrale.[74]

The limited influence of Beaucaire and Dumaine reflected the diminution of power suffered by the bureaux of the Centrale during Delcassé's period. Before 1898, and especially during Hanotaux's ministry,
they had acted as powerful forces in the formulation of French foreign
policy. Their curtailment in the years 1898–1904 was due far less, however, to reorganization than to the personality of Delcassé. The Minister
was determined to control policy-making as fully as possible. As long as
Delcassé remained foreign minister he had little interest in reorganization, and it was noticeable that the transition from nineteenth to
twentieth century was decidedly piecemeal. Yet the Quai d'Orsay's
power remained important and even increased in overall terms, largely
because of the new ambassadorial triumvirate (Barrère, Jules, and Paul
Cambon) and their intimate collaboration with the Foreign Minister.
The Delcassian period witnessed, therefore, not a destruction of the
Quai d'Orsay's power but rather a shifting of the balance between the
Centrale and the Republic's leading ambassadors.

[72] Dumaine to Delcassé, 30 September 1904, AE Delcassé MSS, 4. Dumaine had asked
to have his post given to Le Marchand, but Soulange-Bodin received it. Le Marchand was
made president of the French delegation of the Commission des Pyrénées.
[73] M. Paléologue, *Au Quai d'Orsay à la veille de la tourmente* (Paris, 1947), p. 48.
[74] Dumaine to Jusserand, 30 August 1902, AE Jusserand MSS, 60.

4

Delcassé and the Ambassadorial Élite, 1898–1904

While Delcassé's love of work, his secrecy, and his will to power ensured that he was in control of the diplomatic machinery in Paris to the exclusion of the political division, Parliament, the cabinet, and even the *président du conseil*, it would be fallacious to suppose that Delcassian diplomacy was purely or even mainly his work. Rather, the formulation of policy in the years 1898–1904 owed much to an intimate collaboration between Delcassé and his leading ambassadors: Barrère, the Cambons, Constans, and Jusserand.

The search to find who initiated Franco-Italian or Anglo-French policies loses much of its meaning when the community of views between Delcassé and his principal ambassadors is taken into account. Delcassé, Barrère, and the Cambons were all close members of the fellowship that had as its origins the influence of Léon Gambetta, the shock of France's military defeat at Sedan in 1870, and the desire to atone for the territory and prestige lost during the Franco-Prussian war.

The personalities of Delcassé and his ambassadors encouraged a close working relationship. As one first-hand observer succinctly remarked, Delcassé was not 'un de ces hommes qui ne voudrait peut-être pas avoir l'air de poser les questions'. Nevertheless, he was 'très heureux qu'on lui donne spontanément l'aide'.[1] This is precisely what men such as Barrère and Paul Cambon did, often proffering advice without the request of the Minister. At the same time none of these men would have allowed Delcassé to dictate policy. Moreover, they conceived of their ambassadorial role in terms which precluded any attempt on Delcassé's part to treat them as mere letter boxes.

Friendship was also an important factor in bringing about an intimate collaboration between Foreign Minister and ambassadors. Delcassé liked his most powerful ambassadors and identified with them both socially and politically.[2] Barrère had met Delcassé and supervised him

---

[1] Daeschner to Doulcet, 21 Feb. 1913, AE Doulcet MSS, 20.
[2] C. de Chambrun, *L'Esprit de la diplomatie* (Paris, 1944), p. 42.

when the latter was a fledgeling journalist on the *République française*. Later, Delcassé called him his closest friend in public life, and Barrère acted as Delcassé's *témoin* at his wedding. The Cambons, too, had met the Minister in the offices of Gambetta and were later to call on Delcassé socially on many occasions.

More importantly, confidence in their professional merit encouraged the Foreign Minister to give his leading ambassadors a large part in the making of high-level decisions. He fully appreciated their zeal, intelligence, loyalty, and advice. This admiration did not mean, however, that he abdicated final responsibility or allowed himself to be intimidated by his ambassadors. Barrère's complaint once that he had received no personal note from Delcassé for some time did not provoke a spate of letter writing on Delcassé's part. Equally, Delcassé could be found 'absent without leave' when Paul Cambon came to Paris to lecture him. When he felt it necessary he could put his foot down and act decisively, as he did with Barrère over the Tripolitania–Morocco barter. He was not averse to keeping information from Barrère and the Cambons when it suited him.[3] Generally, however, there was a broad consensus on the major issues.

Conversely, ambassadorial confidence in a Republican foreign minister had never been so high. French diplomats were conscious of Delcassé's limitations, his vivid imagination, and his inflexibility.[4] Nevertheless, they were highly appreciative of his ability to set definite policy goals, to see them through ministerial crises, and to handle Parliament and the press with adroitness.[5] Mutual support and friendship ensured that the diplomatic machinery worked well in these years and usually precluded an ambassadorial hostility capable of sabotaging or hindering the policies of the government.

Undoubtedly, the expertise of the principal ambassadors, their personalities, and their community of views and friendship with Delcassé did much to strengthen their authority. Yet to a considerable extent their power was also derived from the fact that they were 'political' ambassadors, representatives of the Republic who advocated clear lines of policy: Franco-Italian *rapprochement*, Anglo-French friendship, and Franco-German *détente*. The removal of any one of them would have

---

[3] Barrère to Delcassé, 5 May 1901, AE Barrère MSS, 4.

[4] P. Cambon to J. Cambon, 17 Jan. 1899, Louis Cambon MSS.

[5] Ibid., P. Cambon to H. Cambon, 23 July 1898; J. Cambon to Delcassé, 23 Jan. 1905, AE Delcassé MSS, 4.

been considered as a reversal of policy on the part of the French government.[6]

Barrère and the Cambons formed an inner diplomatic cabinet that was to remain unbroken until after the First World War. They not only advised the minister, often when no such request had been issued, but at times lectured and intimidated him.[7] If hindered, they were capable of trying to force his hand through external pressure. They regularly convened in Paris, especially in moments of crisis, and few foreign ministers between 1898 and 1914 made a major decision without consulting them.

They were also extremely powerful within the Quai d'Orsay. They regularly advised the minister on personnel changes, and only rarely did he ignore or contravene their wishes. This privilege gave them tremendous leverage, enabling them to place their supporters in the most prominent positions.[8] Such patronage became increasingly important to Jules Cambon and Barrère in later years due to the fact that the central bureaux were often against their policies of *détente* with Berlin and Rome. Despite the increasing importance of the political director, especially after 1907, the fact that he was technically inferior in grade and had worked under at least one member of the triumvirate ensured that their influence over the central administration remained largely intact. It also ensured that they had the minister's ear and that the political director would not normally challenge their power.

Paul Cambon was clearly the undisputed master of the group and the *éminence grise* of the Quai d'Orsay. He and his brother Jules were born in the 1840s (Paul on 20 January 1843, Jules on 4 April 1845) to middle-class parents. Their father Martin was a leather merchant without great wealth or important connections. Their mother Virginie Larue held very liberal opinions and was a tolerant clerical. Their grandfather on their mother's side had been a captain in the national guard under Louis-Philippe. The early life and career of the two Cambon brothers reflected their thoroughly bourgeois origins. Both rejected the philosophies of the socialists and the reign of Louis Napoléon. Within the

---

[6] P. Cambon to J. Cambon, 6 June 1912, *Paul Cambon: Correspondance* (Paris, 1940–6), iii. 17; A. Gérard, *Mémoires d'Auguste Gérard* (Paris, 1928) p. 513; G. Louis, *Les Carnets de George Louis* (Paris, 1926), ii, 20 May 1915, p. 190; P. Cambon to J. Cambon, 8 Dec. 1908, Louis Cambon MSS.

[7] P. Cambon to his mother, 27 Jan. 1896, *Correspondance*, i. 400; P. Cambon to H. Cambon, 13, 18 June 1906, Louis Cambon MSS.

[8] For the Manneville affair, see P. Cambon to H. Cambon, 16, 17 Mar., 20 Apr., 12 May, 9, 29 Nov. 1904, 26 Apr. 1905, Louis Cambon MSS; Dard to Gérard, 28 Sept. 1910, AN 329 AP 20 Gérard MSS; P. Cambon to J. Cambon, 19 Jan. 1912, AE J. Cambon MSS, 25.

family there were close connections with the Catholic Church. Their uncle was a future bishop of Langres, and Cardinal Lavigerie was a frequent visitor to the Cambon household. For all this religious fervour, however, neither the parents nor the children were narrow fanatics. Virginie raised her children with as much independence of spirit and depth of reflection as Christian ardour.[9] Undoubtedly, this diverse cultural milieu largely explained their pragmatic, non-doctrinal approach to life and their remarkable flexibility. Their school education strengthened these characteristics. After attending Boniface Boarding School both became day students at Louis le Grand. After receiving the *baccalauréat* they went to the Faculté de droit, during which time they participated in the Molé–Tocqueville Conference, a seminar that produced many government officials.[10]

The years immediately prior to and after the Franco-Prussian war had a profound influence on their political orientation. In the final years of the Second Empire they met Republican leaders Camille Pelletan and Jules Simon. They were frequent visitors to Thiers, Gambetta, and the Ferry family, with whom they had particularly close links. This loose band of Republicans incorporated in their philosophy the teachings of Kant, Michelet, Comte, and Proudhon. Their arena was often the Luxembourg gardens, a simple café, or the Théâtre Bobinotou.[11]

The two most important influences were, however, the Franco-Prussian war and the pervasive authority of Gambetta. The Cambons' later efforts were directed to ensuring that France was in a strong enough diplomatic and military position to prevent a second fiasco. Gambetta was the natural leader. As Jules Cambon told the Académie française in his reception speech: 'Comment ne pas subir la séduction de cet homme éloquent et généreux, dont l'âme était ardente et qui portait en lui un sentiment si vif de la grandeur de la France?'[12]

Paul Cambon's relations with various Republican leaders did much to further his career once the Republic had been established. After being a simple law clerk for a number of years, he became Ferry's secretary when the latter was an administrator in Paris in 1870. Later he had a succession of prefectoral jobs in the Alpes-Maritimes, the Aube, the Doubs, and the Nord. Though politics tempted him throughout his early career, and although he was eventually offered the post of foreign

[9] G. Tabouis, *Jules Cambon par l'un des siens* (Paris, 1938), pp. 7–15; R. I. Weiner, 'Paul Cambon and the Making of the Entente Cordiale', Ph.D. thesis (Rutgers University, 1973) pp. 2–6.

[10] Weiner 'Paul Cambon', 2–6.   [11] Ibid.

[12] Tabouis, *Jules Cambon* p. 15.

minister, he refused to leave government service.[13] He was the first resident minister in Tunis between 1882 and 1886, and became ambassador to
Madrid, 1886–91, ambassador to Constantinople, 1891–98, and finally
ambassador to London, where he stayed for twenty-two years.

While Cambon was a religious man he was never dominated by religion
and could show a tolerance remarkable for the period. As prefect of the
Nord he had refused to implement fully the harsh Ferry laws against
religious orders. The anti-clerical laws of Combes in the early 1900s and
the disastrous effect they had overseas appalled him. Furthermore, although he himself was anti-Jewish and initially convinced of Dreyfus's
guilt, he was prepared to reverse his decision by 1899.[14]

This moderation was also reflected in his political beliefs. He was liberal
by upbringing but conservative by nature. Despite the fact that he had
clearly come out against the Napoleonic regime and blamed it for
France's deplorable performance in the Franco-Prussian war, and although he was generally Republican in sympathy, he was by no means a
radical. First, he was never convinced that universal suffrage was the
answer to France's political problems. The masses were ignorant, and the
bourgeoisie was incapable of ruling France through a democratic parliamentary system. The events of 1848 had amply demonstrated this to him.
The Seize mai crisis and the general purging of the nobility filled him with
the deepest apprehension, and he considered that these events had advanced the socialist cause by fifty years. He viewed the Church as the only
institution left to counter this democratic trend, 'la seule construction
établie sur des assises traditionnelles dans une nation si peu hiérarchisée, si
peu disciplinée, si peu respectueuse de ses institutions'. He fully agreed
with Premier Briand's policy of social order and with the suppression of
strikes by force. In 1911 he begged Pichon to remain in the cabinet for fear
that the Radicals, under men like Caillaux, would lead the country too far
towards the left. Equally, he was concerned with the deleterious effects on
the diplomatic corps of the aristocratic decline. Apart from the fact that
the aristocracy had a natural ability to lead, he considered that they were a
necessity in foreign missions.[15]

[13] P. Cambon to his mother, 1 June 1894, Louis Cambon MSS.
[14] P. Cambon to his wife, 16 Aug. 1880, *Correspondance*, i. 114. Also pp. 131, 144, 255,
315–16, 372–3; P. Cambon to J. Cambon, 16 June 1899, Louis Cambon MSS.
[15] P. Miquel, *Raymond Poincaré* (Paris, 1961) p. 263; Mme Saint-René-Taillandier,
Silhouettes d'ambassadeurs (Paris, 1953), pp. 2, 3; K. Eubank, *Paul Cambon: Master Diplomatist* (Norman, Okla., 1960), p. 3; P. J. V. Rolo, *Entente Cordiale* (London, 1969), p. 93; P.
Cambon to H. Cambon, 8 Oct. 1904, Louis Cambon MSS; P. Cambon to his wife, 14 Nov.
1880, P. Cambon to his mother, 24 May 1894, 24 Feb. 1898, *Correspondance*, i. 131, 372, 437.

At an early stage in his ambassadorial career, Paul Cambon had developed a highly intricate and carefully considered conception of diplomacy. It was his consistency in applying it which helped to provide French foreign policy with a certain continuity. His advice was usually heeded by politicians who had little time to reflect on the nature of international politics. In essence, Cambon was committed to the ideal of peace. He viewed the art of diplomacy as involving the peaceful settlement of differences between nations.[16] Flexibility, practicality, good sense, moderation, compromise, patience, and steadiness were all essential characteristics of a good diplomat. It was these qualities rather than unbending righteousness or social aplomb which ensured the protection of diplomatic interests. In this sense he appreciated the *realpolitik* and pragmatism of Bismarck. Nothing was ever absolute, finished, or straightforward. He mistrusted the search for brilliant diplomatic victories, the advancement of fanatical doctrinal policies, and the unnecessary humiliation of other foreign powers, believing that the natural evolution of things, aided by skilful and patient diplomacy, would provide the necessary benefits.[17]

His view of the ambassador's role is extremely important in explaining his influence. His lament in 1901 that diplomatic history was only a long recital of attempts by agents to achieve something in the face of resistance from Paris was revealing. In part, this emphasis on individual initiative and independence was the result of his Tunisian days, when he had struggled alone and unaided. He was not a subaltern. As he tersely explained to Foreign Minister de Selves in the middle of 1911, he considered himself to be the equal of the Minister. He often burnt his instructions when he disagreed with them, fought doggedly with men like Clemenceau and Poincaré, frequently acted on his own instructions, and sometimes improved on those of his minister. He believed that, had Benedetti delayed the formal instructions of Gramont for a short while, the Franco-Prussian war could have been avoided. Nevertheless, he never carried on a personal policy against the express wish of the government. Ultimately, he was mindful that the government, in the form of the premier or foreign minister, was sovereign. If he was unable to persuade it to follow him, he was prepared to submit. This rarely occurred, however, as no one could provide an

[16] Eubank, *Cambon*, p.10; P. Cambon to J. Cambon, 19 Jan. 1899, *Correspondance*, ii. 18.
[17] P. Cambon to his son H. Cambon, 10 June 1904, 16 Sept. 1904, *Correspondance*, ii. 24, 53–5, 272; Cambon to Dr Meunier, 28 Dec. 1913, iii. 57.

acceptable alternative to the form of Franco-British friendship that he espoused.[18]

Undoubtedly, his sense of self-importance and his gravity became more pronounced over the years.[19] Commentators remarked rather unfavourably on these features. Clemenceau's biographer Martet believed that Cambon was a bit inclined to dominate and be rather a bore.[20] W. S. Blunt considered him a 'poseur'[21] while Lord Salisbury felt that he was inclined to pontificate.[22] Cambon did not hesitate to consider himself as the elder statesman, the purveyor of advice, and, as Nicolson noted in his memoirs, very much 'monsieur le préfet'.[23] This seriousness was, in part, the result of the early death of his father and of the fact that he assumed the position of head of the family at the tender age of 6. He developed a stern exterior in early political life because he had been thrust into high office at an early age. Furthermore he was sensitive about his bourgeois origins, and about his lack of independent wealth and social position.[24]

Despite a rather cold exterior, Cambon was a passionate man who displayed warmth to those who were close to him. In the 1890s his letters to his wife, who was dying of tuberculosis, clearly demonstrated his capacity for compassion, love, and emotion. He treated his personnel well, and the loyalty they showed him in later years was sufficient testimony to his ability to evoke a warm response in people.[25]

Moreover, his qualities of mind transcended his petty authoritarian ways. He was a highly intelligent man. He possessed 'un grand sens juridique ... la clarté, la rectitude, et la raison'.[26] Added to an instinct for order and organization was an ability to recognize and to dominate the most difficult questions. Although not particularly adept at handling men, he understood them well. All these qualities made for a strong,

---

[18] C. M. Andrew, *Théophile Delcassé and the Making of the Entente Cordiale* (London, 1968), p. 130; I. Halfond, 'Maurice Paléologue' (Temple University, 1974), 174; Eubank, *Cambon* p. 202; B. Auffray, *Pierre de Margerie (1861–1942) et la vie diplomatique de son temps* (Paris, 1976), p. 250; P. Cambon to J. Cambon, 4 Dec. 1917, AE J. Cambon MSS, 25; P. Cambon to H. Cambon, 1 Apr. 1905, *Correspondance*, ii. 181; P. Cambon to Delcassé, 25 Jan., 1 July 1899, 7 Jan. 1900, AE Delcassé MSS, 3.
[19] Mme Saint-René-Taillandier, *Silhouettes*, p. 3.
[20] J. Martet, *Clemenceau* (Paris, 1930) p. 140.
[21] W. S. Blunt, *My Diaries* (London, 1919), i. 387.
[22] J. A. S. Grenville, *Lord Salisbury and English Foreign Policy* (London, 1964), p. 232.
[23] Tabouis, *Jules Cambon*, pp. 14, 31–5.
[24] P. Cambon to his wife, 2 Apr. 1884, *Correspondance*, i.
[25] A. Thierry, *L'Angleterre au temps de Paul Cambon* (Paris, 1961), p. 27.
[26] Ibid.

realistic, and flexible personality, full of initiative and patience in carrying out policies.

His relationship with his brother was particularly close and was one in
which Jules tended to defer to him. Since the death of their father Paul
had acted as a substitute parent, calling his younger brother 'mon cher
enfant', advising him on his career, protecting his interests, and severely
admonishing him at times.[27] After the Algerian episode, where Jules had
met strong opposition to his rule as governor-general, Paul was able to
prevent him from being disgraced. Later, he worked successfully on
Delcassé to recall Jules to Europe after the mild exile of Washington.[28]
During the Poincaré period he became a mediator between the Foreign
Minister and Jules Cambon and stopped his brother from resigning.
Though Paul was usually the master, Jules never lost his independence
of thought and judgement and was responsible for many important
initiatives. The fact that Paul Cambon was enraged (in certain circumstances) by his brother testifies to the fact that Jules could and did go his
own way. Most of the time, however, the two men shared the same basic
views. If Jules was adamant about a particular issue which met with
ministerial or administrative opposition, Paul threw his very considerable weight behind his brother.

Paul Cambon's relationship with his colleagues involved awe, respect,
and jealousy, but rarely affection. Barrère and Paul Cambon had a
mutual admiration for each other, as each respected the zeal, intelligence, independence, and vision of the other.[29] Nevertheless, Barrère
was interested in the London Embassy after 1902, when he felt his main
work in Italy was accomplished. He seems to have talked to people like
Delcassé and Pichon about the position but was apparently unwilling to
seek it through intrigue. In the 'inner cabinet' Barrère's voice was loudly
and often heard, but Paul's was usually decisive on most matters.

Cambon had strong views about most of his colleagues. Raindre was a
'paper boy' in Paul's opinion, and the Ambassador always went directly
to Delcassé. With Cogordan it was somewhat different. Cambon
thought highly of the political director and worked closely with him. He
was 'aimable' and 'excellent' and had fostered Henri Cambon's
career.[30] Louis impressed him as an administrator, but he disliked his
general independence. Cambon considered Paléologue to be intelligent
and competent but dangerously imaginative for a diplomat. In 1914

[27] Tabouis, Jules Cambon, pp. 10, 24–7.
[28] P. Cambon to H. Cambon, 23 July 1898, Louis Cambon MSS.
[29] Ibid.   [30] Ibid., P. Cambon to H. Cambon, 25 Mar. 1904.

Cambon erroneously believed that, if Paléologue were shifted from the Centrale to the St Petersburg Embassy, he would be capable of doing less damage to French foreign policy.

Cambon inspired loyalty in his subordinates, undoubtedly because of his professionalism and his vision but also because he fostered their careers. De Fleuriau, Geoffray, Bompard, Thierry, Daeschner and Jusserand were all indebted to him. Nevertheless he sometimes aroused tremendous jealousy, mostly because of his tendency to interfere in areas outside his immediate competence and partly because of his haughty manner. In 1908 and 1913 there were attempts to remove him, both in political circles and in the Quai d'Orsay. On the first occasion prolonged sickness made him vulnerable, and in 1913 Poincaré, now at the Élysée, apparently considered his removal.[31] He weathered both storms remarkably well.

In London, Cambon maintained a regular routine. Each morning he rode in Hyde Park, often meeting (not by accident) important English officials and dignitaries. On returning, he carefully scrutinized the day's correspondence and, after consulting his colleagues, sent off official dispatches. After a long lunch he went to the Foreign Office. Since he could not speak English (and believed that to speak it showed a cultural deficiency) he kept his interviews to five or ten minutes. It was noted with much humour in London that Cambon insisted that the simplest words like 'yes' had to be translated into French by his interpreter before a response was forthcoming. The brevity of interviews, however, also reflected his view that what had to be said could be said tactfully but succinctly. At night he wrote his private correspondence, voluminous to say the least. Foreign Minister Pichon once received a letter over twenty pages in length. Moreover, not a single topic of importance to French policy ever eluded his attention.[32] Indeed, he acted as an *éminence grise* and sometimes as *de facto* foreign minister. Every two weeks and at crucial times he journeyed to Paris to talk with his ministers, to oversee the work of the political director, and to keep a close watch on the bureaux. As his subordinate Geoffray remarked in 1906: 'Depuis huit ans qu'il est à Londres, l'ambassade est pour ainsi dire à Paris.'[33]

In 1898 Cambon had hardly been enthusiastic about going to London

[31] Taigny to de Fleuriau, 26 Oct. 1908, AE P. Cambon MSS, 12.

[32] P. Cambon to H. Cambon, 15 Nov. 1907, Paul Cambon to his mother, 23 Feb. 1899, Louis Cambon MSS.

[33] Remark made to Brugère, 5 June 1906, by Geoffray in G. Kreis, 'Frankreichs republikanische Großmachtpolitik, 1870–1914' (Basle University, 1980), notes, p. 136, n. 390t.

and had earlier refused the post. He thought that in the circumstances of 1898 there was little that could be done in London. Moreover, he liked Constantinople and believed that he could arrest the erosion of French influence which had occurred under Hanotaux. Finally, his wife did not want to live in London, and he himself, not speaking English, did not relish the prospect of English society. Delcassé's insistence and the lack of an ambassador during the emerging Fashoda crisis convinced Cambon to move.[34]

Cambon's role in the making of the *Entente Cordiale* of 1904 was decisive. The actual nature of the *Entente*, the translation into action of Delcassé's ideas, and the specific timing of the agreement were Cambon's doing. As Saint-Aulaire noted, he supported Delcassé with 'une adhésion active et éclairée. Il exécutait d'autant mieux ses instructions qu'il les inspirait dans une grande mesure.'[35]

The second of the powerful triumvirate was Jules Cambon. A lawyer by profession, he was attached in 1874 to the Director-General of Civil Affairs in Algeria. On his return in 1879, he was appointed secretary-general for the Prefecture of the Police. In 1882, he was made prefect of the Nord and then became prefect of the Rhône in 1887. In 1891 he accepted the governor-generalship of Algeria, a rather controversial and thankless position given colonial intrigues in Algeria and Paris. Finally Hanotaux offered him the Washington Embassy in 1897, an exile to be sure, but a welcome relief from Algerian squabbles.

As a youth, he had 'plus de feu, de malice gaie, de diversité et de flâneur capricieux' than his brother.[36] In later years he developed into a man of perception, realism, justice, moderation, and compromise.[37] His colleagues inside and outside the Quai d'Orsay recognized his perspicacity, and he quickly developed a reputation for being a skilled negotiator.[38] He was deeply imbued with an almost spiritual love of France and wished to promote the grand destiny which the nation had begun centuries before.[39] He was equally passionate about peace and continually haunted by the Franco-Prussian war. His natural optimism,

[34] P. Cambon to his mother, 20 Jan., 20 Apr. 1893, 26 May 1898, P. Cambon to H. Cambon, 6, 8 Aug., 16 Sept. 1898, Louis Cambon MSS; Delcassé to P. Cambon, 14 Sept. 1898 P. Cambon to Delcassé, 29 Sept. 1898, AE Delcassé MSS, 3.
[35] Comte de Saint-Aulaire, *Confessions d'un vieux diplomate* (Paris, 1953), p. 72.
[36] Mme Saint-René-Taillandier, *Silhouettes*, p. 6.
[37] M. Paléologue, *Au Quai d'Orsay à la veille de la tourmente* (Paris, 1947), p. 214.
[38] A. Ferry, *Les Carnets Secrets d'Abel Ferry* (Paris, 1957), p. 20; Dumaine to Jusserand, 30 Aug. 1902, AE Jusserand MSS, 60.
[39] J. Cambon to Reinach, 23 Jan. 1911, BN (NAF 24875), Reinach MSS.

combined with his deep pacific sentiments, made him strive hard in the interests of peace.[40] He believed that no war was inevitable and that no situation was irretrievable if skilful and patient diplomacy was applied.[41]

None the less, Cambon had his faults. His optimistic nature could work against him. He might often walk into the midst of a storm without an umbrella, as his brother once aptly phrased it. He did not measure his words enough and could sometimes speak impulsively.[42] His private correspondence testifies to this impulsiveness. His second draft of a letter was often considerably more moderate in tone than the first. Nevertheless, in letters to his government, and in his attitude towards those who disagreed with him, he could become extremely impatient. Finally, he was secretive, lacked self-confidence, and took criticism personally.[43] Yet these characteristics should not be exaggerated. It was a measure of the man that when asked at a tea party in Washington whether he favoured one side or the other in the Spanish–American War he cheekily replied 'ni thé ni chocolat'.

His life and career were always linked with his brother's and he owed much of his influence and prestige to being 'le frère de l'autre'. Like his brother he was Republican but not radical, and, if anything, he was even more severe on Radical politicians, blaming their intrigues and personal ambitions for the political instability of the Republic and the lack of continuity in the Republic's foreign policy. Unlike his brother he always considered Dreyfus guilty and would have been glad to have buried him once and for all for the sake of France's diplomatic prestige.[44]

Jules Cambon's prestige in the Delcassian period, under his brother's tutelage, took a turn for the better and he was highly influential in Mediterranean affairs. He formed a close friendship with Delcassé and wrote voluminously to him on American and Spanish affairs.[45] Later, when posted to Madrid, he was often absent from his post and regularly joined his brother and Barrère in visiting Delcassé. Delcassé, for his part, shared Cambon's rather jaundiced view of American ambitions in the

[40] Ibid.

[41] Ibid; Tabouis, *Jules Cambon*, p. 156. For information on Cambon, I am indebted to Mr Jean Cabet, former colleague of Jules Cambon in the Banque de Paris et des Pays Bas where Cambon was a director.

[42] P. Cambon to J. Cambon, 4 Nov. 1912, AE J. Cambon MSS, 25.

[43] Ferry, *Carnets*, p. 20.

[44] J. Cambon to his mother, 20 Sept. 1898, AE J. Cambon MSS, 26.

[45] Delcassé actually encouraged such personal letters and both Cambons complied willingly. The tone of their letters, their voluminousness, and their advice marked them out from people like de Courcel in London, and Patenôtre, who tended to write informative letters with much less advice.

Mediterranean and had relied on his expertise in handling the Spanish-American ambitions in the Mediterranean. Later, after Delcassé had shifted Cambon to Madrid, the two worked closely together in negotiating the 1904 Franco-Spanish accord over Morocco. This collaboration was in marked contrast to Patenôtre's earlier embassy in Madrid.

Cambon worked successfully with most of his colleagues. Paléologue was a relative, Jusserand and Bompard friends. Dumaine, the *sous-directeur du Nord*, was highly appreciative of Cambon's wisdom and worked closely with him.[46] Cambon does not seem to have held Raindre or Cogordan in high esteem; neither received the private letters which were later sent to Paléologue and Louis.[47] Barrère and Jules Cambon were also on friendly terms, but the latter tended to consider the Rome Ambassador as rather aggressive and short-sighted at times.[48] In Jules Cambon's opinion, Barrère was too responsive to the wishes of the Italian government.

Cambon, like his brother, was convinced of the importance of his ambassadorial role, believing that the government was incapable of properly formulating or implementing policy. At times he considered himself above the instructions of the Quai d'Orsay if they did not take into account his status and his efforts. He made it plain that he was not a postal service but rather the chief executor of policy in a specific area. In later years, as he became increasingly frustrated, he was even more willing than his brother to ignore directives from the Centrale and to initiate personal policies.

Cambon's manner of working clearly reflected his professionalism. He was on excellent terms with his staff, as Manneville, his Berlin secretary, noted in 1914, and went to extreme lengths to protect and further their careers.[49] Indeed, the Cambon brothers appear to have developed a rotation system for placing their protégés in posts under them or in crucial positions in the Centrale. However, despite the Cambons' overall control, their subordinates were allowed substantial independence in their work and were not expected to be mere couriers.

Jules Cambon was a perpetually busy man. His belief in secret diplomacy and in the necessity of personal contacts kept him this way.[50] He developed a daily habit of consulting with his staff while strolling in public parks. On returning to the embassy he would receive visitors and

[46] Dumaine to Jusserand, 30 Aug. 1902, AE Jusserand MSS, 60.
[47] J. Cambon to Louis, 24 Aug. 1908, AE Louis MSS, 2.
[48] Ibid.   [49] Manneville to Doulcet, 26 Apr. 1914, AE Doulcet MSS, 21.
[50] De Margerie to Jusserand, 8 June 1902, AE Jusserand MSS, 22.

study questions to be discussed later at the Foreign Office. It was either in the afternoon or at night that his personal correspondence was written.[51] He frequently invited dignitaries to dine in the hope of furthering his diplomatic ends. Cambon wrote lengthy letters and annotated systematically. The first draft of his letters contained a rough summary of his ideas. The second draft, always in his hand, was a much more refined and balanced project. What was noticeable in his letters was the extent to which he played on the vanity of the Foreign Minister to achieve his ends.

The final member of the triumvirate was Camille Barrère. Born in October 1851, he developed into a lanky, bearded man who resembled Henri IV. His physical appearance contributed to what was a formidable presence.[52] Barrère possessed exceptional intelligence.[53] He loved painting, literature, and music, and learned to play the violin while based in Stockholm. He was also an ardent sportsman, a passionate huntsman, and a competent horse rider who enjoyed conducting diplomatic business on such social occasions.[54]

His life and career involved considerable variety. He came from a long line of Republicans, his father being particularly outspoken and his grandfather being the Barrère of the Convention.[55] After Napoléon III's *coup d'état* the family had fled to Britain, his mother's native country, where his first nineteen years were spent. His English was flawless and later he wrote to Jusserand in the language. Returning to France during the Franco-Prussian war, he became involved with the Paris Commune and wrote for the extreme left-wing paper *La Sociale*.[56] Afterwards he returned to Britain to write for the *Manchester Guardian*, the *Fortnightly Review*, and *Fraser's Magazine*. In 1877 he was the London *Times's* correspondent assigned to cover the Russo-Turkish war. Gambetta gave him employment on *La République française*. In 1880 he was sent as French commissioner of the Danube to Galatz. He worked successfully there with the brother of Thomas Sanderson, later British permanent under-secretary, and was useful in arranging some parts of the Treaty of

[51] Tabouis, *Jules Cambon*, p. 173.

[52] Mme Saint-René-Taillandier, 'Avant le sacerdoce: Le Vicomte Chaptal diplomate', *La Revue des deux mondes* (Aug. 1943), p. 392. Also *Silhouettes*, p. 14; L. Nöel, *Camille Barrère* (Bourges, 1948), p. 77; J. Laroche, *Quinze ans à Rome avec Camille Barrère (1898–1913)* (Pans, 1948), p. 11.

[53] Thomas Sanderson to Rosebery, 18 Apr. 1894, NLS, Rosebery MSS, 10135.

[54] Nöel, *Camille Barrère*, pp. 80–1.

[55] Sanderson to Rosebery, 18 Apr. 1894, NLS Rosebery MSS, 10135.

[56] Ibid.; also de Maugny to Ring, Apr. 1885, AE Ring MSS.

London of 1883. He then became consul-general in Cairo, where he made himself thoroughly disagreeable to the British, something he later tried to excuse.[57] Later, he filled posts in Stockholm, Munich, and Berne. Rome, however, had become his main objective. When Billot retired in 1897, he eagerly accepted Hanotaux's call.[58]

Though Barrère had leftist inclinations in his early days, he was later to become an Opportunist and conservative Republican. He considered, unlike Delcassé, that any future domestic threat to the Republic would come more from the Left than the Right.[59] What primarily concerned Barrère was the necessity for governmental stability, and he called for a pragmatic electoral programme and a united front of moderate parties. Fiscal, military, and administrative reforms were to be undertaken and political questions, such as the separation of Church and State and the income tax, were to be adjourned.[60] Once ambassador to Italy, he took great pains to assure Italian King Umberto that French republicanism was not for export and that French democracy was basically conservative.[61] This was an accurate reflection of his political convictions. Although he appears not to have had precise religious notions, he fully supported France's religious protectorate in the Levant.[62] Barrère had an extreme distaste for politicians and Parliament, vowing to Delcassé in 1886 that he would never enter a ministry of adventure whose days were numbered.[63] While Delcassé shared Barrère's eagerness for Franco-Italian *rapprochement*, and made suggestions, it was largely Barrère whose influence was decisive in the Franco-Italian economic accord of 1898, the Mediterranean accord of 1900, and the neutrality agreement of 1902. Delcassé concentrated on scrutinizing the parliamentary scene, preparing public opinion and promoting Barrère's views at the Centrale.[64] Not only did Barrère guide French policy but, by 1902, the Germans were apprehensive about his influence on Italy.[65] Barrère's conception of the ambassadorial role encouraged him to take an active part in policy formulation. Writing to

[57] Sanderson to Rosebery, 18 Apr. 1894, NLS Rosebery MSS, 10135.

[58] Barrère to Paul Cambon, 15 Nov. 1895, Louis Cambon MSS.

[59] Barrère to Delcassé, 6 Feb. 1887, AE Delcassé MSS, 1; Sanderson to Rosebery, 18 Apr. 1894, NLS Rosebery MSS, 10135.

[60] Barrère to Delcassé, 15 Dec. 1886, AE Delcassé MSS, 1.

[61] Barrère to Hanotaux, 31 May, AE NS 'Italie', 13.

[62] Mme Saint-René-Taillandier, *Silhouettes*, p. 14.

[63] Barrère to Delcassé, 15 Dec. 1886, AE Delcassé MSS, 1.

[64] J. Cambon, *The Diplomatist* (London, 1931), p. 678; E. Charles-Roux, 'L'Oeuvre diplomatique de Camille Barrère', *La Revue des deux mondes*, (1941).

[65] Charles-Roux, 'L'Oeuvre diplomatique'.

one foreign minister he clearly expressed his belief in an almost absolute ambassadorial power: 'Cette maison est quelque chose de plus qu'une ambassade ... elle est presque un Gouvernement dans le sens légitime que l'on peut donner à l'expression par rapport à une représentation étrangère.'[66]

Equally important, during the period 1898-1904, was the intimacy of his relationship with Delcassé, a relationship even more intimate than that which existed between Delcassé and the Cambons. This closeness allowed Barrère liberties that other ambassadors would not have dared to take. He often lectured his Minister, severely chastising him for laxity, indiscretions, or unwelcome points of view.[67] He offered advice and interfered frequently in personnel movements.[68] During the most crucial discussions he carried on negotiations without explicit instructions from Delcassé. In February 1900 Barrère told Delcassé in the middle of the Mediterranean negotiations: 'Vous pouvez d'ailleurs vous confier à ma prudence. Rien ne sera signé sans vous avoir été préablement soumis.'[69]

The fact that Barrère graciously consented to submit the document for his Minister's signature must have bemused Delcassé. Yet Delcassé did little to curb his Ambassador's activities. Far from abdicating responsibility, he had full confidence in Barrère. Moreover, the Ambassador was staunchly loyal to Delcassé and, in 1905, abruptly refused to accept the Foreign Ministry when it was offered to him by Premier Maurice Rouvier.[70]

Though not forming a part of Delcassé's inner cabinet, Jean-Jules Jusserand was nevertheless an important ambassador in the years 1898-1914. A man of high moral fibre, undoubtedly the result of his strict Catholic upbringing, he was regarded as something of an intellectual giant, a 'mouton à cinq pattes'. Apart from taking degrees in law, letters, and science, he knew four languages and developed into an expert on English medieval society. To the task of diplomacy he brought meticulous care, carefully scrutinizing correspondence received and making numerous drafts in his own hand before sending off a dispatch.[71]

---

[66] Barrère to Pichon, 20 Jan. 1908, Inst. de Fr., Pichon MSS, 1.

[67] Barrère to Delcassé, 5 May 1901, AE Barrère MSS, 4.

[68] Barrère to Delcassé, ii, 30 Dec. 1900, 18 July 1903, AE Delcassé MSS, 2.

[69] Ibid. 9 Feb. 1900.

[70] P. Cambon to H. Cambon, 8 May 1905, Louis Cambon MSS.

[71] Notes, AE Jusserand MSS, 21; in a memorial to Jusserand in 1937 Franklin D. Roosevelt stated: 'I was amazed by his culture.' His major works were *English Wayfaring: Life in the Middle Ages, Piers Plowman*, and *A Literary History of the English People*. Cf.

Born in Lyons in 1855, he was educated at the Collège des Chartreux and spent his vacation months at his family's residence of Saint-Haon-le-Chatel (Loire). Until his last days he returned regularly to this property. Though his family was affluent, he received little support after his father died and no diploma from the École libre des sciences politiques. Thus he was forced to enter the career through the *concours des consulats*. After finishing first in his class, he spent two years in the Centrale, largely copying drafts of telegrams. He was then sent in 1878 as *élève-consul* to London. By 1881 he was chief of the *Bureau de la Tunisie*, working intimately with Paul Cambon (who became a lifelong friend) in the establishment of the protectorate. Between 1890 and 1898 he was Sous-directeur du Nord, doing good work for Nisard. With Delcassé's arrival he was shifted to Copenhagen.[72]

Delcassé had a high regard for Jusserand's abilities and offered him Washington in 1902.[73] Jusserand was not at all impressed, having for so long dealt with European affairs, and believing that American diplomacy little affected the main lines of French policy.[74] Though he accepted and remained ambassador in Washington until 1924, he was never to influence decisions in the same manner as the triumvirate or even as he had done while *sous-directeur du Nord*. Being so far away, it was impossible for him to join in the regular conferences the triumvirate had with various foreign ministers. Furthermore, the Quai d'Orsay in general little understood the importance of America and found it difficult to discern where the United States belonged in the older European configuration.

Nevertheless, Jusserand's achievements were significant. He was quick to recognize that the United States would eventually become a world power, and he meticulously developed Franco-American links, especially by cultivating Theodore Roosevelt. The American President trusted him implicitly, and, because of Roosevelt's unflattering opinion of uninformed diplomats, he made a special effort to keep him *au courant* of affairs at all times.[75]

Though Jusserand found the British very exacting at times, a legacy of

E. G. Smith, 'An Ambassador of the Republic of Letters', *Blackwood's Edinburgh Magazine*, 176 (1904), pp. 490–500. He frequented the company of Gaston Paris, Taine, Renoir, Sorel, Boutroux, France, Boissier, and Lemaître.

[72] AE Jusserand MSS, 21; J. J. Jusserand, *What Me Befell* (New York, 1933), pp. 3–44, 59.

[73] Delcassé to Jusserand, 23 Mar. 1904, quoted in E. V. Wiley, 'Jean Jules Jusserand and the First Moroccan Crisis, 1903–1906', Ph.D. thesis (University of Pennsylvania, 1959) p. 5.

[74] Jusserand to Delcassé, 16 Aug. 1902, AE Delcassé MSS, 4.

[75] Jusserand to Pichon, 12 Dec. 1906, 6 Mar. 1907, Inst. de Fr., Pichon MSS, 3; Wiley, 'Jusserand' pp. 258–9.

his London days when Franco-British relations were not at their best, he had a natural affinity with the English-speaking world.[76] Not so with the Germans, and one of his principal tasks was to point out at length the nature and strength of German groups and agents in America. At every point he struggled to counteract such influence by joining America more closely to France. This was especially apparent during the First Moroccan Crisis, when he successfully achieved American support for France and involved Roosevelt more comprehensively than the President initially intended.[77]

Another ambassador of considerable independence and initiative was Ernest Constans, ambassador to Constantinople between 1898 and 1909. Described unflatteringly by one subordinate, F. Charles-Roux, as 'vieillard, encore robuste, appesant de corps et ventru', he was a diplomat known for his energy and skill.[78] Before his appointment he had been a businessman and a politician of stature. Elected deputy in 1876 and senator in 1889, he had been minister of the interior during the Boulangist movement.[79]

Though he was a friend of Delcassé in 1898, it was only upon the insistence of de Freycinet, minister of war, that Constans was appointed.[80] As an *intru* he constantly attracted heavy criticism from the career diplomats. His contempt for them was no less marked. A man of generally anti-Russian views, he had few prejudices against the Hamidian Empire. He was too cynical and realistic to transport 'des professions de foi électorale' to the Turkish capital.[81] He found a certain irony in his position. A former anti-clerical, now commissioned to defend the religious protectorate in Turkey, he was required to take his seat on the throne in the cathedral. As one contemporary, L. Einstein, wrote: 'No one more than Constans enjoyed the humour of the situation.'[82] His defence of the Catholic Church reflected this paradox and was more the product of show than substance.

---

[76] Jusserand, *What Me Befell* p. 83.   [77] Ibid. pp. 40, 223–59, 281–97.

[78] *Dictionnaire diplomatique*, 'Constans', p. 5.

[79] On Constans, see L. B. Fulton, 'France and the End of the Ottoman Empire', in M. Kent (ed.), *The Great Powers and the End of the Ottoman Empire* (London, 1984).

[80] See Kreis, 'Frankreichs Großmachtpolitik', iii, n.321.

[81] Cogordan to Collin de Plency, 13 Aug. 1886,; Paléologue to Collin de Plency, 19 Aug. 1886, AE Collin de Plancy MSS, 4; Louis to Pichon, 21 Aug. 1909, Inst. de Fr., Pichon MSS, 3; Constans to Étienne, 28 Jan. 1902, BN (NAF 24237), Étienne MSS; Delcassé to Constans, 16 Mar. 1909, AE Constans MSS, 3.

[82] L. Einstein, *A Diplomat Looks Back* (New York, 1968) p. 66.

Throughout, his realism and financial acquisitiveness were hall-marks of his embassy and he was preoccupied with safeguarding French economic interests.[83] He was also cognizant of the important role French loans could play in attaining commercial concessions. In general, his stature, his adroitness, and his political following at home allowed him to be an exceptionally independent ambassador. In 1901, after failing to persuade the Sultan to settle a number of financial disputes, he peremptorily left his post and returned only after a French occupation of Mytilene had forced Sultan Abdul Hamid to yield.

Constans was clearly enthusiastic to ensure French participation in the Baghdad railway and quite successfully pressed his views on Delcassé in the early months of 1899.[84] Nevertheless, the two men were not in complete agreement. Delcassé wanted the enterprise to be shared equally by France and Germany, but Constans was con-tent to enjoy a limited participation. Thereafter, the Ambassador misled his Minister at certain vital stages of the Baghdad railway negotiation.

By 1903 Constans found himself at odds with Delcassé's policy, which had the support of both the cabinet and the Quai d'Orsay. In subsequent years, leading members of the Quai d'Orsay (including Paul Cambon and Stephen Pichon) clashed directly with him.[85] He was considered too hostile to the Young Turk Revolution of 1908 and too much compromised by pecuniary involvement in pre-revolu-tionary policies. Moreover, he came under increasing attack from the Centrale for not doing enough to expand and safeguard French indus-trial interests. All these differences, despite his repeated warnings as to the difficult nature of obtaining commercial concessions, made him *persona non grata* at the Foreign Ministry and had much to do with his resignation in 1909.[86]

The fact that Constans often acted at Constantinople with remark-able independence was further testimony to an ambassadorial power which was particularly evident in the cases of Barrère and the Cam-bons. Delcassé certainly curtailed the powers of the bureaux, but it was

[83] See AE Constans MSS, 3; BN (NAF 24237), Étienne MSS.

[84] Constans to Pichon, 13 Dec. 1906, AE NS Turquie, 339.

[85] P. Cambon to Xavier Charmes, 8 Feb. 1909, *Correspondance*, ii. 277; Dard to Gérard, i, 13 Oct. 1909, AN, 329 AP 20 Gérard MSS, 2.

[86] Louis to Pichon, 28 Aug. 1909, Inst. de Fr. Pichon MSS, 3; J. Cambon to Pichon, 7 March 1910, AE J. Cambon MSS, 16.

during his first period as foreign minister that an ambassadorial élite rose. It was above all Barrère and the Cambons who translated his broader ideas into specific policies. They were a unique group of men with strong views about their ambassadorial roles and they left their mark on almost all areas of French foreign policy in the years 1898–1904.

5

Foreign Policy under Delcassé, 1898–1904

Unavoidable haggling over the social status of a lobster
(J. J. Jusserand on the *Entente Cordiale* (*What Me Befell*, p. III))

As suggested in earlier chapters, Delcassian diplomacy between 1898 and 1904 can hardly be seen as emanating from Delcassé alone. Certainly he had fixed ideas: underlying suspicion of Germany; the strengthening of the Franco-Russian alliance; concentration on the Mediterranean region as a field for French expansion; and, after 1902, the necessity of an *entente* with Britain. No doubt he was more sensitive to the wishes of St Petersburg than many of his ambassadors. However, the main achievements of the period, the *Entente Cordiale* of 1904 and the Franco-Italian *rapprochement*, resulted from an intimate collaboration between Delcassé and his senior ambassadors.

Delcassé's anti-German sentiment determined much of his foreign policy. The impact of the Franco-Prussian war on his mind cannot be emphasized enough. In the 1880s, at a time when he was relatively free to expound his ideas, hostility to Berlin was a constant theme. This hostility derived from the belief that Germany was basically pursuing a *Weltpolitik* which would end in a war desired by important decision-makers in Berlin. During the 1890s he had consistently warned the Chamber of Deputies of Germany's growing naval potential and of her desire to intimidate France at every turn.[1] Moreover, he fully realized that any real *rapprochement* with Berlin was dependent on France giving up Alsace-Lorraine once and for all. Not that he was basically *revanchiste*, rather, he thought that if a war did eventuate there was always the possibility that the lost provinces might be returned to France.[2] Furthermore, he had been warned in no uncertain terms that any agreement with Berlin which resulted in the return of the lost provinces would be seen by

[1] C. M. Andrew, *Théophile Delcassé and the Making of the Entente Cordiale* (London, 1968), p. 126.
[2] Ibid.; P. J. V. Rolo, *Entente Cordiale* (London, 1969), p. 82.

Russia as sufficient justification to break off the Franco-Russian alliance.[3]

Whereas Delcassé considered Russia as a safe bet, the alternative path of a *modus vivendi* with Berlin seemed to him strewn with difficulties, all of Germany's making. Berlin was clearly deceitful. She refused to engage in any concrete negotiations or to take any appropriate initiative. Generally, she undermined French prestige in the Levant and refused to support France's stand against Britain in Egypt. Finally, Germany's ambitions in the Mediterranean, triggered by the anticipated collapse of the Austro-Hungarian Empire, aroused his deepest suspicions. Although Delcassé was at times prepared to talk with Berlin, he usually had tactical considerations in mind, whether it was a matter of bringing Britain to her senses or of obliging the Spanish government to negotiate over Morocco.

The Münster note of June 1898, which envisaged Franco-German co-operation to forestall the Anglo-Portuguese agreement on Portuguese colonies, set a lasting trend. Delcassé certainly knew of the contents of the note, but against the advice of his political director summarily dismissed it. The occasion was seen by some as a 'missed opportunity' for Franco-German *rapprochement*. In later years Delcassé maintained that no such note had ever come to his knowledge. On another occasion he suggested that he had replied to the note in the affirmative but that the Germans had not responded positively.[4] Though not perhaps consciously so, both statements were false. Delcassé believed that, even if overtures had been made to him, they were neither genuine nor formal, having usually taken the form of *démarches* from the Paris Embassy or of social talk at functions in Berlin.[5] By March 1900, as a result of limited and unsuccessful attempts to involve Germany in a united stand against Britain in the Boer War, Delcassé became convinced of the futility of talking even on minute issues with Germany. Thereafter, he believed that her empire was expanding at France's expense.

Delcassé's hostility towards Germany meant that he attached great importance to the Franco-Russian alliance, an attitude which owed very little to the ambassadorial élite. His first priority was strengthening this alliance. From his period as foreign minister, and afterwards until his

[3] Montebello to Delcassé, 28 July 1899, AE Delcassé MSS, 5.
[4] Senate speech, 20 Mar. 1902, in C. W. Porter, *The Career of Théophile Delcassé* (Philadelphia, 1936), p. 117.
[5] Delcassé to Noailles, 30 Oct. 1899, AE Delcassé MSS, 10.

death, he viewed the Russian alliance as the cornerstone of French policy. In this sense his outlook was markedly different from Gambetta's.[6] He was also more supportive of Russia than any other statesman at the time and was prepared on occasions to sacrifice French interests in favour of Russian.[7] His support for Russia was essentially political, founded upon his perception of French interests and the great fear of Germany.[8] Nevertheless, he was not immune to the flattery of the Russians, and occasionally succumbed to their wooing. Despite criticism from home and abroad, especially from Maurice Bompard, a commercial director who was appointed ambassador to St Petersburg in 1903, Delcassé was a staunch advocate of French loans to Russia.[9] Moreover, he was blind to the prospect of a Russo-Japanese war in 1904. When hostilities commenced he believed that Russia would easily emerge victorious.[10] He went much further than the Quai d'Orsay advised by allowing Russian ships to stop in French ports. After Russia's defeat Delcassé was loath to suggest peace negotiations to St Petersburg for fear of alienating France's only ally.[11]

Though the Russo-Japanese war brought home to Delcassé the often precarious nature of the Franco-Russian alliance, he had become aware of this problem soon after assuming office and had sought to change the terms of the alliance. He had been moved to do so by the lack of support accorded by St Petersburg in the Fashoda crisis and by the way that Russia had suggested a disarmament conference at The Hague in 1899, without prior consultation with France.[12] Fears that an impending Austro-Hungarian collapse would shift the balance of power in Germany's favour clearly played on Delcassé's mind as well. Through reciprocal visits of French and Russian dignitaries the alliance was altered so as to go beyond the mere duration of the Triple Alliance. In essence, the revised Franco-Russian alliance provided for a distribution of power more favourable to France, with specifically anti-British and anti-German clauses.[13] While Montebello, French Ambassador to St

[6] *La Petite République*, 3 Jan. 1884.

[7] 'Notes journalières', 26 Jan. 1914, BN (NAF 16026), Poincaré MSS.

[8] Andrew, *Delcassé*, p. 119.

[9] Hardinge to Sanderson, 29 Mar. 1905, Cambridge University Library, Hardinge MSS.

[10] Porter, *Delcassé*, p. 204; E. N. Anderson, *The First Moroccan Crisis* (Urbana, Ill., 1930) p. 100; P. Cambon to H. Cambon, 10 Feb. 1904, *Paul Cambon: Correspondance* (Paris, 1940–6), ii. 121.

[11] Paléologue to Jusserand, 16 Feb. 1905, AE Jusserand MSS, 60.

[12] Andrew, *Delcassé*, pp. 122–6.

[13] Ibid.

Petersburg until 1903, had created a favourable atmosphere for the agreement, the new terms of the alliance were clearly and definitively the result of Delcassé's unceasing efforts.

Another of Delcassé's fixed ideas was that of expanding French influence in the Mediterranean area. The issues he faced upon assuming office (the settling of the Spanish–American war, Franco-Italian *rapprochement*, and the religious protectorate in the Levant) as well as the later question of Morocco were all approached with this basic notion in mind.[14] His concern with the shores of the Mediterranean derived primarily from a belief that France's North African empire was a unique entity and that it was the natural extension of the mother country. To a lesser extent Delcassé's thinking was strategic. To Delcassé, France was above all a continental power. Although he had seen the merits of expanding into areas of Asia before becoming foreign minister, by 1898 he believed that the French navy could not defend Indo-China.[15] He turned what was essentially a deaf ear to the appeal of Pichon, the minister in China, for a carving up of China.

The Spanish–American war (1898) was the first issue to be tackled from the perspective of Delcassé's Mediterranean ambitions. Undoubtedly he took up Jules Cambon's appeal to mediate in the belief that such intervention would secure French prestige and provide him with a personal success to mark the beginning of his term.[16] However, Delcassé was more concerned with what might happen if America was to enter the Mediterranean, directly attack Spain, and subsequently remain in the region.[17]

A Franco-Italian *rapprochement* was viewed as a means of increasing French power in the Mediterranean. Delcassé believed that *rapprochement* was utterly necessary. Not only was Britain's Mediterranean influence based on the mutual antagonism between France and Italy but, at the same time, this hostility allowed Germany and Austria to encroach into the region. A Franco-Italian *rapprochement* would effectively annul one of the main reasons Italy had joined the Triple Alliance (fear of French predominance in Tripoli). *Rapprochement* would also allow Delcassé to propose a quid pro quo in the form of a French Morocco.[18]

The religious protectorate in the Near East was yet another element

[14] Ibid. p. 87.
[15] Ibid.; A. Néton, *Delcassé 1852–1923* (Paris, 1952) pp. 149–59; *JOC* 12 Dec. 1896 and 1 Feb. 1898.
[16] Delcassé to his wife, 27 July 1898, AE Delcassé MSS, 1.
[17] *DDF*, (1), xiv. 240.
[18] Andrew, *Delcassé*, p. 83, 138–43.

of Delcassé's Mediterranean vision. Though he himself was anti-clerical, he strongly defended the protectorate in front of Parliament and sought to soften foreign reaction to the anti-clerical measures of Premier Combes.[19] He was instrumental in having the Vatican change its mind about having representation at the Porte. He used Cardinal Langénieux, a Frenchman, to solicit support for the French National Committee for the Conservation and Defence of the French Protectorate. This organization was designed to counter the Kaiser's visit to Palestine in October 1898. Later, after various incidents in the Holy Land in the latter part of 1901 and early 1902, Delcassé refused to listen to arguments from the political division that France could not in fact protect foreign nationals against their will. He remained convinced of the need to maintain French prerogatives.[20]

Undoubtedly the acquisition of Morocco was the ultimate goal of Delcassé's Mediterranean policy. Since his time as colonial minister, he had followed an established plan of action. It envisaged a distinction between the international question, which he hoped to settle first, and action in Morocco itself. Even here he believed that, although the Sultan of Morocco should be made to accept aid from France alone, France should proceed in agreement with the Sultan and in such a way as to increase his prestige.[21] Originally, there was to be a preliminary agreement with Italy followed by a partition of territory with Spain. Later steps envisaged taking possession and then organizing a new Moroccan administration.[22] At first Britain was to be offered nothing apart from the neutrality of Tangier and commercial equality, but by 1903 Delcassé showed himself disposed to talk with Britain, using the Egyptian question as a barter. As for Germany, Delcassé was inclined to offer African territorial compensation at a time when Franco-German co-operation seemed possible, during the Boer War. After March 1900, however, he was not willing to offer Germany any compensation whatever.

Delcassé was in no hurry to implement his Moroccan plans and fully agreed with Paul Cambon's assessment that Morocco would become French by the natural evolution of things. Until the signing of a Franco-Spanish accord in October 1904 he was cautious, discouraging plans by

[19] Delcassé to his wife, 12 July 1898, AE Delcassé MSS, 1.
[20] Ibid.; 'Note pour le Ministre, les incidents du 4 Novembre 1901, au Saint-Sépulcre et le protectorat religieux de la France en Orient', 5 June 1902.
[21] Delcassé to Étienne, 18 Aug. 1904, BN (NAF 24237), Étienne MSS.
[22] 'Mémoire' by Delavaud, undated, attached to a note of 15 Aug. 1900, AE Delcassé MSS, 4; *DDF* (2), ii. 382; Delcassé to Barrère, 28 Feb. 1900, AE Delcassé MSS, 1.

industrial concerns such as Schneider, the Allard banking group, and the Banque de Paris et des Pays-Bas.[23] Thereafter he offered encouragement, but on condition that these business interests worked closely with government policy.[24] During the summer of 1904 he found himself in a serious dispute with Étienne, leader of the Colonial party, and Jonnart, governor-general of Algeria, both of whom were criticizing his cautious policy and seeking to force the issue by deploying troops on the Algerian border.[25] It was Delcassé rather than Étienne or the Governor-General of Algeria who subsequently triumphed. After October 1904 Delcassé allowed a more forward policy primarily because he thought the international aspect of the question had been sufficiently settled to warrant *pénétration pacifique*, as it came to be known. The Colonial party appears to have had little to do with his decision.

The other fixed notion of Delcassé was the necessity of arriving at an *entente* with Britain. While Russia was the natural counterbalance to Germany, Berlin feared Britain most. Delcassé realized the importance of Britain in counteracting any German pretensions to hegemony in Europe. Moreover, Britain was the key to France's aspirations in the Mediterranean. Finally, there was a natural community of social and political interests which bound the two nations together. Though many French Republicans might be critical of the constitutional monarchy which existed in Britain, they sympathized with the country's increasingly democratic spirit, a spirit which contrasted with the more autocratic political systems of Central and Eastern Europe. Gambetta's belief that Britain was a natural ally against Germany dominated Delcassé's thinking, and his desire to achieve an *Entente Cordiale* stemmed from careful reflection during the years prior to his arrival in power.[26]

Revisionist attitudes need to be dismissed. Undoubtedly, Delcassé played the diplomatic game as a *realpolitiker*, but he was far from being an opportunist who, as S. C. Hause has suggested, was prepared to align himself with the Germans against the British. Whereas he sometimes considered the British as rivals, Germany was always regarded as an

---

[23] P. Guillen, *Les Emprunts marocains, 1902–1904* (Paris, 1974) pp. 42–4; Andrew, *Delcassé*, p. 264.

[24] Delcassé to Étienne, 13, 16, 18 Aug. 1904, also undated letter 1904, BN (NAF 24237), Étienne MSS; Jonnart to Defrance, Nov. 1905, AE Defrance MSS, 3.

[25] A note of 5 Feb. 1902, AE NS 'Maroc' p. 209.

[26] See especially Barrère to Delcassé, 27 Jan. 1900, AE Delcassé MSS, 1; manuscript and unpublished section of 'La Chute de Delcassé' in Barrère's handwriting, AE Barrère MSS, 5; Delcassé to his wife, 7 Oct. 1898, AE Delcassé MSS, 1; conversation between Delcassé and Jean Doulcet, Jan. 1914, AE Doulcet MSS, 23.

enemy—the enemy.[27] If, at times, Delcassé was prepared to adopt a distinctly anti-British stance with the assistance of Berlin this in no way meant that he had abandoned his basic attitude. Political circumstances were clearly unfavourable between 1898 and 1901 for a *rapprochement* with Britain, and Delcassé was not so inflexible as to be unable to employ different strategies in what was a complicated chess game.

Upon arrival in office in July 1898, in the middle of the Fashoda crisis, Delcassé was eager not only to effect a settlement of the immediate dispute but to lay the basis, where possible, for a general resolution of conflicts with Britain.[28] The prospect of a major Anglo-French war over some 'rogatons' of land in the Sudan did not enthuse him. Paul Cambon, the newly appointed ambassador to London, was 'empowered' to discuss all general issues with the British government. Despite the opposition of Nisard, Delcassé decided to yield to London in the hope that Britain would accord France compensation in the Bahr El Ghazal. Even so, by late October, when it was apparent that London would consider no such compensation, Delcassé was privately prepared to accept an almost unconditional surrender.[29] The prospect of war was an important factor in his thinking.[30] However, as Andrew has pointed out, the attitude of Germany was more crucial.[31] The success of the French scheme to convene a European conference to reopen the Egyptian question depended above all on the attitude of Germany. Delcassé recognized that Anglo-German relations were so cordial that Germany would do nothing substantial to stand in Britain's way.[32]

By the spring of 1899, however, Delcassé was beginning to take a decidedly anti-British stance. He continued to be adamant over the Egyptian question despite the fact that the Colonial party was swinging over to the attitude that a Morocco–Egypt barter was possible. During the Boer War he sought to rally Russia and Germany against the British Lion. The new terms of the Franco-Russian alliance, while largely dealing with Germany and the possibility of the collapse of the Austro-

[27] M. Paléologue, *Three Critical Years, 1904–1906* (New York, 1957), 29 Dec. 1898, p. 10. The revisionist thesis is developed in S. C. Hause, 'Théophile Delcassé's First Years at the Quai d'Orsay' (Washington University, 1969), pp. 1–20.

[28] Delcassé to Barrère, 2 Mar. 1899, AE Delcassé MSS, 1; *BD*, i. 262; *DDF* (1), xiv. 577.

[29] Note by Delcassé to Jusserand, 7 Sept. 1898, AE Jusserand MSS, 21; Delcassé to his wife, 23, 24 Oct. 1898, AE Delcassé MSS, 1.

[30] Delcassé to Jusserand, 22 Sept. 1898, AE Jusserand MSS, 21.

[31] Andrew, *Delcassé*, p. 93.

[32] Ibid. p. 97. See also R. G. Brown, *Fashoda Reconsidered: The Impact of Domestic Politics on French Policy in Africa, 1893–1898* (London, 1969).

Hungarian Empire, also threatened the British empire at certain vital points, especially near Persia and India. In February 1900 he even went to the point of drawing up military proposals, which, though not submitted to cabinet, were brought to the attention of the French Premier and the President of the Republic.[33] The reasons for this dramatic change of attitude were numerous. Primarily, Delcassé believed that the British government was hostile to France for the moment and would consider a *rapprochement* inopportune. For a time, he even viewed Britain as a distinct threat to world peace, and remarked to Jules Clarétie, a journalist friend, in March 1900 that it was necessary to take a stand for the good of civilization.[34] There was, however, something personal, inflexible, and almost pathological in his approach. He became extremely suspicious of British influence in the Mediterranean, believing that Britain was against Franco-Italian *rapprochement*, desirous of sabotaging France's agreements with Spain, and hopeful of implanting herself in Morocco.[35] One of the specific instructions that Saint-René-Taillandier received for his mission to the Maghzen in 1901 was to keep a close watch on the British.[36] Finally, but not least importantly, Delcassé appears to have been personally wounded by the way in which he was treated by the British during the Fashoda crisis.[37]

Thus, though Delcassé still believed in the overriding necessity of the *Entente Cordiale*, he did not resume his pursuit of such an agreement until the beginning of 1903. Paul Cambon, often acting in secret and without the instructions of his Minister, did more to initiate the *Entente* of 1904 than Delcassé. But Cambon did not drag a rather unwilling Delcassé behind him. The Foreign Minister was slow to do anything concrete until 1903 because of the imminence of the Russo-Japanese war. Yet, at bottom, he fully agreed with Cambon's general aims.

In addition to his fear of Germany, Delcassé was driven to act by his interest in Morocco. Unless France and Britain quickly reached a Moroccan *modus vivendi* which safeguarded France's political rights, the British would be able to gain a substantial foothold in Morocco as well as in Egypt. Economic considerations were also at work. Delcassé believed that it was too risky to place all France's financial eggs in the 'Russian

[33] Memorandum by Delcassé, 28 Feb. 1900, AE NS Grande Bretagne, 12.
[34] Jules Clarétie, 'Journal', 8 Mar. 1900, published in *La Revue des deux mondes* (Nov. 1949) p. 130.
[35] Andrew, *Delcassé*, pp. 188–9; *DDF* (2), ii. 57.
[36] *DDF* (2), i. 337, ii. 115, 121, 443, 448.
[37] Ibid. (1), xiv. 428, 433.

basket'. The *Entente* with London was in part an attempt to remedy this imbalance.[38]

The conception of the *Entente Cordiale* was as much Cambon's as Delcassé's.[39] He had envisaged the arrangement as early as 1888. Cambon was thoroughly apprehensive of Germany's *Weltpolitik* in the Mediterranean and deeply concerned by the possibility of Russo-German *rapprochement*. Britain, in Cambon's opinion, was the only safeguard against such an eventuality, and he believed Anglo-German differences could not easily be patched up.[40] Finally, he was suspicious of British ambitions in Morocco and considered that if Morocco was not secured by concessions over Egypt, then both tips of the southern Mediterranean would be irreparably lost.[41] Thus, to a very large extent, Cambon shared Delcassé's virtual obsession with the Mediterranean area.

Cambon's assessment was based on hard material interests rather than Anglophilia. He never disguised his almost pathological suspicion of Britain in Morocco. He could not speak English, abhorred British food, and argued against the establishment of French schools in Britain, on the curious ground that Frenchmen raised in Britain were mentally deficient.[42] Nevertheless, he believed that the Franco-British community of interests could be used to make the British loyal friends, and that they would be a welcome and necessary relief from the Russians.

Cambon had arrived at his convictions as early as 1888, when he was ambassador to Madrid. In that year he had initially wanted to counter German influence in the Spanish Universal Exhibition in Barcelona, but the initial proposal gave way to the wider notion of a Latin union embracing Italy, France, and Spain. Cambon wanted Britain to adhere to the agreement.[43] Soon after, he argued more strongly for improved relations with the British. Though Goblet, the foreign minister, supported him, the move failed, basically because the Italians were not prepared as yet to undermine the Triple Alliance.[44]

Cambon began to exercise a powerful influence soon after taking over the London Embassy. He restrained Delcassé's eagerness in the early

[38] W. Hallgarten, *Imperialismus vor 1914* (Munich, 1951), i. 562.

[39] P. Cambon to H. Cambon, 19 Aug. 1904, Louis Cambon MSS.

[40] P. Cambon to H. Cambon, 13 May 1904, *Correspondance*, ii. 136.

[41] Ibid. 2 Aug. 1904.

[42] P. Cambon to Pichon, 10 Dec. 1909, Inst. de Fr. Pichon MSS, 2.

[43] P. Cambon to Goblet, 1 May 1888, Louis Cambon MSS; P. Cambon to his wife, 9, 13 Aug. 1888; P. Cambon to Lavisse, 17 Nov. 1888, BN, (NAF 25166), Lavisse MSS.

[44] P. Cambon to Spuller, 11 Mar. 1889, AE P. Cambon MSS; P. Cambon to Lavisse, 9 Jan. 1891, BN (NAF 25166), Lavisse MSS.

months of 1899 and successfully redirected Franco-British discussions to
the settling of the immediate problem, that of the Sudan.[45] Not that he
disagreed with Delcassé's aims. On the contrary, from 1898 until the end
of his career Cambon told all who would listen that he was intimately
associated with Delcassé's diplomatic goals. He regarded Delcassé's
downfall in 1905 as a serious blow to himself. However, he practised the art
of the possible. The British were in no mood to speak of *rapprochement* in
1898, and, as a result of the Dreyfus affair, they believed that France was
incapable of maintaining a stable ministry. The British government also
viewed the French conquest of Madagascar and the protectionist Méline
tariff with considerable dissatisfaction. Consequently, when Lansdowne,
the British foreign minister, actually brought up the general question of
Newfoundland fishing rights early in 1899, Cambon did not grab at the
bait.[46]

   Not until the Fashoda crisis was over did Cambon envisage the actual
basis of the 1904 *Entente Cordiale*. He had hoped to speak with the British
over Egypt, a measure which differentiated him from Nisard and the
Centrale, but he did not aim at anything less than the total evacuation of
the country.[47] By 1901 he had changed his view and had begun to work on
Delcassé to accept an Egypt–Morocco barter. He was one of the first to
realize that Egypt was definitively lost.[48] Moreover, his own assessment of
the Moroccan question was that the North African territory had to be
secured against further British encroachment. His trip to Morocco in
1902, ostensibly to holiday with his son Henri, who was stationed there,
was actually a pretext to gain first-hand knowledge and to evaluate British
influence. His trip confirmed his belief that speedy action was necessary.[49]

   By March 1901 he was conducting a skilful policy. On the one hand he
was encouraging the British to discuss the liquidation of Morocco while,
on the other, he was convincing Delcassé of the need to give up Egypt and
to reach a general settlement. He clearly acted on his own initiative.[50] He
continued this campaign relentlessly and, in the summer of 1902, Monson,

   [45] *DDF* (1), xv. 19; P. Cambon to Delcassé, 25 Jan. 1899, AE Delcassé MSS, 3.

   [46] *DDF* (2), xiv. 565, 577; xv. 115. In a letter to Jules, 17 Jan. 1899, he said that Delcassé
did not have 'l'esprit tout à fait juste', and that he was 'trop imaginatif' (Louis Cambon
MSS).

   [47] R. I. Weiner, 'Paul Cambon and the Making of the Entente Cordiale' (Rutgers
University, 1973), pp. 60–6, 94.

   [48] Andrew, *Delcassé*, p. 181; F. V. Parsons, *The Origins of the Morocco Question, 1880–1900*
(London, 1976), p. 626.

   [49] P. Cambon to Delcassé, 23 July 1902, *Correspondance*, ii. 73.

   [50] Lansdowne to J. Chamberlain, 16 Mar. 1901, Joseph Chamberlain MSS, University
of Birmingham, JC 11215.

the British ambassador to Paris, aptly remarked to his Minister, Lord Lansdowne, that Cambon was proceeding with a general exchange of views over Anglo-French difficulties in Morocco despite Delcassé's caution: 'He himself has improved upon his instructions by filling in the picture with details of his own.'[51] Towards the end of 1902 the London Ambassador stepped up his campaign to win Delcassé to the idea of territorial compensation. He deliberately distorted interviews with Lansdowne in order to suggest that the British were considering a Newfoundland–Morocco barter.[52]

When, in October 1902, Lansdowne seemed reluctant to discuss the liquidation of the Moroccan question, Cambon failed to notify Delcassé.[53] By the summer of 1902 he was utterly convinced of the form the *entente* should take, and was playing 'very much from his own hand', confident that he could ultimately obtain Delcassé's approval and support.[54]

During 1903 Delcassé fell into line with Cambon's thinking, in no small part because of the Ambassador's persistence. Delcassé accepted Cambon's notion of a 'territorial compensation' in the form of an Egypt–Morocco barter, and Cambon controlled the timing and contents of the negotiation to the very end. When, at the close of December 1903, Delcassé was keen to achieve a final settlement, the London Ambassador restrained his enthusiasm, not because he had had second thoughts, but because he was playing the traditional French game of winning just a bit more.[55]

In the final analysis Paul Cambon's influence in forging the *Entente Cordiale* was decisive, but he was assisted by Saint-René-Taillandier, the French minister in Morocco. Saint-René was clearly worried about British involvement in Morocco and was instrumental, with Paul Cambon, in initiating measures which would push the British out.[56] He reported to Delcassé in January 1902 that it was absolutely necessary to combat Britain in Morocco. France, he said, should lead the way in promoting Moroccan reforms, and he encouraged Delcassé to let Britain know that France viewed with displeasure Moroccan depend-

[51] Monson to Lansdowne, 23 Aug. 1902, PRO, FO Lansdowne MSS, 9.
[52] P. Cambon to Delcassé, 12 Aug. 1902, AE Delcassé MSS, 3.
[53] *DDF* (2), ii. 456.
[54] Monson to Lansdowne, 31 Dec. 1902, Lansdowne MSS, 9.
[55] Paul Cambon to H. Cambon, 10 Dec. 1903, *Correspondance*, ii. 101.
[56] Delcassé to Étienne, 16 Mar. 1904; Saint-René-Taillandier to Étienne, 31 July 1903, BN (NAF 24237), Étienne MSS; Nicolson to FO, 20 Jan. 1902, FO 99/39, confidential print; Rolo, *Entente Cordiale*, pp. 133–4.

ence on London. Saint-René went much further, however. Paul Cambon visited him in the summer of 1902 and together they worked out a plan of action whereby a more forward policy could be pursued without creating opposition in London.[57]

In marked contrast to Paul Cambon's and Saint-René-Taillandier's efforts were those of the political director, Georges Cogordan. Indeed, Cogordan's anti-British sentiments impaired his judgement. As F. V. Parsons and Christopher Andrew have remarked, he was the 'main proponent of the illusion that Great Britain, who in her weak position would never risk war, could be forced out of Egypt by combined international pressure'.[58] Certainly he was not alone in believing that Britain sought nothing less than global domination. Men like Delcassé, Noailles, and Defrance also considered Britain highly dangerous at the turn of the century. But he was one of the last to realize that Britain was not prepared to abandon Egypt. He remained highly critical of the March 1899 agreement and wanted to embarrass Britain during and after the Boer War in order to force her to leave Egyptian soil. Until 1903 Delcassé appears to have accepted this view.[59]

Cogordan's role in 1903 appears unclear. Cambon noted the way the political director facilitated talks and co-ordinated a variety of strategies. Delcassé, Cambon, and he appear to have held intimate and regular meetings during the period of negotiation. Yet, despite his active co-operation, he retained misgivings until his death, believing that the Egyptian question was crucial to French security in the Mediterranean. He was also annoyed at the 'rogatons' the British proffered as territorial compensation and feared that the *Entente Cordiale* would reward France with little.[60]

If Paul Cambon and Delcassé disagreed, it was over the Franco-Russian alliance. Cambon would much have preferred the Lion to the Bear as an ally, and he showed a remarkable lack of enthusiasm for Russia. He thought that French and Russian interests were often in conflict and that the Russians treated the French in an extremely shoddy and sometimes disloyal manner. Yet for all his criticism his divergence with Delcassé was more a matter of form than of substance. He recognized that

[57] P. Guillen, *L'Allemagne et le 'Maroc', 1870–1905* (Paris, 1969) p. 674; *DDF* (1), vi. 56.

[58] Parsons, *The Origins of the Morocco Question*, p. 559; Andrew, *Delcassé*, p. 111; Rennel Rodd, *Social and Diplomatic Memories* (London, 1923), ii. 6–7, 96.

[59] P. Cambon to Nisard, 10, 13 Mar., 28 May 1897, AE Nisard MSS; P. Cambon to Jusserand, 28 Feb. 1900, AE Jusserand MSS, 22; P. Cambon to Reinach, undated, BN (NAF 13534), Reinach MSS.

[60] Cogordan to Paul Cambon, 29 Nov. 1903, 29 Feb. 1904, AE P. Cambon MSS, 11.

there was no viable alternative to the Russian alliance in the foreseeable future. As he said to Foreign Minister Spuller in March 1889, when one could not have what one liked, one had to like what one had.[61]

His aversion to Russia came to a head when he was ambassador to Constantinople. Primarily, he disliked the subordination of French political and economic interests to St Petersburg in Constantinople and was generally disgusted at the tendency of Russian ambassadors (whether Morenheim or, later, Isvolsky) to act as *de facto* foreign ministers in the French capital.[62] He had considerable differences with Russia over the troublesome Armenian and Cretan question and generally believed that Russia's policy of destroying the integrity of the Ottoman Empire could only have disastrous consequences.[63] Apart from differences over policies, he thought that St Petersburg was reluctant to use her diplomatic and military weight on behalf of France.[64] During the Fashoda crisis of 1898, Russia had not lifted a finger in support of her ally.[65]

Russia's internal conditions also seriously disturbed him. Though no radical himself, the insensitivity of the Romanov dynasty to the political, economic, and soical plight of its people seemed to him utterly appalling. In the immediate aftermath of the 1905 Revolution he thought the monarchy would survive and overcome its difficulties. By 1906, however, he was more pessimistic, considering that revolutionary ideals had gone much further than the intellectuals and middle classes and had now been accepted by the peasantry.[66]

Whe the Russo-Japanese war arrived in 1904, he was hardly supportive of Russia in any sense. In the main, this attitude was due to his fears of Franco-British entanglement in the Far East. Like Delcassé, he overestimated the military might of Russia. Ultimately, too, he was resistant to helping the Russians in the war of their own making.[67] The war clearly frightened him. It acted as the most powerful catalyst for the eventual Triple *Entente* of Russia, Britain, and France. The idea was firmly embedded in Delcassé's mind, but Cambon was no less convinced of its necessity, even though he sometimes thought that the inherent diffi-

[61] Cambon to Spuller, 11 Mar. 1889, AE P. Cambon MSS; P. Cambon to H. Cambon, 2 Dec. 1903, 26 Feb. 1904, Louis Cambon MSS.

[62] P. Cambon to Bompard, 1 July 1891, *Correspondance*, i. 314; K. Eubank, *Paul Cambon* (Norman, Okla., 1960), pp. 37, 54, 55, 57.

[63] Eubank, *Cambon*, pp. 37, 54, 55, 57.

[64] P. Cambon to H. Cambon, 26 Feb. 1904, Louis Cambon MSS.

[65] Ibid. 11 Feb. 1905.   [66] Ibid. 22 Jan. 1905, 30 Aug. 1906.

[67] Ibid. 2 Dec. 1903, 26 Feb. 1904.

culties were insurmountable. Cambon feared that without an Anglo-Russian *rapprochement* Germany would separate Russia from France and reconstitute a revived Three Emperors' League. Furthermore, France would be the major victim in any Anglo-Russian conflict in the Far East.[68]

Cambon's avid espousal of the *Entente Cordiale*, his acceptance, though somewhat less enthusiastic, of the Franco-Russian alliance, and his belief in the necessity of a Triple *Entente* were largely the product of a fundamental mistrust of Germany. The Franco-Prussian war had made a lasting impression on him. Gambetta, his mentor, had convinced him that it was not with Germany that an alliance could be made. Thus Cambon was continuously apprehensive of German attempts to isolate France by alternatively wooing Russia and Great Britain.[69]

Yet for all his concern about German ambition, he did not think Germany inherently warlike. In this respect he struck a note of objectivity, which contrasted with the Quai d'Orsay's tendency to distort German intentions. Certainly he was critical of Wilhelm II, blaming him for Germany's inconsistent policies and labelling him contemptuously as a 'sharp travelling salesman who wished to dazzle the gallery by his knowledge'.[70] However, in spite of the Kaiser's vanity and ambition, he was not, in Cambon's opinion, malicious or aggressive to the point of war.[71] Hence, Cambon was moderate enough to be prepared to talk to Germany. In essence, he wanted to be on courteous terms with Berlin and to keep channels of communication open. Tensions could be eased and concrete arrangements of mutual, if limited, benefit could be made.[72] Though the Triple *Entente*, in Cambon's mind, was primarily designed to give France security from German attack, it was also a means of giving France sufficient authority to talk to Berlin from a position of strength.[73] Cambon would not have gone further than a limited *détente* with Germany. A peaceful coexistence was the most that could be hoped for without a renunciation of France's claim to Alsace-Lorraine. Furthermore, as was apparent in

[68] Ibid. 8 July 1904.

[69] P. Cambon to H. Cambon, 30 Aug. 1906, *Correspondance*, ii. 224.

[70] P. Cambon to Mme Hippolyte Cambon, 24 Oct., 1 Nov. 1898, ibid. i. 442–6.

[71] P. Cambon to H. Cambon, 9 Apr. 1904, 1 Apr. 1905, Louis Cambon MSS; P. Cambon to Pichon, 23 Nov. 1906, Inst. de Fr. Pichon MSS, 2.

[72] P. Cambon to H. Cambon, 25 Apr. 1909, *Correspondance*, ii. 29.

[73] P. Cambon to J. Cambon, 9 Mar. 1909, 4 Nov. 1912, AE J. Cambon MSS, 25; P. Cambon to H. Cambon, 28 Apr. 1904, Louis Cambon MSS.

1908 and 1912, there was always the danger that Russia might miscon-strue Franco-German conversations.

Cambon's attitude towards Italy underwent considerable evolution from the time of his embassy to Madrid. Although enthusiastic about making an *entente*, or even an alliance, with Italy in the late 1880s, he came to see more of Rome's fickle nature later on and argued against attaching Italy to the *Entente* powers. Primarily, he considered Italy 'moins utile qu'embarrassante',[74] and her detachment from the Triple Alliance might encourage Germany to woo Russia. Left as she was, Italy was a weakness in the Triple Alliance. Her aspirations opposed her to Austria-Hungary. Cambon correctly assessed that Italy would remain neutral in the event of a general war until it was possible to distinguish the victorious side.[75]

Spain seemed to Cambon equally fickle. Nevertheless, Spanish rights in Morocco were justified, and Cambon ensured that whenever France made a move in the Mediterranean Spanish susceptibilities were soothed. The prospect of Germany championing Spanish pretensions if these were denied by France was also a strong factor in his desire to cultivate Madrid.[76] Finally, being on friendly terms with both Italy and Spain was a means of winning the respect of Britain, whose interest in the Mediterranean was considerable.

Barrère, like Paul Cambon, had an important part in formulating French foreign policy during the years 1898–1904. Contrary to Langer's opinion, it was in the Barrère–Delcassé period rather than in the Hanotaux–Billot period that a Franco-Italian *rapprochement* was effected. During Hanotaux's ministry a *détente* was reached but little else. Hanotaux had shown limited interest in gaining Italy's goodwill when negotiating the Tunisian treaty of 1896.[77] Billot's preoccupation with Italy's political alignment had impeded a successful conclusion to the commercial treaty. Barrère, however, believed the economic agreement to be a prerequisite for the political.[78] Unlike Billot, he welcomed Italian eagerness.[79]

[74] P. Cambon to Poincaré, 25 Jan. 1912, AE NS 'Italie', II p. 175.

[75] Ibid.; Eubank, *Cambon*, p. 143; P. Cambon to H. Cambon, 7 Feb. 1908, Louis Cambon MSS; J. F. V. Keiger, 'Raymond Poincaré and French Foreign Policy, 1912–1914' (Cambridge University, 1980), p. 99.

[76] P. Cambon to Pichon, 6 Feb. 1909, Inst. de Fr. Pichon MSS, 2; P. Cambon to H. Cambon, 2 Aug. 1904, Louis Cambon MSS.

[77] W. L. Langer, *The Diplomacy of Imperialism* (New York, 1960), p. 293.

[78] *DDF* (I), xiv. 120.

[79] T. Tittoni, 'Visiti ad ambasciatori', *Nuova antologia*, 108/4 (1903), p. 147.

Germany dominated Barrère's thinking, and he wanted to achieve her diplomatic isolation. As ambassador to Rome his ultimate goal was to end the Italo-German alliance, a goal not shared by Paul Cambon. Barrère had been deeply affected by the Franco-Prussian war and by Gambetta's ideas.[80] He was both a Germanophobe and a *revanchiste*. Before becoming ambassador to Italy he had believed that Alsace-Lorraine could only be regained by force, though later, as he matured, he hoped for a diplomatic solution.[81] He advocated the strengthening of the French army, but, unlike the Cambons, was not imbued with pacific sentiments.[82] On the contrary, Social Darwinist theories, so popular at the time, had a powerful hold on his mind. While he was mainly concerned with isolating Germany diplomatically, he was more prepared than most of his ambassadorial colleagues to unsheathe the sword.[83]

To Barrère, Italy was of crucial importance in the isolation of Germany. A full decade before becoming ambassador to Rome he had conceived an ambitious scheme to cut the links between Italy and the Dual Alliance.[84] He had a high regard, perhaps exaggerated, for Italy's political influence and military strength. Though he felt little could be done about the Dual Alliance, the assistance of Italy could decide the fate of any future war against France.[85] Barrère, therefore, was hoping for far more than Italian neutrality. He wanted Italy to abandon the Triple Alliance in favour of an alignment with France.

At the time of his arrival in Rome in 1897 Barrère was convinced that the key to Franco-Italian political *rapprochement* lay in an economic accord. Italy, apart from her own internal economic problems, was suffering from the tariff warfare between the two countries. When Delcassé came to power in June 1898 Barrère's views were more positively received, and an economic agreement was signed in November 1898.[86] In the years following this accord Barrère remained cognizant of the role of economics in Italy's policies and consistently pressured Delcassé to have French markets opened to Italian products. This lowering of France's tariff barriers, he thought, might convert Italy into a French

---

[80] 'La Chute de Delcassé', *La Revue des deux mondes* (Aug. 1932), p. 603.

[81] Barrère to Ribot, 23 Mar. 1892, AE NS 'Bavière', 273; Barrère to Hanotaux, 14 Mar. 1890, AE Hanotaux MSS, 17; *DDF* (i), vii. 453; x. 371.

[82] Barrère to Pichon, 30 June 1898, AE Barrère MSS, 4.

[83] Barrère to Spuller, 12 Dec. 1889, 13 Apr. 1890, AE NS 'Bavière', 268; Barrère to Delcassé, 31 May 1903, 21 June, 30 Dec. 1904, AE Delcassé MSS, 1.

[84] *DDF* (i), x. 68; Barrère to P. Cambon, 15 Nov. 1895, Louis Cambon MSS.

[85] L. Noël, *Camille Barrère* (Bourges, 1948), p. 38, Barrère to Ribot, 1 June 1890, AE NS 'Bavière', 270.

[86] *DDF* (i), xiv. 52, 120, 253, 512.

dependency. Later, he linked the flotation of Italian government bonds on the Paris Bourse to political advantages.[87]

It was Barrère's enthusiasm which led to the signing of the Franco-Italian accords of 1901, though Delcassé was in broad agreement. After the commercial accord, Barrère urged the Foreign Minister to concede the Italians Tripoli, where France had few interests and which was one of the causes of Italian participation in the Triple Alliance. The Ambassador believed that a formal declaration of French disinterest in Tripoli would lead to a Franco-Italian *rapprochement*. During the negotiations conducted in the course of 1900 Barrère largely had his way. Despite Delcassé's initial refusal to accept a formal declaration, Barrère succeeded in winning him over.[88] Delcassé agreed to an exchange of letters based on the London Convention of 1889. He then endorsed Barrère's objections to the wording of the documents, which, in the Ambassador's opinion, failed to safeguard the North African aspirations of the two powers.[89] Finally, Barrère was personally responsible for France's insistence that, in exchange for a free hand in Tripoli, Italy should undertake not to go to war against France in Europe.[90] Ultimately Italy confined the 1901 agreement to the Mediterranean, but the basis of the 1902 neutrality accord had been laid. Certainly Barrère could not prevent Delcassé from including Morocco in the agreement of 1901. He doubted the need to link Morocco and Tripoli, but, in the face of Delcassé's determination, he accepted the most prudent of commitments, an exchange of letters.[91]

The Mediterranean agreement of 1901 was highly significant in Barrère's eyes. It not only modified the distribution of power in the Mediterranean to France's advantage but also greatly improved Franco-Italian relations, since Tripoli had long figured prominently in the calculations of Italian statesmen. Even so, Barrère was keen to go further by changing the terms of the Triple Alliance and by arranging a Franco-Italian neutrality accord. He went to work on two fronts. First, he sought to win the goodwill of the Italian government through a determined policy of courtesy and cordiality. The visit of the Italian fleet

---

[87] Barrère to Delcassé, 2 Apr. 1900, AE NS 'Italie', 15; Barrère to Delcassé, 31 Oct. 1901, AE Delcassé MSS, 1.

[88] Barrère to Delcassé, 9 Feb., 2, 9, 21 May, 9, 20 June, 12 Nov., 7 Dec. 1900, AE Barrère MSS, 2.

[89] Barrère to Delcassé, 27 Jan., 9 Feb. 1900, AE Delcassé MSS, 1.

[90] Ibid., Barrère to Delcassé, 9 May 1900.

[91] Note on a letter of 19 Nov. 1930 from the Quai d'Orsay to Barrère, AE Barrère MSS, 2.

to Toulon in the spring of 1901 was largely of his doing.[92] He also encouraged Prinetti, the Italian foreign minister, to modify the terms of the Triple Alliance so as to remove French objections. Despite Prinetti's words of assurance to the German Ambassador, Barrère exercised a powerful influence over the Italian Foreign Minister. The neutrality accord, signed in June 1902, owed much to Barrère's work, and would probably not have been effected without him. Delcassé, for his part, allowed Barrère remarkably free rein. The Foreign Minister was content to make suggestions, supervise the work of the Centrale, and ensure parliamentary approval.

After the 1902 agreement Barrère considered his main task at an end, and the next years were spent in consolidating the friendship he had built up. He was instrumental in negotiating a series of treaties and agreements of a minor nature, such as the Franco-Italian Arbitration Treaty of December 1903 and the 1904 Labour Treaty, which protected the health and rights of Italian labourers in France.

As the isolation of Germany by the realignment of non-German powers was the focal point of Barrère's policies, Russia and Britain played an important part. Barrère held quite strong anti-British sentiments but he was not unconciliatory.[93] During the Boer War he was expounding an aggressive policy against Britain, arguing that the British listened little to reason and detested weakness.[94] By 1903, however, he was decidedly enthusiastic about the *Entente Cordiale*, seeing that Britain joined to the Dual Alliance would make 'nécessairement craquer ce qui reste de la triplice'.[95] Barrère was sometimes critical of the Russians. To one mainly concerned with the balance of power in Europe, their expansion into Asia was hardly welcome. Nevertheless, though he thought the Russians fickle, and disliked the Russo-Japanese war, he advocated as much support for them as possible. He was mindful that any other policy would enable Germany to suggest to the Russians that the French were unsupportive allies.[96]

Generally, then, Barrère worked intimately with Delcassé and had a very significant voice in Franco-Italian relations. Certainly there were differences between the two men, but these were mainly differences of emphasis. Delcassé, for his part, felt that Barrère was overly concerned with wresting Italy from German domination. Barrère was interested

[92] Ibid.   [93] Sanderson to Rosebery, 18 Apr. 1894, NLS Rosebery MSS, 10135.
[94] Barrère to Delcassé, 31 Dec. 1899, 27 Jan., 9 Feb. 1900, AE Delcassé MSS, 1.
[95] Ibid. 11 May 1900.
[96] Ibid., Barrère to Delcassé, 27 Jan. 1900, 20 Feb. 1904.

primarily in the European balance of power and was less interested than Delcassé in expanding the French empire. But ultimately both men had the same goal, that of restoring as fully as possible the power and prestige lost to Germany in 1871.

The third member of the ambassadorial triumvirate, Jules Cambon, also had Delcassé's ear. In the years 1898–1904, however, his influence was not as far-reaching as that of the other two. Cambon's embassy to Washington largely paved the way for closer Franco-American relations in ensuing years, despite the fact that even in this period most did not consider America as an important world influence. He had accepted the mission from Hanotaux in October 1897 only with some hesitancy, because he did not wish to leave Europe and because he was unable to speak English.[97] When he arrived in Washington he was dismayed with what he saw. The Americans were the new barbarians, badly educated, puerile, and vain.[98] He quickly worked his way into the confidence of Hay, the secretary of state, and of successive presidents, McKinley and Roosevelt. They did not impress him. To Cambon, Hay was very ignorant and created difficulties which did not exist. McKinley, for his part, was a weakling, unable to wield authority over his government.[99]

Cambon's two major ideas in this period were closely connected with his jaundiced view of America. The country's national solidarity and dignity impressed him,[100] but her ambitious and aggressive tendencies made him believe that she would dominate the world's affairs within fifty years.[101] More specifically, Cambon thought that the Mediterranean, France's major field of expansion, was threatened by American infiltration as a result of the Spanish–American war. Cambon vociferously warned Delcassé that the United States would seek to establish herself in Morocco and to open an embassy in Constantinople if she attacked Spain.[102] Delcassé, always suspicious of foreign ambitions in Morocco, heeded his Ambassador's advice and hastily endorsed a Spanish plan for Cambon to act as mediator. Cambon immediately urged the Spanish to yield as quickly as possible.[103]

Cambon believed that the USA was bent on a policy of world imperialism. When she took the Philippines in 1899 he thought that this was

[97] G. Tabouis, *Jules Cambon par l'un des siens* (Paris, 1938), p. 16.
[98] J. Cambon to Delcassé, 8 July, 5, 12 Aug., 23 Sept. 1898, AE Delcassé MSS, 2.
[99] Ibid. 5 Aug., 23 Sept. 1898.   [100] Tabouis, *Jules Cambon*, p. 86.
[101] J. Cambon to de Margerie, dated 1901, AE de Margerie MSS.
[102] J. Cambon to Delcassé, 5 July 1899, AE Delcassé MSS, 2.
[103] Ibid. 17 Mar. 1899.

merely the first step to wider domination in Asia and China specifically.[104] He propounded 'une sorte de doctrine de Monroe au profit de l'Europe' (Germany, Britain, France) against America, but Delcassé was unenthusiastic to move in China for various reasons and did not fully take up the suggestion. The forces sent to put down the Boxer Rebellion included Germans and British but also Americans, and Delcassé was not interested in spheres of influence.[105]

Cambon had mixed feelings about leaving Washington for Madrid in the summer of 1902. He had established considerable influence in Washington but, on the other hand, relished the prospect of returning to Europe.[106] Delcassé, who fully shared Cambon's preoccupation with the Mediterranean, relied heavily on him during the ensuing Franco-Spanish *pourparlers*, which led to an accord in October 1904 and which defined respective spheres of influence in Morocco. Cambon did not, however, agree with the central administration's belief that Spain was at the centre of everything in these years. As he told de Margerie in August 1902, 'Je n'ai pas l'opinion qu'on a au département où l'on me paraît croire que la clef du monde est en Espagne et que le reste ne compte pas.'[107] His evaluation of Spain and her interests reflected his contempt. She was vain, fickle, jealous, and cherished pretensions she could not hope to achieve.[108] Equally, Spain could not be neglected. A dissatisfied Spain would be vulnerable to German blandishments, and he believed that any agreement on Morocco had to satisfy Spanish aspirations.[109] Consequently, he pressed Delcassé well before the *Entente Cordiale* was signed to accommodate Madrid, maintained this pressure after agreement was reached, and had an important part in negotiating the Franco-Spanish accord of October 1904. To strengthen French influence he even suggested that Russia and Spain concert in an *entente platonique*, but this idea never appeared to get off the ground.[110]

Like his brother, Jules was a fervent believer in the *Entente Cordiale* and considered that France's diplomatic strength in the world was a function of Anglo-French relations.[111] In the crisis periods of 1905 and 1911 he turned, not without response, to London rather than St Petersburg. Like

[104] Ibid. 9 June 1899.   [105] Ibid. 17 Mar., 30 May 1899.
[106] J. Cambon to de Margerie, 22 Aug. 1902, AE de Margerie MSS.
[107] Ibid.
[108] Ibid.; J. Cambon to Delcassé, 5 Aug. 1898, 14 Apr. 1904, 24 May 1905, AE Delcassé MSS, 2.
[109] Ibid. J. Cambon to Delcassé, 28 Feb. 1903.
[110] Ibid. 17 Aug. 1903, 9 Apr. 1904, 8 Apr. 1905, 30 Oct. 1911.
[111] J. Cambon to Louis, 24 June 1907, AE Louis MSS, 2. J. Cambon to Pichon, 22 Apr. 1907, 17 Mar. 1909, 18 Nov. 1910, Inst. de Fr. Pichon MSS, 2.

so many French diplomats in the 1890s, he had been critical of British actions in the Mediterranean and of her support of America in the Spanish–American war.[112] But he viewed the 1904 agreement with enthusiasm, having been thoroughly convinced of the necessity of Britain's friendship. While recognizing Britain's faults, her reserve, her self-righteousness, and her ambitions in certain political and economic fields, he deeply admired her respect for the given word, her unbending loyalty, and her moral leadership.[113] Britain was also the perfect foil against German intimidation.

Though Cambon was influential in the determination of Mediterranean policy and often gave sound advice, he lacked the moderation, objectivity, and experience of his later years in Berlin. His passionate preoccupation with the Mediterranean made him overly suspicious of American, British, and Spanish designs. It was in this period that his mistrust of Germany, greater than his brother's, was most apparent. It was not until 1907, when he came face to face with the Germans, that he realized that his earlier judgements had sometimes been unfair to Berlin.

Delcassé, in spite of his secretiveness, accepted for the most part the advice proffered by the ambassadorial triumvirate and acted as the co-ordinator of policies personally initiated by Barrère and the Cambons. Consequently, the *Entente Cordiale*, Franco-Italian and Franco-Spanish *rapprochements*, and the Quai d'Orsay's general anti-Germanism were as much his leading ambassadors' work as his own. Certainly, Barrère was more concerned with the balance of power in Europe than with imperial expansion into North Africa, but the Cambons fully shared Delcassé's virtual obsession with the Mediterranean. Yet, as influential as each leading ambassador was, Delcassé always retained ultimate authority, and his thoroughgoing enthusiasm for the Russian alliance was largely of his own making. In addition, as the Moroccan question became more complicated after 1904, there was a distinct tendency on Delcassé's part to ignore warnings from the Centrale and from his leading ambassadors that Germany would refuse to be a negligible factor.

[112] J. Cambon to Delcassé, 5 July 1898, AE Delcassé MSS, 2.

[113] Ibid. 1 Mar. 1904, 16 May 1905, 30 Oct. 1911; J. Cambon to Pichon, June 1908, Inst. de Fr. Pichon MSS, 2; J. Cambon to Poincaré, 3 March, 27 Nov. 1912, AE J. Cambon MSS, 16; J. Cambon to de Margerie, 14 Nov. 1906, AE de Margerie MSS.

6

The First Moroccan Crisis, 1904–1906

The year 1904 marked a turning point in the history of French foreign policy and in the administration of the Quai d'Orsay. Not only were the *Entente Cordiale* and the Franco-Spanish accords signed, thus signalling the beginning of French *pénétration pacifique* in Morocco, but the death of Cogordan in 1904 led to a considerable reshuffle of personnel and to increased influence on the part of certain officials. Georges Louis became political director, and Soulange-Bodin was made *sous-directeur du Nord*, replacing Dumaine, who was sent to Munich. The new team was solidly anti-German and supported Delcassé's resistance to German pressure in 1905. Despite the eventual downfall of Delcassé in 1905, his policies were not overturned, nor was the influence of the Quai d'Orsay seriously diminished despite a temporary loss of power during Rouvier's early months. On the contrary, it continued to have a predominant role because of German intimidation, Premiers Rouvier's and Bourgeois's inexperience, and the Quai's professional expertise. Also, though Paul Revoil, Philippe Berthelot, and Jules Cambon led the defence of officialdom, they were supported by almost all their colleagues. Unlike the Second Moroccan Crisis, the first revealed great unity in the ranks of permanent officials.

It was during the years 1904–5 that Delcassé was most noticeably influenced by Maurice Paléologue, *sous-directeur adjoint du Midi*. Paléologue's early life and origins were shrouded in mystery, secrecy, and romanticism. He was born in 1859, the only son of a man of Greek extraction exiled for political reasons from Romania and of a woman, probably Jewish, who had been a Belgian musician. There were conflicting stories concerning his ancestry, he emphasizing the antiquity of his name. His critics, of whom there were very many, stressed his thoroughly disreputable background.[1]

---

[1] 'Souvenirs: Russie, ancien régime' p. 10; 'Notes concernant le Quai d'Orsay, 1930–1944' p. 118, AN de Robien MSS.

Paléologue was baptized in the Greek Orthodox Church and became a naturalized citizen of France during his adolescence. He went to the Lycée Henri IV and later, in 1876, to Louis le Grand, where he met Millerand and Poincaré. In June 1880, he came first in the *concours* despite some unfavourable comments by his judges, and he was assigned to the foreign minister's cabinet, partly because of his friendship with Saint-René-Taillandier, his later superior, and perhaps because his family knew Foreign Minister de Freycinet. Barthélemy Saint-Hilaire, de Freycinet's successor, became one of his patrons and, as a noted expert on classical philosophy, encouraged his literary career. However, until Delcassé 'discovered' him, his diplomatic career was rather dull. A note by Francis Charmes suggests that in this period 'pendant de longues années, il demeure hors des cadres, condamné par son grade à ne faire que de la copie'.[2] His most important responsibility was the keeping of secret files, especially those related to the Franco-Russian alliance and to liaison between army and Foreign Ministry intelligence services. During the Dreyfus affair he was official delegate and observer for the Foreign Minister at the Cour de cassation and Council of Rennes. It was here he seemed to make many political enemies, and certain senators took their revenge by having him exiled to Sofia in 1907.[3]

Though most of his career was spent in the Centrale, he had some experience in external posts. After his initial year's training he put in four months as third secretary in Tangiers. In May 1885 he was sent to Rome, but Cogordan specifically requested his presence in the special mission to China in August 1885.[4] After this period he returned to and languished in the Centrale until Delcassé made him *sous-directeur adjoint du Midi* in charge of military affairs.

Paléologue was a thoroughly unsavoury character little suited to the task of conducting diplomacy. He had an alert intelligence which was nevertheless too imaginative. His erudition was astonishing. He had a degree in law, knew English, German, and Italian well, and was encouraged by his mother to become a *littérateur*. As de Robien, a colleague in the years 1914 to 1917, noted, 'sa vue exacte de choses ne s'obscurcissait que lorsqu'il voulait le lier à une formule'. Unfor-

[2] Note by F. Charmes dated 28 Oct. 1912 but probably written earlier, AE *dossier personnel*, Maurice Paléologue.
[3] See his published journal, *My Secret Diary of the Dreyfus Case, 1894–1899* (London, 1957).
[4] Paléologue to Jusserand, 15 Nov. 1885, 27 Nov. 1898, AE Jusserand MSS, 21.

tunately, this was too often the case. His superb literary flair, while it enabled him to write an impressive range of books, was associated with a romanticism and imagination which adversely affected his work and judgement.[5] His despatches always reflected a fluent prose style. In both his despatches and his private journal he employed a direct conversational technique. The trouble was that diplomatic conversations were usually too subtle to be transmitted in this question-and-answer form.[6]

Though his excessive imagination and rash judgements were noticed by friends and enemies alike, his vanity, excitability, and secrecy were no less marked. He always loved to praise himself. De Robien noted in his diary a story by Paléologue: 'Il me rappelait qu'un jour où il devait être reçu par le czar, il voulait que le télégramme puisse partir dès son retour à l'ambassade pour arriver à Paris à l'heure où il ferait le plus d'effet.'[7] Paléologue, far from discounting such stories, spoke openly to colleagues about the historical importance of his role. In 1898, writing to Jusserand from his bed, where he was recovering from an illness, he unabashedly claimed: 'Du fond de ma chambre, où l'on m'apportait les dépêches, je régissait notre empire: la moitié du monde.'[8]

Undoubtedly Paléologue cherished his independence. His many years as guardian of the secret files and his intimate knowledge of Franco-Russian relations and of German military plans imbued him with the notion that he was accountable to France rather than to a foreign minister, whose knowledge, experience, and tenure of office were limited. He believed that a diplomat could influence great movements or events and had no qualms when he acted without or against instructions. Though this unaccountability was extremely dangerous, his conception of the ambassadorial role was also beneficial at times. He instilled a high sense of responsibility in his officials, allowed them to collaborate, and never treated them as page boys, as later chiefs did. Though his indiscretions were sometimes described as 'almost incredible', what dropped from his plate were mostly a few tit-bits meant to

---

[5] 'Notes concernant le Quai d'Orsay' pp. 121–2; 'Souvenirs: Russie, ancien régime', p. 10, AN de Robien MSS.

[6] 'Souvenirs: Russie, ancien régime', 10, AN de Robien MSS; also Taigny to de Fleuriau, 26 Oct. 1908, AE P. Cambon MSS, 4; J. Cambon to P. Cambon, 16 Dec. 1912, AE J. Cambon MSS, 19; Manneville to Doulcet, 23 Jan. 1914, AE Doulcet MSS, 21; newspaper article on Paléologue in AE Doulcet MSS, 20.

[7] 'Souvenirs: Russie, ancien régime', 10, AN de Robien MSS.

[8] Paléologue to Jusserand, 27 Sept. 1898, AE Jusserand MSS, 21.

amuse the salons he frequented. Many colleagues, while detesting his manner, respected his old-world professionalism.[9]

Though his other faults were bad enough, it was his taste for the catastrophic which was most dangerous. Just about all foreign and French commentators were unanimous in recognizing the dire consequences of his deep pessimism. He was a thorough Germanophobe who believed that war was inevitable given Germany's character. As Danoff, a colleague in Sofia, later reported to Jules Cambon, there was always wild talk of 'horizon, de nuages, d'orages menaçants'. It reached at times such frightening proportions that it suggested a mental disequilibrium.[10]

Paléologue's humble origins and the fact that he was considered an *intru* encouraged him to try and make his mark in the world. Already his family had important links through marriage. One sister, Pernelot, married J. Cambon. The other, Zinka, married André Lebon, an influential politician of the Third Republic.[11] Paléologue surrounded himself with members of the highest aristocracy—including Eugénie, Napoléon III's wife—and made a point of his special relationship with Poincaré. He entertained a lot, giving the most lavish dinners. He invited colleagues, visiting officials, and even politicians to lunch but normally made it abundantly clear that they did not belong to his inner group. His custom of telling them when the lunch was over insulted many. His dinners were designed only for his intimate coterie. The salon, where classical concerts were performed and high diplomacy discussed, was the setting in which Paléologue revelled as raconteur and *amant*.[12]

[9] I. Halfond, 'Maurice Paléologue' (Temple University, 1974), pp. vii, xiv, 104; conversation between Paléologue and de Robien, 27 Feb. 1914, AE Doulcet MSS, 23; Paléologue to Jusserand, 27 Sept. 1898, 19 June 1901, AE Jusserand MSS, 21, 22; notes by de Robien, 'Souvenirs: Russie, ancien régime', p. 16, AN de Robien MSS.

[10] In all the reports on Paléologue there was hardly one which praised him. His social behaviour was no secret in diplomatic circles. See e.g. J. Cambon to P. Cambon, 16 Dec. 1912, AE J. Cambon MSS, 19; Manneville to Doulcet, 23 Jan. 1914; Daeschner to Doulcet, 25 May 1914: 'il aura été précédé aussi de trop de mauvais rapports pour que la confiance s'établisse,' AE Doulcet MSS, 21; Bertie, writing to Grey and using Geoffray and Findlay (British minister in Sofia) as sources, referred to Paléologue as 'excitable, inclined to spread sensational and alarmist rumours', and a 'marchand de canards', 26 Jan., 15 June 1912, FO 371, France 3958; PRO, FO 800/165, Bertie MSS.

[11] G. Tabouis, *Jules Cambon par l'un des siens* (Paris, 1938), p. 34.

[12] 'Souvenirs: Russie, ancien régime', p. 17 *bis*, 17 *ter*, AN de Robien MSS; M. Paléologue, *Three Critical Years, 1904–1906* (New York, 1957), pp. 20–7, 249; also conversation between Paléologue and Doulcet, AE Doulcet MSS, 23. Paléologue brought along his personal chef when he went to Russia in an attempt to impress Russian high society.

It was this last aspect which dominated his social life. Like Berthelot, he had a passionate love for women. Eventually his liaison with Mme Bartet, a Parisian socialite, became famous. She imbued him with her snobbery and conquered his friendship by flattering his vanity. In return he confided in her. He often drew pretty pictures on telegrams drafted during the day, being careful, however, to pencil out important diplomatic messages. Later, when he was posted abroad, she acted as a communicator of gossip for him, keeping his memory alive in high circles.[13]

His relations with most of his colleagues were strained to say the least, and even normally mild British diplomats referred to him as the 'marchand des canards'. He could, however, sustain friendships with selected and important persons and could be faithful, devoted, and generous. He worked successfully with Saint-René-Taillandier (his chief in the Sous-direction du Midi between 1895-1901), a personal friend who advanced his career. Jusserand and Paléologue were close friends, and the latter, when he left the Centrale, acted as a source of information for the former. The Cambons were linked to Paléologue by marriage. They were certainly mindful of his shortcomings but still considered him a competent agent. Dumaine was his 'ami spirituel', and the *sous-directeur du Nord* pushed hard for his advancement. Cogordan, for his part, admired Paléologue and both worked closely with Delcassé. Paléologue's relationship with Louis was similar, though they seem to have fallen out a bit after Louis did little to defend him during the 1906 purges.[14]

The relationship between Paléologue and Delcassé was intimate. Paléologue, while conscious that Delcassé did not have a great mind, highly respected his patriotism, his skill at negotiating, and his non-doctrinaire approach. He had more confidence in him than in any other minister, though this did not prevent him from trying to exercise undue influence over Delcassé. The Foreign Minister, for his part, singled out Paléologue for special treatment and valued his assistance more than that of anyone else in the Centrale. Basically they shared the same views, especially on Germany, and Paléologue reinforced Delcassé's attitudes.

[13] 'Souvenirs: Russie, ancien régime', p. 17 *bis*, 17 *ter*, AN de Robien MSS.

[14] Ibid. p. 17; also note by Raindre, 1902 and by Dumaine, 1901, with corrections by Raindre, AE *dossier personnel*, Paléologue; on his friendship with Louis see letters in AE Louis MSS, 1, 2; on his friendship with Jusserand, AE Jusserand MSS, 21, 22; Halfond, 'Paléologue', p. 14; letters between Paléologue and Collin de Plancy, 1886, AE Collin de Plancy MSS, 4.

During the Russo-Japanese war there were noticeable differences, but Delcassé, always his own man, stood his ground.[15]

Paléologue was often strongly influenced by his deep-seated pessimism. He considered Germany basically aggressive in character, with a policy dominated by Holstein, the *éminence grise* of the Wilhelmstraße. Paléologue differed substantially from those like Paul and Jules Cambon who considered Wilhelm II to be peace-loving but inconsistent. Though Jules Cambon disclosed the famous Albert–Wilhelm conversations of 1913, it was Paléologue who thoroughly publicized their dangerous aspects. Finally, he was concerned that the Germans would not tolerate a lasting British–French combination.[16]

He fully shared, therefore, Delcassé's dedication to a strong diplomatic position and a more effective military force. He lauded the *Entente Cordiale*, faithfully upheld the Franco-Russian alliance, and would have liked Italy to come over to France's side. National considerations and pride were considerably more important than peace or the nature of the regime. He deplored Combes's anti-clerical measures, which he thought would have dire consequences for French prestige in the Near East. He disliked the policies of General André, then minister of war, who, he thought, was not only inflicting a sort of 'pogrom' on the military but reducing French military capacity.[17]

Paléologue had Delcassé's ear, but Soulange-Bodin, the *sous-directeur du Nord* from 1905 and later the first *sous-directeur d'Europe, d'Afrique, et d'Océanie* in 1907, was less fortunate. Delcassé had decided, for reasons hardly discernible, not to give Dumaine, the obvious candidate, the leadership of the political division and had instead appointed Soulange-Bodin as deputy director. Nevertheless, the new deputy director made very little mark. Though he reinforced Delcassé's anti-German views, he seems to have done little else. He formulated few notes and even fewer ideas, and appears to have shown hardly any initiative. Delcassé continued to turn to Paléologue. Rouvier later ignored Soulange-Bodin.[18]

[15] Paléologue, *Three Critical Years*, pp. 153, 264; Halfond, 'Paléologue', pp. 51–61; C. M. Andrew, *Théophile Delcassé and the Making of the Entente Cordiale* (London, 1968), p. 66; note by Raindre, 1902, AE *dossier personnel*, Paléologue; Paléologue often lunched with Delcassé and developed a useful friendship with Francis Charmes, ex-political director (G. Louis, *Les Carnets de Georges Louis* (Paris, 1926), 7 Mar. 1908, p. 8).

[16] Paléologue to Jusserand, 16 Feb. 1905, AE Jusserand MSS, 60.

[17] Paléologue to J. Cambon, 13 Nov. 1908, AE J. Cambon MSS, 15; Paléologue, *Three Critical Years*, pp. 15, 25, 66.

[18] A.E. *dossier personnel*, Soulange-Bodin. This dossier contains only one document relating to his birth and his entry into the 'career'; Revoil to Poincaré, undated, BN (NAF 16015), Poincaré MSS.

Soulange-Bodin was born in May 1855 and was the son of a diplomat of the Second Empire. His father was friendly with the Duc Decazes and used this influence in December 1873 to have his son admitted to the service. Soulange-Bodin's most important posting was to Berlin in the 1890s under Jules Herbette, where he was noted for being a brilliant *raconteur* and developed his decidedly anti-German views. Later he became friendly with Hanotaux and was made his cabinet director in 1897.[19] With the coming of the Clemenceau ministry he fell into disfavour because the Premier considered him a reactionary clerical.[20]

Soulange-Bodin was a Germanophobe. He was critical of Wilhelm II, believing him to be a particularly vain and egotistical person. During his long stay in Berlin he had had first-hand experience. He considered the German character to be basically aggressive and viewed the power wielded by military and naval leaders as 'le fanatisme le plus rétrograde'. The state was absolutist and run for the maintenance of the social position of the *Junkers*. He was against the movement for *détente*.

Georges Louis, Cogordan's successor as political director in 1904, shared Soulange-Bodin's anti-German views and confirmed Delcassé's reading of German intentions during the Moroccan crisis. Born in March 1847, he had entered the central administration in 1881 as a *rédacteur* after having taken a degree in law. Like so many other diplomats of the period, he was bourgeois in origin. His father, Pierre Philippe Louis, was 'un avoué près du tribunal civil d'Epernay' and most of his ancestors had been *avoués* or *notaires*.[21] He and the influential politician Léon Bourgeois were neighbours and very close friends. Moreover, Louis's rise during the early 1900s appears to have been assisted by Bourgeois's influence.

In the same year that he entered the Quai d'Orsay, Louis was nominated to the position of *sous-directeur à la direction des affaires commerciales*, a task he filled with distinction until 1893. Named as *ministre plénipotentiaire deuxième classe*, he then became *directeur de la caisse de la dette publique egyptienne*, a post he held until August 1902.[22] He was thus in a powerful position to counter the English stranglehold on Egypt. Delcassé valued his services highly, recalling him to the position of commercial director in

[19] Soulange-Bodin to Hanotaux, 10 July 1897, AE Hanotaux MSS, 29; Soulange-Bodin to de Billy, 5 Mar. 1894, AE de Billy MSS, 28.

[20] See Deschanel to Pichon, 29 Jan. 1909, AE *dossier personnel*, Defrance.

[21] 'Extrait du registre de l'état-civil-Épernay sur Marne', 23 Mar. 1847, AE *dossier personnel*, Georges Louis.

[22] Ibid., text of agreement between Ahmed Mazloum Pasha, minister of finances, Egypt, and Georges Louis, 20 Apr. 1902.

1902 and then appointing him political director in April 1904 after Cogordan's death. Delcassé found him a sound administrator, and the two worked closely together.[23]

Louis was an excellent administrator, a man of deep reflection, experienced and conscientious. He spurned the social world where high diplomacy took place and preferred the confines of his bureau, where he felt policy ought to be made. He was later recognized in many quarters as having been the most thorough and efficient political director in the decade before the war.[24] His intimate knowledge of the workings of finance, industry, and commerce derived from his experience in the commercial division, and his seat on the Egyptian Debt Commission had been combined with a clear vision of France's security needs and diplomatic future. Though he could be inflexible, he carefully thought out and followed through policies.[25] Deputy directors were convoked daily to his office to explain every aspect of their work. Written notes were expected and clear instructions were subsequently issued.[26] Moreover, Louis did not only concern himself with the broad outlines of diplomacy—which his position theoretically freed him to do—but plunged into the mass of daily details and conducted important negotiations, especially the Mediterranean accords of 1907.[27] By 1910 this determination to supervise all aspects of the Quai d'Orsay's diplomatic and administrative activity was having a deleterious effect on his health.[28]

Louis's desire to maintain strict control over the diplomatic machinery was evident from the beginning. He distrusted the press, rarely allowed himself to be interviewed by journalists, and preferred to

[23] Ibid., Delcassé to Louis, 6 Sept. 1902, 19 Aug. 1904.

[24] Ibid., Pichon to Louis, 26 June 1910.

[25] P. Cambon to H. Cambon, 3, 28 Apr., 10 June 1904, Louis Cambon MSS; A. Gérard, *Mémoires d'Auguste Gérard* (Paris, 1928), p. 447; G. P. Gooch, *Recent Revelations in European Diplomacy* (London, 1924) p. 136. As an example of Louis's working technique, see Louis to Pichon, 14 July 1910, AE *dossier personnel*, Louis; R. Poincaré, *Au service de la France* (Paris, 1926–33), iii. 116.

[26] On his obstinacy, see P. Miquel, *Raymond Poincaré* (Paris, 1961), p. 271; on the clarity of his vision, Doumergue to Louis, 17 Jan. 1914, AE *dossier personnel*, Louis; on his outstanding mind, see Paul Cambon to his son, 'Louis . . .voit toujours le pour et le contre' and 'Louis ne peut dire ni oui ni non à rien sans enterrer la terre entière' (30 Jan. 1906), Louis Cambon MSS; report by Radolin, 10 Dec. 1906, Bonn, F. 108, vol. 16, 'Er ist ein durchaus ausstehend denkender.'

[27] 'Projét des notes', 11 Apr., AE NS 'Espagne', 41. See other letters from Apr. to May in same series.

[28] Pichon to Barrère, 14 Dec. 1909, AE *dossier personnel*, Piccioni; P. Cambon to H. Cambon, 7 Feb. 1909, Louis Cambon MSS; P. Cambon to J. Cambon, 26 Mar. 1906, AE J. Cambon MSS, 25.

leave public relations to Pichon or Herbette.[29] Apart from summoning the other deputy directors to his office daily, he worked alone, carefully reading dispatches, marking them, but writing very few comments or transmitting very few internal notes. He clearly feared the endemic indiscretions of the Centrale. Dispatches were usually written in his own hand on all manner of issues. When he felt that an ambassador was trying to encroach upon his responsibilities, he carefully edited or omitted despatches that would have kept the relevant posts *au courant*. Both the Cambons were to complain of Louis's penchant for administering everything, especially during the Near Eastern crisis of 1908 when Pichon's views were hardly known.[30]

Not that Louis was disliked by most of his colleagues. On the contrary, Paléologue (despite his later betrayal of Louis), Revoil, and Raindre were all close friends. Barrère considered Louis an excellent administrator, having worked with him in December 1903 at a technical conference.[31] His relationship with the Cambons was somewhat cooler largely because they found themselves being challenged for the first time by someone in the Centrale. Nevertheless, they liked his good sense, moderation, and modesty. Understandably, his deputy directors did not fully appreciate his careful scrutiny of their work between 1904 and 1906.

Another important official in the period 1904–6 was Philippe Louis Berthelot, son of the eminent scientist and former foreign minister Marcellin Berthelot. Born in October 1866 at Sèvres (Seine-et-Oise), he eventually went on to obtain degrees in arts and law, was proficient in German, English, and Portuguese, and had a good working knowledge of several oriental languages.[32] His haughtiness, sarcasm, and cynicism earned him many enemies, but these deficiencies were balanced by his extreme intelligence, industry, and loyalty to his friends, few though they were. While certainly cold and reserved on the outside, he knew how to be affectionate to an inner group of friends.[33]

As a youth he had been rather dissolute 'en compagnie des enfants gâtés de la République, les carabins et en particulier le juif Léon

[29] Louis to Pichon, 18 Aug. 1909, Inst. de Fr. Pichon MSS, 3.

[30] J. Cambon to Louis, 23 Oct. 1908, AE Louis MSS, 2; P. Cambon to Barrère, 17 Oct. 1908, *Paul Cambon: Correspondance* (Paris, 1940–6), ii. 246.

[31] Barrère to Delcassé, 15 Dec. 1903, AE *dossier personnel*, Louis.

[32] AE *dossier personnel*, Philippe Berthelot.

[33] P. G. Lauren, *Diplomats and Bureaucrats* (Stanford, Calif., 1976), p. 85; D. Langlois-Berthelot, 'Philippe Berthelot, 1886–1934', *La Revue des deux mondes* (June 1976), p. 576; G. A. Craig and F. Gilbert, *The Diplomats* (New York, 1972), p. 71; A. Bréal, *Philippe Berthelot* (Paris, 1937), pp. 13, 52, 54; P. Claudel, 'Philippe Berthelot', *Bulletin de la Société Paul Claudel*, 28 (1967), pp. 8, 48.

Daudet'.[34] Though he eventually married Hélène Linder just before the First World War, he had enjoyed many mistresses. Indeed, it was widely rumoured that one such lover had received the German Declaration of War as a token of affection.[35] His home was a natural meeting place for everything *décadent*. Berthelot furnished his apartment with oriental furniture and took an active interest in cubism and futurist literature.[36] His circle of friends included Barrès, Claudel, Giraudeau, Léger, Paul Morand, and Jean Cocteau. He contributed anonymously to the *Grande Encyclopédie* and also wrote articles in *Le Matin* under the name of Jean d'Orsay.[37] Undoubtedly his political opinions owed much to the influence of his father. He viewed himself as the spiritual son of the Revolution, almost as a Jacobin. Rejecting Catholicism as a tool of the monarchists, he espoused a sort of spiritualism based on Freemasonry. Though he was on excellent terms with the nationalist Barrès, he considered the *Action française* to be dangerous. Not that he was any less sparing in criticism for politicians of the Left. He made a clear distinction between the form of government which he advocated, republicanism, and the way in which the France of his day was being governed. The fact that he spent most of his career in Paris and was often in the company of ministers seems to have done nothing to moderate his dislike of the parliamentary regime.[38]

Berthelot was an extremely ambitious man and his career reflected the importance of patronage in Republican France. He had failed twice to pass the *concours* in 1889, and had entered the career through the back door, the consular service, because of his father's influence.[39] He was received coldly at first by the career men, who considered him something of an *intru*.[40] He failed to distinguish himself in Lisbon, where he had a junior position. In fact it was rumoured that he had siphoned funds from the Lisbon chancellery to pay outstanding debts.[41] When his father became Foreign Minister in 1895 his record was whitewashed and

[34] 'Notes concernant le Quai d'Orsay, 1930–44' p. 72, AN de Robien MSS.

[35] Ibid.

[36] Ibid.

[37] M. J. Rust, 'Business and Politics in the Third Republic: The Comité des forges and the French Steel Industry, 1896–1914' (Princeton University, 1973), p. 26; Bréal, *Berthelot*, p. 54.

[38] 'Notes concernant le Quai d'Orsay', p. 73, AN de Robien MSS; B. Auffray, *Pierre de Margerie (1861–1942) et la vie diplomatique de son temps* (Paris, 1976), pp. 251–4; article from *Le Figaro*, 23 Nov. 1939 (by Wladimir d'Ormesson), in AE *dossier personnel*, Berthelot.

[39] Daeschner to Doulcet, 18 Nov. 1895, AE Doulcet MSS, 17; Marcellin Berthelot to Delcassé, 14 Dec. 1901, AE Delcassé MSS, 6.

[40] 'Notes concernant le Quai d'Orsay', p. 72, AN de Robien MSS.

[41] Ibid.; also Bertie to Grey, 14 Feb. 1916, PRO, FO 800/168, FR/16/17, Bertie MSS.

he was attached to the ministerial cabinet. It was at this time that he transferred from the consular to the diplomatic corps. Under Hanotaux he worked in the Service de l'analyse, which evaluated correspondence for the Foreign Minister. After working as a secretary in the legation in Brussels in 1902, then travelling on a special observation mission to China between 1902 and 1904, he never again left the Centrale and had an absolute horror of foreign posts.[42]

Apart from the influence that his father and his brother André were able to exert, Berthelot was able to win the favour of many foreign ministers. Delcassé was impressed and assigned him the position of *rédacteur* under Fonques Duparre, then in charge of Asian affairs.[43] On the latter's retirement, Berthelot was to take over his position.

Although Germany and France were rivals in Morocco before 1904, it was in this year that the Moroccan crisis began to take shape. Delcassé had already signed agreements with Great Britain and Italy concerning France's privileged position in Morocco. Consequently, after the signing of the Franco-Spanish accord in October 1904, the Foreign Minister pressed ahead with his Moroccan ambitions. He attempted to force the Sultan of Morocco into accepting reforms for the police, the banks and the army, all to be carried out with French assistance. By the new year it appeared that France was intent on excluding Germany from Morocco without offering compensation there or anywhere else. Delcassé handled the Germans very clumsily, hardly notifying Berlin of French actions and showing little inclination to enter into talks, let alone negotiations. Von Bülow, the German chancellor, reacted angrily. According to him, France was defying the Madrid Convention of 1880 which guaranteed Moroccan independence. More to the point, German political and economic interests in Morocco were being disregarded.

As a result, at the urging of the Wilhelmstraße, the Kaiser rather reluctantly interrupted a Mediterranean cruise and in March 1905 stopped in Tangier, where he declared the Sultan of Morocco to be a free and independent agent. The German intention was to inflict a series of humiliations on France and to force the resignation of Delcassé. The French Foreign Minister, with surprisingly little support from cabinet

[42] Bréal, *Berthelot*, pp. 53–61.

[43] Marcellin Berthelot to Delcassé, 14 Dec. 1901, André Berthelot to Delcassé, 18 Mar. 1899, AE Delcassé MSS, 6; René Renoult to Delcassé, 5 Apr. 1905, AE *dossier personnel*, Berthelot.

colleagues, was obliged to resign in June 1905. Even with Delcassé gone, the German government refused to settle the issue through direct Franco-German negotiations and insisted upon an international conference of the Great Powers at Algeçiras. In this forum Germany hoped to achieve a great diplomatic victory over France and to secure her economic and political interests in Morocco. Despite considerable internal haggling at the Quai d'Orsay, the French government finally conceded. In September 1905 both governments sent representatives to work out a programme for a conference to be held in January 1906.

The advice proffered to Delcassé in late 1904 and 1905 by some influential permanent officials and ambassadors may have encouraged him in the belief that he could undertake an expansionist policy in Morocco without attempting meaningful negotiations with Germany. But the actual decision not to negotiate was ultimately his own, and was in keeping with both his determination to make policy and his inalterable anti-German feeling.

Late in 1904 Saint-René-Taillandier, French minister to Morocco, had signalled to the Centrale that Germany appeared to harbour no political designs on Morocco.[44] He encouraged Delcassé to maintain his line of conduct with firmness and resolution and refused to take seriously warnings by the German diplomat Kühlmann, who, he added, was proffering purely personal opinions.[45] Delcassé seems to have taken this opinion to heart and to have believed that he could pursue a forward policy in Morocco, especially after the treaty with Spain had been signed in October 1904. In essence Saint-René's advice was correct, but Delcassé, far from making concessions as he had done with Italy, Spain, and Britain, virtually ignored Berlin, informing her in the most unflattering manner of his intentions. His refusal to modify his Moroccan policy was strengthened by Saint-René, whose disillusionment, after his initial hopes, appears to have been strong.

Paul Cambon's influence was even stronger than Saint-René's. As former minister in Tunis and ambassador to Madrid, he held firm views on the Moroccan question. In the 1880s he had developed the theory that Morocco would come under French domination over a period of thirty to forty years. Slow progress and the maintenance of the status

[44] H. Nicolson, *Sir Arthur Nicolson Bart, First Lord Carnock* (London, 1948), pp. 159–60, Saint-René-Taillandier to Delcassé, 26 Mar., 21 June 1904, AE NS 'Maroc', 172.

[45] Saint-René-Taillandier to Delcassé, 26 Mar., 21 June 1904, AE NS 'Maroc', 172. By Feb. 1905, Saint-René was a bit worried about the 'menées' of the German legation which could 'sans heurter de front notre politique, nous créer de graves embarras'.

quo were therefore essential.[46] Morocco would be a valuable possession but, surprisingly, Cambon did not believe that Germany would seek to intervene. On the contrary, he was confident that German policy was all bluff and designed simply to bring about Delcassé's downfall. In addition, he was convinced that Britain would support France in a war and that such backing would readily deter the Germans. Though he was critical of Delcassé's undiplomatic handling of the Germans, he supported his superior's refusal to make concessions as German pressure mounted.[47]

Barrère, too, strengthened Delcassé's resolve. Though he did not believe that Wilhelm II was bellicose and considered Europe against Berlin, there were alarming signs of pending war. Barrère thought that conversations with Germany would be useless and would merely result in subservience. He called on Delcassé to combat measures such as the two-year military law, which he thought weakened the French army. He counselled the Foreign Minister to talk over all eventualities with Britain.[48]

Paléologue disagreed with Paul Cambon's intransigence and seems to have had a serious difference of opinion with Delcassé about what should be done. Unlike Cambon, he believed Berlin was not bluffing, and that the Kaiser was overtaken by forces he could no longer control. He suggested that Italy, Britain, or Russia be used to mediate between France and Germany. When Delcassé firmly rejected this proposal, Paléologue supported the search for British assistance. However, he urged the Foreign Minister to seek British aid, not for the purpose of deterrence but rather as a means of resisting an eventual German invasion.[49]

Saint-René, Cambon, Barrère, and Paléologue, in the final instance, strengthened Delcassé's resolve to oppose German intimidation by eliciting diplomatic and possibly military support from London. The French Ambassador to Berlin since 1902, Georges Bihourd, had very different ideas. Bihourd's desire for an *entente* with Germany corresponded with Premier Rouvier's wishes and was in complete opposition

[46] P. Cambon to Revoil, 25 Mar. 1887, AE Revoil MSS, 1.

[47] P. Cambon to H. Cambon, 1 Apr. 1905; P. Cambon to Louis, 3 July 1905, *Correspondance*, ii. pp. 180, 200; K. Eubank, *Paul Cambon* (Norman, Okla., 1960), p. 103; P. Cambon to Delcassé, 8, 18 May, 6 June 1905, AE Delcassé MSS, 3.

[48] Barrère to Delcassé, 30 Dec. 1904, 30 Apr. 1905, AE Delcassé MSS, 1; Barrère, 'La Chute de Delcassé' (in manuscript form), AE Barrère MSS, 5.

[49] Paléologue to Jusserand, 10 Feb. 1905, AE Jusserand MSS, 60; Halfond, 'Paléologue', p. 68; Paléologue, *Three Critical Years*, pp. 233, 242, 280, 308.

to Delcassé's hard line. During the Moroccan affair he had persistently warned Delcassé of the madness of not informing, let alone including, Germany.[50] He was haunted by the military defeat of 1871 and terrified by the resolve of the German government, especially that of von Bülow and of the permanent official, Richthofen. Bihourd was keenly aware that Germany had the capacity to overrun Paris in fifteen days. His solution was to appease Germany and the Kaiser's *amour propre* in particular. In his opinion, a visit to Paris by the Crown Prince would flatter both the Kaiser and his son and eliminate the venomous words currently being exchanged.[51]

Undoubtedly the fact that relations had deteriorated so seriously could be attributed in part to Bihourd's timidity and apathy. He could have done something to alleviate the tension, but, unlike most ambassadors, was unwilling to act without specific instructions.[52] In addition, he was subject to a bad nervous condition and was somewhat overawed by the brusqueness of the Germans.[53] More importantly, he showed little interest in his task. In the thick of the crisis it was reported that at no time had Bihourd raised the question of Morocco during a dinner with von Bülow. He wanted to leave his post, supposedly because of his condition, to enjoy a peaceful retirement in his house at Nice.[54]

Bihourd's authority in Paris was negligible and it was no more substantial in Berlin. The Germans were scornful of his timidity. Moreover, as one parliamentarian wrote to Princess Radziwill in June 1904, 'Bihourd ne connaît personne, ne représente rien.' His only intermediary was the Hungarian Szechenyi, and the fact that they met in some disreputable brothels in Berlin was enough to set the German establishment against the Ambassador.[55]

Nevertheless, Bihourd's inefficacy was not at the root of the problem. It was Delcassé's refusal to consider negotiations which made Bihourd's task impossible from the beginning. Only in March 1905, with the visit of the Kaiser to Tangier, did Delcassé feel obliged to broach the subject with Germany. In April he informed the Chamber of Deputies that France might offer Germany a written guarantee of commercial freedom. Nothing more substantial was forthcoming, however. It was

[50] Notes by Bihourd, pp. 9, 10, 40, AE Bihourd MSS; *DDF* (2), v. 1, 28, 44, 62, 68, 77.

[51] Notes by Bihourd, pp. 10–11, AE Bihourd MSS.

[52] Ibid.; P. Cambon to H. Cambon, 1 Apr. 1905, AE Louis Cambon MSS.

[53] Paléologue, *Three Critical Years*, p. 229.

[54] Report by Radolin, 10 Dec. 1906, Bonn, F. 108, vol. 16; Daeschner to Revoil, 27 Feb. 1906, AE Revoil MSS, 2.

[55] Unknown to Revoil, 17 Aug. 1905, AE Revoil MSS, 2.

only when pressure was applied by Rouvier and his cabinet colleagues, whom he had hitherto ignored, that he did anything direct.[56] Bihourd himself was not supplied with sufficient information, and what appears to have been an organized campaign to discredit the Ambassador for career reasons and policy differences was begun.[57]

Although Delcassé had survived crises before, he had always managed to secure some parliamentary, cabinet, or presidential support. It was a different story in 1905. His downfall was above all the result of a clash between himself and Premier Maurice Rouvier. Rouvier viewed himself as a natural diplomat and leader. His clandestine talks with the Germans and his campaign to discredit Delcassé were, to some extent, a bid for power. Also, Rouvier blamed Delcassé for the heavy losses which his Banque française pour le commerce et l'industrie had incurred during the Russo-Japanese war, when the Foreign Minister had failed to foresee the Russian defeat. Besides ambition and personal animosity, Rouvier's financial background led him to disagree with Delcassé. Rouvier prided himself on his economic expertise. As a banker he viewed the world as an area of international co-operation for financial gain and was especially sympathetic to the idea of improving economic relations with Germany. Delcassé and he had had a series of arguments over financial matters. The Foreign Minister had vetoed French involvement in the German-controlled Baghdad railway, something Rouvier had wanted, and he had ignored Rouvier's advice concerning the handling of the Moroccan loans.[58]

Finally, in 1905, Rouvier was decidedly less hostile to Germany than Delcassé. The Premier told Jules Cambon in the middle of the crisis that, even if there was an 80 per cent chance of French military success, he would still choose the path to peace.[59] He was interested in principle in working more closely with Berlin. Soon after coming to power as foreign minister, he suggested the internationalization of the Moroccan financial system.[60] Though firmly convinced that Germany was not

[56] Andrew, *Delcassé*, pp. 272, 273, 274.

[57] J. Cambon to Louis, 16 Oct. 1908, AE J. Cambon MSS, 15; notes by Bihourd, p. 41, AE Bihourd MSS.

[58] P. Cambon to H. Cambon, 29 Apr. 1904, Louis Cambon MSS; W. Hallgarten, *Imperialismus vor 1914* (Munich, 1951), p. 525; Rouvier, as the *chef de file* of the French bank Commerce et industrie, was interested in achieving a French participation. Andrew, *Delcassé*, p. 306.

[59] J. Cambon to de Margerie, 15 Feb. 1906, AE de Margerie MSS.

[60] P. Cambon to Louis, 3 July 1905, *Correspondance*, ii. 206.

bluffing during the Moroccan crisis,[61] he was hopeful of negotiating a Franco-German *détente*.

Rouvier's actions in his first weeks as foreign minister were decisive enough. He pushed aside Delcassé's principal advisers, Cambon and Barrère. He forbade Paul Cambon to continue military and naval conversations with the British, and ignored Louis and Paléologue. He tried to do much himself. Dossiers were to be kept in a complete state for his perusal. Most important telegrams were written by him. Notably, he sent telegrams urging both the Japanese and Russian governments to end their war. Paléologue, who detested Rouvier, cattily remarked to Louis that Rouvier dreamed of being 'un personnage historique'. Certainly he undertook some significant initiatives. Saint-René-Taillandier's plan for a military and naval operation against the Sultan of Morocco was shelved. Without prompting, Rouvier dispatched notes to the Germans that even they did not expect. There was indeed something a little naïve about his expectation that diplomacy could be restricted to a few simple conversations and directives.[62]

Paul Cambon was virtually ignored by Rouvier during this period. He, in turn, disavowed Rouvier's policies. He was too deeply committed to Delcassé's views not to feel politically and personally injured. During Rouvier's period Cambon showed a distinct lack of interest and initiative in the Moroccan negotiations, rarely gracing the Quai d'Orsay with his presence. He did make one suggestion in June 1905 which Rouvier accepted. This was to reply to Germany's request for a conference by saying neither 'yes' nor 'no' but by stipulating that any conference should be preceded by a prearranged agreement. On the whole, however, Cambon remained firmly convinced that to accept a conference was a mistake. When Rouvier finally overruled him he appears to have been piqued, to have isolated himself, and to have restricted his diplomatic activities to saving the *Entente Cordiale*. On a lesser note, he did try to moderate the talk of 'enterrement', the 'propos alarmistes', and the 'prédications funèbres' which were flourishing at the Centrale. He judged correctly that the crisis would not end in a Franco-German conflagration.[63]

---

[61] Paléologue, *Three Critical Years*, p. 280; E. N. Anderson, *The First Moroccan Crisis* (Urbana, Ill., 1930), p. 212; J. Caillaux, *Agadir* (Paris, 1919), p. 22; Bihourd notes, pp. 10–11, AE Bihourd MSS; Andrew, *Delcassé*, p. 286; Barrère, 'La Chute de Delcassé', p. 122.

[62] Paléologue to Louis, 30 Aug., 2 Sept. 1905, AE Louis MSS, 1; P. Cambon to Louis, 3 July 1905, *Correspondance*, ii. 202.

[63] Paléologue to Louis, 2 Sept. 1905, AE Louis MSS, 1; P. Cambon to Louis, 3 July 1905, P. Cambon to J. Cambon, 22 June 1905; P. Cambon to H. Cambon, 15 June 1905, *Correspondance*, ii. 197, 198, 200.

Louis's influence also suffered. After Barrère and Cambon had washed their hands of Rouvier, he was the main proponent of the view that a conference would be dangerous. First, he thought that Germany's main aim was the humiliation and isolation of France. A conference would not alter her objectives. Secondly, Germany was bluffing. A conference would play into her hands. Thirdly, he refused to accord too much credit to Berlin's conciliatory words after Delcassé's fall. Finally, as Germany had provoked the crisis, it was not France's role to champion the idea of a conference. A determined opposition would make Berlin climb down from its high horse.[64] Rouvier, however, ignored his political director's advice, and Louis was kept busy with the form rather than the content of negotiations. Whether by choice or compulsion he took his annual holidays in August and September, leaving Paléologue to fill in the details with private letters.[65]

Though Barrère, Cambon and Louis were temporarily pushed aside, it was Paléologue who was the recipient of most of Rouvier's criticism. There was a mutual detestation. Paléologue was contemptuous of his superior's ignorance of foreign affairs, while Rouvier distrusted Paléologue's intriguing nature. The biographer of Paléologue, Halfond, put Rouvier's distrust down to the fact that he had been consulted by Paléologue behind Delcassé's back and now feared a similar fate. The two men seem to have clashed violently on several occasions. Rouvier lectured Paléologue severely for his pessimism, removed him from further involvement in the Moroccan question, and refused to do more than employ him in such minor tasks as the drafting of dispatches and the gathering of secret information.[66]

Clearly, Paléologue's activities needed to be curtailed. He was like a 'Sibyla diplomatrice' prognosticating doom. Throughout, he considered that Germany's conciliatory words would not be matched by deeds and that the aim of German policy was to reduce France to dependence. Even if France were to cede, there would be no guarantee that similar incidents would not arise in the future. Admittedly he was less pessimistic during the later part of September when Rosen, the German representative, and Revoil, Rouvier's new confidant at the

---

[64] P. Cambon to H. Cambon, 27 Jan. 1906, Louis Cambon MSS; Paléologue to Louis, 16 Sept. 1905, AE Louis MSS; Louis to J. Cambon, 22 Aug. 1907, AE J. Cambon MSS, 15; Louis to Revoil, 12 Jan. 1906, AE Revoil MSS, 2; Paléologue, *Three Critical Years*, p. 242; Louis to Revoil, 12 Jan. 1906, AE Revoil MSS, 2.

[65] Notes by Bihourd, pp. 10–12, AE Bihourd MSS.

[66] Paléologue to Louis, 30 Aug., 2 Sept. 1905, AE Louis MSS, 1; Halfond, 'Paléologue', p. 76; Gavarry to Revoil, 16 Feb. 1906, AE Revoil MSS, 2.

Centrale, came together to discuss a programme for a conference. His secret sources had conveyed information suggesting that Wilhelm II had decided upon a policy of conciliation in order to undermine Franco-British friendship. Paléologue's optimism lasted less than a week. When the meetings dragged on for eight hours a day without result, he began to work behind the scenes for a tough stand against Germany. As Jean Doulcet, then in the political division, commented: 'Paléologue est un âne, beaucoup plus occupé de faire blinder des pièces que de suivre une négociation.' It is interesting to note that Paléologue always referred to the *Entente Cordiale* as the 'alliance franco-anglaise', that he used this term in the strict sense of the word, and that he was convinced that the British would support France in a continental war.[67]

Delcassé's old team had been effectively, if momentarily, pushed aside, but the corollary was not that the Quai d'Orsay's influence was diminished. On the contrary, Revoil was specifically brought in to advise the Foreign Minister. Though his initial hopes for a *détente* were high, he soon reversed his stand. Rouvier himself hardened his attitude with remarkable rapidity, in part because of Revoil's advice but also because of the influence of his *chef du cabinet* Émile Daeschner and his *chef adjoint* Philippe Berthelot. New men had been brought onto the scene, but their advice differed little from that proffered by Paul Cambon, Louis, Barrère, and Paléologue.

The most important of the new men was Paul Revoil, one of Rouvier's Marseilles friends and the person to whom the Foreign Minister entrusted the handling of the crisis.[68] A lawyer by profession, he was a confident man who rarely betrayed excitement. It was his finesse and subtle persuasiveness which made him effective. He was able to gain acceptance for his views through firmness, competence, and good humour.[69]

His career had been quite spectacular and reflected both his ambitious nature and his intimate links with influential politicians. In 1893 he had been Jules Develle's *chef du cabinet*, and in October of that year he had replaced Louis as *sous-directeur des affaires commerciales*. Hanotaux was a close friend and made him *directeur du cabinet* in 1895. Though sent to Tunis as *adjoint au résident-général* in 1896, he became minister in

[67] Paléologue to Jusserand, 2 Feb. 1906, AE Jusserand MSS, 37; Paléologue to Louis, 5, 12, 16, 20 Sept. 1905, AE Louis MSS, 1; Letter by Doulcet, 12 Oct. 1905, AE Doulcet MSS, 15.
[68] Gaillard to Revoil, 22 June 1905, AE Revoil MSS, 2.
[69] L. Einstein, *A Diplomat Looks Back* (New York, 1968), p. 14.

Tangier some four years later. He was offered the governor-generalship of Algeria in 1901. He refused it at first, arguing that the task would tax his health too much. Ill-health, in fact, dogged him throughout his life. He was also anxious to complete the task he had begun in Morocco the year before. At last, however, his friends, Delcassé, Waldeck-Rousseau, and Millerand, prevailed upon him. After undertaking a special mission to study Tunisian agricultural production, he was disgraced by Combes because he was considered to be too closely linked to moderate Republicans and because he was thought to favour an aggressive policy in Morocco. His career languished until Rouvier attached him to the Centrale in June 1905.[70]

Revoil was known for his competence in economic and financial questions but was still more highly esteemed for his profound knowledge of Morocco and the Mediterranean. As minister to Tangier he advocated a forward policy in Morocco, which he was prepared to realize by the use of force. When he moved to Algeria, he encouraged disorder on the Moroccan border. Indeed, his preoccupation with Morocco made him an early and influential advocate of the *Entente Cordiale*. With Saint-René and Paul Cambon, he warned Delcassé of British-German infiltration and of the necessity of reaching a settlement with Britain.[71]

Like Daeschner, Bompard, Regnault, Geoffray, de Margerie, Jules Cambon, Paléologue, and Jusserand, he formed a part of a loose alliance whose general direction came from Paul Cambon. He had collaborated with the master in Tunis and formed a close friendship with Regnault. It is significant that, although Cambon himself temporarily fell out with Rouvier, his followers remained in the most vital positions. Daeschner was *chef du cabinet*; Revoil was ambassador to the Algéçiras Conference and a special adviser to Rouvier; de Margerie and Regnault were Revoil's assistants; and Jules Cambon was ambassador to Madrid. As a result, a tough stand was taken against Germany in the end, the *Entente Cordiale* was saved, and Delcassé and Cambon were vindicated.

The early weeks (June–July) of Rouvier's ministry witnessed something of a power struggle between Louis and Revoil. Unlike Delcassé and Louis, Revoil believed it was possible and desirable to converse with Germany about Morocco, and he counselled Rouvier to accept a con-

[70] AE *dossier personnel*, Paul Revoil; E. Weber, *The Nationalist Revival in France, 1905–1914* (Los Angeles, 1968), p. 33; J. C. Allain, *Agadir* (Paris, 1978), pp. 152, 154, 162; P. Guillen, *L'Allemagne et le Maroc, 1870–1905*, (Paris, 1969), p. 565; article by Jean Carrère, 6 Dec. 1906, AE Revoil MSS, 29.

[71] Guillen, *L'Allemagne et le Maroc*, pp. 565, 674; Revoil to Étienne, 13 Aug. 1904, BN (NAF 24237), Étienne MSS.

ference. He stressed the argument that Germany was not about to
unleash a war. The Quai d'Orsay, he pointed out, had been informed by
a decipherment of the *cabinet noir* that Berlin intended to settle the affair
peacefully. There was also something personal in his struggle to reach
the Minister's ear. Though he was friendly with Louis, he considered
himself the leading expert on Morocco, and was always passionately
involved with the question. Furthermore, he was seeking an opportunity
to re-establish his career after its collapse during the Combes period.
According to Paul Cambon, Rouvier was torn between the two but
finally opted for Revoil's arguments.[72]

Revoil, for his part, appears to have been strongly influenced by
Eugène Regnault, at that time stationed in Tangier under Saint-René-
Taillandier. He and Revoil were intimate friends, and the latter took
care to nominate him as his chief adviser at the Algéçiras Conference.
During negotiations his composure came to the fore, and foreign diplomats noted that he enjoyed more sympathy with the English-speaking
delegations than Revoil.[73]

Although Revoil listened attentively to Regnault's advice, there was
an important area of difference between the two men. Regnault had not
been in favour of an international conference. On the contrary, he
believed that it would restrict French expansion in Morocco. But he
counselled Revoil to speak directly with Berlin, so as to prevent the
Germans from becoming more obstructionist later on. Though he
thought that none of the public services in Morocco should be accorded
to Germany, reasonable satisfaction should be given to German colonial
opinion through 'adjudications publiques pour les entreprises de
travaux publics et de fournitures sans distinction de nationalité'. Moreover, concessions could be made outside of Morocco. Regnault warned
Revoil against a military plan devised earlier by Saint-René which involved military incursions into Moroccan territory. He considered that
such a scheme would merely reinforce the German argument that
France was flouting international accords. Finally, the Franco-Spanish
and Franco-British accords should remain untouched.[74]

[72] Bihourd notes, pp. 10–12, AE Bihourd MSS; Revoil to Poincaré, 24 Sept. 1905, BN
(NAF 16015), Poincaré MSS; P. Cambon to H. Cambon, 3 Apr., 22 June 1905, Louis
Cambon MSS; F. V. Parsons, *The Origins of the Morocco Question, 1880–1900* (London, 1976),
p. 534; Andrew, *Delcassé*, p. 261; Weber, *Nationalist Revival*, p. 96; notes by Gavarry, AE
Revoil MSS, 2.
[73] De Margerie to J. Cambon, 26 Jan. 1906, AE J. Cambon MSS, 3; Einstein, *A
Diplomat*, p. 15.
[74] Regnault to Revoil, 18, 29 May 1905, AE Revoil MSS, 2.

Though Revoil had urged acceptance of the conference and though he was prepared, with Rouvier's backing, to make limited concessions, he was by no means reluctant to oppose German wishes. He strongly defended France's prior agreements and refused to yield to German pressure for greater mutual involvement in Morocco. Indeed his firmness was to be seen in Rouvier's decisions.[75] Within six weeks Rouvier had been alienated by German insistence on a conference and generally disappointed by Berlin's lack of goodwill. He commissioned Paul Doumer, then a parliamentarian, to make it plain to Abbé Wetterlé, an intermediary between Berlin and Paris, that if Germany was not conciliatory, France was ready for war. Britain would send 100,000 troops and Italy would remain neutral. Such toughness certainly had the desired effect on Radolin, German ambassador to Paris. According to Wetterlé, Radolin erroneously wrote 300,000 and not 100,000 for the British expeditionary force.[76]

Revoil, for his part, proceeded to adopt a firm stand in the Rosen–Revoil September *pourparlers* which arranged a programme for the conference. The Germans had expected details to be finalized in three or four days. However, Revoil, now very emotional and sad as a result of German inflexibility, dug his heels in, and an agreement was reached only after one and a half months of tortuous bargaining. According to Revoil's report to Poincaré in September 1905, France had not undertaken a single engagement of any sort regarding the conference. According to Joseph Reinach, Revoil went even further and stated that 'il était opposé à toute entente avec l'Allemagne sur quelque sujet que ce soit'. Rosen found Revoil a man with whom it was almost impossible to make an agreement. As a result Germany proposed (albeit unsuccessfully) Jules Cambon as French ambassador to the conference.[77]

Revoil's tenacity and firmness clearly took the German government by surprise, and his authority over Rouvier was noted. As for Rouvier, who had expected to keep the Foreign Ministry for a few short weeks, he had become weary and worried by September and much more willing to listen to the almost unanimous voice of the Quai d'Orsay.[78] He felt that

[75] Revoil to Poincaré, 3 Apr. 1906, BN (NAF 16015), Poincaré MSS; Paléologue to Louis, 5 Sept. 1905, AE Louis MSS, 1; Comte de Saint-Aulaire, *Confessions d'un vieux diplomate* (Paris, 1953), p. 152.

[76] Abbé Wetterlé to H. Cambon, dated 1925, Louis Cambon MSS.

[77] E. Roche to Revoil, 14 Dec. 1905; note on undated conversation with Rosen, AE Revoil MSS, 2; Revoil to Poincaré, 24 Sept. 1905, BN (NAF 16015), Poincaré MSS; J. Reinach to Mme Revoil, 5 Feb. 1906, AE Revoil MSS, 2.

[78] Paléologue to Louis, 16 Sept. 1905, AE Louis MSS, 1; Daeschner to Revoil, 1906, dossier, 'Mardi', AE Revoil MSS, 2.

the Germans had deceived him, and he now favoured the same strengthening of Anglo-French links desired by his permanent officials. By December 1905 the Cambons, Barrère, and Louis had returned to favour with the Foreign Minister. They met in closed session to plan strategy for the conference.[79] Paul Cambon, hitherto ignored by Rouvier, told his brother that he saw Rouvier every day at 6 p.m.[80] By January 1906, Daeschner and Berthelot, with Revoil now attending the Algéçiras Conference, had become so influential that they were able to shape Rouvier's ideas and to write his dispatches.[81]

Quite apart from Rouvier's fatigue and disappointment, the Quai d'Orsay, or more precisely Jules Cambon, played a skilful and under-handed game to secure approval for its views. Cambon was utterly convinced that war was imminent. Pressure on Wilhelm II, whom Berlin society was labelling a Napoléon without any victories, was mounting, and he was becoming increasingly belligerent. Cambon worked out a twofold strategy: military conversations with Britain in preparation for war and the encouragement of a full-scale revolution in Spain, then fickle and unsupportive. Louis was given the details of Jules Cambon's plans, but they were deliberately kept from the Foreign Minister. Paul Cambon burned his brother's memorandum after talks with high government officials in London. For the moment, Louis and the Cambon brothers worked on Rouvier to accept the principle of British support.[82]

Their campaign was totally successful. Rouvier, exasperated by German manœuvres, was willing to listen. He had reversed his opinion of the British, and now considered them loyal and steadfast. When the Belgians complained to him about British interference in the Congo, he sent their ambassador packing. He not only admitted the principle of reaffirming Anglo-French links but approved with few reservations Jules Cambon's call for serious military conversations. British support, ignored in June 1905, had become crucial to Rouvier in December, and the Quai d'Orsay had done much to bring about this volte-face.[83]

[79] P. Cambon to J. Cambon, Dec. 1905, AE J. Cambon MSS, 25.

[80] P. Cambon to Revoil, 1 Dec. 1905, AE Revoil MSS, 2.

[81] Ibid., Daeschner to Revoil, 1906, dossier, 'Mardi'; Bréal, *Berthelot*, pp. 71-2.

[82] P. Cambon to J. Cambon, 22 Dec. 1905, J. Cambon to P. Cambon, 18 Dec. 1905, 1 Mar. 1906, AE J. Cambon MSS, 9, 19.

[83] Ibid. 19, 15, J. Cambon to P. Cambon, 18 Dec. 1905, P. Cambon to J. Cambon, 9 Jan., 19 Mar. 1906; Anderson, *First Moroccan Crisis*, p. 256; J. Cambon to de Margerie, 15 Feb. 1906, AE de Margerie MSS; A. Thierry, *L'Angleterre au temps de Paul Cambon* (Paris, 1961), p. 67; P. Cambon to H. Cambon, 13 June 1906, Louis Cambon MSS; Berthelot to Revoil, 6 Feb. 1906, AE Revoil MSS, 2.

The conference which Germany had demanded began in January 1906, and was held at Algeçiras, a rather seedy port at the bottom of Spain. Revoil, Regnault, and Pierre de Margerie were France's main representatives. Russia, Great Britain, Austria-Hungary, Italy, the USA, and Spain were all participants, along with several minor powers. From the outset Germany demanded equal representation in a Moroccan international bank. She also refused to envisage a Franco-Spanish organization of the police of major Moroccan ports, especially in Casablanca. When this second demand failed to secure majority support, the Germans proposed that seven Moroccan ports be placed under Franco-Spanish police control and the Casablanca police be subject to the authority of an inspector chosen from one of the small powers.[84]

Rouvier, in Revoil's absence, turned to Daeschner for advice and support. Daeschner, the *chef du cabinet*, was generally regarded as the protégé of Paul Cambon, formerly being Cambon's assistant in London. Rouvier, like Cambon, admired his talent for writing and his gift of command. From the beginning, Daeschner was utterly convinced of the necessity of holding firm at the conference, and Rouvier accepted most of his advice. It was Daeschner who provoked the negative response which Rouvier gave on the Moroccan police issue. The Foreign Minister was ultimately prepared to break up the conference and to place France's case before European public opinion.

Rouvier was never as intransigent as Daeschner, however. The *chef du cabinet* was struck by a report from Bompard, French ambassador to St Petersburg, which argued that the Russians had learned that Berlin did not envisage war during the conference. Such an assurance, Daeschner thought, allowed France to demand whatever she wanted. Rouvier remained more moderate. He even went as far as requesting de Courcel, now a retired ambassador, to travel to Berlin and Copenhagen to arrange a meeting with Wilhelm II. De Courcel, appalled at the recent anti-clerical measures of the government, especially the separation of Church and State, consented with great reluctance. He made it clear to Rouvier that he disliked serving a government which, in his own estimation, struck down women and children in churches. Nothing came of the trip. De Courcel found the German position justified and counselled Rouvier to yield. Daeschner, however, had accompanied de Courcel,

[84] For a thorough evaluation of Franco-British relations between 1905 and 1911, see K. A. Hamilton, 'Great Britain and France, 1905–1911', in F. H. Hinsley (ed.), *British Foreign Policy under Sir Edward Grey* (Cambridge, 1977); P. Cambon to J. Cambon, 19 Jan. 1912, J. Cambon MSS, 25.

and was able to use his influence with Rouvier to have de Courcel's efforts nullified.[85]

Berthelot, the *chef du cabinet adjoint*, fully supported Daeschner, and he convinced Rouvier that France had to stand firm against Berlin. The limit of concessions had been clearly reached. During the conference, Rouvier allowed Berthelot to draft dispatches of the most important nature and was content to sign the texts submitted. Berthelot's influence was at its zenith in March when Revoil, physically exhausted and emotionally drained, appeared on the verge of giving ground on the question of the police. Berthelot, working with Daeschner, telegraphed energetic instructions to hold firm.[86]

Undoubtedly, Revoil had stumbled during the period 7 to 14 March. As Daeschner noted, he was inclined to avoid confrontations. The French government, too, was undergoing a political crisis cooked up by 'cet animal Ribot', as Jules Cambon contemptuously remarked. In view of France's uncertain situation, the British were having second thoughts. Revoil could thus be excused, but his weakening was short-lived and more in form than in substance. Overall, as the Germans themselves acknowledged, he maintained a policy of firmness. He was fully committed to safeguarding France's position in Morocco, the Franco-Russian alliance, the *Entente Cordiale*, and the friendships with Spain and Italy.[87] In this sense he agreed with Jules Cambon's assessment that what was at stake was not only Morocco but more crucially the whole basis of France's diplomatic system. In the final analysis, Morocco was a function of European relations.[88]

Though Jules Cambon, Daeschner, and Berthelot all feared that he might not be strong enough, Revoil attacked the German stance through clear and precise arguments. He meticulously cultivated friendly relations with Nicolson, then British representative, and usually concerted with him before each day's plenum session. He closely scrutinized Spain's movements, bringing her quickly into line with the French position when she strayed. He collaborated closely with White, Visconti-Venosta, and Cassini, the American, Italian, and Russian rep-

[85] P. Cambon to J. Cambon, 19 Jan. 1912, J. Cambon MSS, 25; Daeschner notes, dossier, 'Mardi' 1906, Gavarry to Revoil, 2, 16 Feb. 1906, Daeschner to Revoil, 27 Feb. 1908, AE Revoil MSS, 2.

[86] Bréal, *Berthelot*, pp. 71–3; Daeschner to de Billy, 22 Jan. 1906, AE de Billy MSS, 27.

[87] Revoil to Poincaré, 3 Apr. 1906, BN (NAF 16015), Poincaré MSS; Revoil to Tardieu, 24 Mar. 1907, AN 324 AP 14 Tardieu MSS.

[88] See letters from Revoil to J. Cambon, 1906, in AE J. Cambon MSS, 11; J. Cambon to Revoil, 1901, AE Revoil MSS, 2.

resentatives. Ultimately, his attention to detail, and the fact that he knew the most difficult Moroccan issues intimately, enabled him to leave the Germans floundering.[89]

Revoil's work was crucial, but without Jules Cambon's constant support it is to be doubted that the conference would have been such a success for France. As de Margerie, formerly Cambon's secretary in Madrid and now a French delegate to the conference, told Revoil, Cambon was influential enough to make or break his efforts. Revoil was extremely careful not only to flatter the Ambassador but to take his advice to heart. Through de Margerie, Revoil kept Cambon *au courant* of the minutest details. Cambon, for his part, felt that Revoil was a little weak and therefore frequently but discreetly intervened in an attempt to bolster him. De Margerie was sent specifically to keep an eye on Revoil and to brief Cambon. In Madrid, Cambon bribed the Spanish press and applied pressure to the Spanish government. In Paris, he counselled Rouvier, and was instrumental in maintaining a firm and unified French policy. When Louis, Revoil, and Rouvier appeared tired, he was quick, as was his habit, to send despatches admonishing them for their weakness.[90]

Cambon's belief that war might break out at any moment did not moderate until he came face to face with the Germans as Berlin ambassador in 1907. Before the conference, he warned Revoil that German pretensions might be excessive and told him that, whatever minor transactions were to be made, firmness should be his guiding principle.[91] Though much concerned with the question of the Moroccan police, Cambon's principle aim was to keep Germany out of Morocco. The Atlantic was essential to France's security, and it was inadmissible that Germany or any other power should threaten her coastline. More than any other person it was Jules Cambon who prevented the French government from breaking up the conference during the difficult February period. He disagreed strongly with his brother on this point. Whereas Paul believed that the worst solution would be to yield to the Germans and to allow the conference to continue, Jules thought that the worst solution would be its dissolution without conclusion. He was perhaps the only one who truly believed that the conference would

[89] De Margerie to J. Cambon, 17, 27 Jan., 3 Feb. 1906, AE J. Cambon MSS, ii, J. Cambon to Revoil, 30 Dec. 1905, AE Revoil MSS, 2.
[90] De Margerie to de Billy, 23 Nov. 1905, AE de Billy MSS, 63.
[91] J. Cambon to Revoil, 30 Dec. 1905, 1, 29 Mar. 1906, AE Revoil MSS, 2.

continue and that the Germans would give way. If Paris was tired, so was Berlin, and he considered that France's traditional diplomatic custom of dragging out negotiations and haggling over everything would serve her well. It did.[92]

The Algeçiras Conference, despite its difficult moments, went according to Cambon's expectations until the Left and Right combined to bring down the French government in March 1906. Political instability in Paris seriously undermined the French position, and with the arrival of Bourgeois as foreign minister in the Sarrien cabinet it was not certain that France could hold her ground.

The new Foreign Minister was hardly well suited to the post. The Germans thought that he would be a pushover, and indeed the fact that he was once described as a negotiator by temperament and a person shunning responsibility augured badly for the French position. Paul Cambon, who had become appreciative of Rouvier's resolution, thought Bourgeois totally indecisive. The Fashoda crisis, according to Cambon, had been the product of his weakness.[93]

The policy which France pursued in the Moroccan crisis during Bourgeois's ministry derived equally from the Foreign Minister's thinking, some of which envisaged general co-operation between nations, and from the Quai d'Orsay's prodding. While Bourgeois was on friendly terms with Radolin, conciliatory, and interested in harmonizing international relations, he did not see how he could begin his ministry with unpopular concessions. His study of the Moroccan dossier firmly convinced him that he had arrived at the limit of acceptable transaction. He was prepared to envisage some flexibility on the issue of an international bank, but he was not prepared to accept an agreement worse than the current status quo. On the crucial issue, the question of mixed police in the ports, he consistently instructed Revoil to remain firm. Only Franco-Spanish police were acceptable, Casablanca could not be abandoned, and the eventual inspector was to have no right of

---

[92] J. Cambon to P. Cambon, 18 Dec. 1905, J. Cambon to de Margerie, 24 Jan., 1, 15 Feb., 8 Mar., 14 Nov. 1906, AE J. Cambon MSS, II, 19; P. Cambon to H. Cambon, 4, 22 Feb. 1906, Louis Cambon MSS.

[93] A. Tardieu, *La Conférence d'Algéçiras* (Paris, 1907), p. 322; A. L. Donnelly, 'France and the Society of Nations', Master's thesis (Trinity College, 1980), p. 51; P. Cambon to H. Cambon, 13, 18 June 1906, Louis Cambon MSS; Bourgeois to Gérard, 11 Apr. 1907, 18 Sept. 1913, AN 329 AP 18, 20, Gérard MSS; Bourgeois to Étienne, undated, BN (NAF 24237), Étienne MSS; Bourgeois to Reinach, 28 July 1907, BN (NAF 24876), Reinach MSS.

command. Thus, he had clearly rejected the most important of the German claims.[94]

The Quai d'Orsay, clearly apprehensive of the possible results of Bourgeois's indecisiveness, set out, as it had done with Rouvier, to force the Foreign Minister's hand. Jules Cambon descended upon him like a vulture and offered guidance as well as information. Louis, a mentor and close friend, was instrumental in having Bourgeois take a firm and steady line.[95]

Berthelot's actions were also influential. The *chef adjoint* had found it difficult to remain in his position when Bourgeois came to power. He had, according to Paul Cambon, a grudge against the Foreign Minister because of his father's replacement in the 1890s. Nevertheless, a *rapprochement* took place between Bourgeois and Berthelot, and it was one which enabled the latter to retain his influential position. Berthelot strengthened his hand still further by leaking to *Le Temps* Rouvier's last instructions to Revoil.[96]

The influence of the diplomats and permanent officials was, therefore, large even in the closing stages of the Algeçiras Conference. France's relative success was due largely to their efforts. Despite Austria-Hungary's support, Germany found herself relatively isolated and, apart from winning some commercial concessions, did not erect barriers to France's political or economic penetration. The Act of Algeçiras of April 1907 secured for France and Spain control of all eight Moroccan ports with the proviso that those at Casablanca and Tetuan should have mixed police with a Swiss officer appointed by the Sultan as inspector. A state bank was established which was open to the capital of all nations but which offered special privileges to France.

Though the crisis was over by May 1906, the Moroccan problem was not resolved, and the Cambons, especially Jules, worked on a larger Mediterranean agreement which would safeguard French influence in Morocco. Paul always considered Algeçiras a disaster and thus urged the London government to reaffirm the relevance of the *Entente Cordiale* to Morocco. For Jules, Morocco had always been an emotional issue

[94] See L. Bourgeois, *La Société des nations* (Paris, 1911); P. Cambon to J. Cambon, 19 Mar. 1906, J. Cambon to de Margerie, 15 Mar. 1906, de Margerie to J. Cambon, 14 Mar. 1906, AE J. Cambon MSS, ii, 25; Anderson, *First Moroccan Crisis*, p. 385; Tardieu, *La Conférence d'Algeçiras*, p. 327.
[95] M. Paléologue, *Au Quai d'Orsay à la veille de la tourmente* (Paris, 1947), p. 32.
[96] P. Cambon to J. Cambon, 19 Mar. 1906, AE J. Cambon MSS, 25. This measure resulted from Bourgeois's refusal to entertain Marcellin Berthelot's request for Anglo-French talks over Egypt.

and he had long been involved in expanding French influence there. He remained pessimistic about the future, and was convinced that a war might well be initiated by Berlin. It was he who suggested the idea of the Mediterranean agreement with Spain, a plan which he had conceived as early as the Spanish–American war of 1898. Significantly, the threads of the 1907 (Anglo-Spanish and Franco-Spanish Mediterranean) negotiations remained in his hands, and, even after he left Madrid for Berlin during the spring of 1907, he received and dispatched vast amounts of information on the subject.[97]

In sum, the Quai d'Orsay was extremely influential during the First Moroccan Crisis. Delcassé needed no prompting to adopt his intransigent stance against Berlin. His decision to refuse talks was, in form at least, uniquely his own. Yet the advice coming from his permanent officials strengthened his mistaken belief that he could ignore Berlin. Apart from Bihourd (and de Courcel), none of his leading advisers envisaged substantial negotiations or concessions. The demise of Delcassé signalled a waning of the Quai d'Orsay's influence. This was short-lived. Rouvier changed horses but not stables, and his new advisers, Revoil, Berthelot, and Daeschner, proved in time as inflexible as Barrère, Louis, the Cambons, and Paléologue. Rouvier not only listened to their arguments and accepted their advice but, by the end of his ministry, had reversed his stance so considerably that the Cambons, hitherto highly critical of him, wanted his maintenance in office. In fact, by December 1905 Rouvier was heeding the advice proffered by the two Cambons, Louis, and Barrère.

Bourgeois's accession to power brought renewed apprehension and consternation but, as before, Bourgeois was taken in hand by his permanent officials and came to adopt their views. In essence, though Delcassé fell like Lucifer from the heavens in disgrace, his diplomacy was maintained by the competence, determination, and intrigues of the Quai d'Orsay and the diplomatic élite. Ultimately, the First Moroccan Crisis reflected the extent to which the leading diplomats and their colleagues at the Centrale were, in crisis situations, able to impose a shared outlook on foreign ministers.

[97] Hardinge to Grey, 10 Apr. 1907, PRO, Hardinge MSS, 10; J. Cambon to Pichon, 9 Mar. 1907, Inst. de Fr. Pichon MSS, 2; J. Cambon to Pichon, 24 Feb., 1, 9 Mar., 17 May 1907; AE NS 'Espagne', 41; J. Cambon to P. Cambon, 2 Jan. 1907. AE P. Cambon MSS, 11; D. J. Miller, 'Stephen Pichon and the Making of French Foreign Policy' (Cambridge University, 1976), p. 151. For an excellent analysis of the agreements, see K. Hamilton, *Bertie of Thame: Edwardian Ambassador* (Woodbridge, 1990), pp. 127–39.

7

The 1907 Reforms

Comme au lendemain des révolutions, l'esprit du conservatisme remplissait toute la maison. Il n'est plus question des réformes. Beati possidentes!

(Paléologue to de Billy, October 1907)

Although Delcassé toyed with the notion of reforming the Quai d'Orsay, it was not until 1907 that ideas were translated into action. Implementation owed something to criticism by the Radicals, who wished to purge the Quai d'Orsay of non-Republican elements and to make it more open to the influence of Parliament and public opinion. However, the real impetus came from inside the Quai d'Orsay in the person of Philippe Berthelot, who was determined to modernize thoroughly and to create a Foreign Ministry which would be led by a new breed of professionals administering departments where global, economic, cultural, and political issues were intimately linked. As for the changes in personnel associated with Berthelot's reforms, they owed much to Premier Clemenceau's personal prejudices and to intrigues inside the Foreign Ministry.

Undoubtedly Radical criticism played an important role in persuading Parliament, public opinion, and the press to give consideration to reform. In the early 1900s there had been a shift in power in favour of the Radicals. Cognizant of the necessity of creating institutions more in line with Republican philosophies, especially after the Dreyfus case and the Church–State conflict, some Radicals called for a wholesale purge. There had been numerous criticisms of the Quai d'Orsay before 1907 from Dubief, in introducing the annual budget for 1902, from Gervais, and from Deschanel, the president of the Commission des affaires extérieures et des protectorats.[1] Much of the displeasure voiced had dealt

[1] *JOC Rapport* 2640 (1902).

with the concern that the Quai d'Orsay was not sufficiently representative of the Republic and that it did not reflect the new shift to the left. Yet the influence of such criticism should not be exaggerated. It was only natural that Dubief, Gervais, and Deschanel, all budget *rapporteurs*, should fulfil their tasks. Only Deschanel remained in a position of power sufficiently long to sustain his criticism. Widespread support was not forthcoming from Parliament, and much criticism was the work of Radicals who were not in office. Those in power were a good deal more moderate. There is no evidence to suggest that such pressure as the Radicals mounted was sufficiently concentrated to force change. As Lauren himself admits, such attacks could not be sustained in public debates or over a period of time, since politicians viewed their constituencies rather than the diplomatic map as a major area of concern.[2] No politician sat on the newly instituted Commission des réformes administratives.

Radical criticism, then, should not be regarded as the major determinant of the 1907 reforms. It was not confined to the Quai d'Orsay and extended to the Ministries of the Interior, War, Public Works, and Posts and Telegraphs.[3] In addition, the charge that the Quai was inefficient and incapable of handling France's vital interests in the twentieth century was thoroughly squashed by its superb handling of the First Moroccan Crisis at a time when the politicians and the government itself were found wanting. Moreover, despite howls in 1904–5 over Delcassé's secret diplomacy, by 1907 there was general approval of the Quai d'Orsay's line of thinking, which had clearly blamed Berlin for the crisis.

The Radical party itself was hardly in a position to see through reforms it espoused. Foreign Minister Pichon acted as a shock absorber for much of the Radicals' invective. Apart from the fact that he identified very closely with the career, having been in it for over a decade, he soon came to realize the difficulties that parliamentary and cabinet encroachment posed to his own position.[4] By 1908 he was thoroughly determined that Parliament should not meddle in such delicate matters.

The Radical party, too, was incapable of seeing through its wishes effectively. The period between 1906 and 1911 was one of concentration on the political arena rather than on the diplomatic stage. Polarization in the Radical party on issues such as progressive income tax, unions, the

---

[2] P. G. Lauren, *Diplomats and Bureaucrats* (Stanford, Calif., 1976), p. 47.
[3] *JOS*, 5 Nov. 1906.
[4] Pichon to J. Cambon, 10 July 1908, AE J. Cambon MSS, 16.

socialist threat, and strikes precluded any continual surveillance of the progression of Foreign Ministry reforms.

Essentially, outside criticism was of limited importance. The reforms of 1907 were primarily the product of positive approaches to twentieth-century administration from within the Quai d'Orsay itself. This internal factor differentiates French reforms from those carried out in the British and German foreign offices. There, reform was the result of belated measures imposed from outside on a rather unresponsive, unenthusiastic central administration. With the Quai d'Orsay it was an entirely different matter and reflected the way in which that institution led the diplomatic world into the twentieth century.[5] As with other reforms in the years 1898–1914, not a single parliamentarian nor public figure sat on the Commission des réformes administratives, set up by Pichon in November 1906. The members, Thiébaut, Gavarry, Crozier, and Berthelot, were all permanent officials.

Premier Clemenceau's role in the reforms cannot be minimized, but stemmed more from personal prejudices than from a Republican zeal for reform. Certainly throughout his career he had struggled against clerical and reactionary forces in the civil service and government, Paul Cambon explaining his behaviour as a 'manie épuratoire'. On assuming power, Clemenceau made it clear that French foreign policy must be republicanized. Yet his speech of 5 November 1906 did not single out foreign policy as being the most neglected area. He was concerned with modern society as a whole, the need for civil liberties, social justice, the protection of the working masses, and the creation of a new ministry of labour.[6]

The Commission des réformes administratives, established the next day, reflected the new Republican spirit. Crozier, Gavarry, Thiébaut, and Berthelot all held Republican views. The last, Philippe Berthelot, who dominated the commission's work, was particularly sympathetic to the Republican cause. His report to Parliament gave far more than lip service to the ideal of a diplomatic machinery which would be more accountable to Parliament and public alike.[7] Writing privately to Claudel in August 1907, he emphasized what was to him the essential point—the creation of a new breed of aggressive professional men with Republican sympathies: 'Tout est question de personnes. Qui nom-

[5] Berthelot to Claudel, 4 Aug. 1907, AE Berthelot MSS, 23.

[6] *JOS* 5 Nov. 1906; P. Cambon to H. Cambon, 22 July 1906, Louis Cambon MSS; P. Cambon to H. Cambon, 26 Oct. 1906, *Paul Cambon: Correspondance* (Paris, 1940–6), ii. 226.

[7] *JOC* 3 May 1907, 'Commission des réformes administratives'.

mera-t-on? C'est là l'important, et presque même la seule question importante.'[8] Berthelot's emphasis on individuals and Clemenceau's mania for purges resulted in a widespread personnel movement after 1907. Paléologue was exiled to Sofia, while his friend Dumaine was sent to Mexico. A supposedly dangerous clerical, de Margerie, learned from a newspaper that he had been exiled to Siam. Soulange-Bodin and Beaucaire went north to occupy Stockholm and Copenhagen. Those known for their Republican sympathies were given important ambassadorial posts. Jules Cambon was accorded Berlin; Aunay, Berne; and Revoil, Madrid.

The reasons for this purge, however, were far more complex than a simple desire to republicanize France's diplomatic institution. Clemenceau's personal prejudices played an important role. He was particularly suspicious of de Margerie, Paléologue, Beaucaire, Soulange-Bodin, Dumaine, and Geoffray, and he wanted their removal from Europe quickly effected. As late as 1914 he was complaining to Poincaré and to Doumergue about them.[9] Clemenceau's bias against Geoffray was reflected in the inordinately long time he had to remain in London as Cambon's counsellor. It was only a personal meeting between Clemenceau and Geoffray in 1908 that made possible the continuation of Geoffray's career.[10] Barrère, too, was the subject of much suspicion. Clemenceau disliked his friendship with Gambetta and Delcassé and the two immediately fought over the possible purchase of the Rome Embassy. Barrère's replacement was openly discussed in 1907.

That the movement of personnel was not necessarily directed against the aristocracy was mirrored in the way that Count Stephen Pelletier d'Aunay was recalled from inactive service and placed in Berne. Clemenceau, moreover, attacked staunch Republicans who did not conform to his particular opinions. As Jean Allemane, a Socialist deputy in the Chamber and a man little prepared to support personnel of non-Republican sympathies, commented to Pichon: 'trop de républicains ont été frappés au ministère des affaires étrangères, non parce qu'ils n'étaient pas à la hauteur de leur tâche, mais à cause de leurs opinions politiques.'[11] The fact that certain officials did not agree whole-

---

[8] Berthelot to Claudel, 4 Aug. 1907, AE Berthelot MSS, 23.

[9] B. Auffray, *Pierre de Margerie (1861–1942) et la vie diplomatique de son temps* (Paris, 1976), p. 167; 'Notes journalières', 6, 7 Jan. 1914, BN (NAF 16026), Poincaré MSS 16026.

[10] Report, Lancken to Wilhelmstraße 1910, Bonn, F. 108, vol. 19; J. Laroche, *Quinze ans à Rome avec Camille Barrère (1898–1913)* (Paris, 1948), p. 205; Barrère to P. Cambon, 10 Jan. 1907, AE P. Cambon MSS, 11; report by von Wedel, 5 Jan. 1907, Bonn, F. 108, vol. 18.

[11] *JOC* 5 Dec. 1907.

heartedly with Clemenceau's policies while still espousing Republican sympathies was enough to condemn them to the four corners of the world.

Personal prejudice, intrigue, and ambition within the Quai d'Orsay itself were also powerful factors in the diplomatic movement. Paléologue's exile to Sofia was as much the result of his cold relations with Berthelot as of his political and religious views. Bihourd's enemies in the Quai d'Orsay were equally as numerous.[12] The denial of an embassy to Beaucaire appears to have been due to Louis's animosity towards him.[13] Revoil's and Crozier's ambitions were also important factors. As president of the Commission des réformes administratives, Crozier was in a strong position to take over Vienna, a position he coveted. Revoil sought a posting to Madrid by having Jules Cambon replace Bihourd in Berlin.

Even the supposed widespread move against the aristrocracy in 1909–10 was more personally than politically motivated. Undoubtedly there was a movement emanating from the private ministerial cabinet under Dutasta and from Gavarry in the Affaires administratives to suppress the remaining nobles. Dutasta was employing *Le Matin* to urge the revision of titles, which he thought would facilitate the elimination of nobles.[14] A committee was, in fact, set up by Gavarry to investigate the abuse of titles. It decided to recognize only titles of the heads of families and only titles acknowledged by a legal decision.[15] As Dard, a permanent official, commented sarcastically to Gérard, 'à ce compte il ne restera, dit-on, que le Baron Labure'. By 1910, forty-seven out of fifty-one titles had disappeared from the *Annuaire diplomatique*.[16]

Yet the movement was directed against the person of Beaucaire himself rather than against the aristocracy in general. As Beaucaire informed a friend, of the 600 agents in the Quai d'Orsay only thirty-three were aristocrats. The Quai had been republicanized years before, especially in the 1890s. Of the remaining aristocrats, there were only three or four who could not prove their titles. Moreover, Beaucaire himself, despite his aristocratic background, was a Republican member of the Conseil général de la Mayenne.[17] The so-called measures against

[12] Notes, AE Bihourd MSS; Berckheim to Gérard, 5 Jan. 1907, AN 329 AP 20 Gérard MSS.

[13] Beaucaire to Undetermined, 29 Jan. 1909, AE Beaucaire MSS, 10.

[14] *Le Matin*, 19 Apr. 1909.

[15] Gavarry to Beaucaire, 15 Jan. 1909, AE Beaucaire MSS, 10.

[16] Dard to Gérard, 22 Feb. 1909, AN 328 AP 20 Gérard MSS.

[17] Note of Beaucaire's, 29 Jan. 1909, Beaucaire to Pichon, 8 Feb. 1909, AE Beaucaire MSS, 10.

the aristocracy were an attempt by two of his colleagues to smear his name and to ruin his chances for an embassy.[18]

There is little doubt that Berthelot was the guiding spirit behind the main reforms. His proposals of 6 November 1906 (enacted in April 1907) encompassed a wide range of administrative issues as well as important personnel changes which were designed to make the Quai more responsive to the economic and political problems of the twentieth century. To Berthelot, the pivotal point of the 1907 reforms was the perennial problem of the 'choix de personnes'. If he had had his way totally, the purges would have been more widespread, with a view to replacing diplomats of the older period when court diplomacy had been vitally important. What was now needed, Berthelot thought, was a new breed of aggressive agents who viewed finance and economics as highly significant.

Already the number of men trained in matters of finance, commerce, and industry who held high-ranking positions was impressive. Significantly, Bompard, a former commercial director, became ambassador to St Petersburg and then ambassador to Constantinople. It was a measure of the importance of the role that economic questions were to play in these two areas. Similarly, the political director, George Louis, had also been a former commercial director. According to Berthelot, however, there were still many diplomats in European posts who were ill-attuned to the economic needs of twentieth-century France. The new breed, men such as Conty, Bapst, Regnault, and Revoil, were given important postings to the newer colonial and commercial areas.

The necessary corollary to flooding the Quai d'Orsay with new men of exceptional economic expertise was the thorough transformation of institutions. The virtual separation of political and commercial affairs was seen by Berthelot as intolerable. He emphasized in his report to the Chamber of Deputies that the division was artificial and damaging as 'la concurrence internationale abrite des visées politiques derrière des entreprises commerciales'.[19] In oriental, African, and American countries this was clearly the case, but even in Europe politics and commerce were becoming intertwined. To Berthelot, finance and industry were powerful weapons in the arsenal of national interest.[20] He had been a fervent advocate of an aggressive economic diplomacy in the newer

[18] Ibid. 29 Jan. 1909. For other indications of the personal rivalries affecting career advancement, see Bourgeois to Reinach, 28 July 1907, BN (NAF 24874), Reinach MSS.

[19] 'Réorganization de l'administration centrale du Ministère des affaires étrangères'; decree, 29 Apr. 1907, *Annuaire diplomatique et consulaire* (1907).

[20] *JOC* 3 May 1907, 'Commission des réformes administratives'.

regions of the globe for many years.[21] In this regard, there was a qualitative difference between the French and German cases. In Germany
businessmen pressured reluctant governments into seeking new opportunities and protecting existing areas.[22] In the French case, diplomats
and permanent officials often encouraged and supported, for reasons of
national prestige, the external ventures of reluctant financiers and industrialists.

In view of the interconnection of geography, politics, and economics,
the most important of the 1907 reforms was the amalgamation of the
political division and commercial division under one director. The
Sous-direction du Nord and the Sous-direction du Midi were replaced
by the Sous-direction d'Europe, d'Afrique et d'Océanie, the Sous-direction d'Asie, the Sous-direction du Levant, and the Sous-direction
d'Amérique. Other reforms consisted of the establishment of a Direction des affaires administratives et techniques and of a Bureau des communications, as well as the reorganization of the private ministerial
cabinet and the Bureau du personnel. For the first time attempts were
made to standardize conditions of service and to introduce the interpenetrability of the diplomatic and consular divisions.

Clearly, the most significant enactment was the establishment of a
Direction des affaires politiques et commerciales. This was a revolutionary measure in relation to other European foreign offices which
trailed far behind. Henceforth, the political division and the commercial
division were amalgamated and matters hitherto kept separate were
treated together. In this way matters handled in isolation without the
knowledge of other departments gave way to more co-ordinated
policies. The creation of the position of *conseiller commercial et financier*
ensured that, if deputy directors did not have sufficient competence in
handling certain economic matters, they could seek advice from an
expert. The responsibilities of the new position included advising all
geographical bureaux on the economic consequences of policy, preparing treaties of commerce, observing international financial fluctu-
ations, and collecting reports on foreign market conditions. The *conseiller*
was also to handle affairs with business associations which had substantial interests overseas.[23]

Though Berthelot was the guiding spirit of the reforms, not every-

---

[21] A. Gérard, *Mémoires d'Auguste Gérard* (Paris, 1928), p. 455; Berthelot to Claudel, 4
Aug. 1907, AE Berthelot MSS, 23.

[22] See L. Cecil, *The German Diplomatic Service, 1871–1914* (Princeton, NJ, 1976). This work
provides a good comparison between German and other foreign offices.

[23] *JOC* decrees of 29 Apr., 3 May 1907; *JOC Rapport* 2015 (1909).

thing went his own way. For example, he wished to raise the status of commercial relations to a Sous-direction des rapports commerciaux and to maintain the prerogatives of the Quai d'Orsay against the Ministry of Commerce in certain important economic questions. The proposed subdivision would have responsibility for the flow of imports and exports, for accords and conventions with other countries, and for the development of France's commercial relations in general. It was not until after the war, in 1919, that such a subdivision was established. Moreover, despite Berthelot's criticism of proposed *attachés commerciaux* as 'mauvaises doublures' for consuls, such positions were created and placed under the authority of the Ministry of Commerce.[24]

Indeed, the Ministry of Commerce was beginning to play an increasingly significant role in pre-war French foreign policy. By 1906 this ministry had the right to intervene in matters of commerce in overseas posts. It corresponded directly with consuls and advised them on matters pertaining to foreign trade, industry, and finance.[25] The attachés posted overseas conducted studies on local customs, sale and delivery conditions, transportation facilities, raw materials, the activities of competitors, and the availability of new markets. They also sought opportunities for investment and provided all possible assistance to chambers of commerce and other business organizations. Consequently, there was substantial bickering over relative responsibilities between the consuls and the attachés, and between the Quai d'Orsay and the Ministry of Commerce. Moreover, the Quai was forced increasingly to share its information with commerce, its offshoot, the Office national du commerce extérieur, and the economic section of the État-major de l'armée. To some extent, however, these offices acted rather as sources of information for the Quai, which jealously retained the initiative in the area of formal decision-making.[26]

An inherent part of the increased intertwining of economics and politics was the ending of formal divisions between the diplomatic corps and the consular service. The latter was seen in the old system as a compensation for those not intelligent enough to pass all the diplomatic examinations. As a result, intellectual and social barriers had seriously affected the co-ordination of policies.[27] Though the need to achieve

[24] Berthelot to Claudel, 4 Aug. 1907, AE Berthelot MSS, 23.

[25] *Le Temps*, 1 Nov. 1906.

[26] Lauren, *Diplomats and Bureaucrats*, pp.167–8; AN Ministère du commerce et de l'industrie, carton F12, 9288, 'Office national du commerce extérieur'.

[27] H. Pognon, *Lettre à M. Doumergue au sujet d'une réforme du Ministère des affaires étrangères* (Paris, 1914), pp. 111–12.

greater equality between the two services was pointed out by parliamentarians and by various chambers of commerce, the real driving force behind reform was once again Berthelot.[28] Indeed, his desire to end divisions between the services was largely the product of an unpleasant personal experience. He was a former member of the consular service who had entered the diplomatic corps with his father's help, and who had been regarded with hostility as an *intru*.[29]

Despite the intentions of Berthelot, the complaints of the Chamber of Commerce about the inefficiency of the consuls, and constant criticism of the élitism of the diplomatic corps by parliamentarians such as Deschanel, the results achieved were rather disappointing. Before 1907 there had been a total separation of the careers. Not only were there separate examinations for the two services, but personnel had distinct bureaux to handle their careers. Berthelot's suggestion that the same examination be given to diplomats and consuls was a welcome proposal. Yet the fact that entry into the two services still depended upon a candidate's aggregate mark created a situation in which the most successful invariably opted for the diplomatic career. The same old jealousies persisted because of a technical fault in an otherwise admirable reform. In 1914, the condescension of the diplomatic corps towards the consular remained strong.[30]

Calls by informed critics such as Deschanel for the interpenetrability of the services were only heeded slowly. Only in 1913 were the first rather primitive steps taken to create an equivalence of rank, when agents were allowed to exchange positions at a corresponding level.[31] Most reforms were not introduced until after the war, and total amalgamation was not realized.[32] Moreover, interpenetrability created more problems than it solved. Claudel, an experienced consul in China, argued just before the war that the mingling of the two branches in fact widened the rift. Consuls were seen as second-rate citizens and not as technical economic experts. They were not expected to provide diplomatic analysis or leadership.[33]

---

[28] *JOC Rapport* 2015 (1909); *Rapport* 337 (1908); Lauren, *Diplomats and Bureaucrats*, p. 87; *Le Temps*, 15 May 1912; Bertie to Grey, 26 Dec. 1907, FO 371/250; Abteilung IA, Frankreich 108, vol. 18, disp. 188, Lancken to von Bülow, 16 May 1907; *JOC Rapport* 333 (1907).

[29] 'Notes concernant le Quai d'Orsay', p. 72, AN de Robien MSS.

[30] Ibid. p. 122.

[31] Decree, 22 Sept. 1913, *Annuaire diplomatique* (1914).

[32] Lauren, *Diplomats and Bureaucrats*, p. 109.

[33] Note, Claudel, 3 May 1914, AE Thiebaut MSS.

Reforms relating to overseas posts provided further evidence that well-meaning intentions were often not translated effectively into action. Berthelot had originally envisaged a global reorganization. The former concentration of the central administration on European affairs was to be replaced by a more balanced treatment of international relations, which took into account the growing importance of Asia and Africa. Bourgeois and Pichon had solicited the opinions of diplomats overseas with a view towards eradicating traditional posts and creating new ones.[34] The Cambons, too, were conscious of the shift from European affairs eastward to the Near and Middle East, Asia, and Oceania, and southward to Africa. They were only in the forefront, however, of a mood of general dissatisfaction with posts in existence. As one consul noted in 1909, the Russo-Japanese war had profoundly affected the political and economic conditions prevailing in east Asia.[35] Another, in a similar report to the Chamber of Deputies, lamented the fact that the imperialist partition of Africa in the nineteenth century had not been matched by the creation of diplomatic missions corresponding to Africa's new importance.[36] Others pointed out that while France had eighteen consular missions in Spain, she maintained only seven or eight in the United States.[37] The 1907 reforms did something to rectify this situation. Some missions in Europe, either obsolete or usually costly, were terminated, and new missions were created in Paraguay, Argentina, South Africa, the Congo, Liberia, Egypt, Afghanistan, Japan, Canada, and the United States.[38] Nevertheless, the process begun in 1908 could hardly be termed as rapid. Most changes came after the First World War and were the result of a whole new set of circumstances. As Berthelot complained to consul and author Claudel in August 1907, 'J'attends un moment favorable et quelqu'un de disposé non pas même à agir mais seulement à écouter pour exposer un programme d'action.'[39]

Despite the reforms of 1907, most diplomats continued to be placed at a great disadvantage in comparison with their more fortunate colleagues in the central administration. Pognon, a prematurely retired consul, was certainly correct in contending that agents abroad were largely incapable of defending their rights, of arguing their cases, and of securing

---

[34] *Le Temps*, 17 Nov. 1906; *JOC, Rapport* 2015 (1909).
[35] *JOC Rapport* 2015 (1909).
[36] Ibid.   [37] *JOS* 16 Jan. 1907.
[38] *JOC Rapport* 2015 (1908); *Rapport* 3318 (1914); *Rapport* 6339 (1919); *Rapport* 2020 (1921).
[39] Berthelot to Claudel, 4 Aug. 1907, AE Berthelot MSS, 23. On the reorganization of consular posts in Asia Minor, the Interprétariat, and the Drogmanat in the Levant, see AE Bonin MSS, 12.

objective treatment.[40] Deschanel's remark that there were in essence two careers, one for those who basked in the sun in Paris and one for those who were forgotten in foreign posts, was even more evident after 1907. Formal regulations required an agent to spend a minimum period of time abroad before being promoted. Yet influential men such as Piccioni and Gavarry were easily able to further their careers in the Centrale without ever leaving its confines. Berthelot, who became secretary-general for a record period in the 1920s and 1930s had left the Centrale on only two occasions early in his career. Pichon's attempt to force Piccioni to accept a foreign post in 1908–9 was a dismal failure. By 1909 he had been elevated to the position of *sous-directeur d'Amérique*. Lauren's contention that after 1907 the highest administrative jobs were given only to those with substantial overseas experience is therefore misleading.[41]

Nor was the standardization of overseas agents' wages and conditions effected as quickly as envisaged. As late as 1913, agents abroad were still speaking of their salaries as insufficient, as absurdly low, and as the 'wages of famine'. Anomalies abounded in the years after 1907.[42] While a *conseiller d'ambassade* in London and St Petersburg was receiving 24,000 francs per annum, his colleague in Rome was being paid 10,000 francs less. Undoubtedly, measures put into practice before 1914 provided for standardized payment based on grade and took into consideration distance required to travel, size of family living costs, and the nature of a post. Yet it was only in September 1913 that the first rather primitive decrees resembling a *statut de la carrière* were enacted.[43] Later decrees were a response to the radically changed circumstances which existed after the First World War.[44] Nor should the enactment of formal decrees be seen as a reliable indication that the actual position of agents was improved. As Arnavon, an official in the central administration, told Doulcet, the Quai d'Orsay in 1912 was in no position to pay for an attaché's travelling expenses, let alone the wages of a more high-ranking official.[45]

[40] Pognon, *Lettre à M. Doumergue*; Daeschner to Doulcet, 23 Mar. 1913, AE Doulcet MSS, 20.

[41] For Piccioni's and Gavarry's struggle, see Pichon to Barrère, 11 Dec. 1908, 14 Dec. 1909, AE *dossier personnel*, Piccioni; note also a series of letters from Gavarry and Ribot, AE *dossier personnel*, Gavarry; Lauren, *Diplomats and Bureaucrats*, p. 102.

[42] AE Direction du personnel, carton 85, 'Textes et projets de réforme antérieurs à 1912'; *JOC Rapport* 148 (1913).

[43] Decree, 22 Sept. 1913, in *JOC* 27 Sept. 1913.

[44] Decrees, 15 Nov. 1920, in *JOC* 28 Nov. 1920.

[45] J. Arnavon to Doulcet, 28 Nov. 1912, AE Doulcet MSS, 20.

Undeniably, the reforms relating to French commerce around the world were substantial and the most impressive of the reforms of 1907. The manner in which French diplomats encouraged French trade and actively sought industrial orders was criticized by some foreign commentators, praised by others, but noticed by all. Some of the aggressive salesmanship of these 'economic missionaries' derived from their personal pecuniary interests. National interests, however, still predominated, and the handling of economic matters in general by the Quai d'Orsay was far more forward looking than that of the Foreign Office or of the Wilhelmstraße. Nevertheless, even in this area, there was a divergence between the theory and practice of reform. As Deschanel himself admitted, the number of attachés after 1907 was restricted and it was not until 1919 that their use became widespread.[46]

The attempted reform of the central administration offered a further example of how revolutionary ideas and enactments often ran into difficulties. The new position of political and commercial director was a classic case. The amalgamation of *affaires commerciales et politiques* was designed to create a highly powerful official who would exercise control over all aspects of the central administration. He would co-ordinate the work of all departments so as to meet one of Berthelot's major criticisms, the lack of liaison between the various branches.[47] Thus, the political and commercial director, 'dégagé du travail matériel, appuyé sur des spécialistes, secondé par le sous-directeur chargé des instructions de politique générale', would 'suivre dans leur ensemble les affaires d'Europe qui sont solidaires'.[48] In practice, however, the results were different. The subsequent increase in the power of the newly created *sous-directeur d'Europe, d'Afrique, et d'Océanie* created a natural rival. The new deputy director, while not technically a *directeur adjoint*, was now the chief administrator of European, African, and Pacific affairs and effectively assumed the power of the previous political director. While theoretically able to be the supreme authority (apart from the minister) in formulating and executing policy in its totality, the director in practice might find himself excluded from the day-to-day details of diplomacy which were so vital for well-informed judgement. Both Louis and Bapst, in an effort to avoid this fate, plunged themselves into the

[46] *JOC Rapport* 333 (1907).
[47] 'Réorganization de l'administration centrale du Ministère des affaires étrangères', decree, 29 Apr. 1907, *Annuaire Diplomatique* (1909–10), p. 326.
[48] Ibid.

hurly-burly of mundane details. Moreover, the director's relationship with the minister's private cabinet and the ambassadors remained ill defined. He continued to be inferior in rank and prestige, with the result that these diplomats were still well capable of initiating private policies. Only the creation of a powerful secretary-general of superior rank could remedy this situation. Unfortunately such an office did not become a permanent feature of the central administration until the mid-1920s.

The relationship between the foreign minister's private cabinet and the political and commercial director was strained. Although officially the *chef du cabinet* had no say in policy matters, he was the personal secretary and confidant of the minister and could therefore have more influence than the political director. By 1911 a man such as Herbette was able openly to usurp the director's role and make important decisions on a whole range of policy matters.

The creation of four new subdivisions—Europe, Afrique, et Océanie; Asie; Levant; and Amerique—to replace the traditional Nord and Midi was revolutionary in character and was later to be emulated by almost all other major foreign offices. This reorganization reduced to a minimum the difficulties or errors of attribution and made possible a more effective centralization and co-ordination of policy-making.[49]

A most important result of the 1907 reforms, apart from the changes relating to commercial interests, was the actual increase in power of the departments of the Quai d'Orsay. The creation of specialized bureaux manned by technical experts and headed by a new *sous-directeur d'Europe, d'Afrique et d'Océanie* led to a situation not envisaged by those parliamentarians who had called for a restriction of the Quai's power. The traditional two-division system leisurely administered by men of the old career quickly gave way to a proliferation of departments far more difficult to manage and run by men intent on becoming little bureaucratic imperialists. In particular, Pichon's close identification with his subordinates, his laziness, Bapst's incompetence, and the formal raising of the status of subdivisions and their chiefs led to a situation in which the authority of the bureaux loomed large. The immediate result of Berthelot's reforms, far from instituting clearly delineated duties, led to personal policies and competition among powerful young deputy directors trying to outdo each other.

The new subdivisions were certainly novel in their creation. The Sous-direction d'Europe, d'Afrique, et d'Océanie was a combination of rational and at the same time illogical features. Like the Nord which it

[49] Ibid.

replaced it was the premier subdivision of the Foreign Ministry and brought together for the first time all aspects of policy relating to the major European powers. This arrangement was definitely an improvement on the former division of Midi and Nord. However, in a move 'assez peu explicable', in a former diplomat's words, the regions of Africa and Oceania were tacked on.[50] It was only in 1914 that both were detached and incorporated respectively in the new Sous-direction d'Afrique and in the Sous-direction d'Asie. Essentially, the original measure was a ploy to allow the Sous-direction d'Europe to consecrate the majority of its time to the Moroccan issue. It is interesting to note that this move adds weight to the view that Moroccan affairs were seen mostly as a function of Franco-German relations.[51]

Other European questions, especially those relating to European and Asian Turkey and the Balkans, were delegated to the Sous-direction du Levant, which was created in 1907 but hastily abolished in 1912. The Levant also dealt with Persia, Egypt, Abyssinia, and Islamic affairs in general. The unstable nature of this subdivision was largely due to two interlocking factors. Firstly, the Levant was to be responsible for the Near East only while the Moroccan question preoccupied the Sous-direction d'Europe. Because of the seriousness of Balkan issues, especially after the Austrian annexation of Bosnia-Hercegovina in 1908, the Levant became increasingly important and the amount of work passing through its offices was enormous.[52] Both the *sous-directeur d'Europe, d'Afrique, et d'Océanie*, whose realm the Near East should have been, and the *sous-directeur d'Asie* (in this case Berthelot, who considered himself an expert on Eastern affairs) looked on its growing importance with suspicion. Berthelot suppresed the Levant on assuming the position of *directeur adjoint* (and thus *sous-directeur d'Europe*) in 1914 and kept all Near Eastern affairs within his grasp.

The Sous-direction d'Asie, which included China, Japan, Indo-China, Korea, and India, naturally went to Berthelot in 1907. This appointment alone made it an extremely powerful department. Major events such as the Russo-Japanese war of 1904–5 and the Chinese Revolution of 1911, combined with the increased involvement of the United States and Japan in the Pacific, added to its importance. Under Berthelot's leadership the subdivision increasingly concerned itself with

[50] A. Outrey, 'Histoire et principes de l'administration française des affaires étrangères', *Revue française de science politique*, 3 (1953), p. 510.

[51] AE unsigned report, 1912, series C, 'Administration' 23, vol. 28.

[52] Taigny to de Fleuriau, 26 Oct. 1908, AE P. Cambon MSS, 12.

commercial matters. The deputy director fully encouraged a more aggressive economic policy in the Asian region. One of the major changes made by this subdivision was to establish an Interprétariat able to handle the newer languages encountered on the Asian continent. Previous training in the École de langues orientales vivantes had involved primarily Arabic, Persian, and other Near Eastern languages.[53]

The Sous-direction d'Amérique, though not of the same stature as the other three, was nevertheless an important innovation. Not only were French commercial interests in South and Central America becoming more substantial, but the rise of the United States to the position of world power demanded more attention. Until 1907, American affairs had been subject to an unstable development. Although a Bureau de l'Amérique et des Indes had been instituted in 1844, it was suppressed in 1848. In 1856 it was restored but underwent considerable change. Finally, the reform of 1907 definitely placed all American affairs, southern and northern, political and commercial, in the hands of the Sous-direction d'Amérique.[54]

African affairs were in a mess. In the nineteenth century the term 'Africa' referred to little else apart from Tunisia and Madagascar. Later, there ensued a battle between the Quai (and elements in it), the Navy Ministry, and the Colonial Ministry for segments of an 'expanding' Africa. The 1907 reforms, for their part, did little to promote the stable handling of African affairs. It was not until 1914, under Doumergue, a former colonial minister and a man very much interested in Africa, that a separate Sous-direction d'Afrique was finally instituted.[55]

One of the most important innovations of the 1907 reforms was the introduction of a Bureau des communications. Its purpose was twofold: to act as a distributor of important communications within the Quai d'Orsay and to liaise with the agencies of the outside world.[56] Before 1907, there had been a small Service de la presse composed of members of the minister's cabinet. One of Berthelot's most severe criticisms had been the way in which artificial barriers had been set up in the Foreign Ministry so that important pieces of information or decisions made in some departments were not generally transmitted.[57] The new bureau collected foreign and domestic press articles which it summarized and analysed along with important decisions. Its work was then transmitted to those most immediately concerned in the Centrale and foreign

[53] Berthelot to Gérard, 6 Dec. 1907, AN 329 AP 19 Gérard MSS.
[54] Outrey, 'Histoire et principes des affaires étrangères', p. 508.
[55] Ibid. p. 509.   [56] *JOC* 3 May 1907.   [57] Ibid.

missions. Information was henceforth filed systematically in dossiers 'using techniques of alphabetical classification to assure rapid retrievability'.[58]

The most basic function of the bureau, however, was that of dealing with the outside world. Undoubtedly criticism from Parliament, the press, and others over the rather vague nature of information emanating from the Foreign Ministry was a powerful motive for change. But Berthelot's conception of the power of the press as a means of influencing public opinion was the predominant factor in reform.[59] This was an innovative notion, as the press in the nineteenth century had been employed more to feel out foreign governments than to influence opinion.[60] The close links established with the press during the Algeçiras Conference had brought home to Berthelot and to other officials the authority which newspapers could wield in major crises. The support of the French press appeared to have contributed to France's success at the conference.[61] After the 1907 reform, links with the press became closer than in the past.[62] The streams of journalists entering the front door of the central administration continued even on Sundays and legal holidays.[63]

Cultural propaganda was also becoming an important facet of pre-war diplomacy.[64] Paul Cambon was not the only diplomat who sincerely believed that the French language was alone in expressing rational thoughts or that French culture was superior to all others. A department of French schools and works in foreign lands, created as a service by a simple *arrêté* in April 1909, was elevated to the rank of bureau by a decree of August 1910. Although money had been allocated for schools and other cultural institutions in previous years, the amounts had been relatively small. Expenditure totalled 353,850 francs in 1900 and only increased to 883,340 francs by 1905. By 1910, however, the total had skyrocketed to 2,227,971 francs.[65]

The 1907 reforms recognized the increasing importance of con-

---

[58] Ibid.; also Lauren, *Diplomats and Bureaucrats*, p. 94.   [59] *JOC* 3 May 1907.

[60] E. H. Carr, *Propaganda and International Politics* (New York, 1939), p. 8.

[61] A. Tardieu, *La Conférence d'Algeçiras* (Paris, 1907), pp. 92 502–4; de Margerie to J. Cambon, letters written between Jan. and June 1906, AE J. Cambon MSS, II.

[62] Grahame to Foreign Office, dispatch 44, in Bertie to Grey, 24 Jan. 1909, FO 371/666.

[63] *JOC Rapport* 2015 (1909).

[64] Gustave Mendel, AE NS 'Allemagne' 18, 'Note sur un projet qui semble propre à fortifier et à étendre l'action économique, intellectuelle et morale de la France dans le Levant', Mar. 1914.

[65] AE 'Comte définitif des dépenses de l'exercice, 1900–1933'.

tentious matters between states. Until 1907 bureaux handling *affaires contentieuses* had undergone several transformations, finally being attached to the political division in 1882. The 1907 reforms maintained it within the competence of the political and commercial division, and it was spread among the various geographical subdivisions. Also, matters relating to *contentieux administratifs* were henceforth permanently attributed to the Direction des affaires administratives et techniques as a Sous-direction des chancelleries et contentieux administratifs.[66]

The Conference of Algeçiras and Bourgeois's philosophies on arbitration were largely responsible for this increased awareness of contentious matters. Many of Germany's diplomatic obstructions at the conference had appeared in the guise of technical, judicial, and commercial arguments. The position of *jurisconsulte*, while not new, was strengthened in administrative status, and came to assume vital importance in the years between 1907 and 1914. Louis Renault, a professor of law at the Sorbonne, was an expert in the field of international law and as *jurisconsulte*, played a significant role in the development of Franco-German relations. Although Renault could at times be preoccupied by the more trivial aspects of his job, in general his influence eased tensions between Paris and Berlin. Undoubtedly his friendship with Kriege, his German counterpart, had a lot to do with this. Each appreciated the other's professionalism and knowledge, and their personal relations were excellent. The most important factor, however, was Renault's own moderation, which acted as a counterpoise to the Centrale's more intransigent attitude. He recognized that, although Germany's diplomatic claims were often inadmissible, many of the legal premises on which they were based were more tenable than most French bureaucrats were prepared to concede.[67]

The Quai d'Orsay wished to centralize disputes within one bureau, and consequently an arbitration bureau was established under the leadership of Jarousse de Sillac, a legal expert. It was attached to the Direction des affaires politiques et commerciales and was responsible for the preparation of French cases submitted to international arbitration, for signing new arbitration treaties, and for planning French participation in international conferences.[68]

Despite Bourgeois's strong hopes that the arbitration bureau might

[66] Outrey, 'Histoire et principes des affaires étrangères', p. 715.
[67] J. Cambon to Pichon, letters, Apr. 1913, AE J. Cambon MSS, 16.
[68] A. L. Donnelly, 'France and the Society of Nations' (Trinity College, 1980), p. 91; also AE Bourgeois MSS, 16.

help in the establishment of a real association of nations, the Quai d'Orsay tended to employ it as a means of unmasking Germany's pretensions before an objective international tribune. Apart from its beneficial propaganda element, neither the bureau nor Bourgeois's various activities were taken all that seriously. The bureau was busied more by a theoretical programme for the proposed 1914 Hague Conference and other arbitration schemes than by actual disputes.[69] Jarousse de Sillac was conservative and traditional by nature, and he tended to dilute Bourgeois's more far-seeing schemes. Moreover, Sillac was against any programme for arms reduction and was equally hostile to the compulsory arbitration of disputes.[70] As an indicator to the world of France's sincere desire for peace, the bureau served a certain purpose, but it was never more than a convenient mechanism of French propaganda.

The final major reform in the combined political and commercial division concerned the Foreign Ministry's archives. Until 1907 archivists had been mainly preoccupied with historical studies of little importance for their time. Archives had been kept in a generally disorganized state. Berthelot's aim was to create an archival system that would lend itself to the study of modern problems and that would take an active part in the formulation of policy. Modern filing systems were created and more up-to-date documents collected so that the archives would become an integral part of the working of diplomacy.

Administrative affairs in the form of the new Direction des affaires administratives et techniques were put theoretically on a level equivalent to political and commercial affairs, and its leader assumed the rank of director. As Gavarry, its first incumbent, noted, its influence was entirely restricted to administrative matters, a 'cul de plomb solennel qui n'a traité que des questions techniques, ne touchant pas à la politique commerciale française à l'étranger. Cette direction pourrait aussi bien être installée à la Justice.'[71] The functional specialists provided for in the 1907 reform were trained in scientific administration and technical affairs, but had little or no say in policy formulation. The division on the whole, therefore, was considered as something of an exile or wilderness in the Centrale, and Gavarry, who was critical of the Quai's policies, found himself restricted to being something of a housekeeper. As the director he took charge of such relatively minor issues as a Franco-

---

[69] See notes relating to an American proposal for compulsory arbitration and limitations of armaments, AE Bourgeois MSS, 4.

[70] Ibid., notes by Sillac, 23 June 1911.

[71] Gavarry, Pro-memoria, 17 Jan., AE *dossier personnel*, Gavarry.

Russian accord on literary and artistic property, or the international sanitary conference of Paris in 1911.[72]

The Direction administrative had a number of subdivisions and divisions. The first, the Sous-direction des unions et des affaires consulaires, had previously been a subdivision in the former Direction des affaires commerciales et des consulats. The 1907 reform removed from it any significance in policy formulation. It was left to handle matters like railways, canals, consular agreements, international rivers, navigation, weights and measures, relief matters, hygiene, labour, policy regulations, maritime security, postal and monetary accords, agricultural diseases, copyright and patent protection, and meteorological and seismological affairs.[73] In the nineteenth century these matters had been of little importance and were treated in isolation. However, the interdependence of nations in the twentieth century made necessary more co-operative efforts in certain areas.

The second division, the Sous-direction des affaires des chancelleries et du contentieux was primarily concerned with legal conflicts, extradition, naturalization, privileges, and immunities. Both parts of the subdivision had been detached from former divisions, Chancelleries from the Direction des consulats and Contentieux from the old political division. Contentieux, therefore, was present in both the political and commercial division and the Direction des affaires administratives et techniques.

The attempt by the Quai d'Orsay to meet the growing demands of twentieth-century diplomacy was reflected in other changes. By 1904, typing ability began to supplant the artwork of the scribe,[74] and by 1907 the 'avalanche du papier' was being handled by increasing numbers of women typists.[75] The new technology also changed the way officials worked. Electric lights, cars, and elevators had appeared by 1907.[76] These were improvements which hardly led to a revolution in diplomatic practice. The telephone and the wireless telegraph did. The former art of salon diplomacy with its formal relationships gave way to

[72] Ibid.   [73] *JOC* 3 May 1907.

[74] According to Charles-Roux, the typing machine had been introduced in 1904 (*Souvenirs diplomatiques d'un âge révolu* (Paris, 1956), p. 91). But Lauren suggests the earlier date of 1900 (Lauren, *Diplomats and Bureaucrats*, p. 38). Also AE 'Comptabilité, décrets et décisions ministeriels', carton 44, no. 74, *arrêté*, 8 Mar. 1900.

[75] *JOC* 3 May 1907, 'Commission des réformes administratives'; AE Personnel, 'Décrets et arrêtés', carton 28, *arrêté* 28, Dec. 1907.

[76] AE 'Comptabilité, décrets et décisions ministeriels', carton 53, no. 113; 'Note pour le Ministre', 25 Mar. 1904. An item for 'frais de voitures' first appears in the budget for the Quai d'Orsay in 1904; AE, 'Compte définitif des dépenses de l'exercice, 1901'.

diplomacy by telephone or telegraphy. Moreover, these innovations gave greater opportunities to foreign ministers to conduct negotiations themselves. Decisions were taken more quickly, but the margin for error was also made greater.

Even minor departments in the central administration reflected the response to the twentieth century. Since many countries were veering away from French as the natural diplomatic language, the Service de traduction was enlarged to cater for other languages. Similarly, the Service géographique seems to have been extremely busy during the 1900s. Whereas the *Annuaires diplomatiques* of the late nineteenth century contained two rather crude maps of Africa and Asia, by 1911 they provided numerous and highly detailed maps. As Jules Cambon noted during the Agadir crisis, rivulets and mountains in Africa once considered 'rogatons' had become of vital importance in the diplomatic struggle.[77]

The arms race, too, was having a profound effect on the administration of the subdivisions. Although the Centrale clearly retained an ultimate authority, it was increasingly forced to discuss issues of a military nature with other organizations such as the Conseil supérieur de la défense nationale. Indeed, the Quai created its own Service des affaires militaires, which was subdivided in 1912 among the European, American, and Asian departments as the Service des attachés militaires et navals. It was designed to handle military and naval attachés and to examine closer links between military and diplomatic affairs. As early as 1909–10 the Quai d'Orsay was considering the military and diplomatic implications of air power and arranging conferences to determine such things as national air space.[78]

The lack of substance which many of the 1907 reforms possessed is perhaps best exemplified by the attempt to alter the role of the foreign minister's private cabinet. The original terms of the reform had called for a private ministerial cabinet 'dégagé du personnel des services annexes' but keeping general control of the Direction du personnel. As all personnel were accountable to the minister in theory, he would have had the final say after taking into account the notes of *chefs de services* and

[77] *JOC* 3 May 1907, 'Commission des réformes administratives'; *JOC Rapport* 3318 (1908), *Rapport* 1230 (1908).

[78] See K. A. Hamilton, 'The Air in Entente Diplomacy: Great Britain and the International Aerial Navigation Conference of 1910', *International History Review*, 3/2 (Apr. 1981), pp. 169–200.

of the political director.[79] These provisions were largely incompatible.
On the one hand there was to be a separate apparatus to handle personnel,[80] which was consonant with practice in most other ministries.[81] On
the other hand, the foreign minister's ultimate authority destroyed whatever objectivity or independence it might have had. Even if the
minister's *chef du cabinet* was himself a career diplomat, he performed a
task which was political. As Keiger has noted, corrupt or politically
motivated chiefs staffed key areas of the administration with loyal
followers or threatened to dismiss those of independent views.[82]

Nor was the rivalry between the ministerial cabinet and the political
division ended. The original idea had been to reduce the status of the
cabinet to that of a link between the bureaux and the foreign minister.[83]
The fact that the cabinet was often staffed by the minister's friends or
family was enough to make this notion untenable in practice. Moreover,
Berthelot himself was *chef adjoint du cabinet* and therefore none too enthusiastic to reduce the cabinet's power.[84] In actual practice the power of
the cabinet greatly increased. Agents themselves were intensely conscious of the power of the *chef du cabinet* and were as much concerned
with establishing friendly ties with him as with carrying out their professional duties.[85] Decisions about personnel were made without prior
consultation of the heads of posts or even of the political director.[86] Moreover, the *chef du cabinet* was sometimes able to supplant the decision-
making authority of the political director.

Though its power increased, the machinery of the minister's cabinet
functioned as badly as ever. Dispatches were not only tardily communicated to the concerned parties but occasionally and inexplicably found
their way quite accidently into the foreign ministries of other countries.
The Madrid Embassy did not possess maps concerning the Algerian
border nor did the Tangier legation have a copy of treaties relating to
the Conference of Algeçiras. Documents concerning the Bosnian crisis
of 1908 ended up in the Russian Ministry of Foreign Affairs.[87] Jules

[79] Decree of 29 Apr. 1909, *Annuaire diplomatique* (1909–10).

[80] *JOC* 3 May 1907, 'Commission des réformes administratives'.

[81] *Le Temps*, 18 Nov. 1911.

[82] J. F. V. Keiger, *France and the Origins of the First World War* (London, 1983), p. 27.

[83] *JOC* 3 May 1907, 'Commission des réformes administratives'.

[84] Lauren, *Diplomats and Bureaucrats*, p. 87.

[85] Berthelot to Claudel, 4 Aug. 1907, 3 Mar. 1911, AE Berthelot MSS, 23; Arnavon to
Doulcet, 28 Nov. 1912, AE Doulcet MSS, 20; Dard to Gérard, 20 Oct. 1908, AN 329 AP
20 Gérard MSS.

[86] *Le Temps*, 18 Nov. 1911.

[87] F. V. Parsons, *The Origins of the Morocco Question, 1880–1900* (London, 1976), p. 663.

Cambon complained that he was not receiving correctly deciphered telegrams. The ministerial cabinet was tampering seriously with the communication system and selectively editing certain telegrams to reinforce the Centrale's point of view.[88]

As if these shortcomings were not enough, the cabinet remained a nest of intrigue and leakage. Jules Cambon sent most of his information to Pichon and Louis in the form of private correspondence which not only reached them directly but avoided classification in the archives and thus the usual *bavardage*. Even with private correspondence, however, there was no guarantee that a member of the minister's cabinet would not pick up the letter and read it. Jules Cambon often complained that words privately said in a letter to someone in the Quai were reported back to him at fourth or fifth hand.[89] Even his brother, who was far less prone to complain to Louis or Pichon about matters of this nature, was clearly concerned by the manner in which traditional leakage was allowed to continue.[90] Much leakage and intrigue was associated with matters of personnel. Men were dismissed from the service or disgraced because of such activity,[91] and by such means individuals were able to achieve promotion without overseas experience.[92]

The cry for better-trained and better-paid diplomats was scarcely heeded in the 1907 reforms.[93] Theoretically, decrees in 1907 and 1911 created fixed levels of payment based on hierarchical rank. One of Berthelot's major objectives had been to encourage regular professional work by experts.[94] In practice little was achieved. Certainly, men were working longer hours and using more advanced techniques, but often they did so with little sense of direction and even in opposition to the work of other bureaux.[95] Undoubtedly, too, pay was increased for attachés so as to make it easier for those with merit to enter the hallowed portals of the central administration.[96] Yet little was done to fix in practice objective criteria for payment internally or abroad. It was not until September 1913 that a professional approach was taken towards

[88] Panafieu to Louis, 4 Nov. 1908, AE Louis MSS, 2.

[89] J. Cambon to Louis, 29 June 1906, 25 Jan., 8 Feb. 1909, AE Louis MSS, 2.

[90] Ibid., P. Cambon to Louis, 19 Nov. 1907.

[91] Pognon, *Lettre à M. Doumergue*. On personal intrigues in the Lamartinière affair, see Gavarry to Reinach, 23 July 1908, BN (NAF 13540), Reinach MSS.

[92] Pro-memoria by Gavarry, 17 Jan. 1907, AE *dossier personnel*, Gavarry.

[93] *JOC Rapport* 2661 (1906).

[94] Decree of 29 Apr. 1909, *Annuaire diplomatique* (1909–10).

[95] AE 'Comptabilité, décrets et décisions ministeriels', carton 52; 'Note pour le Ministre', Hamon to Pichon, undated.

[96] *JOC Rapport* 333 (1907).

problems such as leaves of absence, recall or transfer to the central administration, retirement, and promotion. This delay occurred in spite of the fact that an Association professionelle des agents du Ministère des affaires étrangères had existed since 1907. This organization was little more than an ultimate resort for those seriously disadvantaged. It was in no sense a trade union urging the government to establish permanent rules, and it acted more as a social club than as a pressure group. A full three years after the 1907 reforms were enacted Hamon, the *chef de la comptabilité*, noted the lack of *esprit de corps* caused by uncertainties over such matters as advancement and vacations. In 1908 de Margerie was constantly bringing before the Bureau du personnel the fact that his salary for the Siam position had still not been fixed in a 'definitive' manner.[97] Jules Cambon would have been forced to spend his own money on diplomatic and political publications had he not made a personal appeal to Foreign Minister Pichon.[98]

This sorry state of affairs was in large part due to the fact that costs were expanding along with personnel. Admittedly expenditure had been raised since 1900, when it was 16,898,042 francs. Between 1905 and 1910 the total had risen from 18,356,852 to 21,613,947 francs. Nevertheless, this increase was largely swallowed up by the costs of new embassies, the establishment of new consular missions, the buying of technological equipment, and cultural propaganda.[99] Moreover, the Division des fonds et de la comptabilité was inefficient. Despite the fact that Hamon had been brought in from Finances to manage the Quai d'Orsay's funds, there was little or no public accounting. On occasion Hamon himself was the personal beneficiary of money waiting to be used.

The entry requirements for new personnel remained illogical. The idea of making all attachés serve a probationary period of three months under the watchful scrutiny of the Commission du stage was laudable. Yet the examination was so rigorous that it was frequently failed by candidates who would have made desirable diplomats. Usually it was seventeen hours in length, the stiffest given in any government service. Only the *concours* for the *lycée* and the professor's examination rivalled it.[100] Its weakness, however, owed more to the nature of its questions than its length. A preoccupation with the smallest technical, economic,

---

[97] Ibid.; Hamon to Pichon, 26 Dec. 1910, AE 'Comptabilité, décrets et décisions ministeriels', carton 51; de Margerie to the Quai d'Orsay, 1908, AE *dossier personnel*, de Margerie.

[98] J. Cambon to Pichon, 7 Feb. 1910, AE J. Cambon MSS, 16.

[99] 'Compte définitif des dépenses de l'exercice, 1880–1930'; *JOC Rapport* 3318 (1916).

[100] W. R. Sharp, *Civil Service Abroad* (New York, 1935), p. 145.

and political trivia made the exam a mere memory test while ignoring those qualities most needed in a diplomat: sound judgement, initiative, original thought, intelligence, and plain common sense.[101] The test was so disheartening that the original idea of creating objective tests open to men of talent irrespective of wealth or rank was almost totally submerged by an avalanche of work and paper. In the end, the old system of nepotism and political favouritism was allowed to continue because the alternative was unrealistic and unworkable. Only in 1914 was serious consideration given to overhauling the entire examination programme.

Overall, although the positive aspects of the 1907 reforms must be recognized, they should not be exaggerated. More spectacular results could hardly have been expected in view of the highly restricted membership of the reform commission. The reforms were the work of permanent officials who were more concerned with innovations in administration and professionalism than with the more political demands of the Radicals for Republican diplomacy. Certainly, in his report Berthelot gave more than lip service to the call for increased accountability to the public and Parliament, but this did not mean that they then came to control foreign policy. Nor did it naturally follow that the actual power of the Quai d'Orsay was curtailed. Berthelot least of all would have envisaged such a diminution.

Even within the areas of administration and professionalism Berthelot was the first to acknowledge that his reforms were not as far-reaching and as effective as he had expected. Even before the reforms were put into effect he was lamenting to Claudel, his friend in China:

Ce qui est fâcheux, c'est que l'on ne me laisse pas tout dire; déjà dans mon premier rapport bien des choses ont été modifiées et atténuées ...Vous ne pouvez imaginer les difficultés, ennuis et résistances de toutes sortes rencontrés pour faire aboutir la pauvre réforme. Et l'exécution est à peine entamée: La mollesse de P. [Pichon], les intrigues des personnes, rendent tout compliqué.[102]

As Berthelot suggested, not only did Pichon become increasingly lukewarm, but the conservatism and resistance to change of officials and diplomats alike was a formidable obstacle. Bapst was wary about taking over the directorship while everything was in flux. The influential Cam-

---

[101] Eichtal to Bourgeois, 17 May 1913, Bourgeois to Pichon, 3 June 1913, AE Bourgeois MSS, 4; *JOS* 16 Jan. 1907; *JOC Rapport* 333 (1907).
[102] Berthelot to Paul Claudel, 4 Aug. 1907, AE Berthelot MSS, 23.

bons became more hostile to the reforms as time went by. As early as October 1907 Paléologue could cynically comment to de Billy that 'comme au lendemain des révolutions, l'esprit du conservatisme remplissait toute la maison. Il n'est plus question des réformes. Beati possidentes!'[103]

A growing international tension was a further problem for the reform movement. At a time when relations with Germany were strained and when the Balkans were in full turmoil, there was a reluctance to introduce changes. In view of the darkening horizon no one was in a hurry to meddle with a machinery which, while not perfect, at least worked. Time and more stable circumstances were needed.

The importance of personnel changes should certainly not be over-emphasized. In the long run Clemenceau's measures were largely neutralized. De Margerie, though temporarily unable to return to the Centrale, was given the important position of minister to Peking. Under the constant pressure applied by the Cambons and Reinach, he became *directeur adjoint* under Poincaré and political and commercial director under Doumergue. De Margerie's career was an excellent example of how the career remained open to aristocrats who were prepared to take a conciliatory approach towards the Republic. His new position in 1909 in Peking clearly contradicted a note made in the British Foreign Office that, under the present regime, 'only diplomatists of approved republican opinions could hope for advancement'.[104] Soulange-Bodin was another interesting case. Though he fell out of favour with Clemenceau, he chose his own post and was reconciled with Clemenceau in a very short time.[105] Paléologue and Dumaine both went on to highly successful careers. Dumaine became ambassador to Vienna and Paléologue became political and commercial director, ambassador to St Petersburg, and finally secretary-general. Geoffray, whose clerical leanings Clemenceau suspected, succeeded Revoil in Madrid. Henri Cambon was able to report to his father in January 1908 that Clemenceau had no intention of removing Barrère from Rome.[106]

If the results of the appeal for more Republican diplomacy admin-

[103] Paléologue to de Billy, 10 Oct. 1907, AE de Billy MSS, 3; J. Cambon to Louis, 8, 18, 24 Feb. 1908, AE Louis MSS, 2; P. Cambon to H. Cambon, 22 July 1907, 20 Sept. 1906, Louis Cambon MSS.

[104] Note on cover of S17/788 in FO 371/24.

[105] Dard to Gérard, 22 Feb. 1909, AN 329 AP 20 Gérard MSS; Deschanel to Pichon, 29 Jan. 1909, AE *dossier personnel*, Defrance.

[106] Barrère to Pichon, 28 Jan. 1912, Inst. de Fr. Pichon MSS, 1; Henri Cambon to P. Cambon, 15 Jan. 1908, Louis Cambon MSS.

istered by representatives of the Republic were disappointing, this was partly because of the conservatism of Pichon (and the officials themselves) as well as a certain mellowing by Clemenceau. The statements made while in opposition often bore little resemblance to policies enacted when in government. This was the case with both Pichon and Clemenceau. The two men became aware of the enormous difficulties which structural reforms would involve and of the effect which wholesale purges would create. Before coming to office, and even during his initial months in power, Pichon's espousal of Republican diplomacy was unequivocal.[107] By 1908 he was decidedly unenthusiastic. Writing to Jules Cambon in July 1908 he stated that he much preferred to rely on secrecy. He constantly acted as a shock absorber for Clemenceau's invective. Rather ineffective in the first months, he had tamed the ageing tiger by the end of his term as premier.[108] Pichon's 'mollesse' also derived from his laziness, and despite his beliefs he was by temperament unsuited to the implementation of major administrative reforms. As his term increased he became progressively indolent, often absent from the Quai d'Orsay.

Surprisingly, Clemenceau mellowed considerably during his years in office. As D. R. Watson, his biographer, acknowledges, the Premier's foreign policy was less intransigent towards Germany than generally recognized. He was no different in matters of personnel. Paul Cambon's observation that Clemenceau was responsive to reasonable arguments if one stood up to him was correct.[109] Moreover, as Clemenceau came into contact with the agents he vilified, some, if not all, of his prejudices were moderated. Equally important, Clemenceau's commitment to open diplomacy while in opposition changed dramatically after he took the reins of government. His almost autocratic temperament prevented any abdication or lessening of government prerogative.

Ironically, the formal recruitment policies of the Quai d'Orsay were in total contradiction with the avowed policies of the Radicals. Between 1905 and 1907, of the 192 men appointed to the diplomatic and consular services, 153 came from the École libre des sciences politiques.[110] At that

[107] *La Révolution française*, 45 (26 Feb. 1879); see Marcel Hutin's article in *L'Écho de Paris*, 18 Nov. 1906.

[108] Bertie to Grey, 29 Oct., 17 Nov. 1906, FO 371/74; Pichon to J. Cambon, 10 July 1908, AE Cambon MSS, 16.

[109] D. R. Watson, 'The Making of French Foreign Policy during the First Clemenceau Ministry, 1906–9'. *English Historical Review*, 86 (1971); P. Cambon to J. Cambon, 26 Nov. 1908. AE J. Cambon MSS, 19.

[110] Sharp, *Civil Service Abroad*, p.105; F. L. Schuman, *War and Diplomacy in the French Republic* (New York, 1931), p. 38.

institution the predominant philosophy was nationalism, and a certain hostility to parliamentarianism and democracy was carefully cultivated. The Radicals were unsuccessful in reducing the flow of Sciences-po graduates into the Quai d'Orsay. Indeed, it was not until September 1913 that a decree definitively created a regular system of formal examinations ensuring competence and professionalism. The loopholes available for candidates with sufficient patronage remained many.

On balance, the reforms actually introduced were disappointing, and what had appeared so promising in 1907 had largely crashed around the reformers' ears by 1911. The gap between theory and practice was not altogether surprising since the reforms were essentially the work of men inside the Quai d'Orsay. Clemenceau's personal prejudices, the character of Pichon, and intrigues and resistance within the Quai d'Orsay all worked against substantial change. The Radicals, in general, played very little part in either the enactment or the implementation of reform. Their cries for open diplomacy were hardly heeded. Moreover, the nature of the parliamentary game prevented any continuous scrutiny over the reforms proposed. Certainly, in the areas of internal and external administration, the achievement was relatively impressive, and France acted as a beacon for other European foreign ministries. Yet, even in this restricted sense, a distinction needs to be clearly made between the theory and practice of reform. Illogicalities, personal intrigues, power politics, internal resistance, and outright corruption all seriously diminished the importance and scope of Berthelot's accomplishments.

8

Pichon's First Ministry, 1906–1909

Despite the practical problems inherent in the 1907 reforms, the years 1906-9, Pichon's first ministry, were marked by the consolidation of the authority of the Quai d'Orsay and by a relatively stable foreign policy. Although the Foreign Minister enjoyed long tenure of office (1906-11), he collaborated closely with and depended largely upon his most important officials, Louis, the Cambons, and Barrère in particular. As a result of their efforts, there were significant developments: attempts at Franco-German *détente*, culminating in the 1909 Franco-German economic accord; a continued improvement of relations with Italy and Britain; the pacific settlement of the 1908 Near Eastern crisis; the gradual penetration of Morocco; and the formation of the Triple *Entente*.

The fact that the 1907 reforms proved to be disappointing on the whole was to a considerable extent the responsibility of Stephen Pichon. The Foreign Minister's Republicanism and his desire to reform the Quai d'Orsay were not in question. Although a man imbued with flexibility, foresight, and moderation, his laziness and his lack of forcefulness seriously reduced his effectiveness.

Pichon was born in Burgundy in 1857, the son of a local tax collector. As an only child, he was given surprisingly little attention, a situation exacerbated by his father's death when he was only 12 years of age.[1] After early schooling at the Collège d'Arnay-le-Duc and the Lycée Besançon, he went to Louis le Grand in 1874 and there met Poincaré, Paléologue, and Millerand. He subsequently spent two years at the École normale supérieure.[2] In 1879 he joined the newspaper *La Révolution française* with the help of Clemenceau, whom he had met the previous year. By 1885 he had entered Parliament, where he remained until the election of 1893, when a Socialist opponent brought about his defeat. He

---

[1] D. J. Miller, 'Stephen Pichon and the Making of French Foreign Policy' (Cambridge University, 1976), pp. 2–3; *The Times*, 25 May 1908.
[2] *The Times*, 19 Sept. 1933; Pichon to Lycée Louis le Grand, 5 July 1902, AE NS 'Tunisie', 323 *bis*.

turned his hand to a diplomatic career, serving as minister to Brazil and China and as resident-general in Tunis, before returing to the Senate.

In his earlier years, Pichon's political views had been those of the extreme left, and *La Révolution française* was a left-wing paper whose collaborators included Marx's brother-in-law Charles Longuet. Pichon had reasonably close relations with such Leftists as Jules Guesde and Louis Blanc. In Paris he was a highly visible supporter of Jules Michelet, who was an idol of the Republican extremists, and a critic of both Marshal MacMahon and the political opportunism of Gambetta.[3]

Pichon was not a revolutionary, however. Much of his political philosophy can be explained by his devotion to Republican institutions. His brand of reform did not envisage violence. He adopted such causes as the release of the Communards, freedom of the press, free and secular education, separation of Church and State, suppression of the Senate, a reformed magistrature, and social welfare.[4] By 1889 Pichon's enthusiasm for reform seems to have moderated to a large extent. Undoubtedly the Republic was not in as much danger as it had been during the formative years of the 1870s and early 1880s. He had married into a wealthy banking family and had plumped for capital rather than the workforce during the Decazeville strike of 1886. By the late 1880s he was closely allied with the Radicals in general and Clemenceau in particular. During the 1890s, whether because of lack of support by the socialists in his election bid of 1893 or because of ideological conviction, he had become bitterly hostile towards socialism, which he considered to be the 'danger de demain'.[5]

Though Pichon was a Republican, he was not an avid advocate of the parliamentary game, which partially explains why he was unwilling to hand over the formation and execution of foreign policy to Parliament. Once again his electoral defeat in 1893 seems to have influenced his thinking. Writing to Poincaré in 1895, he contemptuously referred to Parliament as the 'domaine du coq à l'âne de l'intrigue et de l'absurdité'. In 1901 he was critical of the atrocious number of political factions.[6] He had greater faith in public opinion but, despite his journalistic background, did not propose a democratic control of foreign policy.[7]

Clemenceau's decision to place Pichon at the Foreign Ministry clearly

[3] Miller, 'Pichon', p. 4.

[4] *La Justice*, 2 Aug. 1880; *La Révolution française*, 22 Mar. 1879.

[5] A. Ranc, *Souvenirs: Correspondance* (Paris, 1913), p. 406.

[6] Pichon to Poincaré, 13 Nov. 1895, BN (NAF 16011), Poincaré MSS; Pichon to Millerand, quoted in Miller, 'Pichon', p. 22.

[7] *La Justice*, 15 Jan. 1890, 10 Oct. 1891.

reflected the Premier's desire to wield Excalibur himself.[8] Pichon was thoroughly loyal to Clemenceau, lacked forcefulness, had a constant need for reassurance and guidance, and enjoyed little, if any, parliamentary prestige. Moreover he lacked ministerial experience and had only just returned to political life.[9] Clemenceau, recognizing Pichon's vulnerability to cabinet intrigues and parliamentary politicking, had first offered the Foreign Ministry to de Selves and Poincaré.[10] Given his inclination to intervene in the formulation of foreign policy, however, it is not surprising that he settled on Pichon. Ultimately, the two men achieved something of a common outlook. As D. R. Watson has indicated, the view that the Franco-German *détente* of February 1909 was the result of Pichon dragging an unwilling Clemenceau behind him requires serious re-evaluation. There was little conflict if any over the necessity for *détente* or over other policy matters.[11]

On the other hand, the view that the Premier imposed his will upon the diplomatic machinery is no less fallacious. In fact, Clemenceau modified his position towards both Germany and Russia in an effort to satisfy the professionals of the Quai d'Orsay. This accommodation went much further than a mere crossing of the floor from the opposition to the government benches. Clemenceau's criticism of Berlin and St Petersburg had been loudly voiced for many years and was the result of deep-seated feelings. Nevertheless, he became a strong supporter of the Franco-Russian alliance despite the hostility this stand aroused within his own party. He fully concurred with Jules Cambon's attempt to arrive at a *détente* with Berlin. Clemenceau always had the final say, but the decisions he took were usually in accord with what the Quai d'Orsay was advocating.[12]

Pichon's relationship with the Quai d'Orsay and the manner in which he viewed his role as foreign minister were tempered by several factors: his relations with colleagues, his lack of initiative and forceful-

---

[8] P. Cambon to H. Cambon, 26 Oct. 1906, *Paul Cambon: Correspondance* (Paris, 1940–6), ii. 226.

[9] Bertie to Grey, 25 Oct. 1906, FO 371/71; Bertie to Grey, 4 Nov. 1906, PRO FO 800/164, Bertie MSS; Barrère to Pichon, 26 Oct. 1906, Gérard to Pichon, 25 Oct. 1906, Inst. de Fr. Pichon MSS, 1, 3; P. Cambon to Barrère, 26 Oct., 4 Nov., AE Barrère MSS, 1.

[10] *Le Temps*, 24 Oct. 1906.

[11] See D. R. Watson, 'The Making of French Foreign Policy during the First Clemenceau Ministry, 1906–9', *English Historical Review*, 86 (1971), pp. 775–82; P. Cambon to Pichon, 23 July 1909, Inst. de Fr. Pichon MSS, 2.

[12] It is to be noted that although Clemenceau was kept *au courant* about the 1907 Mediterranean agreements, and agreed in principle, he did nothing more. Bertie to Grey, 7 Apr. 1907, FO 800/179, Bertie MSS; also 15 Apr. 1907, FO 425/300, confidential print.

ness, and his natural laziness. His horror of work was apparent from his first days in office. Writing to Joseph Reinach only days after becoming foreign minister, he lamented about the crushing workload which appeared to overwhelm him.[13] One week later he complained of extreme fatigue. As time went on, Pichon preferred to sign work which had been carried out in his name and which he should have undertaken himself. By the time of the Briand ministry in 1909 he was frequently absent from the Quai d'Orsay.

Clearly Pichon was not an initiator of events, being better suited to co-ordinating the efforts of others. As both British Ambassador Bertie and Arsène Henry, a former commercial director, noted, Pichon depended far too much for enlightenment and direction on his advisers. He was very accessible to counsels of a moderate nature and was prepared to go along with them when they were not in formal contradiction with his wider philosophies. Even when he had definite opinions on certain issues, he was hardly forthright in promoting them. If he persisted, the Quai d'Orsay often manipulated parts of the Paris press, which Pichon feared, to change his mind.[14]

The influence of the Quai d'Orsay was thus strengthened not only by Pichon's personality and working habits, but also by the friendships he maintained with his subordinates. As a diplomat with ten years' experience, he had collaborated with leading officials, in particular Conty, the *sous-directeur d'Europe, d'Amérique, et d'Océanie*. These close working relationships extended to the salon and the dinner party, and men such as the Cambons, Barrère, and Louis were frequently seen on social occasions with the Minister.[15]

The relationship between Pichon and Louis, the political and commercial director, was particularly intimate. The Minister admired his *directeur's* competence and professionalism and, while having the final say in most negotiations, usually concurred with the view of his colleague.[16] Louis was given a free hand in the implementation of day-to-day details as well as in the broader area of policy formulation. As Pichon's ministry lengthened, he increasingly left the Quai d'Orsay in Louis's hands and was largely content to act as a sounding board for Louis's ideas. On many occasions it was Louis who formulated the official response to an issue. Dispatches were transmitted to Pichon for

[13] Pichon to Reinach, 31 Oct., 7 Nov. 1906, BN (NAF 13527), Reinach MSS.

[14] Henry to Revoil, 30 Dec. 1911, AE Revoil MSS, 5; Bertie to Grey, 12 Mar. 1910, FO 425/335, confidential print.

[15] Nicolson to Cartwright, 20 Feb. 1911, PRO, FO 800/347, Nicolson MSS.

[16] Pichon to Louis, 8 Aug. 1904, AE Louis MSS, 2.

his approval. There is no evidence to suggest that he diverged from his director's assessment on any major question. In fact, Louis felt sufficiently in control to send dispatches in Pichon's name without the Minister's prior approval.[17] The authority enjoyed by Louis stemmed in part from Pichon's conception of the role of the political and commercial director.[18] He considered the position to be of vital importance, 'le plus important, le plus délicat et le plus sérieux de notre diplomatie ... le chef d'état-major général du ministère'.[19]

Pichon's relations with the Cambons and Barrère were generally very good. Though not as apprehensive as Jules Cambon about going to Ems or Fashoda, Pichon fully agreed with Cambon's belief in the necessity of some sort of *détente* with Germany and constantly supported his efforts to achieve better relations. He appreciated both Cambon's skill as a diplomat and his deep commitment to peace. He openly acknowledged that the Ambassador's task was singularly difficult. As a mark of his personal affection for Cambon, Pichon sought to reward him with the *grand cordon de la Légion d'honneur*.

There was no personal friction between Paul Cambon and Pichon. Nevertheless, relations between the two could hardly be described as intimate, and, at times, Cambon was able to overwhelm the rather unforceful Pichon. On many occasions the Foreign Minister modified his views in accordance with Cambon's advice, particularly in the field of Franco-Japanese relations, where Pichon had wanted a political as well as a commercial agreement.

Pichon was closer to Barrère, with whom he shared a similar political outlook and a liking for Italy. Just before leaving the Foreign Ministry in January 1911 he wrote to Barrère:

Ce sera l'une de mes satisfactions principales lorsque je quitterai le ministère d'avoir fortifié l'amitié qui m'unissait à vous. Je n'ai pas besoin de vous dire combien j'apprécie votre caractère, la fermeté et la sûreté de vos vues ... Nous n'aurons pas de peine à rester d'accord puisque nous avons le même but et les mêmes desseins.[20]

---

[17] Louis to Pichon, 14 May 1907, 5, 11, 19 Aug. 1909, Inst. de Fr. Pichon MSS, 3; Pichon to Louis, 27 Aug. 1909, AE Louis MSS, 2. In May 1909 Pichon wrote as follows about Louis: 'Il est universellement connu, apprécié par les représentants des puissances avec lesquels il entretient en France les relations les meilleures.' Pichon to Touchard, 25 May 1909, Inst. de Fr. Pichon MSS, 4.

[18] Louis to Pichon, 22 Dec. 1909, Inst. de Fr. Pichon MSS, 3.

[19] Quoted in Miller, 'Pichon', p. 34.

[20] Pichon to Cambon, 18 July 1907, AE J. Cambon MSS, 16; Pichon to Barrère, 6 Jan. 1911, AE Barrère MSS, 4.

The most powerful official in the central administration after Louis was Philippe Berthelot, *sous-directeur d'Asie*. His relationship with Pichon also appears to have been close. As a deputy in the early 1890s Pichon had been on friendly terms with his father Marcellin Berthelot. Pichon and Philippe Berthelot had a similar attitude towards the parliamentary Republic. Berthelot considered Pichon far-sighted, sensible, and a diplomatic statesman of the first order.[21] Pichon appreciated Berthelot's logical and brilliant mind, his unfailing will, his industry, and his ability to formulate clear policies. Under Pichon, Berthelot was able to chair meetings in his name and to give orders to officials much higher in rank than himself. On most subjects the two men found themselves in agreement, and Berthelot's influence extended to Asian, Near Eastern, and even Moroccan affairs.[22]

Berthelot's relationship with his colleagues was not as fruitful. His ambitious nature, his penchant for intrigue, and his condescension towards many colleagues made him highly unpopular. Bertie referred to Berthelot as 'that skunk' who was 'without judgement but of pushing and intriguing nature'.[23] In later years he was feared rather than respected, and his ability to place cronies in the most advantageous posts made him as many enemies as friends.[24] For all that, he appears to have worked successfully with both de Margerie and Gérard, who were posted respectively to China and Japan. Gérard was a devoted friend, who praised Berthelot's industry and his clear direction of Asian affairs.[25]

As an administrator Berthelot was almost in a class by himself. Only Louis was able to match his prodigious memory and intelligence. Though Berthelot could be unduly cynical, his faith in the power of logic was unswerving, and it was this quality which made him a man of vision. He had little time for sentimental policies of any kind, and based his judgements upon a careful weighing of the evidence. His favourite Chinese proverb, 'le chou est né pour être malheureux car sa tête est

[21] Berthelot to Revoil, 21 Sept. 1913, AE Revoil MSS, 4.

[22] A. Bréal, *Philippe Berthelot* (Paris, 1937), p. 78; Berthelot to Pichon, 27 Sept. 1916, Inst. de Fr. Pichon MSS, 1; Pichon to Delcassé, 14 Dec. 1901, AE Delcassé MSS, 1.

[23] Bertie to Hardinge, 28 Sept. 1916, Bertie to Grey, 14 Feb. 1916, PRO, FO 800/188, Bertie MSS, FR 16/17.

[24] 'Notes concernant le Quai d'Orsay', p. 72, AN de Robien MSS.

[25] A. Gérard, *Mémoires d'Auguste Gérard* (Paris, 1928), p. 455; see correspondence exchanged between Berthelot and Gérard, 1907–14, AN 329 AP 19, 20, Gérard MSS.

trop près de son cœur', reflected his almost obsessive preoccupation with logic and rationality.[26]

Not surprisingly, Berthelot excelled at formulating policies which were based on clear arguments. However, he displayed certain weaknesses. If he had a special aptitude for the general area of policy formulation, the daily execution of policies bored him.[27] Furthermore, his ignorance of the machinery of overseas posts and his cynicism blinded him to other, equally valid, viewpoints and to the technical difficulties inherent in the execution of policy.

Berthelot combined with a very precise notion of the general principles of policy formulation an absolutely amazing industry. He considered rest as the most dangerous treatment for any sickness. Consequently he slept only three to four hours nightly.[28] On arriving at the Centrale very early in the morning, he would personally review all incoming dispatches related to his own department and then scrutinize the daily press as well as the dispatches of departments not directly concerning him. Almost all his dispatches were drafted in his own hand.[29]

His desire to dominate both the machinery of the Centrale and men's minds was often evident. His liking for personal interviews reflected his will to power. Instead of conferences, he preferred intimate meetings with individuals, which enabled him to obtain a clearer impression of a problem.[30] Though he rather fancied himself a story-teller and would sometimes leak information, he generally did so for social rather than political reasons. The indiscretions he allowed himself were usually insignificant. On the whole, he worked in secrecy, rarely descending from the magisterial offices of the fourth floor and very rarely discussing his views with other colleagues.[31]

Berthelot's handling of his colleagues also reflected his determination to dominate. During a year in China in 1903 he had gained a reputation for lording it over consular officials.[32] As *sous-directeur d'Asie* his dis-

---

[26] Berthelot to de Billy, 17 Nov. 1911, AE de Billy MSS; article by R. Recouly in *Le Gringoire*, 30 Nov. 1934, AE *dossier personnel*, Berthelot; B. Auffray, *Pierre de Margerie (1861–1942) et la vie diplomatique de son temps* (Paris, 1976), pp. 251–5.

[27] Auffray, *De Margerie*; notes by Billot in 1889 and Gavarry in 1902, AE *dossier personnel*, Berthelot.

[28] Berthelot to Revoil, 21 Sept. 1913, AE Revoil MSS, 4; Bréal, *Berthelot*, p. 13.

[29] Bréal, *Berthelot*, 52, 78.

[30] Ibid. p. 8.

[31] G. A. Craig and F. Gilbert, *Diplomats* (New York, 1972), p. 65; P. Claudel, 'Philippe Berthelot', *Bulletin de la Société Paul Claudel*, 28 (1967), p. 48.

[32] Bréal, *Berthelot*, pp. 51, 59.

patches were always courteous but often decidedly authoritarian.[33] Though he tended to favour agents involved in Near Eastern matters, he was condescending towards most subordinates.[34] Moreover, he carefully supervised all aspects of his deputy directors' work, clearly trusting very few.

It was in the area of Far Eastern affairs that Berthelot's influence predominated, and he became the chief architect of Far Eastern policy. In 1903 he had spent a year in China making an account of the historical development of the country, interviewing warlords and officials alike, observing Chinese life, and even visiting Tibet. His trip convinced him that China was perhaps the only real market in the world available for economic exploitation, and he advocated an aggressive economic diplomacy there.[35] The apparent decadence of the Chinese empire, he thought, made it imperative to get a foothold before the British, Americans, and Russians carved up the country.[36]

Berthelot had an even greater impact on Franco-Japanese relations. He had initially objected to the Franco-Japanese treaty of 1907 not so much on political grounds, or because Russia would be hurt, but because he felt that the economic clauses did not provide sufficient compensation for French industry.[37] The decision to ratify the treaty had been made, however, before he became *sous-directeur d'Asie*. He was powerless to change Pichon's mind; but by 1910 he had persuaded Pichon that loans to Japan as well as the forthcoming Franco-Japanese commercial treaty should be accompanied by both substantial industrial orders and a lowering of customs barriers.[38] Admittedly, Pichon was able to hold out against his deputy director in the initial loan of 1910, but had to admit soon after that future loans could not be as freely given. The Franco-Japanese commercial treaty signed in the summer of 1910 clearly reflected the influence of Berthelot.[39] Not only did Pichon play a minimal role in the negotiations, but Berthelot was able to lower Japanese customs barriers substantially.

Though Albert-Jules Defrance's term as *sous-directeur du Levant* at the Quai d'Orsay lasted only two years, 1907–09, he was moderately influ-

[33] Auffray, *De Margerie*, p. 252.

[34] Bréal, *Berthelot*, pp. 12, 51; J. d'Aumale, *Voix de L'Orient: Souvenirs d'un diplomate* (Montreal, 1945), p. 40.

[35] Bréal, *Berthelot*, pp. 59–61; article by R. Recouly in *Le Gringoire*, 30 Nov. 1934, AE *dossier personnel*, Berthelot.

[36] Berthelot to Claudel, undated, AE Berthelot MSS, 7.   [37] Ibid.

[38] 'Note au sujet d'un emprunt japonais', 23 Apr. 1910, and 'Les Futurs Emprunts japonais', 10 June 1910, AE NS 'Japon', 56.

[39] Ibid. Pichon to Minister of Finance, 29 Apr. 1910, Pichon to Gérard, 17 May 1910.

ential in the formulation of Near Eastern policy. Born in 1860, he had entered the Quai d'Orsay in December 1880 as an *attaché autorisé à la direction politique*.[40] In the next twenty seven years he had several postings in Europe, South America,[41] Asia,[42] and the Near and Middle East, which was his area of speciality.[43]

His career languished in the early 1900s, but Pichon's arrival was a godsend. Defrance's wife was on close terms with Madame Pichon. Defrance was subsequently made *sous-directeur du Midi* in January 1907, and then *sous-directeur de Levant* in December of that year.[44] In January 1909 he apparently got 'itchy feet' again and asked for a posting to either Cairo or Athens, presumably because he wished to plunge more deeply into Near Eastern affairs. He was given Stockholm. Surprisingly, when Cairo became free in June 1910 he no longer wanted the post. Nevertheless, he was sent there.[45]

- Defrance was a very capable diplomat. He had an excellent knowledge of commercial questions. His immediate superiors in his various posts noted that he was an agent of tact, firmness, and intelligence, who kept *au courant* of the latest developments and was a good drafter of dispatches. It was, however, his energy which struck most of his colleagues, and he was always vehement in whatever stance he took. This was not without its inconveniences, as the other side of the coin was that he always appeared to have a chip on his shoulder when discussing his career (he was an extremely ambitious man) or the policies of other powers. Indeed, this tendency sometimes led him to misjudge the motives of others.[46]

Defrance advocated an aggressive policy of seeking spheres of influence in Asiatic Turkey at the expense of Britain and Germany and of supporting the Balkan states against the influence of the German powers, in particular Austria-Hungary. Throughout his career he was a rabid colonialist and espoused an aggressive economic and diplomatic policy in the Near and Far East as well as in the Americas. Though he was highly suspicious of Germany, his interest in the colonial areas made him equally distrustful of Great Britain. His reports from Cairo,

[40] AE *dossier personnel*, Defrance; Defrance to Hanotaux, undated, AE Hanotaux MSS, 2.

[41] Defrance to Hanotaux, 22 Nov. 1886, 1 June 1893, 21 June 1894, AE Hanotaux MSS, 2.

[42] Ibid. Defrance to Hanotaux, 21 Apr. 1896.

[43] Note from Delavaud to Rouvier, 26 June 1905, AE *dossier personnel*, Defrance.

[44] Berckheim to Gérard, 5 Jan. 1907, AN 329 AP 20 Gérard MSS.

[45] AE *dossier personnel*, Defrance, 19 Apr. 1891.

[46] Ibid., reports by Bacourt to Ribot, 2 Aug. 1891, Imbert to Ribot, 25 May 1891.

Bangkok, Santiago, and Tehran were full of British duplicity.[47] He was, however, unsuccessful in stopping the British advance in either Siam or Egypt. As *sous-directeur de Levant*, he was able to have a greater impact on French policy. He advocated and facilitated French involvement in the Abyssinian question in 1907, clearly mindful of the fact that it was another area where Britain could extend her colonial influence yet conscious of the economic rewards that could be gained by agreeing with Italy and Great Britain.[48] As minister to Cairo he continued to combat British colonial influence, advocating the acquisition of the Ottoman territory of Syria even though most French diplomats were unwilling to envisage the dissolution of the Ottoman Empire at any time before the First World War.[49]

As for so many other French foreign ministers, the focal point of Pichon's attention was Berlin. Before and during his two ministries in 1906-11 and 1913 his suspicion of Germany remained constant. Basically, this sentiment was derived from his childhood days during the Franco-Prussian war of 1870-1. The memory of his native Burgundy under German occupation stayed with him.[50] The authoritarian spirit of Prussia offended his democratic and republican convictions.[51] Moreover, he regarded Germany's diplomatic campaign to break the *Entente's* encirclement by improving her relations with Britain and Russia as an attempt to isolate France and make her subservient to Berlin's whims.

On principle Pichon was not against *détente* with Germany. He fully applauded and encouraged Jules Cambon's attempts to establish meaningful channels of communication with Berlin. He found the prospect of world conflagration thoroughly repugnant. Yet it was clear that he was sceptical about what could be achieved. He was more sympathetic to Louis's caution than to Cambon's optimism. If fact, he was mildly critical of Cambon's obsession with preventing any future Franco-German conflagration. He found it difficult to accept his assessment that not all was rotten in Schleswig-Holstein. He was not fully convinced that there were influential Germans bent on peace and sincerely desirous of *rapprochement*. Theoretically, then, he sensed the need for a general *détente*, but in practice he was sceptical about Germany's long-term

[47] Defrance to Hanotaux, 22 Nov. 1886, 4 Nov., 3 Dec. 1895, AE Hanotaux MSS, 21.

[48] Defrance to Chevandrier de Valdrome, 15 Jan. 1907, 12 Feb. 1908, AE Chevandrier de Valdrome MSS.

[49] Defrance to Lemonnier, 15 Oct. 1908, AE *dossier personnel*, Defrance.

[50] Miller, 'Pichon', p. 4.

[51] Pichon to Hanotaux, 24 Mar. 1898, AE Hanotaux MSS, 28.

sincerity and did not expect a cordial relationship to develop. He was convinced that the best way to deal with Berlin was through a position of diplomatic and military strength. The main objective was to achieve greater security by strengthening existing ties with Russia and Britain and by seeking agreements with other powers such as Italy and Japan.

That Pichon's goals were limited was apparent from the outset of his ministry, when Cambon went to Norderney (situated off the German mainland), to discuss with Chancellor von Bülow a range of issues leading to *rapprochement*. Pichon stressed in his instructions the need to be extremely circumspect. While not rejecting out of hand any concrete proposal by Berlin, he made it clear that Cambon was not to take the initiative.[52] After the meeting, a *communiqué* which was drafted by Cambon and which spoke of a 'parfait accord des vues' was reduced by Pichon to a rather meaningless note to the press.[53] As he explained to the Ambassador in July 1907: 'Mais quant au fond, je reste malheureuse-ment convaincu que l'Allemagne ne poursuit qu'un but dans l'impuiss-ance où elle est: nous attacher à elle par une alliance, se réserver les moyens de créer une division de notre côté le jour où elle serait conduit à un conflit avec l'Angleterre.'[54]

A series of incidents in Casablanca, which erupted in 1907 and continued until 1909, intensified Pichon's distrust of Berlin. The first incident began in the summer of 1907, when anti-foreign outbreaks led to the murder of a French national, Dr Émile Mauchamp. France retaliated with the bombardment of Casablanca, and the occupation of Uida (north-west Morocco) and the whole of the Shawia region on the Atlantic coast. Then, in September 1908, tension arose when three German deserters from the French Foreign Legion were taken forcibly from the custody of a German consular official. Germany's public announcements that she would not aggravate the general situation in Morocco were not matched by the actions of her agents.[55] When Jules Cambon suggested the idea of an economic agreement which would recognize France's political ascendancy, Pichon had serious reserva-tions. At first he wanted to include Spain and Great Britain in the conversations, and took the view that any economic agreement with Berlin would give her *carte blanche* to meddle further in the affairs of the Maghzen. At any rate, Germany's economic interests there were

[52] Pichon to J. Cambon, 18 July 1907, AE J. Cambon MSS, 16.
[53] Pichon to J. Cambon, 22 July 1907, AE NS, 'Allemagne', 3.
[54] Pichon to J. Cambon, 18 July 1907, AE J. Cambon MSS, 16.
[55] Pichon to Barrère, 25 May 1907, Inst. de Fr. Pichon MSS, 4.

inferior to France's and any collaboration would need to take this fact into account.[56]

By the end of 1908 Cambon's attempts to convince Pichon that Berlin was not totally insincere were having greater success.[57] Indeed, in February 1909 France and Germany signed an accord which reaffirmed the independence and integrity of Morocco. What was perhaps more to the point, Germany recognized France's predominant political influence in the territory while in return France agreed to safeguard Germany's commercial interests and to include German nationals in future economic concessions. Admittedly, during the weeks which preceded the agreement, Pichon remained highly suspicious, needing to be personally convinced by Cambon.[58] Even after it was signed he emphasized to Paul Cambon that it meant 'absolument rien', and mocked those who saw it as the beginning of a Franco-German fraternity.[59] He seems to have been moved by several considerations in accepting the accord. A growing internal opposition was accusing him of being Delcassé's successor and heir.[60] *Combisme* had enfeebled the French army. Russian military weakness after the Russo-Japanese war of 1904 and her diplomatic blundering in the Near Eastern crisis of 1908 had, for the moment, made her something of a negligible quantity. Finally, tension caused by events in the Balkans and Morocco made some sort of Franco-German *modus vivendi* essential. Indeed the political aspect outweighed the economic.[61]

It was with such ideas in mind that Pichon briefly envisaged a liquidation of the Baghdad railway affair. He recognized that a settlement of the problem would be advantageous. It would be more difficult for Germany to seek political squabbles with France when the two countries had just signed a major economic agreement. Besides, London and St Petersburg appeared to be conniving behind Paris's back. Feelings of loyalty were yielding to fears that France would be left out. In the end, however, Pichon's suspicion of Germany reasserted itself, and he came to see Baghdad railway discussions as something of a trap.[62] France's

[56] Pichon to J. Cambon, 22 July 1908, AE NS 'Allemagne', 31.

[57] Miller, 'Pichon', p. 210.

[58] Louis to Pichon, 14 Jan. 1911, Inst. de Fr. Pichon MSS, 3.

[59] Pichon to P. Cambon, 22 Feb. 1909, Inst. de Fr. Pichon MSS, 2.

[60] Comte de Saint-Aulaire, *Confessions d'un vieux diplomate* (Paris, 1953), p. 204.

[61] Pichon to Paul Cambon, 22 Feb. 1909, Inst. de Fr. Pichon MSS, 2. See also E. W. Edwards, 'The Franco-German Agreement on Morocco 1909', *English Historical Review*, 81 (1966).

[62] Pichon to J. Cambon, 1 Aug. 1907, 1, 10 July 1908, 26 Jan. 1911, J. Cambon to Pichon, 29 Nov. 1909, AE Cambon MSS, 16.

policy of a four-power internationalization of the loan remained in effect.

At the same time, Pichon was hardly enamoured of St Petersburg. Had there not been a signed agreement between the two countries, Pichon mused, one would hardly have known that Russia was France's ally. Although diplomatic considerations were uppermost in his mind, ideological or political factors contributed to his distrust of Russia. As a young left-wing Radical defending the Republic in the nineteenth century, he had been critical of the autocratic and repressive system of the tsars.[63] As a diplomat in China, he had opposed the manner in which the Russian government pursued its aims to the detriment of the Franco-Russian alliance. When he became foreign minister, this attitude did not completely disappear. The Near Eastern crisis of 1908-9, as much the product of the intrigues of Russian Foreign Minister Isvolsky as of the Austrian Minister Aehrenthal, strengthened his mistrust of St Petersburg. By the time of the Russo-German Potsdam talks in 1910 he was very seriously concerned over the state of the alliance despite his optimistic remarks to the Chamber. Although he was convinced that the talks would fail in the end, this did not excuse the 'légèreté' of Russia. It was evident to him that France had no choice but to scrutinize the behaviour of her ally with considerable vigilance.[64]

Undoubtedly, Pichon's dislike of Russia moderated somewhat as he became older. As foreign minister, he viewed the Franco-Russian alliance as the cornerstone of France's security and sought to make it an effective diplomatic and military instrument.[65] On the other hand, his endorsement of the alliance did not mean that he was prepared to be subservient to Russia. It took no less than a twenty-one-page private letter from Paul Cambon in 1907 to persuade him to drop a scheme for a Franco-Japanese political agreement which would in no way be regarded as favourable to St Petersburg.[66]

London was much more to Pichon's liking. He had been critical during his youth of the British monarchy, but was generally sympathetic to Britain's democratic system. More importantly, however, he felt that Great Britain was the key to keeping Germany in check. Even in the 1880s, when most French politicians were advocating the evacuation of

[63] *La Justice*, 18 Jan. 1890, 11 Oct. 1891.

[64] Pichon to P. Cambon, 25 Jan. 1911, AE P. Cambon MSS, 4; Pichon to J. Cambon, 26 Jan. 1911, AE Cambon MSS, 16.

[65] Bertie to Grey, 29 Oct. 1910, FO 371/74.

[66] *La Justice*, 18 Jan., 11 Oct. 1891; P. Cambon to Pichon, 3 July 1907, Inst. de Fr. Pichon MSS, 2.

Egypt by Britain, Pichon favoured a Franco-British *rapprochement*.[67] When the *Entente Cordiale* came into operation he enthusiastically supported it.[68] Throughout his ministry he attempted to strengthen Franco-British links, primarily by urging an Anglo-Russian *entente* but also by promoting the Anglo-Spanish Mediterranean agreement of 1907. His proposal for a political treaty with Japan was largely motivated by the hope that such an agreement would meet with British approval.[69] Equally, his fear of improving Franco-German relations was in part derived from his belief that it was not the most suitable period to test the British friendship excessively.[70] Although Britain was not as energetic as he might have wished, he admired her respect for the given word and her loyal behaviour towards friends.

Pichon's sympathies towards Italy were no less conspicuous. He was an Italophile by nature and believed that the two nations had an identity of race and a community of aspirations and interests.[71] Though the Italian government was still committed to the Triple Alliance, the majority of the Italian public looked to Paris rather than to Berlin for friendship.[72] Even before the agreements made in the Delcassian period, he had advocated the detachment of Italy from the Triple Alliance.[73] He appeared to envisage nothing less than a Franco-Italian alliance, and on assuming the Foreign Ministry he spoke of improved relations with Italy as 'l'un des points essentiels de ma tâche, un de ceux qui me préoccupent personellement le plus'.[74] Consequently, he attached a high priority to the work of Barrère and, despite his desire to transfer Legrand from Rome to the central administration in 1909, he deferred to Barrère's wish to retain him. The Franco-Italian agreement of 1907 was used almost uniquely to strengthen Franco-Italian relations.[75] In later years Pichon's affinity with Italy remained strong. After resigning in 1911 he undertook a trip to Italy and became a member of the Comité France-Italie, whose avowed aim was the improvement of Franco-Italian relations.[76]

Pichon's attitude towards Austria was less consistent. In the two years before the Near Eastern crisis of 1908-9 he tended to agree with Ambas-

---

[67] Miller, 'Pichon', p. 44.
[68] Pichon to Delcassé, 13 Apr. 1904, AE Delcassé MSS, 5.
[69] Pichon to Gérard, 23 Nov. 1906, AE NS 'Japon', 72.
[70] Pichon to Louis, 22 July 1907, AE Louis MSS, 2.
[71] *La Justice*, 12 Oct. 1883.   [72] Bax-Ironside to Grey, 24 July 1909, FO 371/668.
[73] *La Justice*, 12 Oct. 1883.
[74] Ibid.; Pichon to Barrère, 16 Jan. 1907, 8 June 1908, AE Barrère MSS, 4.
[75] Miller, 'Pichon', p. 143.   [76] Ibid.

sador Crozier's view that Vienna was more than the plaything of Berlin. He praised Austria's refusal to be Germany's instrument during the First Moroccan Crisis, and he was anxious not to alienate Austria in seeking better relations with Italy.[77] The Balkan crisis, however, appears to have opened his eyes. By July of 1909, Bax-Ironside, British minister to Sofia, could report to Grey that, diplomatically, Pichon saw little difference in policy between Berlin and Vienna.[78] Saint-Aulaire was recalled from Morocco and sent to Vienna to keep an eye on Crozier's activities in the Austrian capital.[79] By the end of his ministry Pichon was dismissing Crozier's appeals for tighter links with Austria, and generally felt that Austria's inability to solve her nationalities problem would doom her to destruction or oblivion.

If Austria was incapable of handling her subject nationalities, Turkey simply refused to do so. Pichon was disappointed with the Young Turks who had overthrown the Sultan in 1908, and thought that their failure to make reforms stemmed from an emphasis on nationalism. He believed that the ambition and intrigues of the Committee of Unity and Progress were to blame for many Near Eastern problems, especially the Cretan question.[80]

When the Near Eastern crisis of 1908–9 arose, as a result of the Austrian annexation of Bosnia-Hercegovina and of Bulgaria's declaration of independence, it left French policy under Pichon in something of a quandary. His own pro-Slav bureaux were pushing him away from official disinterest in the area and towards support for Russia, who had not received her quid pro quo, the Straits. Though disillusioned with the Young Turk regime, suspicious of Austria-Hungary supported by Germany, and fearful of Russian disappointment and anger, he did not want to see the breakdown of the Ottoman Empire. At this stage it would lead to war and seriously hinder French interests. Especially under the guidance of Paul Cambon and Louis, Pichon's policy in the end was to restrain Russia and accept the changes already wrought. He was convinced that the only way to avoid war in the Near East was to maintain the status quo by establishing a concert of the major European powers and by following a firm policy towards the Porte.[81]

The Moroccan question preoccupied Pichon more than any other during the period. He intended to observe strictly the agreements made

[77] Pichon to Barrère, 8 June 1908, AE Barrère MSS, 4.
[78] Bax-Ironside to Grey, 24 July 1909, FO 371/668.
[79] Saint-Aulaire, *Confessions*, p. 209.
[80] Pichon to Louis, 17, 27 Aug. 1909, AE Louis MSS, 2.
[81] Ibid., Louis to Pichon, 18, 21 Aug. 1909.

at Algeçiras in 1906, and he thought that the natural evolution of events would work in France's favour.[82] Appeals from men like Minister Regnault, the military, and the Colonial party did little to impress him. Rather, he fully concurred with Cambon's formula of slow but steady progress.[83]

Pichon was more enthusiastic about expansion in Asia than in North Africa. As minister to China in the late 1890s he had unsuccessfully called for a halt to France's open-door policy, arguing that Russia, Germany, and Great Britain were carving up the Manchu empire into spheres of influence.[84] The Russo-Japanese war had clearly transformed the map of Asia, and Pichon believed that Russia's influence would continue to wane. Though it was not he who had sent Gérard to Tokyo, but rather Bourgeois, he fully agreed with Gérard's work and actively supported it.[85]

Though many of his policies in the Far East derived from his personal assessment of French interests, on the whole Pichon was strongly influenced by the Cambons, Barrère, and Louis. Louis's views were predominant in the area of Franco-German relations. He was certainly much more of a Germanophobe than polemical writing suggested after the First World War. His mistrust of Germany made him extremely cautious despite the fact that he was not in principle against a *détente* with Berlin. He had a large part in persuading Pichon to limit the scope of the Norderney talks. Small specific arrangements and courteous conversation were as far as Louis wanted to go. Some minor differences in Central Africa could be resolved, but, apart from that, France had only to listen.[86] Although he agreed that it was necessary to go to Norderney, he did so for tactical reasons. He believed that the Germans were making a rather shallow gesture in response to French criticism that they had never done anything concrete to promote a *rapprochement*. Even if Schön, the German foreign minister, or Wilhelm II were sincere, the Wilhelmstraße, which had convened the meeting, could not be trusted. Finally, France had to be concerned about her relations with Britain and Russia. Even if Berlin was not trying to break up the Triple *Entente*,

---

[82] J. C. Allain, *Agadir* (Paris, 1978), p. 265; Miller, 'Pichon', pp. 178, 231, 232; Pichon to P. Cambon, 29 Jan. 1911, AE P. Cambon MSS, 4.

[83] Pichon to J. Cambon, 22 July 1907, 1 Feb. 1910, AE J. Cambon MSS, 16.

[84] Pichon to Hanotaux, 24 May 1898, AE Hanotaux MSS, 28.

[85] Pichon to Gérard, 29 July 1907, AN 329 AP 20 Gérard MSS.

[86] Louis to Pichon, 17 July 1907, Inst. de Fr. Pichon MSS, 3.

which he felt she was, a Franco-German *rapprochement* might create a negative reaction in St Petersburg and London.[87]

As Louis expected, the Norderney talks produced little in the way of detailed arrangements.[88] The Casablanca incidents, for their part, confirmed his belief that Germany was pursuing an obstructionist policy in Morocco. It appeared to Louis that the German consul had wantonly intervened to aid the escape of Foreign Legion deserters. France's rights in the affair were unimpeachable, and Louis found Jules Cambon's desire for concessions excessive. Not only was he successful in persuading Pichon to adopt a harder line, but he appears to have prevented an early end to the affair by dilatory tactics and leaks to the press.[89]

Louis and Jules Cambon came into direct conflict over Franco-German economic collaboration in Morocco. In principle Louis did not reject the proposal, but he was fearful of upsetting arrangements previously made. Any agreement had to include the British and the Spanish, and only after the other two powers had refused to enter *pourparlers* could bilateral talks with Berlin be considered.[90] Though incapable of blocking an agreement, he prevailed upon Pichon to ensure that the pact was superficial in character. Even after the signing, he warned Jules Cambon that the agreement would raise immense difficulties in Madrid.[91]

Although Louis differed with Jules Cambon over Franco-German relations, he shared the Cambons' assessment of Great Britain as the key to the balance of power on the European continent. He was careful not to undertake any measure that would alienate the British government, and he was highly appreciative of Britain's loyalty.[92] Louis's opinion was that Britain had proven her reliability during the First Moroccan Crisis of 1905.[93] Consequently, he was instrumental in facilitating the Mediterranean agreements with Spain and Britain, and he tried to smooth over difficulties between the Russian and British governments.[94]

[87] Ibid., Louis to Pichon, 21 May 1907; Louis to Cambon, 11 June, 22 Aug. 1907, 18 Oct. 1908, 26 Aug. 1909, 16 Sept. 1911, J. Cambon to Louis, 24 June, 19 July, 27 Aug., 16 Sept. 1907, AE J. Cambon MSS, 15.

[88] Annotation by Louis on J. Cambon's letter to Louis, 29 Oct. 1908, AE Louis MSS, 2.

[89] Ibid.; J. Cambon to Louis, 29 Sept., 27, 29 Oct. 1908, P. Cambon to J. Cambon, 31 Oct., 10 Nov. 1908, AE J. Cambon MSS, 25.

[90] J. Cambon to P. Cambon, 14 Nov. 1908, AE J. Cambon MSS, 19; Miller, 'Pichon', p. 217.

[91] Louis to J. Cambon, 11 Feb. 1909, AE J. Cambon MSS, 15.

[92] Louis to Pichon, 19, 31 Aug. 1909, 24 Dec. 1910, Inst. de Fr. Pichon MSS, 3.

[93] Note by Gavarry, undated, AE Revoil MSS, 2.   [94] Miller, 'Pichon', p. 151.

At times, however, he thought Britain naïve, especially when it came to German naval promises and to her interest in the Baltic.[95]

Louis's role in the 1908 Balkan crisis was substantial. He strengthened and gave effect to Pichon's disinclination to support Russia's adventurism in the Balkans.[96] Indeed, Louis was clearly apprehensive about European peace after the measures undertaken by Bulgaria and Austria-Hungary in response to the Young Turk Revolution. He considered that the status quo maintained by a concert of the major European powers was the only means of avoiding a serious conflagration.[97] Initially he opposed the notion of a conference, fearing that Germany and Austria-Hungary would find such a gathering advantageous. He went so far as to sabotage Jules Cambon's quest for one.[98] By the summer of 1909, however, he had considerably modified his position because he feared the consequences of the Greco-Turkish quarrel over Crete.[99] Though an appeal to Germany and Austria was not without problems, peace could best be maintained by making joint representations to the Porte.[100] Louis regarded Austria as the initiator of most problems in the Balkans, but he thought that firmness was necessary in dealing with the Turkish government.[101]

Although Near Eastern issues were of increasing concern to French policy-makers during the years 1907-09, Franco-German relations continued to receive top priority. It was during this period that Jules Cambon, under the protective wings of Pichon and his brother, sought to impress his views on the Centrale and the government. Undoubtedly, his pleas for improved relations almost single-handedly resulted in the 1909 Franco-German accord. But he continued to meet with resistance from the Centrale. The 1909 agreement was given quite limited substance. The Centrale's obstruction was a constant source of irritation for Cambon. In the final analysis he was forced to recognize that, while he could smooth over repeated difficulties between France and Germany,

[95] Louis to Pichon, 19, 30 July 1907, Inst. de Fr. Pichon MSS, 3.

[96] Pichon to Louis, 27 Aug. 1909, AE Louis MSS, 2.

[97] Louis to P. Cambon, 8 Oct. 1908, AE P. Cambon MSS, 4; Louis to Pichon, 17, 18, 21 Aug. 1909, Inst. de Fr. Pichon MSS, 3; Louis to J. Cambon, 26 Aug. 1909, AE J. Cambon MSS, 15.

[98] Louis stopped the Cambons' pursuit of a conference by having the *Agence Havas* prematurely leak news of their intentions. See P. Cambon to Barrère, 17 Oct. 1908, *Correspondance*, ii. 247.

[99] J. Cambon to Pichon, 3 Apr. 1909, AE J. Cambon MSS, 16.

[100] Louis to J. Cambon, 26 Aug. 1909, AE J. Cambon MSS, 15.

[101] Louis to Pichon, 5, 14, 15, 18 Aug. 1909, Inst. de Fr. Pichon MSS, 3.

he could not usher in a new period in which the two states were no longer 'chiens de faïence'.

As Keiger has remarked, of all the French ambassadors before 1914 Jules Cambon 'alone possessed a policy which actively sought from its inception to avert a European war'. His design was to release tension in Europe by the establishment of more cordial relations between France and Germany.[102] To be sure, Cambon was not seeking a realignment of forces in the traditional way. France would continue to remain strictly faithful to her ally Russia and to her *Entente* partner Britain.[103] A Franco-German *entente* was undesirable, he thought, because Germany might use such an agreement to alienate France's friends and to reduce her to a subservient status. Rather, he advocated an end to mutual hatred and a more systematic attempt to find common ground when diplomatic problems arose; in short, a *détente* in which the two countries would be 'en bonnes termes'. Initially, Cambon envisaged agreements in particular areas of mutual interest, but within a year he had broadened this programme to embrace a more European policy, as he termed it, whereby the traditional alliance systems would eventually be replaced by a rational consideration of the interests of Europe as a whole. While Cambon was far from anticipating the League of Nations and did not propose the setting up of formal diplomatic machinery, he was clearly seeking a new means of overcoming traditional conflicts in order to avoid a world war. He had mocked Bourgeois's concept of arbitration, but by the end of 1908 he felt that there was a place in it for the solution of Franco-German problems.[104]

Undoubtedly, Cambon's pursuit of *détente* was the product of his obsession with the dangers of a general conflagration. When criticized by Pichon for being haunted by the memory of Benedetti and the Ems telegram, he made no attempt to defend himself. He thought that every effort should be made to promote peace. As he told Louis in December 1907, 'au moment où ... elle [Germany] est obligée d'avoir la conversation et de prendre une initiative avec nous ... nous devons éviter à tout prix de prendre celle de l'échec d'une entente'.[105] That this policy was

[102] J. F. V. Keiger, 'Raymond Poincaré and French Foreign Policy, 1912–1914' (Cambridge University, 1980), p. 128. See also J. F. V. Keiger *France and the Origins of the First World War* (London, 1983), pp. 37.

[103] J. Cambon to P. Cambon, 21 July 1907, AE J. Cambon MSS, 19.

[104] Ibid., J. Cambon to P. Cambon, 15, 21 July 1907; J. Cambon to Louis, 4 Feb., 4, 10 May, 11 Oct. 1908, AE Louis MSS, 2; J. Cambon to Pichon, 23 Dec. 1907, 22 Feb., 14 Mar., 21 Sept. 1908, 22 Feb., 24 June 1909, Inst. de Fr. Pichon MSS, 1.

[105] P. Cambon to J. Cambon, 8 Mar. 1912, AE J. Cambon MSS, 25; J. Cambon to P. Cambon, 12 Mar. 1911, AE J. Cambon MSS, 19; J. Cambon to Pichon, 17 June 1908, Inst. de Fr. Pichon MSS, 1; J. Cambon to Louis, 29 June 1907, AE Louis MSS, 2.

largely motivated by a concern for peace is evident in Cambon's justification of *détente*:

Cette entente rendra ce qu'elle rendra, pas grand chose probablement, mais elle aura tout de même pour un temps éclairci l'horizon: cela nous donnera une matinée de printemps où nous pouvons sortir sans parapluie; c'est quelque chose et l'Allemagne trouvera là le prétexte pour se montrer d'une façon explicable aux yeux des chanoines allemands accommodante au Maroc ... Si on ne poursuit pas une politique réaliste, positive, si on poursuit autre chose au temps, qu'on le dise, mais le temps n'aurait pas assez de sûreté pour le ministre qui nous conduirait à la guerre.[106]

Cambon was not a pacifist. Rather, he was pacific. He was not a 'dove', and was the supreme critic of parliamentary, press, and labour representatives who climbed on to the bandwagon of peace and arbitration.[107] Though there was much idealism in his thinking, he was also influenced by military factors. He recognized the military unpreparedness of France and the ineffectiveness of the Franco-Russian alliance after the Russo-Japanese war.[108]

Cambon had been sent to Berlin specifically to repair the damage done by Bihourd, whose sympathy to Germany and whose apparent willingness to talk to Berlin had alarmed the Centrale. A profound transformation had occurred, however, in Cambon's attitudes and was noticeable at the time of the Norderney talks with von Bülow in the summer of 1907. When he came into contact with policy-makers in Berlin, he was surprised to discover that men such as Wilhelm II, Schön, Tschirsky, and Eülenburg appeared sincere in wanting a *détente* with France.[109] Von Bülow, though no friend of France, was too much of a European and too much like a member of the English gentry to begin a general conflagration. It appeared to Cambon that, although Berlin was no lamb, many of the difficulties in Franco-German relations had been caused more by misapprehension than by design. Indeed, of the two powers, France, who was unable to control her press, public opinion, and Parliament, and to follow one line consistently, was primarily at fault.

Cambon was not about to rush into any quick agreement with Berlin, although the opportunity presented itself at Norderney. First, he feared

[106] J. Cambon to Louis, 23 Dec. 1907, AE Louis MSS, 2.
[107] Ibid.; J. Cambon to Louis, 13 Apr. 1909, AE J. Cambon MSS, 15.
[108] Ibid., 4 Feb. 1908.
[109] Ibid. 15, 16, J. Cambon to Paléologue, 13, 20 May 1912, J. Cambon to Pichon, 19 Nov. 1908; J. Cambon to Louis, 22 May, 16 July, 24 Aug. 1908, AE Louis MSS, 2.

that any accord too hastily concluded and not representing the wills of the two peoples would be doomed to failure.[110] Secondly, he feared the personal failure which might result from an initiative on his part.[111] Thirdly, he did not wish to associate himself with the feelers of amateurs like Étienne, who had just made a trip to Kiel to see the Emperor, or with the work of certain journalists who aroused excessive expectations among the French public.[112] Consequently, before the talks at Norderney, he argued that France should be content to discuss and, if possible, agree on matters of secondary importance. Within a year, however, he was envisaging a general European settlement. Whereas in 1907 he believed it was wrong for France to be included in the regatta at Kiel, in the following year he tried to convince Pichon that France's exclusion was inadmissible.[113]

It was apparent to Cambon that justifiable German grievances had not been given sufficient attention by the Centrale. Germany's defence of her industrialists and financiers abroad was not a policy designed to cause continual friction with Paris but one determined by internal considerations. To some extent, acceptance of German expansion overseas would act as a safety valve and help to create an era of *détente* between the two countries.[114] Cambon consistently urged the French government to co-operate with Germany in the Baghdad railway scheme, but after four years he had achieved little. Pichon was too fearful of alienating Russia and Great Britain.[115]

Cambon also had trouble in getting the Centrale to accept his view of the Casablanca incidents. He tried to convince Paris that Germany was largely conciliatory and that much of the blame rested with France herself. Germany was concerned that General Lyautey was giving to his relief column the 'allure de conquête'. Cambon himself was alarmed at the way in which French soldiers and civilians had seen the affair as a pretext for military penetration.[116] His observations were badly received by the Centrale, which thought his attitude far too soft.[117]

Cambon's work was not a total failure. He and his brother were

[110] J. Cambon to Pichon, 23 June 1907, AE J. Cambon MSS, 16.
[111] Ibid., J. Cambon to P. Cambon, 15 July 1907.
[112] Ibid.   [113] Ibid., J. Cambon to Pichon, 24 June 1906, 3 Mar. 1908.
[114] Keiger, 'Poincaré', p. 318; J. Bariéty and R. Poidevin, *Les Relations franco-allemandes, 1815–1975* (Paris, 1972), p. 818; Keiger, *France and the Origins*, p. 39.
[115] J. Cambon to Louis, 24, 29 June 1907, J. Cambon to Pichon, 6 Feb. 1911, AE J. Cambon MSS, 15, 16.
[116] J. Cambon to Pichon, 6 Feb. 1909, Inst. de Fr. Pichon MSS, 3.
[117] J. Cambon to Louis, 26 Jan., 29 Sept., 29 Oct. 1908, AE Louis MSS, 2; J. Cambon to Pichon, 30 Mar., 10 May, 14, 29 Sept. 1908, AE J. Cambon MSS, 15.

successful in persuading Pichon not to rush penetration into
Morocco.[118] Moreover, Jules Cambon converted Pichon to the idea of
German economic collaboration in Morocco. The Foreign Minister
agreed that the German goverment, no longer harassed by industrialists
like the Mannesmann brothers, would cease to make Morocco an issue.
The Franco-German discussion of Moroccan affairs which Cambon
had advocated as early as July 1907 therefore began. Cambon was the
moving force behind the negotiations.[119]

The February 1909 agreement came as a surprise to many French
diplomats. Paul Cambon was astonished that it had ever been reached,
and suspicion and intransigence on the part of Louis and the Centrale
made it an empty letter. The limitations of Cambon's influence were no
less apparent during the Near-Eastern crisis of 1908-9. Admittedly, his
pro-Slav, anti-Austrian sentiments strengthened France's readiness to
champion the rights of the Balkan countries. However, his attitude
merely reflected the majority viewpoint in the Quai d'Orsay. Cambon
considered Austria-Hungary to be doomed and thought that she had
made herself the chief troublemaker in the Balkans not so much to
expand but to survive. Even with Germany's help he believed that
Austria-Hungary would eventually collapse and that, therefore, France
should recognize the power shift in favour of the newer countries, Serbia
and Bulgaria. If Bulgaria was not recognized by France, it would gravi-
tate towards the German sphere of influence.[120]

Admittedly, too, Cambon's attitude towards Russia during the Near
Eastern crisis was of some significance. In general, he was even more
severe on St Petersburg than his brother, and denounced Russian
adventurism in the Balkans. When the St Petersburg Embassy later
became free, Jules wrote emphatically to Paul: 'J'aimerais aller à Rome,
mais je ne veux pas aller à Pétersbourg où tout me déplaît.'[121] Militarily,
Russia was weak. Diplomatically she was disloyal.[122]

[118] J. Cambon to P. Cambon 18 May, 2 Nov. 1908, AE J. Cambon MSS, 19; J. Cambon
to Pichon, 14 Sept. 1908, Inst. de Fr. Pichon MSS, 2.
[119] P. Cambon to Pichon, 6 Feb. 1909, J. Cambon to Pichon, 25 Jan. 1909, Inst. de Fr.
Pichon MSS, 3; J. Cambon to Louis, 19 July 1907, AE Louis MSS, 2. For a full discussion on
the agreement see E. W. Edwards, 'The French–German Agreement on Morocco, 1909',
pp. 483–513.
[120] J. Cambon to Pichon, 25 Jan. 1909, 28 Apr. 1913, Inst. de Fr. Pichon MSS, 3; J.
Cambon to Poincaré, 9 Dec. 1912, AE J. Cambon MSS, 16; G. Tabouis, *Jules Cambon par
l'un des siens* (Paris, 1938), p. 231.
[121] J. Cambon to P. Cambon, 9 Sept. 1912, Louis Cambon MSS.
[122] J. Cambon to Delcassé, 8 Apr. 1905, AE Delcassé MSS, 2; J. Cambon to P. Cambon,
20 Mar. 1909, AE P. Cambon MSS, 12; J. Cambon to Pichon, 4 Aug. 1913, AE Cambon
MSS, 16.

Russia's ambitions in the Balkans, her claim to be the only *interlocuteur* with the Balkan states, and the intrigues of Foreign Minister Isvolsky absolutely horrified him. Cambon contributed to the rather cold reception which the French government gave to Isvolsky's programme and policies. Nevertheless, he advocated strict fidelity to the Franco-Russian alliance if circumstances warranted it.[123] He was mindful that 'si nous voulons garder figure en ce monde, il nous faut rester fidèle à nos obligations d'alliés'. However, he warned Pichon: 'Je doute que nos chambres et notre démocratie aient un sentiment aussi vif de ce que sont les devoirs internationaux. Par suite je doute que le gouvernement puisse entraîner à une guerre à propos de la Serbie notre pays qui sait quel est l'enjeu de la partie et qui ne se croît pas personellement visé comme dans l'affaire de Casablanca.'[124]

Consequently, Cambon did play a significant part in restraining Russia and Austria-Hungary. But the main points of his programme were rejected by the Centrale and by Pichon, who was under the influence of Louis. Cambon's belief that the key to the Moroccan crisis lay in Near Eastern events and that Macedonian unrest was in France's interest was altered by the Austro-Russian collision.[125] Circumstances now required the collaboration of the Great Powers, and nothing should be done to alienate Germany. On this particular point Cambon's influence was minimal. He failed to convince the Centrale that Berlin, while faithfully supporting her ally, was not behind the crisis and that she was equally anxious to keep the peace. His comment that Kaiser Wilhelm was not only willing to talk with Paris but prepared to 'tendre la main en orient et suivre une politique parallèle' fell on stony ground. While Cambon was sufficiently powerful to stop a war breaking out, there was little he could do to reduce the tension in Franco-German relations.[126]

His failure to arrive at a deep and meaningful *détente* was the product of several factors, but at the root of the problem lay the intransigence of the Centrale and the absence of widespread support among his fellow ambassadors. While Pichon and Cambon were in agreement in principle on the necessity of *rapprochement* and though Pichon sincerely sup-

[123] J. Cambon to Poincaré, 29 Dec. 1912, J. Cambon to Paléologue, 18 Mar., 29 Oct. 1912, J. Cambon to Pichon, 3 June 1913, J. Cambon to P. Cambon, AE J. Cambon MSS, 15, 16, 19.
[124] For the British position on the crises see M. B. Cooper, 'British Policy in the Balkans 1908-9', *Historical Journal*, 7 (1964-5); J. Cambon to Louis, 26 Oct. 1908, AE Louis MSS, 2; J. Cambon to Pichon, 8, 10, 12, 17 Mar., 14 June 1909, AE J. Cambon MSS, 15.
[125] J. Cambon to Pichon, 14, 29 Sept. 1908, AE J. Cambon MSS, 15.
[126] Ibid., J. Cambon to Pichon, 5 Oct., 8 Mar., 3 Apr., 12 May 1908.

ported the efforts of his Ambassador in Berlin, the suspicion of officials at the Centrale triumphed in the end. No sooner had the February 1909 agreement been signed than Paris found proof in the Potsdam talks that Berlin was up to her old tricks.[127] The Centrale was quick to incite press attacks against Berlin, to leak important information in order to sabotage negotiations, to delay *pourparlers*, and generally to create an atmosphere which envenomed Franco-German relations. In government circles there were those who disliked him, a legacy of his Algerian days.[128] When Jules wanted something done he usually approached his brother first and the foreign minister later. Moreover, he had made little effort to build up a power base in the Centrale. His obstinacy and his willingness to criticize those who opposed him made him some influential enemies. Despite Cambon's unpopularity, however, he was the only member of the French diplomatic corps who had a concrete, workable programme for avoiding a major war.

While Jules Cambon's fortunes fluctuated, Paul Cambon steadily increased his authority. Pichon was inclined to regard him as his chief adviser and made very few decisions without his approval. Cambon, for his part, wrote voluminous letters to Pichon as he had done with Delcassé, and usually managed to visit Pichon once every two weeks.[129] Though Cambon was critical of Pichon's timidity and of his general laziness, these characteristics could be turned to the Ambassador's advantage. Unlike Delcassé, Pichon seemed incapable of disregarding Cambon's wishes. Moreover, Cambon was the only one who could hold his own with Clemenceau.

Cambon enjoyed considerable success during the years 1907–9. His prestige had suffered somewhat as a result of Delcassé's fall, but events had proved that a firm stand against Berlin did not necessarily lead to war. While the Franco-British military conversations of January 1906 appear initially to have been conceived by Jules, Paul quickly embraced the idea and was happy with the results. He did not regard a Franco-British alliance, for all its appeal, as a serious possibility. Writing to Pichon in Novermber 1906 he remarked that 'des garanties politiques sont sans valeur puisqu'elles n'ont pas de sanction et ne dépendent que de l'humeur des gens'. Apart from this rather resigned attitude, Cambon believed that Franco-British interests naturally coincided and that

---

[127] J. Cambon to Pichon, 18, 24 Nov. 1910, Inst. de Fr. Pichon MSS, 3.

[128] See article by A. Tudesq in *Action française*, Jan. 1912, in AN 329 AP 19 Gérard MSS.

[129] See esp. Pichon to P. Cambon, 22 Nov. 1906, Inst. de Fr. Pichon MSS, 2.

Britain would be a faithful partner anyway. Small technical accords, such as the military conversations of 1906, the Mediterranean agreement of 1907, and the Grey–Cambon letters of 1912, did more to bind the two countries together than any formal alliance.[130]

Cambon's influence was unchallenged during the Franco-Japanese talks of late 1906. Pichon believed that a political *entente* was of vital importance to France's empire in the Orient, to good Anglo-Japanese-Russian relations, and to the undermining of German influence in Japan. Despite the fact that Pichon won Clemenceau's approval for the scheme, Paul Cambon was able to veto the idea and to modify it so that it was limited to an economic *entente*. While the London Ambassador was no lover of St Petersburg and was critical of the manner in which French interests had been subordinated to Russia's, he was nevertheless a supporter of the Franco-Russian alliance. He successfully argued that a Franco-Japanese agreement would unnecessarily irritate the Russian government, which was still smarting from defeat at the hands of Japan.[131]

Paul was not as anti-German as the Centrale. He did not blame Berlin for all the diplomatic difficulties which arose in the period 1907-9. His own assessment, supported by long conversations with his brother, was that France should be prepared to talk to Germany. While he complained of Germany's actions during the Casablanca incidents of 1907-9 and the Near Eastern crisis of 1908-9. he tended to blame the fickle nature of the Kaiser or the inconsistency of leading German officials. Berlin, he thought, was not trying to pick a quarrel with France or to isolate her from Britain and Russia. Consequently, while he had little to do with the 1909 accord, he fully applauded and supported his brother's work. At the same time, however, he did not believe that the two countries could achieve anything more than reasonable and courteous relations. If there were to be additional negotiations, France could only engage in them from a position of strength.[132]

On the whole, Cambon's approach to the Moroccan question remained predominant. His belief that Morocco would be gained through slow and natural advancement, by the sheer evolution of things, re-

---

[130] Ibid., P. Cambon to Pichon, 24 Nov. 1907.

[131] Ibid., Pichon to P. Cambon, 22 Nov. 1906; P. Cambon to Pichon, 21 Nov. 1906, AE P. Cambon MSS, II.

[132] P. Cambon to Pichon, 23 Nov. 1906, AE P. Cambon MSS, II; P. Cambon to J. Cambon, 9 Mar. 1909, AE J. Cambon MSS, 25; Miller, 'Pichon', p. 185; K. Eubank, *Paul Cambon* (Norman, Okla., 1960), pp. 59, 97; P. Cambon to Louis, 20 May 1909, AE Louis MSS, 2; P. Cambon to Pichon, 25 Feb. 1909, Inst. de Fr. Pichon MSS, 3.

mained unchanged. At times he could be energetic, espousing a vigorous policy during the Casablanca incidents. As long as Paris used force as a means of maintaining security in the Maghzen and not as a means to conquest, then Berlin would raise no objections. Though Germany did begin to object and he was for a time critical of his brother's conciliatory approach, his moderation ultimately prevailed. He believed more errors had been made in Paris than in Berlin and he feared that agents in the Centrale and on the spot in Morocco would regard the unrest in Casablanca as *carte blanche* for expansion.[133]

During the Bosnian crisis of 1908, Cambon's role was of fundamental importance and reflected his deeply pacific sentiments.[134] He considered the crisis as yet another example of the way in which the Russians were manipulating the alliance to support their adventurous policies. It was he more than anyone in the Clemenceau government or in the Quai d'Orsay who was responsible for France's refusal to support Russia. He was pleased, in fact, that Isvolsky had been sent packing. Though sympathetic towards the awakening Balkan nations, he was equally conscious of the strain which they placed on the integrity of the Ottoman Empire, whose disintegration, he thought, would seriously endanger European peace. Furthermore, though France was not vitally interested in the Near Eastern crisis, the Balkan states could not be allowed to dictate policy to the Great Powers.[135]

The Eastern question had preoccupied him from the time that he was ambassador to Constantinople. If Turkey was the sick man of Europe, it was largely Austria's doing. He considered Vienna to have been the leading generator of problems in the Balkans, and he was convinced that the day she marched into the area a general conflict would erupt.[136] A substantial effort to maintain the status quo on the part of the Great Powers appeared to him the only way to handle a problem that was largely 'improvisoire' in nature and incapable of a definitive solution in the near future.[137] Thus, the integrity of the Ottoman Empire loomed large in his thinking. As ambassador to Constantinople he had espoused a series of reforms in Armenia, Crete, and Macedonia which would have

[133] P. Cambon to Pichon, 1 Aug. 1907, Inst. de Fr. Pichon MSS, 3; P. Cambon to Jules Cambon, 6 Nov. 1908, *Correspondance*, ii. 251.

[134] Eubank, *Cambon*, p. 128.

[135] P. Cambon to Pichon, 1, 8, 24 Jan., 25 Feb., 20 Mar. 1909, Inst. de Fr. Pichon MSS, 3; P. Cambon to Louis, 28 Oct. 1908, AE Louis MSS, 2; P. Cambon to J. Cambon, 25 Mar. 1908, *Correspondance*, ii. 281.

[136] P. Cambon to Paléologue, 16 Oct. 1908, AE P. Cambon MSS, 12; Eubank, *Cambon*, p. 168; P. Cambon to Pichon, 26 July 1913, Inst. de Fr. Pichon MSS, 12.

[137] P. Cambon to J. Cambon, 11 Aug. 1908, *Correspondance*, ii. 244.

shored up Turkey. The arrival in power of the Young Turks in 1908 did not greatly enthuse him, but he thought that they might achieve some reforms and that they would weaken German influence at Constantinople.[138]

While Pichon, Louis, and the Cambons were primarily responsible for formulating France's policy during the Balkan crisis, Defrance, *sous-directeur du Levant*, played an important secondary role. Though France was not directly involved in the 1908-9 crisis, Defrance acted as an intermediary and helped to mend relations between Turkey and Bulgaria.[139] He thought that St Petersburg had betrayed the interests of the Balkan states in order to further her designs on the Straits. The lukewarm reception which Isvolsky's projects received in Paris was in part the result of Defrance's disgust.[140]

The deputy director's pro-Balkan proclivities derived from several considerations. Most importantly, he feared that Germany was expanding southward to the Mediterranean and Constantinople. The Balkan states would act as a natural buffer to this intrusion. Secondly, he was very much a part of the Sciences-po group in the Centrale, which looked favourably upon the rise of separate nationalities in the Balkans.[141] Finally, he appears to have succumbed to the personal charm of Ferdinand of Bulgaria.[142] In October 1908, in the middle of the crisis, he temporarily replaced Descos in Belgrade. Though he was in no way accredited to the Bulgarian court, he visited Sofia, where Ferdinand received him extremely warmly. Defrance came away convinced of Ferdinand's peaceful intentions and inclined to support his demands.

The influence exercised by Defrance and, to a large extent, by Paul Cambon was indicative of the power and authority of the Quai d'Orsay during the years 1907-9. Admittedly, the Quai was not called upon as was the case during the crises of 1905, 1911, and 1914 to conduct policy almost alone. Pichon enjoyed one of the most stable foreign ministries in the history of the Third Republic. Yet the power of the ambassadorial élite and of the Centrale was in no way diminished. The

---

[138] P. Cambon to J. Cambon, 22 Oct. 1908, AE J. Cambon MSS, 25; P. Cambon to Paléologue, 16 Oct. 1908, AE P. Cambon MSS, 12; Eubank, *Cambon*, p. 53.

[139] *DDF* (2), xi. 492; note in Defrance's handwriting, AE Defrance MSS, 3.

[140] Note, AE Defrance MSS, 3.

[141] Ibid.

[142] 'Entretien avec le Prince Ferdinand de Bulgarie à Sofia ce 23 October 1908', AE Defrance MSS, 3; Taigny to de Fleuriau, 26 October 1908, AE P. Cambon MSS, 12; Defrance to Lemonnier, 15 October 1908, AE *dossier personnel*, Defrance.

reforms of 1907 proved to be of limited importance. If, by 1911, two separate factions, the older ambassadorial élite and the 'Young Turks' of the Centrale, had taken shape and were vying with each other for ultimate power, it was precisely because nothing substantial had been done to alter the machinery of the Quai d'Orsay or the manner in which it functioned.

9

Internal Disarray and External Crisis: The Quai d'Orsay and the Second Moroccan Crisis, 1909–1911

An nescis, mi fili, quantilla prudentia regitur orbis?
(Do you not know, my son, with how little wisdom the world is governed?)

(Count Oxenstierna (1583–1634) to his son)

The collapse of the Clemenceau government in July 1909, Clemenceau's replacement as premier by Aristide Briand, and the arrival of the incompetent Edmond Bapst as the new political and commercial director marked the beginning of period of chaos in the Quai d'Orsay. The seriousness of this disorder became acute after the fall of the Briand ministry in March 1911, when intense governmental instability prevailed and Franco-German tension increased.[1]

In the years 1909–11 the Quai d'Orsay was far from being a homogeneous organization. Jules Cambon, supported by his brother, was able to involve the French government in *pourparlers* with Germany which eventually resulted in the Franco-German treaty of 4 November 1911. However, the clique of 'Young Turks' (Herbette, Bapst, Conty, and Regnault) deprived the treaty of any real importance. Despite its acceptance by Parliament, the Centrale was able to sabotage any long-term benefits which might have resulted and to create an atmosphere where further dialogue was seen as dangerous. The Centrale's attitude was characterized by deep-seated suspicion concerning German policy and by a virulent Germanophobia.

The Quai d'Orsay and the French foreign policy in general were in disarray well before the Agadir crisis of 1911. In fact, the era of incoherence began almost immediately after the fall of Clemenceau's

[1] C. M. Andrew and A. S. Kanya-Forstner, 'The French "Colonial Party"' *Historical Journal*, 19 (1974), pp. 449–50.

government. Although Pichon was retained by Briand as foreign
minister, he had lost his enthusiasm for the job. Indeed, a combination
of indolence and illness kept him away for weeks at a time.[2] He became
reliant on the postal and telephone communications of Louis, who was
able to administer the Centrale without much interference.[3] Whereas
at the commencement of his ministry Pichon had often given interviews to French and foreign diplomats and often gone before Parliament, by 1910 he was decidedly more reticent.[4] Henry, the former commercial director, informed Revoil in February 1911 that Pichon was
gloomy, plaintive, and mistrustful of himself to the point of being
almost totally indecisive.[5]

A major consequence of Pichon's continual absence between 1909
and 1911 was that it enabled young bureaucrats such as Bapst, Conty,
Herbette, and Berthelot to carve out small empires for themselves.[6]
The ensuing rivalries were great, though the Quai d'Orsay's general
lack of cohesion and direction was due in no small degree to Edmond
Bapst, political and commercial director between July 1909 and
November 1911. Born in 1855 in Paris, he was one of the most highly
educated men to enter the Quai d'Orsay. Though of bourgeois origin,
he married into the aristocracy. The Bapst family in its own right was
eminent in the army and literary fields.[7]

After entering the Quai d'Orsay in 1882 as an attaché in the press
bureau, Bapst spent most of his career overseas, especially in the Near
and Far East, and was considered an expert on the affairs of these
regions.[8] Thus, unlike many other officials in the Centrale, he had
ample experience of foreign posts. Despite Joseph Caillaux's scathing
remarks about both Conty and Herbette, he found Bapst thoroughly
likeable, high praise indeed from one whose dislike for the Quai
d'Orsay was intense.[9]

Bapst brought to the position of political director a number of qualities. In the forefront of these was the fact that he was an extemely

[2] Bertie to Grey, 8 Oct., 21 Oct. 1909, PRO, FO 800/61, Grey MSS.

[3] Bertie to Grey, 25 July 1909, FO 371/668; see the letters from Louis to Pichon, Aug.
1909, Inst. de Fr. Pichon MSS, 3; Pichon to Reinach, 12 Sept. 1910, BN (NAF 13527),
Reinach MSS.

[4] Bertie to Grey, 3 Jan. 1910, PRO, FO 800/165, Bertie MSS.

[5] Henry to Revoil, 9 Feb. 1911, AE Revoil MSS, 5.

[6] Pichon to P. Cambon, 7 Mar. 1911, AE P. Cambon MSS, 4; Pichon to Gérard, 20 Apr.
1911, AN 329 AP 20 Gérard MSS; D. J. Miller, 'Stephen Pichon and the Making of
French Foreign Policy' (Cambridge University, 1976), p. 290.

[7] AE *dossier personnel*, Bapst.   [8] Ibid., Bourgeois to Jonnart, 31 Jan. 1913.

[9] Caillaux, *Mes Mémoires* (Paris, 1942–7), ii. 148.

diligent worker. He desired to master all questions pertaining to his office, and despatches were always written in his own hand.[10] This facility for work was usually combined with good sense and sang-froid, which was reflected in the moderation in his views.[11]

Bapst's ability to dissect a question was not without its inconveniences. It often led to a certain intellectual arrogance and to a reluctance to take orders or to listen to advice.[12] There was, moreover, a certain contradiction between Bapst's insistence on having all problems referred to him and the infrequency with which he attempted to answer them.[13] The only result was to sour his relationship with both diplomats abroad and officials under his authority. He resented Herbette and Conty not so much because there was a fundamental difference of views, but rather because he was jealous of their ability to take the initiative away from him. The seriousness of this jurisdictional dispute was compounded by Bapst's outward aloofness, which manifested itself in an inability to maintain good social relations with his staff, his Minister, or foreign diplomats.[14]

If there was, however, one factor more than any other which caused confusion in the Quai and made Bapst possibly the worst political director before the First World War, it was that he had little idea of administration at a time when the 1907 reforms were placing an increased burden on the political division and the transformation of the old system into four separate subdivisions. The amalgamation of the commercial division with the political division clearly overwhelmed him. The crushing workload combined with his lack of initiative and refusal to be advised or to delegate authority resulted in administrative paralysis.[15] A letter by Bapst to Gérard at the end of 1909 indicated the chaos to which both the new system and Bapst's administrative incapacity had contributed:

Le tort a été de vous communiquer tout crémeux ces dépêches sans mentionner que le Ministère n'endossait pas la responsabilité de leur contenu. Je vous prierai d'avoir quelque indulgence pour le directeur politique qui au moment de la signature mise en présence à signer, néglige un peu de revoir les pièces jointes.[16]

---

[10] AE *dossier personnel*, Bapst. For the large number of dispatches in Bapst's hand, see AE NS 'Allemagne', 39.

[11] AE *dossier personnel*, Bapst.

[12] Henry to Revoil, 19 Nov. 1911, AE Revoil MSS, 5.

[13] Bompard to P. Cambon, 7 Apr. 1911, AE P. Cambon MSS, 4.

[14] AE *dossier personnel*, Bapst.

[15] P. Cambon to de Margerie, 21 Aug. 1910, AE de Margerie MSS.

[16] Bapst to Gérard, 22 Nov. 1908, 12 Oct. 1909, AN 329 AP 20 Gérard MSS.

Bapst himself realized at a very early stage that he was unsuited to the position of political director. Less than a year after his appointment he was looking for a post elsewhere. His relations with Pichon were strained, to say the least, and he found himself in disagreement with his Minister on numerous issues.[17] He would have preferred a more aggressive policy in the Near East, Morocco, and the Far East.[18] Undoubtedly his influence grew during the Briand ministry because of the continued absence of Pichon.[19] Yet it is to be doubted that his authority was substantially increased. As Paul Cambon commented, Pichon had made Bapst's position untenable by openly criticizing him and by replacing him temporarily in the summer of 1910.[20] There can be no question that the weakness of French diplomacy at the time of the Potsdam talks between Russia and Germany was largely due to a poor working relationship between Pichon and Bapst.

Bapst left his mark primarily on France's Asian policies, in which he was particularly interested and in the formulation of which Pichon allowed him fairly free rein. As minister to Peking between 1905 and 1907 he had recognized the importance of the Far East in international relations and urged French governments to take a greater interest in Chinese affairs. China, he thought, was a decadent and lost country, and he advocated a policy of loans tied to orders for French industry.[21] Although he was suspicious of Great Britain's influence in China, he saw little alternative to working with her against Japan, whom he considered to be highly dangerous and aggressive.[22] It was on this point that a strong divergence developed between Bapst and Pichon. The latter was also opposed to Bapst's insistence on linking industrial advantages to French loans.

Bapst's attitude towards the Ottoman Empire was similar to his stance on China. Both before and after the Young Turk Revolution of 1908, he regarded Turkey as truly 'the sick man of Europe'.[23] To Bapst Turkey

[17] Bapst eventually resigned himself to an increasing loss of authority. When Pichon called in Louis in the summer of 1910 Bapst raised no resistance (P. Cambon to de Margerie, 21 Aug. 1910, AE de Margerie MSS).

[18] Ibid.; also B. Auffray, *Pierre de Margerie (1861–1942) et la vie diplomatique de son temps* (Paris, 1976), pp. 229, 230; P. Cambon to Pichon, 13 Sept. 1910, Inst. de Fr. Pichon MSS, 2.

[19] Bapst to Gérard, 14 Dec. 1906, 14 Jan., 21 Dec. 1907, AN, 329 AP 20 Gérard MSS.

[20] P. Cambon to de Margerie, 21 Aug. 1910, AE de Margerie MSS.

[21] Bapst to Gérard, 21 Jan. 1908, 2, 20 Oct. 1910, AN, 329 AP 20 Gérard MSS.

[22] Ibid.

[23] Bapst to Doulcet, 29 Aug. 1903, AE Doulcet MSS, 14; Bompard to P. Cambon, 7 Apr. 1911, AE P. Cambon MSS, 4; Constans to Delcassé, 21 Sept. 1904, AE Delcassé MSS, 4; J. Cambon to P. Cambon, 4 Mar. 1911, AE J. Cambon MSS, 19.

was incapable of rejuvenation, and he regarded the Macedonian question as unsolvable within the existing Turkish framework. All that could be done was to share as largely as possible in the liquidation of the Ottoman Empire. He was highly critical of Ambassador Constans, under whom he had served at Constantinople from 1898 to 1904.[24] He was largely responsible for moves aimed at Constans's recall.[25] In Bapst's opinion, Constans had failed to defend those French interests most threatened by German competition: the religious protectorate and industrial ventures. Constans's failure to press for industrial concessions in return for French financial assistance had been especially regrettable. Bapst was almost as quick to find fault with Maurice Bompard, Constans's successor, because Bompard believed in preserving the territorial integrity of the Ottoman Empire.[26]

Surprisingly enough, Bapst's attitude towards Germany was generally moderate. He was not an advocate of needless pinpricks, and on some issues saw the need to undertake serious negotiations. The questions of the Homs–Baghdad railway was an example. He told Jules Cambon in May 1910:

Ce n'est certes pas moi qui pousserai aux désaccords avec l'Allemagne et vous savez que notamment sur la question du Homs–Baghdad, je déplore ce qui a été fait. L'opposition à la ligne allemande [the Baghdad railway] menace d'apres moi d'être péniblement vue par l'empereur et d'être cause de procédés hostiles de sa part et de celle de son gouvernement. Peut-être même l'attitude de ce dernier dans l'affaire de l'emprunt marocain dépend-elle un peu du mécontentement provenant de la lutte engagée en Mésopotamie et Syrie.[27]

However, he drew a distinction between the Baghdad railway and German involvement in Morocco, where he could only see difficulties in Franco-German economic collaboration. Thus, he had never accepted the 1909 Franco-German accord.[28] Nor could he see any reason why France had to share her privileged position with Germany. In case of Spain he seemed willing to concede that she had legitimate rights, but he was as opposed to Franco-Spanish economic co-operation as he was to Franco-German economic co-operation.[29] When the Moroccan situ-

[24] Bapst to Doulcet, 27 Dec. 1904, AE Doulcet MSS, 14.
[25] J. Cambon to de Margerie, 13 Mar. 1905, AE de Margerie MSS.
[26] Bompard to P. Cambon, 7 Apr. 1911, AE P. Cambon MSS, 4.
[27] Bapst to J. Cambon, May 1910, AE J. Cambon MSS, 14.
[28] J. C. Allain, *Agadir* (Paris, 1978), p. 284; Bapst to de Billy, 28 Aug. 1910, AE de Billy MSS, 34; J. Cambon to Pichon, 8 May 1910, AE J. Cambon MSS, 16.
[29] Bapst to Pichon, 16 Sept. 1910, Inst. de Fr. Pichon MSS, 1.

ation came to a head in early 1911, his somewhat aggressive stance was marked.

Alexandre Robert Conty, Bapst's *sous-directeur d'Europe* since the summer of 1909, was different in many respects from his chief. Born in 1864 in Abilly (Indres-et-Loire), he had been educated at the École polytechnique, not usually the learning ground of diplomats.[30] Although he came from a well-to-do, upper-middle-class family, his marriage to Armande Le Roy Liberge (a widow with two children, a château, and eight servants) made him even wealthier. If there was one characteristic which impressed his colleagues, it was his forceful personality. As de Robien, a colleague, noted, Conty was 'trapu, le front haut, protégé par une crinière rebelle au peigne, la face carrée, bassée par une moustache de poil, le corps puissant, il donnait l'impression de force'.[31] His opinions were sometimes expressed in the form of violent displays of temper. Indeed, in China during the First World War, he broke a piece of furniture in a moment of rage.[32] At times he displayed an 'ironie mordante' which spared no one. Yet he was not without intelligence, and he revelled in a light-hearted humour which often became coarse. While at the Quai he often amused colleagues with his unusual programme for an imaginary reception of the Tsar, one which involved: 'D'abord l'hymne russe chanté par tous les polonais de la carrière ... et Dieu sait s'ils y en avaient ... plus un acte d'une pièce célèbre de Brieuns.' The *tour de force* was a choral concert with two choirs singing 'sous tes grandes lois' and 'les cornes d'abondance'.[33] There was, in addition, a bohemian side to his character. Dinners bored him unless they were limited to close friends; rather, he preferred to seek amusement outside the salons and 'high society' of Paris. One of his favourite spectacles was 'the folies Conty', an amateur troupe of diplomats dressed up as transvestites.[34]

Conty had succeeded in entrenching himself in the Centrale after a series of exotic postings.[35] He entered the Quai in 1889 as an attaché to Jules Herbette. Thereafter, Conty was sent to Berlin, Bucharest, Rio de Janeiro, Brussels, and Lisbon. In April 1901 he was placed in charge of American affairs in the Direction des consulats, and was appointed *sous-directeur d'Amérique* after the 1907 reorganization. As a result of Soulange-Bodin's exile and Pichon's patronage, he was made *sous-directeur d'Europe* in September 1909.[36]

---

[30] AE *dossier personnel*, Conty.   [31] Notes by de Robien, AN de Robien MSS.
[32] Ibid.   [33] Ibid.   [34] Ibid.   [35] AE *dossier personnel*, Conty.
[36] See Pichon's glowing reports from Brazil and Tunisia, AE *dossier personnel*, Conty.

His relations with foreign ministers and colleagues were generally excellent. He was very much in favour with Pichon, with whom he had worked in Brazil and Tunis. Pichon appears to have depended more on him than on Bapst.[37] The foreign minister appreciated Conty's intelligence, his industry, his precision, and his economic expertise. Though Conty enjoyed less intimate relations with Pichon's successors Cruppi and de Selves, both men thought highly of him.[38] He and Maurice Herbette were close friends, having been together in Berlin in the 1890s under Ambassador Jules Herbette. Berthelot, too, seems to have liked him.[39] The Cambons increasingly held Conty responsible for the malaise prevalent in the Quai during the period 1909–11, but only a few years before Paul had described him as an upright and distinguished boy despite being an impatient person.[40]

Cambon's comment is helpful in understanding Conty. He was essentially an ardent patriot, dedicated to the advancement of what he considered to be the interests of 'France éternelle'.[41] Trained by the École polytechnique in the virtues of precision, he was an industrious and honest individual who expected his subordinates to display similar qualities. He ensured that agents under his authority did not acquire private economic interests in the country to which they were posted.[42] His independence and forthrightness were exceptional, and were frequently directed towards his superiors.[43] In this sense he was an extremely valuable adviser.

The other side of the coin was that he was too meticulous, too scrupulous and too uncompromising. His education at the École Polytechnique was probably responsible for giving him a tendency towards absolute solutions and towards being logical in the extreme.[44] His scruples ill equipped him to understand countries where bribery was an essential diplomatic tool. Indeed, an excessive attachment to principle made him at times rather naïve and blind.[45]

Conty's ill temper was particularly evident in his dealings with Germany. His hostility to the Germans had developed for the most part under the watchful eye of Jules Herbette, a noted Germanophobe. His early days in Berlin appear to have made a deep impression upon him.

[37] On Pichon's relationship with Bapst, see Pichon to Barrère, 14 Dec. 1909, AE *dossier personnel*, Piccioni.
[38] Comte de Saint-Aulaire, *Confessions d'un vieux diplomate* (Paris, 1953), p. 224.
[39] See Conty's letters to Berthelot, 1923, AE *dossier personnel*, Berthelot.
[40] P. Cambon to J. Cambon, 24 Feb. 1907, AE J. Cambon MSS, 25.
[41] Notes by de Robien, AN de Robien MSS.
[42] Ibid.   [43] Ibid.   [44] Ibid.   [45] Ibid.

He had often gone riding with Bismarck, and in doing so gained a first-hand knowledge of German tactics.[46] What he learned made him deeply suspicious. His commitment to the letter of the law led him to regard Germany as a classic case of deceit, treachery, and downright malevolence. Like Herbette and Bapst, he totally disapproved of the 1909 Franco-German accord because he thought that France was not obliged to share Morocco with anyone, let alone Germany. He was determined to break the accord. He found Germany particularly troublesome in colonial matters, where his initiative was most felt, and he strongly believed that she was insatiable.[47] Though he was unsuccessful in getting Pichon to reconsider his Moroccan policy, like Bapst and Louis before him he seems to have prevailed upon the foreign minister not to seek more than a rather superficial *détente* with Germany.

Another highly influential individual within the Foreign Ministry, and one who became especially powerful during the Agadir crisis, was Maurice Herbette. He headed the press bureau between 1907 and 1911 and later became the *chef du cabinet* of foreign ministers Cruppi and de Selves. Born 1870, the year of French defeat at Sedan, he harboured intense anti-German feelings because of the outcome of the Franco-Prussian war. He was a highly intelligent man who had earned a degree in the humanities and finished first in the *concours* of 1894. Raindre, a former superior, noted that he was a careful worker whose powerful analytical mind was especially evident in his historical memoranda.[48] Nevertheless, Caillaux's description of him as 'niais ventru', while perhaps exaggerated, gave some idea of his will to power, his love of intrigue, and his overriding vanity.[49] Like his father Jules Herbette, a former *chef du cabinet et du personnel*, Herbette earned the reputation of 'Herr Bête' for his ruthless manipulation of appointments.

Herbette had achieved eminence very quickly thanks to patronage and to the fact that most of his career had been confined to the Centrale. He was powerfully supported by his father, a former ambassador in Berlin, and by Charles de Freycinet, an ex-premier and foreign minister.[50] Apart from a few brief postings, his career after 1896 was entirely that of the Parisian bureaucrat. Though Jules Cambon was not always an impartial observer of Herbette, he was nevertheless near the

---

[46] *Dictionnaire diplomatique* (article on Conty).   [47] Caillaux, *Mémoires*, ii. 148.

[48] 'Notes des chefs du poste', AE *dossier personnel*, Herbette.

[49] J. Cambon to P. Cambon, 12 Apr. 1911, AE J. Cambon MSS, 19; Caillaux, *Mémoires*, ii. 149; Lindenlaub to Gérard, 14 Nov. 1911, AN 329 AP 20 Gérard MSS; Delavaud to Barrère, 7 July 1911, AE Barrère MSS, 2. Lindenlaub was a pseudonym for Émile Lautier.

[50] AE *dossier personnel*, Herbette.

mark when he lamented to his brother that 'Herbette est très préoccupé de Paris, des couloirs de la Chambre et surtout de la presse. Il ne sait pas ce qu'on pense à l'étranger.'[51]

Herbette's political views resembled those of his father. He was both a staunch Republican and an anti-clerical. He was opposed to anything which smacked of the *ancien régime*. However, he was no extremist. He regarded socialists with horror and, during the industrial turbulence of 1910, he strongly supported 'social order' and a wide range of repressive measures.[52]

Herbette's power as *chef du cabinet* resulted from his relations with foreign ministers, in particular Cruppi and de Selves, his control of personnel, and his dealings with the press. In the first instance, Cruppi was extremely inexperienced and allowed him free rein in both administrative and political matters. Herbette's authority was still further strengthened when de Selves succeeded Cruppi. There was a mutual admiration between the two, and de Selves was rarely far from his *chef du cabinet*.[53] Herbette's position as *chef du personnel* was also of great importance. Since the reforms of 1907 the position had become extremely important, and bureaucrats and diplomats alike viewed changes to the ministerial cabinet with considerable interest and apprehension.[54] Herbette had no qualms in using his position to further the interests of those who pleased him and to exile those towards whom he was unfavourably disposed.[55] Similarly, the press represented a powerful instrument by means of which Herbette consolidated his position in the Quai and pressed his views upon diplomats and ministers.[56]

As *chef des communications* between 1907 and 1911 Herbette created a situation in which much of the press was prepared to accept his advice.[57] One of his relatives, Jean Herbette, worked for *Le Siècle*, and he had good relations with other newspapers, notably *L'Écho de Paris*.[58] Thus, during the Agadir crisis, he was able to unite much of the press in opposition to the principle of talks with Germany. When proposals were made to Germany they were immediately leaked to Paris newspapers.[59] Herbette used the Paris press to criticize Jules Cambon, who explained this hos-

[51] J. Cambon to P. Cambon, 17 June 1911, AE J. Cambon MSS, 18.

[52] M. Herbette to Delcassé, 3 Mar. 1911, AE Delcassé MSS, 4.

[53] De Selves to Quai d'Orsay, 23 Jan. 1917, AE *dossier personnel*, Herbette.

[54] Berthelot to Claudel, 3 Mar. 1911, AE Berthelot MSS, 23.

[55] Delavaud to Barrère, 7 July 1911, AE Barrère MSS, 2.   [56] Ibid.

[57] Herbette to J. Cambon, 30 June 1907, AE J. Cambon MSS, 15.

[58] E. M. Carroll, *French Public Opinion and Foreign Affairs, 1870–1914* (New York, 1931), p. 266; J. Le Bourd to J. Cambon, 19 Sept. 1911, AE, J. Cambon MSS, 14.

[59] J. Cambon to P. Cambon, 17 July 1911, AE J. Cambon MSS, 19.

tility in terms of 'une antipathie de nature' against him. This was too simplistic a notion.[60] Herbette, though sensitive to the repeated objections which Cambon had made to his administration of the Bureau des communications, was attacking Cambon's policies rather than his person.[61]

During 1911 Herbette assumed a role quite out of keeping with that which normally belonged to the *chef du cabinet*. In fact, he actively encroached upon the powers of the political division. As the *chef du cabinet* he should have restricted himself to such matters as the transmission of correspondence, liaison between the political division and the Foreign Minister, and the handling of personnel matters. He was well aware of what he was supposed to do.[62] Nevertheless, not only did he attend most high-level meetings and offer advice, but on numerous occasions he wrote despatches of an important political nature.[63] In addition, telegrams, *lettres particulières*, and despatches were communicated to him for his perusal and comment. Incoming despatches were often tardily sent to the political division. Sometimes Bapst was not informed of the foreign minister's wishes. Above all, Herbette's advice carried great weight with the Minister.[64] De Selves increasingly depended on him for guidance and for support against the premier, Joseph Caillaux.[65]

Underlying Herbette's action was a Germanophobia which contested even the principle of conversation with Germany. He believed that Germany could not be trusted in any agreement. Indeed, her interest in *détente* was essentially a 'ruse' to separate France from both Russia and Britain.[66] Herbette's views rested on balance-of-power considerations. Nevertheless, his anti-German sentiment was to some extent ideological in nature. He abhorred everything that Imperial Germany represented. Imbued with a deep Republican spirit, he despised Prussia's anti-democrat and authoritarian spirit as well as her tendency to use brute force.

Herbette's thinking was revealed in a laboriously long report which he drafted for Pichon in 1908 entitled 'Relations avec la France 1902–8'. It is to be doubted, given Pichon's laziness, that he read much of it. This

---

[60] Ibid.

[61] Cambon had been highly critical of Herbette's handling of the press since his posting to Berlin in 1907.

[62] Herbette to Delcassé, 3 Mar. 1911, AE Delcassé MSS, 4.

[63] See numerous despatches in AE NS 'Allemagne', 39, 40, especially 13 Aug. 1911.

[64] Delavaud to Barrère, 7 July 1911, AE Barrère MSS, 2; J. Cambon, Notes de voyage, 20–31 Aug., AE J. Cambon MSS, 13.

[65] e.g. J. Cambon to P. Cambon, 17 June 1911, E. J. Cambon MSS, 19; notes in AN 324 AP 2 Tardieu MSS.

[66] 'Relations avec la France, 1902–8', AE NS 'Allemagne', 26.

report appears to have been one of the few documents which, prior to 1914, sought to establish the premisses of German policy towards France. It was probably written in conjunction with the Franco-German negotiations which resulted in the agreement of 9 February 1909. Herbette argued that Germany was unlikely to moderate either her deceitfulness or her disloyal nature.[67] Her behaviour if not totally intractable was irritating and obstructionist.[68] To support his thesis he went back to negotiations over the Congo in 1885 and recalled Germany's attitude towards Britain during the 1880s. Despite their friendly gestures the Germans had been unable to conceal their insincerity and disloyalty.[69] Herbette proceeded to examine the *pourparlers* during Delcassé's ministry and the attempts by Noailles, the French ambassador to Berlin, to modify Delcassé's analysis that no concrete proposal had been made by Germany and that the friendly attitude of the Germans had been designed to damage France's image in Russia.[70] Germany's duplicity had become even more evident in Morocco after 1900. Germany had exhibited a deceitfulness which was in no way a defence of legitimate German interests but rather an irrational hostility towards France.[71] The conclusion to Herbette's over-300-page report is worth quoting in part as it succinctly summarizes his suspicion and hostility towards Germany:

Les sept dernières années ont donc été fertiles en évènements la plupart du temps pénibles et nullement favorables à un rapprochement ... Pendant cette période les rapports Franco-Allemands ont-ils été presque constamment aigres, même tendus. On a vécu, à maintes reprises, des jours troublés comme lors des accès de mauvaise humeur du Prince de Bismarck ou des conséquences de l'Impératrice Frederick à Paris.

L'étude impartiale des documents officiels prouve que la France et ses gouvernants ne peuvent, en aucune façon, être rendu responsable de cette situation. Notre pays a souffert dans sa dignité comme dans ses intérêts de l'intrusion de l'Allemagne dans sa politique intérieure et extérieure. Il est toutefois réconfortant de constater qu'un changement s'est produit dans les rapports Franco-Allemands grâce à l'énergie du gouvernement et de l'opinion publique.

S'il était possible de tirer une conclusion du passé on pourrait craindre néanmoins que l'Allemagne ne persiste pas longtemps dans ses sentiments de détente.

Et l'on doit rappeler tout en espérant un avenir meilleur, ce que M. Jules Cambon, alors Ambassadeur à Madrid écrivait le 8 Mars: 'Nous ne devons pas

---

[67] Ibid. pp. 69, 211, 343.   [68] Ibid.   [69] Ibid. p. 1.   [70] Ibid. pp. 21–4.
[71] Ibid. p. 21.

faire quoi que ce soit qui puisse être considéré par l'Empereur Guillaume comme un désir de modifier notre situation réciproque ... Notre indifférence aura seule raison de son inquiétude.'[72]

With the collapse of the Briand goverment in early 1911, Jean Cruppi became foreign minister. After a career in the magistracy, he had entered Parliament in 1898. In 1911, moreover, he became foreign minister by default. More qualified men had rejected the post. He was included in the cabinet to ensure a balanced representation of parliamentary groups.[73] He was not entirely devoid of the qualities which made for a successful foreign minister. He was usually eager, because of his legal background, to undertake a thorough study of the questions before him. But this virtue was unfortunately accompanied by a legal narrowness which allowed the letter of the law to dominate the spirit of justice.[74] Because of this inexperience, his ignorance of foreign affairs, and his inability to respond rapidly to changing events, he too often took the advice of his permanent officials.[75] The volume of correspondence emanating from his officials and the lack of notes in his own writing suggest that, if he made a conscientious attempt to master diplomatic issues, he was not endowed with a great analytical mind.

Unfortunately for Cruppi, he became foreign minister at a time when France's expansion in Morocco was about to encounter strenuous opposition from the German government. Berlin clearly suspected that France was seeking to destroy the 1909 Franco-German economic agreement. Upon his arrival in office, France refused to accept German participation in the management of Moroccan finances or in Moroccan railway and mining ventures. Cruppi added fuel to the fire by choosing on 17 April 1911 to order an occupation of the Cherifien capital Fez, on the pretext of safeguarding foreign nationals. His decision was made after a meeting with Berteaux, minister of war, and was endorsed with-

---

[72] See also the revealing letter which he wrote to Jules Cambon in June 1907, when the German government was manifesting a certain interest in *détente*: 'on y affirme que l'empereur se montrerait soudain disposé à nous aider au Maroc de façon à arriver à une entente ultérieure sur d'autres points avec nous. Il y avait une tendance à rendre public ce soi-disant revirement. Après entente avec M. G. Louis et Dutasta, il m'a paru préférable d'étouffer l'affaire car nous paraîtrons vouloir encore jeter une amorce. On nous avons subi assez de rebuffades pour être en droit d'attendre qu'on nous saisisse de quelque chose de ferme et de précise.' AE J. Cambon MSS, 14.

[73] Caillaux, *Mémoires*, ii. 43–4; G. Louis, *Les Carnets de Georges Louis* (Paris, 1926), p. 165; E. Burke, *Prelude to Protest in Morocco* (Chicago, 1976), p. 117.

[74] Berckheim to J. Cambon, 15 Mar. 1911, Bapst to J. Cambon, 8 Mar. 1911, AE J. Cambon MSS, 15.

[75] Ibid. 19, J. Cambon to P. Cambon, 17 Apr. 1911.

out discussion by Premier Monis, the only other minister in Paris at the time.

Although it would have been almost impossible to convince Berlin, Cruppi's decision to occupy Fez was by no means a straightforward case of 'adventurism'. Rather, he had been influenced by both emotion and inexperience. Emotionally he felt obliged to act by a sense of responsibility towards the Franco-European colony in Fez. His inexperience led him to reject any local solution, order the immediate intervention of French troops, and to give insufficient thought to consulting either Spain or Germany. It also resulted in his subordination to the French military and to adventurous permanent officials.[76]

In giving his fateful order, Cruppi was convinced that France's intervention would not be an occasion for the overturning of the status quo. As soon as the necessary assistance had been rendered, a situation *status quo ante* would be established.[77] Given this belief, he was thoroughly upset when he learned that Spain had in her turn occupied certain Moroccan regions, especially El Ksar,[78] and that Germany had reacted in hostile fashion.[79]

Cruppi's decision had basically been his alone, but once he had made it, he increasingly abdicated responsibility for policy-making.[80] Presented on his arrival at the Quai with a crisis of which he knew little, comprehending but few of the intricacies of the Moroccan situation, and in no way understanding the international implications of his action, Cruppi was continually forced to depend on his permanent officials and to make decisions whose disastrous consequences he did not foresee.

In the final analysis, Cruppi was prepared to seek a negotiated settlement of the Moroccan crisis. He envisaged substantial concessions in the French Congo long before the Caillaux government took

[76] Ibid., J. Cambon to P. Cambon, 3 Apr. 1911. On his inexperience, see Regnault to de Billy, 19 Apr. 1911, AE de Billy MSS, 37; Cruppi to de Billy, 19 Apr. 1911, AE NS 'Maroc', 112; Andrew and Kanya-Forstner, 'Colonial Party', pp. 123–4. On the need to be firm, see J. Cambon to Cruppi, 9 Apr. 1911, Cruppi to J. Cambon, 20 Apr. 1911, AE J. Cambon MSS, 14. On his intimacy with General Moinier, the commanding officer in Morocco, see Allain, *Agadir*, pp. 269–70. Also, for links with the military, see General Segonzac to Étienne, 25 May 1911, BN (NAF 24237), Étienne MSS.

[77] Regnault to de Billy, 25 Apr. 1911, Cruppi to Moinier, 24 May 1911, AE de Billy MSS, 36, 37; Bertie to Grey, PRO, FO 800/52, Grey MSS; Cruppi to de Billy, 28 Apr. 1911, Cruppi to Moinier, 17 Apr. 1911, AE NS 'Maroc', 213.

[78] Herbette to J. Cambon, 15 June 1911, Cruppi to J. Cambon, 17 Apr. 1911, AE J. Cambon MSS, 14, 15.

[79] Ibid.

[80] J. Cambon, 'Notes de Voyage', 22 June–8 July, AE J. Cambon MSS, 13.

office.[81] Nevertheless, he was opposed to Franco-German economic co-operation in Morocco.[82] Such collaboration, he thought, would prevent France from establishing a complete domination of the territory.[83]

Several members of the Centrale, Bapst, Herbette, Conty, and, for a time, Regnault, took full advantage of Cruppi's inexperience. They now sought to push Germany out of Moroccan affairs altogether. Bapst, whose authority with Pichon was almost negligible, relished the opportunity to enhance his status with the arrival of Cruppi. In fact, Cruppi's assumption of office allowed the political director to 'corner' the Minister and to have his more expansionist policies accepted.[84] Consequently Bapst was largely able to destroy the policy of a cautious *pénétration pacifique* devised by Pichon and the Cambon brothers. Specifically, Bapst pressed Cruppi to dissolve all economic links with Germany in Morocco, which would be a clear violation of the 1909 agreement. In March 1911, under the pretext that Spain and Britain would object, Franco-German collaboration in a railway line between Tangier and Fez was sabotaged by Bapst.[85] As if this action was not sufficient to alienate German industrial interests, he then proceeded to draw up a new financial agreement with Morocco, which was signed on 16 March. This document made no provision for German participation and no reference to other European partners.[86] Finally, a mining agreement which could have furthered Franco-German goodwill and collaboration foundered as a result of Bapst's meddling.[87] As Jules Cambon lamented, Franco-German negotiations were being conducted in an 'esprit de chicane'.

Conty skilfully seconded Bapst's aggressive approach. His role in the 1911 crisis was *néfaste* to say the least. With the advent of Cruppi he successfully pushed for a more forward policy in Morocco to the exclusion of talks with either Spain or Germany.[88] Using an illogical logic, he sought to base France's destruction of the 1909 agreement with

[81] Ibid. 15 J. Cambon to Paléologue, 9 May 1912; notes by Messimy, uncatalogued, AN Messimy MSS; Caillaux, *Mémoires*, ii. 69.

[82] J. F. V. Keiger, 'Raymond Poincare and French Foreign Policy, 1912–1914' (Cambridge University, 1980); also *France and the Origins of the First World War* (London, 1983), p. 34.

[83] J. Cambon to P. Cambon, 17 Nov. 1911, AE J. Cambon MSS, 19.

[84] Bompard to P. Cambon, 7 Apr. 1911, AE P. Cambon MSS, 4.

[85] Bapst to J. Cambon, Mar. 1911, AE J. Cambon MSS, 14; Allain, *Agadir*, p. 282.

[86] Allain, *Agadir*, p. 282.

[87] Ibid.; Bapst to de Billy, 28 Aug. 1910, AE de Billy MSS, 34.

[88] J. Cambon to Paléologue, 13 May 1912, AE J. Cambon MSS, 15.

Germany on the Algeçiras Act. In addition, he pushed for a renunciation of the Franco-German consortium in the Ngokho-Sangha.[89]

Bapst's, Conty's, and Herbette's arguments were strongly supported by Eugène Regnault, the French minister in Tangier. Indeed, he appears to have been almost as influential as Bapst between February and July. With Marcilly, head of the Moroccan section in the Centrale, he had long advocated an expansionist policy in Morocco. Although not a member of the Centrale in 1911, he was in Paris as an adviser on Moroccan affairs to Cruppi and de Selves. During Pichon's first ministry, he had unsuccessfully appealed for a more foward policy in Morocco. He had clashed with Clemenceau over strategy in the Casablanca affair, when he urged the wholesale use of military and naval force.[90] Like the others in the Centrale, he had opposed the 1909 agreement, and justified his attempts to sabotage it by arguing that Great Britain would object to a strengthening of Germany's economic position in Morocco.[91] He insisted that it was necessary to pacify the territory before Franco-German collaboration could begin.[92] His suspicion of German *menées* and intimidation was such that he disliked even the idea of conversations with Germany.[93]

With the advent of Cruppi, Regnault was able to overturn Pichon's policies. The new foreign minister relied heavily upon him and retained him in Paris even though he was due to return to Tangier.[94] As Allain has recently noted: 'Avec Cruppi l'influence de Regnault va s'exercer sans partage, sans concurrence, et sans objections possibles du ministre auquel manque l'expérience directe de l'évolution antérieure.'[95] By Cruppi's own admission, Regnault had encouraged him to order the occupation of Fez.[96]

Regnault's views were somewhat more moderate in 1911 than they had earlier been. His fear of international repercussions led him to advocate the use of police rather than troops.[97] He advised a sounding out of Germany, and when the military were finally employed he hoped that

[89] G. Suarez, *Aristide Briand* (Paris, 1938), p. 342.
[90] Moinier to de Billy, 21 Feb. 1911, AE de Billy MSS, 37.
[91] Ibid., Regnault to de Billy, 25 Apr. 1911.
[92] Ibid., Regnault to de Billy, 16, 25 Feb., 27 Apr. 1911.
[93] Ibid.   [94] 'Note pour le Ministre', 25 Apr. 1911, AE NS 'Allemagne', 34.
[95] Allain, *Agadir*, p. 282; Regnault to de Billy, 28 Mar. 1911, AE de Billy MSS, 37.
[96] Regnault to de Billy, 28 Mar. 1911, AE de Billy MSS, 37; Regnault to de Billy, 16 Feb., 19, 27 Apr. 1911.
[97] 'Note pour le Ministre', 25 Apr. 1911, AE N.S. 'Allemagne', 34; Regnault to de Billy, 19 Apr. 1911, AE de Billy MSS, 37.

they would not occupy Fez.[98] As he told de Billy, the *chargé d'affaires* in Tangier, on 25 April 1911, 'Le gouvernement recommandera au Général Moinier de ne pas occuper Fez, de façon à ne pas déclencher un mouvement hostile parmi nos adversaires et à éviter toute tentative dans ce sens sur le terrain diplomatique.'[99]

In the final analysis, however, Regnault contributed just as much to the Centrale's aggressive policies as Bapst, Conty, and Herbette. While he did not see this occasion as an opportunity for adventurism in Morocco, he had argued strenuously in previous years for an expansionist policy. His distrust of Germany, his contempt for Spain, and his complete rejection of German participation in Moroccan finances added fuel to the fire.

Not surprisingly, a serious rift developed during the Moroccan crisis between the older ambassadorial team and the new breed of 'Young Turks', as Jules Cambon contemptuously labelled them. The Berlin Ambassador had particular reason for dissatisfaction since he had been the chief architect of the 1909 Franco-German agreement. Under Pichon, he had been allowed to formulate a Moroccan policy which involved a gradual penetration and a regular consultation of Berlin. With the advent of Cruppi, however, 'la politique des profits quotidiens et des assurances contre les aventures et la politique attentive et de bonne humeur' gave way to the Centrale's policy of 'pinpricks'.[100] Paul Cambon, Léon Geoffray, ambassador to Madrid, Bompard, ambassador to Constantinople, and Gavarry, *directeur des affaires administratives et techniques*, all ranged themselves behind Jules Cambon.[101] Even Delcassé's help was enlisted. For the time being, however, Jules Cambon was forced to accept the supremacy of the Centrale, which refused to believe that Germany was not seeking to create unnecessary difficulties in Morocco and that she had legitimate economic interests to protect.[102]

Cambon was no more successful in his appeal for a less mean-spirited

[98] Ibid., Regnault to de Billy, 19, 25, 27 Apr. 1911.

[99] Ibid., Regnault to de Billy, 25 Apr. 1911.

[100] J. Cambon to Delcassé, 1, 7 Mar. 1911, AE Delcassé MSS, 3; J. Cambon to P. Cambon, 17 Apr. 1911, AE J. Cambon MSS, 19.

[101] Gavarry, who had virtually no say in political matters, was a consistent opponent of adventurism in Morocco. He also argued against the Germanophobic sentiments of his other colleagues in the *Centrale*. See note by Gavarry, undated, 1906, AE Revoil MSS, 2; Gavarry to Revoil, 2, 16 Feb. 1906, and especially Gavarry to de Billy, 26 Aug., undated, AE de Billy MSS, 34.

[102] J. Cambon to Cruppi, 21 Apr. 1911, J. Cambon to P. Cambon, 17 Apr. 1911, J. Cambon to Delcassé, 7 Mar. 1911, AE J. Cambon MSS, 14, 19.

policy towards Spain. He recognized how difficult the Spanish could be, especially after Moroccan towns had been occupied. They were not necessarily the dupes of the Germans, as Regnault argued. If France dealt generously with the Spanish, they would not assist German penetration of Morocco.[103] In view of Regnault's influence over Cruppi, Cambon was preaching in the desert.

In principle he was not hostile to the idea of intervention in Morocco to repress disorder. Indeed, he urged Cruppi to 'se montrer énergique'. Action, however, had to be preceded by consultations with Great Britain and Germany. The latter had to receive assurances that there was no idea whatever of conquest and that, the mission accomplished, the Algéçiras Act would continue to be fulfilled according to Cambon.[104] Any breach of this act would prompt a hostile reaction on the part of Germany, who was already beginning to feel that she had been duped.[105] Cambon's advice turned quickly to warnings when it became clear that his prudent policy of consulting with Germany and taking limited action in Morocco was being ignored. He came to the conclusion well before the Agadir incident of July 1911 that it was necessary to gain a free hand in Morocco without ceding any Moroccan territory to Germany.[106]

As Jules Cambon had feared, a collision occurred. Despite promises to evacuate Fez, the French remained in the Cherifien capital. On 5 June, after the collapse of Franco-Spanish negotiations, Spain occupied Laraiche and Alcazar. It was only a matter of time before Berlin intervened. The sending of the German gunboat *Panther* to Agadir on 1 July was dramatic, but, as Allain has demonstrated, the action was a 'riposte' to French intransigence and adventurism. Berlin wished to demonstrate to France, Britain, Italy, and Spain that she had 'as much right to compensation in the event of the alteration of the status quo in Morocco'.[107]

To confuse matters, the serious injuries suffered by Premier Monis in an aeroplane crash in June left the French government in a chaotic state. Just a few days before the sending of the gunboat, Joseph Caillaux became premier and chose the inexperienced Justin de Selves as foreign minister. De Selves, an elderly seigneurial type, owed much of his pro-

[103] 'Notes de voyage', 22 June–8 July 1911, AE J. Cambon MSS, 13.
[104] J. Cambon to P. Cambon, 3 Apr. 1911, AE J. Cambon MSS, 19.
[105] Ibid. 21, 22 Apr. 1911.
[106] Ibid. J. Cambon to Cruppi, 9 Apr., 9, 15 May, 12 June.
[107] M. L. Dockrill, 'British Policy during the Agadir Crisis of 1911', in F. Hinsley (ed.), *British Foreign Policy under Sir Edward Grey* (Cambridge, 1977), pp. 271–2.

fessional success to his uncle de Freycinet. He became a prefect in 1880, and during the Clemenceau ministry in 1907 there had been talk of him succeeding Reverseaux in Vienna.[108] In the end his entry into the Senate had given him an opportunity to escape an unpalatable prefectoral position.[109] In 1911, he was accorded the Foreign Ministry only after other prospective ministers had rejected it,[110] and only after Caillaux had decided to appoint a man of the second rank in order to control foreign affairs himself.[111]

De Selves had other ideas. He had prepared himself for the Ministry of Foreign Affairs by maintaining good relations with the diplomatic corps in Paris. In addition, he had most of the qualities of a good ambassador. He had extensively polished manners, spoke a refined French, and displayed considerable discretion.[112] Though inexperienced, he made a conscientious effort to master his dossiers and to be more than Caillaux's voice at the Quai.[113] He kept himself well informed and sometimes took initiatives against the explicit wishes of the Caillaux cabinet.[114]

Such unapproved initiatives could be disastrous, and he was ill suited to the position of foreign minister at a time of prolonged crisis. Beneath a calm exterior there lurked a nervousness, impatience, and impressionability that translated itself into impetuous acts.[115] Equally serious, he was incapable of following a consistent line of thought and was easily influenced by his permanent officials, especially Herbette, for whom he had a filial affection.[116] Initially, de Selves wrote very few of his dispatches.[117] He modified this procedure after he had been repeatedly

[108] Von Wedel, German ambassador, to Wilhelmstraße, 11 Nov. 1906, Bonn, F. 108, vol. 16.

[109] 'Notes de voyage', 22 June–8 July, AE Jules Cambon MSS, 13.

[110] Caillaux, *Mémoires*, ii. 48–9.

[111] Ibid. ii. 79; J. D. Bredin, *Joseph Caillaux* (Paris, 1980), p. 98.

[112] J. Cambon, 'Notes de voyage', 22 June–8 July, AE J. Cambon MSS, 13; Suarez, *Briand*, p. 356; Saint-Aulaire, *Confessions*, p. 227.

[113] Saint-Aulaire, *Confessions*, p. 229; Cambon, 'Notes de voyage', 22 June–8 July, AE J. Cambon MSS, 13.

[114] J. Cambon to Poincaré, 9 Feb. 1912; de Selves to J. Cambon, 12 Sept. 1911, AE J. Cambon MSS, 16; De Selves to J. Cambon, 3 Aug. 1911, AE NS 'Allemagne', 36.

[115] P. Cambon to J. Cambon, 30 July 1911, AE J. Cambon MSS, 25.

[116] De Selves to Herbette, 7 Jan. 1912, de Selves to the Quai d'Orsay, 22 Jan. 1917, AE *dossier personnel*, Herbette.

[117] According to Paul Cambon, 'Selves écrit tous ses télégrammes lui-même, immédiatement, souvent sans réflexion et sous l'impression du moment. Il ne faut pas s'en émouvoir' (AE J. Cambon MSS, 25). In fact, it was Bapst who wrote the overwhelming majority of de Selves's telegrams and dispatches.

depicted as a plaything of his officials, but originality of thought and greater independence were not forthcoming.[118]

A good example of the contradiction between his outward calm and inner nervousness was his impulsive reaction to the sending of the German gunboat *Panther* to Agadir. Though he had been in office only one day before the crisis started, he decided to request the dispatch of a French cruiser.[119] Then, despite his hostility towards Germany, he was prepared at one point to cede the whole of the French Congo without the cabinet's approval.[120]

De Selves provided Jules Cambon with no clear instructions until the end of July. This delay resulted from de Selves's willingness to adopt the views of his permanent officials, who thought that Germany's objective was either to divide France and Britain or to occupy parts of southern Morocco.[121] What dominated de Selves's attitude, therefore, was a deep suspicion of German intentions. This being the case, he was far more interested in strengthening Franco-British solidarity than in engaging in Franco-German *pourparlers*.[122] Once assured of British support he was not averse to adopting a firm, even provocative, stance.[123]

It was only after Jules Cambon had protested to Caillaux that de Selves instructed the Ambassador to begin talks with the German government.[124] Even then, de Selves's attitude was marked by inflexibility and an inability to understand the German point of view.[125] He was determined to obtain all of Morocco without making any serious concessions.[126] Yet as soon as negotiations had begun he was accusing the German government of pettiness and *fourberie*.[127]

---

[118] Ibid. The Cambons were not sparing in their criticism, which led de Selves at one point to write to Jules Cambon that the letter he was receiving came entirely from him: 'tout ceci est de moi et ma pensée personnelle!' (De Selves to J. Cambon, 18 Sept. 1911.)

[119] Caillaux, *Mémoires*, ii. 20. De Selves was particularly enthusiastic about this tactic and persisted in thinking it would have been the best strategy (de Selves to Bapst, 5 July 1911, AE NS 'Allemagne', 35; de Selves to Caillaux, undated, in AN 324 AP 2 Tardieu MSS).

[120] Uncatalogued notes, AN 324 AP 2 Tardieu MSS.

[121] De Selves to P. Cambon, 9 July 1911, AE NS 'Allemagne', 35; de Selves to Caillaux, undated, AN 324 AP 2 Tardieu MSS.

[122] De Selves to P. Cambon, 27 July, 14 Aug. 1911, AE NS 'Allemagne', 36.

[123] Bredin, *Caillaux*, p. 105.

[124] 'Notes de voyage', 22 June–8 July 1911, AE J. Cambon MSS, 13; Caillaux, *Mémoires*, ii. 147–8; de Selves to J. Cambon, 13, 25, 26 July 1911, AE, N.S. 'Allemagne', 36.

[125] P. Cambon to J. Cambon, 30 July 1911, AE J. Cambon MSS, 17.

[126] De Selves to J. Cambon, 18 Sept. 1911, AE NS 'Allemagne', 39.

[127] Caillaux, *Mémoires*, ii. 166; Allain, *Agadir*, p. 374; de Selves to Caillaux, 10, 12, 13, 15 Aug. 1911, AN 324 AP 2 Tardieu MSS. Also de Selves to Bapst, 5 July 1911, to J. Cambon, 25 July 1911, to P. Cambon, 26 July 1911, AE NS 'Allemagne', 35, 36.

As Jules Cambon maintained, however, it was not de Selves but rather the Centrale which formulated French policy during the crisis.[128] De Selves's reliance on Herbette, his *chef du cabinet*, was especially pronounced. In view of Herbette's 1908 report to Pichon, it was not surprising that he disagreed with the 1909 Franco-German economic accord in Morocco.[129] The sending of the gunboat *Panther* to Agadir merely confirmed his deep-seated suspicion of Germany. Like Conty, he thought that the correct response was to 'fight fire with fire' by dispatching to the Moroccan port a cruiser superior to the *Panther*.[130] Herbette's willingness to take this step suggests that he was prepared to risk a European war.[131] Throughout the period of Franco-German talks in August he remained convinced of the insincerity and unreliability of Germany. The bellicosity of de Selves, which led him to call a meeting of military and naval chiefs in the second week of August, was certainly encouraged by Herbette, who thought that Germany was prolonging negotiations as a prelude to implanting herself in certain parts of Morocco.[132] When this occupation failed to take place Herbette became no more inclined to negotiate seriously with Germany, and he continued to aim for an unqualified French domination of Morocco.[133]

When it became increasingly evident that premier Caillaux was determined to come to terms with Berlin, Herbette pressed for the total exclusion of Germany from Morocco, for termination of Franco-German economic co-operation, and for Germany's acceptance of a French protectorate.[134] These demands stemmed from a fear that Germany would seize any pretext to strengthen her influence in Morocco. Herbette disliked the idea of German participation in railway ventures. As long as Germany retained an economic involvement in Morocco, she possessed the means of obstructing French policy.

Herbette's attitude towards Spain was characterized by a comparable suspicion. De Selves commissioned him to prepare the draft treaty which was to be presented to Spain when the Franco-German *pourparlers* concluded. This document, when completed, revealed what Geoffray, French ambassador to Madrid, described as a narrow nationalism and a spirit of meanness. Herbette's reluctance to meet Spain's

---

[128] 'Notes de voyage', 20–31 Aug. 1911, AE J. Cambon MSS, 13.
[129] Caillaux, *Mémoires*, ii. 148–9.
[130] Ibid ii. 148–52.   [131] Ibid.
[132] Herbette to Barrère, 14 Aug. 1911, AE Barrère MSS, 2.
[133] Caillaux, *Mémoires*, ii. 148–52.
[134] See his drafting of notes on the project of treaty, 19 Sept. 1911, AE NS 'Allemagne', 34.

wishes was undoubtedly reinforced by the fear that Germany was supporting Spanish claims in the hope of finding a back door into
Morocco.[135]

Conty, for his part, strongly supported Herbette, and it was he, rather
than Bapst, who had insisted that no substantial concessions should be
made to Germany. Once negotiations were under way and the French
Congo became the centre of *pourparlers*, Conty, because of his
African expertise, became invaluable to de Selves. He was called upon to
act as France's leading representative at the ensuing London talks. It was
he who carried on negotiation with von Lancken, the German delegate.[136] He showed no inclination to be conciliatory, and offered Germany nothing more than limited privileges in the French Congo.[137] The
value of the territory was such, he argued, that the loss of even a part of it
could mean the destruction of France's empire in Equatorial Africa.[138]
Throughout the negotiations he remained firmly convinced that it
would be madness to make substantial concessions. How were such
concessions to be avoided? Conty believed that a policy of standing up to
Germany was the only answer. Indeed, he was convinced that, if Germany did not go to war with France during the Moroccan crisis, she
would do so in the near future. Although the French army was not fully
ready, Conty nevertheless saw the Moroccan crisis as a favourable
opportunity for war. Britain would ultimately be forced to support
France. His confidence was reflected in the Centrale's proposal to send a
French cruiser to Agadir, and it contributed to the convocation of
military and naval chiefs during the second week of August.[139]

Regnault strongly backed Conty and Herbette. His importance diminished after the sending of the *Panther*, which turned a Moroccan conflict into a European crisis. However, he remained an active supporter of
those who opposed talks with Spain and wanted to exclude Germany
from Morocco.[140] Much of the difficulty involved in drafting the
Franco-German treaty of 4 November 1911 was caused by Regnault. He

---

[135] Despite the ambassadorial inquiry of Nov. 1911 into his role at the Quai d'Orsay,
Herbette triumphed over his critics. As a sign of affection, one of de Selves's last acts was to
raise him to the rank of *ministre plénipotentiaire*. After relinquishing the dual posts of *chef
du cabinet et du personnel*, he asked for a leave of three months. On returning, he assumed
the relatively unimportant post of *sous-directeur des unions internationales et affaires
consulaires*. Herbette died of 'angine de poitrine' at the Claridge Hotel in Nov. 1929
(Prefect of Police to Quai d'Orsay, AE *dossier personnel*, Herbette).

[136] Caillaux, *Mémoires*, ii. 150–1.

[137] 'Note pour le Ministre', 21 Sept. 1911, AE NS 'Allemagne', 34.

[138] Ibid.   [139] 'Notes de voyage', 20–31 Aug. 1911, AE J. Cambon MSS, 13.

[140] Regnault to de Billy, 16 Feb. 1911, AE de Billy MSS, 37.

was prepared to dispute everything. Even after the treaty had been signed he envisaged French encroachment on Spanish Morocco.[141]

As early as the end of July it had become evident that the Centrale was receiving limited direction from above. Though Bapst had initially agreed with the Centrale's views, he had lost all control as political and commercial director. His eclipse was the more unfortunate as he was coming to realize the possible consequences of French intransigence. He appears to have been deeply shocked by the sending of the *Panther* to Agadir,[142] and it was at this time that his attitude began to change. Eventually he took the view that a continued refusal to open talks with Germany would lead to a war which was neither inevitable nor desirable. Hence he was opposed to the idea of following the German example and sending a cruiser to Agadir.[143] He had some success in persuading de Selves to undertake serious talks with the Germans. On 19 July 1911, he met the foreign minister and noted that the Minister was frightened by the fact that Germany's original request for frontier rectifications in Western Africa had become superseded by a demand for the entire French Congo. De Selves contended that 'ni lui ni aucun autre ministre ne pourra en face du pays recommander une cession de territoire aussi considérable'. Bapst in turn insisted on the need for both serious negotiations and concessions: 'J'ai manifesté avec force notre sérieuse intention de nous entendre. C'est un but élevé qui mérite un sacrifice. Je ne pouvais que recommander instamment de continuer des conversations en admettant le principe des concessions.'[144] Bapst's opinions, therefore, had diverged sharply from those of Conty and Herbette.

Nevertheless, if Bapst accepted the principle of serious discussion leading to concessions, he was determined, like his colleagues at the Centrale, to ensure that Germany posed no further problems in Morocco. Consequently he maintained his objection to Franco-German economic collaboration and opposed any talk of joint railway ventures.[145]

If the Centrale had had its way no agreement would presumably have been signed with Germany. But the Foreign Ministry was far from homogeneous. As was so often the case before the First World War, the

[141] Grahame to Tyrell, 23 Jan. 1913, PRO, FO 800/53, Grey MSS.

[142] Allain, *Agadir*, p. 334.

[143] A. Tardieu, *Le Mystère d'Agadir* (Paris, 1912), p. 434; de Selves to Bapst, 5 July 1911, AE NS 'Allemagne', 34.

[144] Note by Bapst, 19 July 1911 (transmitted to J. Cambon by Colonel Pellé, French Military Attaché in Berlin), AE J. Cambon MSS, 15.

[145] Additions to draft treaty, 18, 23 Sept. 1911, AE NS 'Allemagne', 34.

Second Moroccan Crisis saw continuous conflict betwen the Centrale, headed by Bapst, Conty, Herbette, Regnault, and Marcilly, and the ambassadorial élite led by the Cambon brothers. The Cambons and their allies recovered from their initial powerlessness to regain the upper hand during the most critical periods of the crisis. As a result, the Centrale had to be content with diluting the agreement of November 1911 and whittling down the concessions made to Germany.[146]

The role of Jules Cambon became preponderant after the sending of the *Panther* to Agadir. It was he who more than any other French diplomat made possible the maintenance of peace and the definitive acquisition of Morocco. His ability to influence Caillaux was very considerable, and he therefore chose to work with the premier rather than with de Selves.[147] Cambon tried to impress upon Caillaux that to some extent the Germans' anger was justifiable: 'les lanternements que nous leur avons opposés les ont persuadés qu'il n'y avait rien à faire avec nous en faits d'accords économiques au Maroc et que par suite l'égalité de traitement des intérêts économiques serait menacée si notre domination s'établissait.'[148]

Cambon sought to apply pressure on the Centrale from outside. Not only did he keep Caillaux *au courant* on every major matter, but in his letters to the premier he attempted to force a modification of behaviour or attitude on the part of de Selves and the 'Young Turks', whom he accused of sabotaging the 'house of Talleyrand' as well as French policy. In addition he bypassed the Centrale and corresponded directly with his brother, whose prestige and authority he mustered in support of his views. Nor was he averse to employing a weapon to which Herbette had frequent recourse: the press.[149]

Cambon's role in early July, when the crisis had begun in earnest, was crucial. It was not that he was any more successful with de Selves than he

[146] *JOC Annexe*, pp. 237, 245.

[147] To make a distinction between Caillaux's and Cambon's contribution to peace is perhaps arbitrary, and Allain has ably demonstrated the close liaison between the two. Cambon advised Caillaux constantly and Caillaux used Cambon as the translator and interpreter of his policy. It is noteworthy that the correspondence between Caillaux and Cambon is warmer and more voluminous than that between the Ambassador and de Selves. See AE J. Cambon MSS, 13.

[148] See Allain, *Agadir*, p. 370; J. Cambon, 'Notes de voyages', 22 June–8 July, AE J. Cambon MSS, 13.

[149] e.g. after receiving a letter from his brother about the possible breakdown of negotiations, Paul wrote to de Selves and seriously rebuked him. In the various meetings held at the Quai d'Orsay Paul gave his brother outspoken support.

had been with Cruppi.[150] However, de Selves was away in Holland with President Fallières, and Cambon, who was in Paris, enjoyed direct contact with Caillaux. He had a large part in frustrating the Centrale's desire to send a French cruiser to Agadir and limiting Franco-German talks to bilateral conversations.[151] When de Selves proposed to take charge of the negotiations in Paris and to raise the question of a conference, Cambon successfully thwarted him.[152] The Ambassador was particularly adamant about the damage a conference would cause. It would result in the strengthening of the German presence in Morocco and in the ultimate loss of the territory. He went on to argue that a furthering of France's commercial interests in Morocco was preferable to the sending of a local cruiser. Such policy would eliminate the possibility of local opposition, tighten France's grip on Morocco, and place responsibility for a crisis squarely on Germany. Cambon's Moroccan strategy was largely accepted by Caillaux. It involved stopping all further military progress and furthering as many economic interests as possible.[153]

Throughout the Franco-German negotiations Cambon relentlessly urged the Quai d'Orsay and the French government to be generous with concessions in the Congo in order to complete France's North African empire. Whereas the Centrale was reluctant to make concessions in the Congo without substantial reciprocal concessions in Morocco, Cambon contended that the best means of securing Morocco was to offer Congolese territory with few 'strings' attached. Some rivulets and isles in the French Congo amounted to little in comparison to a North African empire.[154]

In the final analysis, Cambon's role was decisive in preventing war in 1911. Nevertheless, he was not always successful in obtaining what he wanted most, sincere *détente* with Germany. He could prevent the two

[150] He complained in his private notes of the extent to which Herbette was able to influence de Selves. 'Notes de voyage', 22 June–8 July and 20–31 Aug., AE J. Cambon MSS, 13. For an illuminating examination of Caillaux's controversial role and life between 1911 and 1914 see K. A. Hamilton, 'The "Wild Talk" of Joseph Caillaux: A Sequel to the Agadir Crisis', *International History Review*, 9/12 (May 1987), pp. 195–226.

[151] 'Notes de voyage', 22 June–8 July and 20–31 Aug., AE J. Cambon MSS, 13.

[152] 'Notes de voyage', 22 June–8 July, Cambon to de Selves, 24 July 1911, AE J. Cambon MSS, 13.

[153] Ibid., 'Notes de voyage', 22 June–8 July.

[154] Allain, *Agadir*, pp. 352, 356, 358; also J. Cambon to Delcassé, 4 Oct., AE Delcassé MSS, 4; J. Cambon to Caillaux, 10 July, 20, 23, 27, 29 Sept., 'Notes Voyages', 20–31 Aug., AE J. Cambon MSS 14, 13; G. Tabouis, *Jules Cambon par l'un des siens* (Paris, 1938), pp. 211, 219; J. Cambon to Messimy, 19 Oct. 1911, AN, Messimy MSS; de Selves to J. Cambon, 18, 30 Sept. 1911, 9 Oct. 1911, AE NS 'Allemagne', 39, 40; Henry to Revoil, 25 Nov. 1911, AE Revoil MSS, 5.

nations from coming to blows, but he was powerless before the intrigues of the Centrale to establish cordial relations with Germany. His projected agreement with Germany, which utilized the declarations associated with the *Entente Cordiale*, was rejected by the Centrale, which judged it 'insuffisant'. It was the Centrale's project, motivated by deep suspicion and drafted so as to exclude Germany from Morocco, which became the basis of the 4 November treaty. Despite appeals to Caillaux, Cambon failed to gain acceptance for his idea of a Franco-German economic collaboration involving primarily the joint construction of Moroccan railways. At the insistence of the Centrale he was condemned to petty *marchandage* over minute details in Morocco and the Congo.[155] Meanwhile, the Foreign Ministry formulated several versions of the treaty, and tended to take back with one hand what it offered with the other.[156] The inconsistency and inefficiency of the Quai d'Orsay were such that Kiderlen-Wächter, the German foreign minister, could justifiably remark to Cambon that the manner in which the French had conducted *pourparlers* was unparalleled in his experience.

It was clear that the Quai d'Orsay was ill equipped to handle the lengthy negotiations. It was a house divided against itself, and was reeling under the weight of an administrative disorder caused by Bapst's incapacity and by inherent weakness in the 1907 reforms. There were numerous signs of anarchy. The Foreign Ministry sent out despatches for which it refused to accept responsibility.[157] Important posts were not being kept *au courant*, and telegrams were not being relayed properly.[158] Governmental instructions were sometimes changed if they failed to meet with the approval of permanent officials.[159] Conflicting personal views were published in the Paris press. De Selves, like Cruppi, received partial advice and was often not told of important developments until it was too late to formulate a response.

This chaotic state of affairs could have been prevented by a strong political director. After all, the 1907 reforms had sought to enhance his authority by amalgamating the commercial and political sections. Bapst, however, was ill suited to a position which clearly overwhelmed him. Lacking the respect of his deputy directors, he was incapable of instilling

[155] J. Cambon to Caillaux, 2 Aug., 9 Sept. 1911; 'Notes de voyage', 20–31 Aug., AE J. Cambon MSS, 13, 14.
[156] See AE NS 'Allemagne', 40.
[157] Bapst to Gérard, 12 Oct., 22 Nov. 1909, AN 324 AP 20 Gérard MSS.
[158] Tardieu notes, 1912, AN 324 AP 2 Tardieu MSS.
[159] 'Notes de voyage', 20–31 Aug., AE J. Cambon MSS, 13.

the necessary discipline in the 'house of Talleyrand'. The power which Herbette enjoyed in political decisions stemmed basically from Bapst's timidity, and did not rest on any formal attribution. The 1907 reforms had in no way envisaged the involvement of the *chef du cabinet* in the decision-making process.[160]

Bapst's incapacity therefore stood at the root of a good many problems. Nevertheless, administrative abuses left untouched by the 1907 reforms also contributed to the disarray of 1911. Relatively young men with little experience abroad had been able to dominate the Quai d'Orsay.[161] These were individuals who tended to see everything from a Parisian perspective and who had difficulty in foreseeing the consequences of their proposals. Limitations of this kind were strengthened by the Young Turks' preoccupation with the parliamentary *couloirs* and by their eagerness to build personal empires within the Centrale. Paléologue really reflected the prevailing view when he wrote to Jusserand in 1901: 'J'aimerais mieux assister à de grandes choses dans un grade inférieur qu'à des choses mesquines et inquiétantes dans le grade le plus élevé.'[162]

To some extent, the flawed performance of the Quai in 1911 was caused by the growing power of Herbette. The 1907 reforms had failed to weaken the power of the ministerial cabinet over personnel. Many diplomatic or internal appointments continued to be 'politically' motivated. Victims of the system could easily demonstrate that they had been passed over in favour of those who had the *chef du cabinet's* ear.[163] There was nothing particularly new about this abuse.[164] Under Herbette, however, it was carried to an extreme. Quite apart from the favouritism and political meddling which went on, Herbette was eminently unsuited to hold the position of *chef du cabinet*. He was, after all, a first secretary who had suddenly been empowered to decide the fate of high-ranking officials. Even if he had tried to be more objective, it is doubtful that the Bureau du personnel would have made sounder decisions. His youth and his lack of diplomatic experience were a 'redoutable cause d'erreures d'appréciations et de fautes de jugements de mauvais choix'. Apart from his immediate coterie, he knew few diplomats or the posts they served in, and thus was usually ignorant of the right man for the right job. To make matters worse, he was reluctant to seek advice, and, as *Le Temps* sternly noted: 'Bien plus, ce fonctionnaire

[160] Herbette to Delcassé, 3 Mar. 1911, AE Delcassé MSS, 4.
[161] Pichon to Barrère, 11 Dec. 1908, AE dossier personnel, Piccioni.
[162] Paléologue to Jusserand, 1901, AE Jusserand MSS, 22.
[163] *JOC Annexe*, pp. 237, 245.
[164] Lindenlaub to Gérard, 14 Nov. 1911, AN 329 AP 20 Gérard MSS.

politique ne consulte même pas les directeurs. Ceux-ci donnaient autrefois un avis facultatif.'[165]

During Herbette's ascendancy, the division between the ministerial cabinet and the political division widened. There was a close correlation between Bapst's abdication of responsibility and Herbette's 'empiètements'. The power of Herbette was such that, according to Jules Cambon, he entered de Selves's office whenever he wished.[166] Herbette attempted to maximize his influence by sending dispatches several months late to the political division.[167] He restricted the flow of information to embassies, and thereby deprived ambassadors of an adequate appreciation of problems.[168]

To add to the Quai d'Orsay troubles, 1911 saw the culmination of a series of financial scandals. Several officials had taken advantage of the slack fashion in which the Quai d'Orsay kept its accounts. As Poincaré remarked to Parliament, an incredible administrative disorder had reigned for several years at the Quai d'Orsay, and public accounting rules had been disregarded with unparalleled perseverance. Although Cruppi set up a commission in April 1911 to investigate both Hamon's stealing of Ministry funds and the general mismanagement, the results were meagre. At the end of 1912, one diplomat commented bitterly that the Quai d'Orsay could not even raise enough money to pay for his installation in a foreign country.[169]

Breaches of professional conduct were rife. In March 1911 René Rouet, an agent in the consular service, gave copies of secret Foreign Ministry documents to private French interests in Turkey.[170] Herbette had to answer enquiries into his private income. He admitted to receiving 'un léger supplément de ressources matérielles de quelques milliers de francs' for sitting on the boards of directors of the Société d'assurance mutuelle, the Centre mutuelle, and the Compagnie centrale d'eclairage Lebon.[171] Even the architect of the Quai d'Orsay, Chedanne, was implicated in a scandal involving the extortion of money and the theft of the Quai's tapestries. In all these cases, what stood out was not so much the individuals who had contravened professional ethics, but the fact

---

[165] *Le Temps*, 14 Nov. 1911.
[166] 'Notes de voyage', 20–31 Aug., AE J. Cambon MSS, 13.
[167] Ibid.   [168] Tardieu notes, 1912, AN 324 AP 2 Tardieu MSS.
[169] It was Pichon who began the inquiry into Rouet and Hamon, but the problem was left for Cruppi to solve (Louis, *Carnets*, 12 May 1911, p. 193).
[170] AE, Gout MSS, 14.
[171] AE *dossier personnel*, Herbette (notes of ambassadorial inquiry).

that the Foreign Ministry's system of administration was an open invitation to fraud.

At another time, these scandals might have gone relatively unnoticed, but not when France was in the middle of an international crisis and when its Foreign Ministry was bitterly divided and badly managed. As Théodore Lindenlaub, a correspondent of *Le Temps*, reminded Ambassador Gérard, too many things were going wrong: 'En temps ordinaire on prendrait l'affaire avec légèreté, sans doute; après les quatre mois de négociations avec Berlin aboutissant à une cession territoriale en pleine paix, l'esprit national est froissé, profondément mécontent.'[172]

There was indeed a strong current of dissatisfaction with the Quai d'Orsay, but surprisingly enough it differed greatly from contemporary criticism of the British Foreign Office. Whereas British opinion was calling for open diplomacy, democratization of the service, and a weakening of the Foreign Office's powers, French opinion, in general, took the opposite tack. The Quai's major critic, *Le Temps*, whose campaign led to the establishment of an internal reform commission, wanted to strengthen the Foreign Ministry by appointing a secretary-general. According to *Le Temps*, the problems of 1911 had arisen because the political director lacked clearly defined responsibilities. The influential daily questioned none of the Quai d'Orsay's powers. How could it, asked Lindenlaub, when there had been three ministries in one year?[173]

In 1911, however, public criticism in France was far less boisterous than in Britain, and amounted to a cleaning of dirty laundry rather than the purchase of new clothes. *Le Temps's* campaign was waged primarily by the journalists Tardieu and Lindenlaub, and it was symptomatic of the general reluctance to make changes that Lindenlaub could formulate a more comprehensive project of reform than a Senate commission which had been established to review the November 1911 treaty. Lindenlaub launched a severe attack on 'empiètements d'attributions', 'immixtions injustifiées', and 'pouvoirs factices'.[174] He was especially critical of Herbette, who was described as having an 'appetite for power' and a 'taste for intrigue', and as being 'le maître sans contrôle de la diplomatie Française'. What was needed was a 'Caesarean' operation, whereby the Bureau du personnel was detached from the minister's cabinet and given the status of a special section under independent directorship. This post had to be filled by a minister plenipotentiary or someone of

[172] Lindenlaub to Gérard, 14 Nov. 1911, AN 329 AP 20 Gérard MSS.
[173] Ibid.
[174] Ibid.

even higher rank, who would fix definite rules of advancement and give considerable weight to the notes of superiors. Disputes would be entrusted to an impartial tribune rather than to the judgement of a *chef du cabinet*.[175]

The pivot of Lindenlaub's reorganization was the introduction of a secretary-generalship. This measure would lead to 'le rétablissement d'un fonctionnement normal des services s'aidant et s'éclairant les uns et les autres, au lieu d'agir isolément et parfois de se nuire, volontairement ou non'. Lindenlaub in no way wanted a diminution of the Quai's power. In fact he was prepared, in view of new African and Asian horizons, to assign the Foreign Ministry additional authority. The main objective was not to democratize or weaken the Quai, but to instill unity and *esprit de suite* at the top. This task was to be performed by a secretary-general of proven ability who had 'occupé réellement et pendant un certain nombre d'années de grands postes et attaché son nom à des négociations importantes'.

As this statement suggested, Lindenlaub was apprehensive about the way in which increasing numbers of young officials were staking out their careers in Paris. To combat this trend, he suggested an initial period of two years in the Centrale followed by a minimum of ten years abroad. Such experience, coupled with impartial promotion rules, would mould better diplomats.[176]

Le Temps's campaign was successful in forcing de Selves to convene an internal commission in mid-November 1911. It was assisted when the foreign minister, questioned by the parliamentary committee set up to examine the treaty of November 1911, revealed that he was unaware of Cruppi's official objections to Spain's Moroccan policy.[177] Bapst, who had been on holiday at the time, was no less ignorant. The truth was that Herbette had failed to communicate Cruppi's protests to either de Selves or Bapst, and that the relevant dossier had gone 'astray'. Herbette was then called before the internal commission (composed of Louis, Barrère and Gérard), which considered his activities in addition to the reforms suggested by *Le Temps*.

Very little resulted from the criticism voiced in 1911. Herbette, who was Tardieu's chief target in *Le Temps*, was raised to the rank of *ministre plénipotentiaire*.[178] The campaign of *Le Temps* subsided as quickly as it had

---

[175] Ibid.   [176] Ibid.
[177] Henry to Revoil, 19 November 1911, AE Revoil MSS, 5.
[178] Ibid.

arisen. Indeed, there was a general consensus that it would be dangerous to make substantial changes in view of the ministerial instability so apparent in 1911. While the ambassadorial commission recommended the appointment of a secretary-general, it did so precisely because such an office would be a safeguard against the effects of ministerial instability. No legislation resulted, and leading parliamentarians, including Pichon, Millerand, Poincaré, Ribot, Develle, Cruppi, Dupuy, Méline, and Clemenceau, feared the further erosion of the foreign minister's authority by a Paul Cambon or a Camille Barrère.[179]

An internal commission, of course, was unlikely to envisage a diminution of the Quai d'Orsay's powers. At the same time, such change was inhibited by the intimate relationship between diplomatic and political circles in France. In many cases, diplomats and bureaucrats were the relatives of politicians who used the Quai as the greatest and most prestigious source of family employment. Even without this nepotism, the ties of friendship between official and politician were so strong as to prevent a wholesale *épuration* of men and administration.[180] The British and French cases, therefore, differed greatly. Whereas the reform movement in Britain sought to curb the initiative of the Foreign Office, to make it more democratic, and to inaugurate a period of open diplomacy, French reformers by 1911 were more concerned to improve the efficiency of the Quai d'Orsay and to ensure that its power was more effectively utilized.

[179] A. Gérard, *Mémoires d' Auguste Gérard* (Paris, 1928)

[180] Thierry, d' Aunay, Berthelot, Aynard, and de Margerie were just a few who had political contacts. Others, like the Cambons, Louis, Gérard, counted politicians as their closest friends.

10

Poincaré, Pichon, and Doumergue at the Quai d'Orsay, 1912–1914

After the Moroccan debacle of 1911, it was inevitable that there would be some parliamentary reaction against the Quai d'Orsay, but it was surprisingly mild. Raymond Poincaré, the new foreign minister, rejected the submissions of the ambassadorial commission and created an inner cabinet of confidants, thereby pushing the Centrale aside. In effect, this minor surgical operation resulted more from Poincaré's personal style than from the pressure of outside opinion. Poincaré undoubtedly wished to control the diplomatic machinery and to dominate policy formulation. Nevertheless, his almost total ignorance of foreign affairs, his special ·relationship with Paléologue, newly created political director, and his confidence in men such as de Margerie, *directeur adjoint*, made him, at least, very accessible to the advice of leading officials. Moreover, the very fact that the Quai's power remained largely intact left it with the potential of imposing itself in future on less dominant ministers. This is exactly what happened with men like Jonnart, Pichon, and Doumergue. The Quai's influence was held in check only as long as Poincaré retained his portfolio. Thereafter, its power increased and became concentrated in the hands of Paul Cambon's grouping. Although the 'Young Turks', mostly products of the École libre des sciences politiques, were challenging the older brigade for power, the ambassadorial élite was largely successful in maintaining its influence until the First World War.

Poincaré was not interested in radical schemes to reform the Quai d'Orsay. He wanted minor administrative changes that would facilitate his work. Such changes would be a reflection of his personal style rather than the result of discontent arising from the events of 1911. The machinery would be left intact while personnel changes were made. The idea of a secretary-general was shelved, primarily because a Cambon or a Barrère might utilize the increased authority to challenge the power of Poincaré.[1] The foreign minister proceeded to shuffle his

[1] A. Gérard, *Mémoires d'Auguste Gérard* (Paris, 1928), p. 448.

officials. Conty was sent to China as *ministre plénipotentiaire*. Bapst, put 'à la disposition' in 1912, was eventually exiled to Christiania. Herbette returned to the Direction des affaires administratives. However, a wholesale reform of the bureaux was impractical. Advised by the Cambon brothers, Revoil, and Barrère, Poincaré decided to follow a different course and to create an 'inner cabinet' of loyal and trustworthy men.[2] Paléologue, an intimate friend of Poincaré's since their school days at Louis le Grand, was recalled from Bulgaria and accorded the position of political director.

This was a very substantial increase in power for Paléologue. After Delcassé's fall in 1905 his star had waned considerably and he was exiled to minor posts.[3] Although Poincaré was certainly mindful of Paléologue's faults, especially his excessive imagination, he was nevertheless confident that he would be a loyal and intelligent subordinate.[4] De Margerie, for his part, was recalled from China after the Cambons had brought considerable pressure to bear on Poincaré, and the new position of *directeur adjoint* was specifically created for him. Although Conty had filled the position of *sous-directeur d'Europe* and thus *sous-directeur adjoint*, the new position gave de Margerie authority over all the deputy directors and put him naturally in line for the top spot when an embassy had been found for Paléologue.[5]

Poincaré's 'inner cabinet' was initially to consist of a representative of each member of the ambassadorial triumvirate. Paul Cambon, who came up with this idea, wanted to ensure efficient communication between the Centrale and the diplomatic posts and to strengthen the influence of the ambassadorial élite. However, only his representative, Daeschner, eventually entered the Minister's cabinet, where he was made *chef du cabinet*.[6]

Despite the closeness with which the ambassadorial élite and Poin-

---

[2] J. F. V. Keiger, *France and the Origins of the First World War* (London, 1983), pp. 48–54; Cambon wrote to his brother, 'Nous avons parlé presqu'uniquement de l'organisation intérieure du ministère.... Il a des idées très saines. Il m'a demandé un directeur et un chef du cabinet' (19 Jan. 1912), AE J. Cambon MSS, 25. According to Louis, it was on Revoil's recommendation that Daeschner was made *chef du cabinet* (*Les Carnets de Georges Louis* (Paris, 1926), 8 June 1914, ii. 125).

[3] Paléologue to Dutasta, 7, 23 Jan. 1910, AE *dossier personnel*, Paléologue; Berckheim to Gérard, 5 Jan. 1907, AN 329 AP 20 Gérard MSS.

[4] Keiger, *France and the Origins*, pp. 49–50; *Notes Journalières*, 4 Mar. 1914, BN (NAF 16027), Poincaré MSS.

[5] De Margerie to Paléologue, 6 Apr. 1912, AE *dossier personnel*, de Margerie; *Le Journal*, 23 July 1912.

[6] Undated conversation between Paléologue and Doulcet, AE Doulcet MSS, 23; P. Cambon to J. Cambon, 19 Jan. 1912, AE J. Cambon MSS, 23.

caré co-operated in the piecemeal reform of the Quai d'Orsay, the inner cabinet soon began to function as the mouthpiece and counsel of Poincaré to the exclusion of the ambassadors. Poincaré relied overwhelmingly on the judgements of its members. Paul Cambon's initial approval of the Foreign Minister turned to sharp criticism as the year went by. Poincaré's avowed intention of cleaning out the 'Augean stable' was merely a means of stamping his personal authority upon the machine, and in this he was magnificently successful. Even the doyen of ambassadors, Paul Cambon, was forced to incline before the master. As he complained to Jules in Berlin: 'Je ne suis pas de son avis sur tout, il s'en faut, je lui ai dit mais comme il tient à ses idées je suis bien obligé de m'incliner devant ses instructions formelles et je me suis borné à lui exprimer poliment et franchement mon opinion sans le lui imposer, ce n'est pas mon rôle.'[7] Poincaré's relations with Barrère and Jules Cambon also worsened, but this deterioration was the result of policy differences rather than of a personality clash as was the case with the elder Cambon.[8]

Not only had the ambassadors' projected reforms backfired but Poincaré was successfully employing his inner cabinet to push the Centrale totally aside. As Berthelot remarked to Gérard, the deputy directors were kept busy with matters of little importance, and the real decisions were taken at the top by Poincaré after careful consultation with Paléologue and, to a lesser extent, with de Margerie.[9]

Had Poincaré been decisive, then clear and reasonable policies could have been expected, but, despite his determination to rule the Foreign Ministry, he was inclined to submit even the most mundane daily decisions to the scrutiny of his government. Again, this was almost uniquely the result of Poincaré's personality and hardly reflected any inclination to practise a more open diplomacy. His fear of personal responsibility made him basically equivocal. Paul Cambon underlined the problem in a letter which was never sent, probably because of its reproachful tones:

Je vous avouerai que je trouve bien gênante pour vous-même l'habitude que vous avez pris non pas de tenir le conseil au courant de vos pourparlers d'une façon générale, mais de lui demander des décisions sur tout et de vous enlever à vous-même tout aisance. Mais réclamer son approbation journalière pour tous vos

[7] P. Cambon to J. Cambon, 4 Nov. 1912, AE J. Cambon MSS, 23; Delavaud to Gérard, 25 Dec. 1912, AN 329 AP 20 Gérard MSS.
[8] Keiger, *France and the Origins*, pp. 59–81; P. Miquel, *Raymond Poincaré* (Paris, 1961), pp. 262–4.
[9] Berthelot to Gérard, 26 Mar. 1912, AN 329 AP 20 Gérard MSS: 'Le département est calme: ... les bureaux sont tenus à l'écart. Toutes les tractations d'orient se décident entre le président [du conseil] et le directeur.'

actes ... et vous considérer comme lié par ce que vous appelez des décisions du gouvernement, alors que sur ces détails de la vie diplomatique quotidienne, il ne peut y avoir de décision définitive puisque la situation se modifie à chaque instant, c'est vous interdire la possibilité de négocier.[10]

Despite Paul Cambon's advice and the report of the ambassadorial inquiry, little was done to resolve the problems which had emerged during 1911 and which were largely due to the *chef du cabinet*. The powers of the political director were left intact, as amorphous and as dependent as ever upon his relationship with the foreign minister. In keeping with his desire to be his own master, Poincaré had initially decided to appoint a counsellor rather than a *chef du poste*, and Legrand, rather than Paléologue, had been his first choice.[11] Nothing was done in the decree of July 1912 to clarify the political director's position.

Nor were problems relating to the ministerial cabinet and personnel attacked. Before the war the ditch between the cabinet and the political division remained as wide as ever. Daeschner and Paléologue waged constant warfare in vying for the Minister's ear and in sabotaging each other's work.[12] The situation was made even more ludicrous in later years, when Berthelot and de Margerie held the two positions alternately. In the years before 1913, most *chefs du cabinet* had not held high positions in the political division. This was certainly the case with men like Dutasta, Beau, Daeschner, and Thiébaut. However, de Margerie and Berthelot, while acting as *chef du cabinet*, were at the same time either political and commercial director, as in de Margerie's case, or *directeur adjoint*, as in Berthelot's case. Despite initial hopes that the combination of the two high-level jobs would lead to a smoother running of the Centrale and to a better liaison between the ministerial cabinet and the political division, it tended to create, on the contrary, a more intense rivalry. By 1916 the situation had become unworkable. One commentator noted that 'Berthelot rédige toutes les réponses aux postes, pour les affaires importantes. Le reste, il l'expédie à la direction politique, au troisième étage; fureur de Margerie, qui n'a plus que du travail courant.'[13]

[10] P. Cambon to J. Cambon, 4 Dec. 1912, AE J. Cambon MSS, 25. In a speech to the Senate on 5 Feb. 1912 Poincaré indicated that he intended to formulate foreign policy with the support of public opinion and the press. Yet, as Millerand pointed out, this statement was motivated by 'la phobie de la responsabilité' (quoted in Keiger, *France and the Origins*, p. 45).

[11] Louis, *Carnets*, ii. 211–12.

[12] P. Cambon to H. Cambon, 20 May 1912, Louis Cambon MSS. Kreis, 'Frankreichs republikanische Großmachtpolitik, 1870–1914' (Basle University, 1980), notes, pp. 134–6, n. 390, 0–9. [13] Quoted ibid., notes, p. 135, n. 390r.

As for personnel, there was little change. The Bureau du personnel remained under the authority of the *chef du cabinet* and it was given an independent chief only in 1918. Until that time cries of favouritism remained rife, and men like Berthelot continued to promote their friends.[14]

In other areas, too, those who had appealed for widespread reform and purges were disappointed. The reorganization of the Quai enacted in July 1912 and in 1914 was a 'mere re-distribution of the work of the sub-directors', as the British Foreign Office was informed.[15] The Sous-direction du Levant was abolished and incorporated into the Sous-direction d'Europe. This last, which had previously been the Sous-direction d'Europe, d'Afrique, et d'Océanie, was reorganized in 1914 so that Africa became a separate subdivision and the Pacific was added to Asia. The Sous-direction d'Amérique remained the same with minor internal reorganization in 1914. Thus, immediately before the war, a more logical system based on geographical and economic needs had evolved from the 1907 reforms, but the exact nature of each department's responsibilities and the amount of initiative it possessed were not subjected to close scrutiny. In the final analysis, everything was dependent on a particular minister or director and his relations with his subordinates.[16]

Another area where reform was certainly necessary but not forthcoming was that of existing personnel. De Margerie was correct when he argued that one of the major problems of the Quai d'Orsay was the presence within it of an ill-suited combination of men. What was required was not the removal of a limited number of individuals, but a wholesale purge of the 'House of Talleyrand'. Apart from personal rivalries and the constant overstepping of functions there was the added difficulty of a certain narrowness in the Centrale, mostly directed against Germany. Such a limitation meant that the Centrale was often incapable of pursuing any more than one negotiation or one line of thought at any given time. Yet, as de Margerie complained to Reinach in February 1912, it was to be doubted that anything substantial would be done about the sad state of affairs as long as certain functionaries were

[14] H. Pognon, *Letter à M. Doumergue au sujet d'une réforme du Ministère des affaires étrangères* (Paris, 1914), p. 37. Pognon was a prematurely retired consul who had suffered under the system. On Berthelot's ability to advance his friends see 'Notes concernant le Quai d'Orsay, 1930–44', dossier Chambrun, pp. 27–9, AN de Robien MSS.

[15] Minute on Carnegie to Foreign Office, 26 July 1912, FO 371, France 1368; *Le Temps*, 23 July 1912.

[16] Daeschner to Doulcet, undated, 1913, AE Doulcet MSS, 21.

supported by influential politicians.[17] In view of the fact that the internal
commission set up in 1911 had been supportive of the Quai, and since
powerful influences were behind many functionaries, it was not surprising that the guillotine had fallen infrequently.

The partial demotion of three men was hardly sufficient to create a
more professional department.[18] As Poincaré's term advanced, he was
gradually to realize that this was the case, but his attempt to eradicate
resistance to his policies in the Centrale met with determined opposition. Resistance was led by the Sciences-po group, which were strongly
sympathetic to Balkan nationalist aspirations. With the onset of the
Balkan wars their influence on affairs was to become an increasingly important factor and, in the ensuing years, they were to maintain a running battle with the team led by the Cambons. Although in 1912 only 18
per cent of all diplomats were graduates of the Sciences politiques, 45 per
cent of those in the ministerial cabinet and the political and commercial
division had attended this prestigious *grande école*.[19] Eight of the sixteen individuals attached to the private ministerial cabinet were Sciences-
po graduates. Under Jonnart and Viviani, a similar ratio prevailed.[20]

While Poincaré was foreign minister, the Sciences-po group was to a
large extent held in check. However, they were able to assist the Balkan
states during the First Balkan War of 1912 by releasing to the press details
of negotiations between the Great Powers.[21] Throughout late 1912 and
during the various Balkan crises links with Tardieu, himself pro-Balkan,
and other members of the Paris press were particularly close.[22] The
Centrale, dominated by the Sciences-po group, not only used the press
against Poincaré but also kept him ill informed.[23] At the same time, it
was critical of both Italy and Austria-Hungary, the traditional enemies

[17] De Margerie to Reinach, 26 Jan., 25 Feb. 1912, BN (NAF 13547), Reinach MSS;
Geoffray to de Margerie, 29 Feb. 1912, AE de Margerie MSS.

[18] Bapst was put 'à la disposition', then exiled to Christiania in 1913. Conty was removed
only slowly from European affairs and was eventually sent to China. Herbette returned to
administrative affairs.

[19] W. R. Sharp, *Civil Service Abroad* (New York, 1935), p. 105.

[20] In Jonnart's private cabinet, 9 out of 18 were Sciences-po graduates. In the central
administration the ratio was as follows: Sous-direction d'Europe, d'Afrique et d'Orient, 4
out of 13; Asie, 2 out of 5; Amérique, 2 out of 5; Bureau du Maroc, 3 out of 5. Viviani's
private cabinet, which had a total of seventeen members, contained 10 individuals trained
at the Sciences-po. In the political and commercial division, the proportion was 16 out of
40. (*Annuaire diplomatique et consulaire* (1911, 1913, 1914).)

[21] Nicolson to Hardinge, 9 Oct. 1912, PRO FO 800/359, Nicolson MSS; Grahame to
Tyrell, 15 Dec. 1912, FO 800/53, Grey MSS; Bertie to Nicolson, 21 Oct. 1912, FO 800/165
Bertie MSS.

[22] Avon to Tardieu, 30 Sept. 1911, AN 324 AP 18 Tardieu MSS.

[23] Lindenlaub to Gérard, 14 Nov. 1912, AN 329 AP 20 Gérard MSS.

of the Balkan states. It played a large part in the recall of Crozier from Vienna, sabotaged Jules Cambon's policy of *détente* to such an extent that Cambon was forced to rely on private letters to Poincaré, Pichon, and Paléologue, and seriously jeopardized the work of Barrère in Rome. Bompard, who, as ambassador to Constantinople, was striving to preserve the Ottoman Empire, was also a target of the Sciences-po grouping in the Centrale.[24]

The sympathy which these influential officials felt for the Balkan nationalities was derived from their teachers at the École libres des sciences politiques. Many professors at the school were not only nationalist[25] but had a fervent belief in the Slavic world. Dard, a high-ranking official, unabashedly stated his convictions as follows:

Je croyais comme beaucoup d'élèves des Sciences-po à l'avenir du monde slave, qui m'avait été révélé par Vogüé, Léger, Ernest Denis, Rambaud, Mackenzie-Wallace. Déjà on considerait comme prochaine la fin de François-Joseph, et l'on échafaudait des systèmes sur les Tchèques et les Yougoslaves enfin autonomes. Et puis le partage de l'empire Ottoman permettrait de satisfaire toute la société chrétienne.[26]

This last point was in direct opposition to Poincaré's policies. In fact, the foreign minister was largely unsuccessful in stamping out resistance, and after his accession to the Presidency of the Republic in 1913 the Sciences-po group came into its own. They could have been permanently suppressed only by a complete reorganization of the central administration. Their influence was not restricted to the Balkan bureaux and was solidly established in many branches of the Centrale. The bureau du Maroc and the Bureau de la Tunisie contained many graduates of the École libre des sciences politiques.[27]

Though the Centrale, under the influence of its Sciences-po element, was clearly challenging the older ambassadorial élite, it did not triumph prior to the First World War. Instead, the ambassadors, under Paul Cambon's leadership, actually increased their authority. Since the 1890s Cambon had been placing his men in key positions. By 1914, many of the top spots were filled by his supporters. Although none of these diplomats would have taken orders from Paul Cambon, they generally shared and

---

[24] J. Cambon to Pichon, 21 Nov. 1909, Inst. de Fr. Pichon MSS, 2; Bompard to Paul Cambon, 7 Apr. 1911, AE Paul Cambon MSS, 4.
[25] Comte de Saint-Aulaire, *Confessions d'un vieux diplomate* (Paris, 1953), p. 11.
[26] Dard to Gérard, 28 Sept. 1910, AN 329 AP 20 Gérard MSS.
[27] R. Poincaré, *Au service de la France* (Paris, 1926–33), i. 98; Louis, *Carnets*, 22 June 1916, ii. 112; Keiger, *France and the Origins*, p. 33.

supported his views. As a result, his influence was strongly felt in the Quai d'Orsay immediately prior to the war. He imparted to the Foreign Ministry a desire for peace, moderation, and, above all, a sense of discipline. Though insufficient reform had been enacted and a more reckless Sciences-po grouping was coming to the fore, Paul Cambon was able to establish and maintain a certain unity and professionalism in the years immediately prior to the First World War.

Of the limited reforms introduced between 1912 and 1914, some of the most significant were designed to resolve the numerous problems arising from the newly created protectorate in Morocco. Not only was a resident-generalship created and earmarked for General Lyautey, but the Bureau du Maroc was established under Dupeyrat's direction. The main tasks of this office were to co-ordinate the policies of the resident-general and the Centrale and to handle practical matters concerning police, the statute of Tangier, and economic and judicial matters. From the outset, the Bureau du Maroc encountered enormous difficulties. Irrespective of who was making the decisions in France, Lyautey by and large was unprepared to accept external direction. Dupeyrat nevertheless wished to concentrate power in Paris. The ensuing conflict between two equally stubborn men was bound to cause confusion in France's Moroccan policy.[28] Lyautey was not the only one who opposed the new bureau, and it was weakened by the traditional jealousy of other functionaries, especially Saint-Aulaire in Tangier, Jules Cambon in Berlin, and Louis Renault, the *jurisconsulte*.[29] Because he had direct access to Poincaré, Dupeyrat was seen as a direct challenge by all three men. With the appointment of de Margerie as political director they were able to diminish his importance. In fact, Dupeyrat and the Bureau du Maroc were brought under the control of the political director.[30]

Other reforms had an equally limited impact. The *concours* itself continued to be a hindrance to the recruitment of suitable individuals. A committee was set up to study it and comprised Bourgeois, d'Eichtal, a professor at the Sciences politiques, Berthelot, Claudel, Lemonnier, a consul, and Jarousse de Sillac of the arbitration bureau. This committee agreed that the *concours*, based on rote-learning, was not attracting the

---

[28] Ribot to Tardieu, 28 Apr. 1912, AN 324 AP 14 Tardieu MSS; B. Auffray, *Pierre de Margerie (1861–1942) et al vie diplomatique de son temps* (Paris, 1976), p. 271.

[29] Saint-Aulaire, *Confessions*, p. 231; Saint-Aulaire to Chevandrier de Valdrome, 30 July 1913, AE Chevandrier de Valdrome MSS; Saint-Aulaire to de Margerie 16 Jan. 1914, AE de Margerie MSS.

[30] J. Cambon to Pichon, 12 July 1913, AE J. Cambon MSS, 16; Saint-René-Taillandier to de Margerie, 26 Jan. 1914, AE, de Margerie, MSS.

right candidates. Both d'Eichtal and Claudel were critical of the scope of the test, which had been 'encyclopédique' in order to classify more easily the growing number of candidates. Instead of a *concours* which sought out the 'érudites', who were conspicuously theoretical in approach, the committee called for an examination in which judgement, originality of thought, good sense, and the ability to make a quick decision were uppermost.[31] In essence, the general culture of the candidate would be assessed rather than his ability to remember large quantities of fact. The reports of the Commission du stage on the individual qualities of each candidate were to have added weight.[32]

The decree of 22 September 1913 gave effect to many of the criticisms voiced by the committee. It regularized formal examinations and tremendously improved their quality. Consequently, greater opportunity was given to candidates of merit. On the other hand, patronage and the right of the foreign minister to nominate did not disappear, a state of affairs for which the coming of the First World War was partly responsible.[33]

Perhaps more was expected of Poincaré than of any other foreign minister during the years 1898–1914. The man was a peculiar mixture of many elements. He was the product of a liberal bourgeois background and, not surprisingly, he developed a secular outlook. He excelled in his studies at the Lycée Bar, adopting an exceptionally serious and meticulous approach to his work. After studying at the Lycée Louis le Grand, he obtained a law degree, contributed to Paris newspapers, and entered Parliament. Apart from entering a few cabinets, he preferred to wait on the political sidelines for the most part until the appropriate moment.[34] He was by nature grave, uncommunicative, and little given to pleasantries or the expression of emotion. Though certainly austere, he did not have a rock instead of a heart, as Waldeck-Rousseau once remarked, and he was not as insensitive as was later made out. What Poincaré often regarded as natural courtesy was seen by others as aloofness, even coldness. Undoubtedly he suffered from a natural timidity and shyness. Even during later life the prospect of public speeches filled

---

[31] Note by Claudel, 3 May 1914, AE Thiébaut MSS, 2.

[32] Ibid., notes: meeting of committee, 23 Apr. 1913.

[33] Ibid., Claudel note of 3 May 1914.

[34] Miquel, *Poincaré*, pp. 26, 41, 52; G. Wright, *Raymond Poincaré and the French Presidency* (Los Angeles, 1942), pp. 17–18; Poincaré, *Au service*, i. 7; Keiger, *France and the Origins*, pp. 44–5.

him with such anxiety that he ceremoniously rehearsed and learned them by heart.[35]

Another trait which characterized Poincaré was lack of flexibility.[36] Perhaps because of his legal training, he was at times unable to compromise on even the most trivial of issues. When crossed, he lost his head and used a cutting, condescending tone which made him unpopular even with friends.[37]

Nevertheless, as Paul Cambon grudgingly admitted, although Poincaré was headstrong and to the point, he was not ill willed.[38] His legal background had been a useful preparation for the administration of the Quai d'Orsay. Though his meticulousness could be carried to extremes, almost to puritanical rigidity, the other side of the coin was that he had an intuitive notion of what was not only right but just. Despite his ardent patriotism and his ancestral links with the lost provinces, he found the idea of war repulsive and he rarely lent his name to the more strident forms of nationalism. That part of his personality which made him stubborn, uncompromising, and rigid also made him an ardent supporter of the legal process and, more importantly, a supporter of peace.[39]

Poincaré's political ideas were moulded in the 1870s and 1880s, when the reaction against the Second Empire was strongest. He wanted the Republican party devoid of both reactionary and collectivist influences. This 'progressist' outlook became increasingly anti-socialist. He refused President Loubet's invitation to enter the Waldeck-Rousseau ministry in 1899 because of the presence of a Socialist, and in the 1900s he was apprehensive of a socialist revolution. Despite these anxieties, he was imbued with a liberal philosophy which subscribed to the idea of progress and which consequently foresaw a diminution of the socialist threat. His liberalism was far more than just a socio-economic analysis of society,[40] and contained a substantial element of idealism.[41]

During his first days in office, Poincaré let it be known that he was in control of the Foreign Ministry. He had no particular love of career men, having had to deal with them and their intrigues as *rapporteur* for

---

[35] Miquel, *Poincaré*, pp. 86, 89, 187; Wright, *Raymond Poincaré*, p. 24; notes p. 89, AN 151 AP 44 Deschanel MSS.

[36] 'Notes journalières', 10 Feb. 1913, BN (NAF 16024), Poincaré MSS.

[37] Gérard, *Mémoires*, p. 451; P. Cambon to J. Cambon, 4, 5 Nov. 1912, AE J. Cambon MSS, 25.

[38] P. Cambon to J. Cambon, 4, 5 Nov. 1912, AE J. Cambon MSS, 25.

[39] Keiger, *France and the Origins*, pp. 44–6; Miquel, *Poincaré* p. 86.

[40] Miquel, *Poincaré*, pp. 84, 143, 145, 171–2; Wright, *Raymond Poincaré*, p. 22.

[41] Miquel, *Poincaré*, pp. 192, 251; Wright, *Raymond Poincaré*, p. 21.

the Senatorial Reform Commission of 1911. Suspecting their loyalty and competence, he set out to rule them very firmly. Starting work early each day at the Quai d'Orsay, he insisted on perusing even minor dossiers, studied them all, and wrote to the ambassadors himself. In addition, he annotated dossiers and personally opened letters meant for his perusal. Before he arrived at a decision subordinates had to furnish written advice or information. As Paul Cambon observed, Poincaré was definitely no diplomat, but he was an excellent administrator with a tidy legal mind and a thorough sense of discipline.[42]

However, Poincaré's legal training had its drawbacks. Accustomed to working with precise dossiers and texts, he felt ill at ease with diplomatic language, whose apparent fluidity irritated him. He was not adept in the way he phrased his telegrams. The ambassador receiving such items often felt that he had been treated like a naughty child. Even Paléologue was moved to complain to Paul Cambon that 'il ne comprend pas que dans nos habitudes une désapprobation à peine indiquée portée d'un blame. Son besoin de précision rend ses télégrammes désagréables de même qu'il rend toutes ses propositions inacceptables.'[43]

His handling of ambassadors reflected the rigidity that was so much a part of his character. He sometimes treated them as though they were there to act as a letter box for the government. In this respect, he was particularly suspicious of the initiatives of Barrère and the Cambon brothers, and was determined to bring them to heel.[44] Yet even with other ambassadors the mistrust was equally as great. As he noted in his diary in January 1914, 'tous nos représentants acceptent trop volontiers le point de vue du gouvernement auprès duquel ils sont accrédités'.[45]

Poincaré's wish to dominate diplomats who had become accustomed to a large measure of independence was one of the major reasons for the lack of policy co-ordination which developed during his stay at the Quai d'Orsay. Another was the contradictory nature of Poincaré himself, at once 'quelque chose de Napoléon' in his administration of affairs yet ambivalent over the correct foreign policy to pursue.[46]

[42] Miquel, *Poincaré*, p. 266; Gérard, *Mémoires*, p. 454; Keiger, *France and the Origins*, p. 53; P. Cambon to J. Cambon, 4 Nov. 1912, AE J. Cambon MSS, 25.
[43] P. Cambon to J. Cambon, 4 Nov. 1912, AE J. Cambon MSS, 25; Keiger, *France and the Origins*, p. 53.
[44] Louis, *Carnets*, ii. 212.
[45] 'Notes journalières', 29 Jan. 1914, BN (NAF 16026), Poincaré MSS.
[46] P. Cambon to J. Cambon, 6 Feb. 1913, Louis Cambon MSS.

Though he certainly used the press and public opinion, Poincaré found it difficult to resist the pressure of men such as Tardieu and Judet.[47] This contradiction of a domineering personality constrained by fear of responsibility had almost disastrous effects during the Second Balkan Crisis, when clear and reasonable foreign policy was essential.

Poincaré's relations with his subordinates were a peculiar function of his administrative expertise and his inexperience in policy formulation. Initially, he had opted for Legrand as political director. Indeed, it was only after Legrand had compromised himself that Poincaré considered Paléologue. According to Paul Cambon, Poincaré appreciated and liked Paléologue, but found him to be a little too imaginative—a serious criticism in Poincaré's opinion.[48] Paléologue proved more reliable than expected. Though Poincaré was jealous of Paléologue's prerogatives, his inexperience forced him to rely increasingly on the advice of his political director. Ultimately Poincaré made the decisions, but usually he did so only after careful consultation with Paléologue, to the exclusion of the bureaux.

Poincaré maintained excellent relations with de Margerie, the new *directeur adjoint*. Poincaré thought him a particularly able agent, and the two men held similar attitudes on most policy questions.[49] Nevertheless, though de Margerie was usually consulted as a member of the inner cabinet, the decision-making process was largely restricted to the combination of Paléologue and Poincaré.

Poincaré and Berthelot disliked each other. They were also deeply divided by the question of banking interests in China. Poincaré continued to support a consortium of powers, while Berthelot favoured increased participation by a Franco-Belgian group in which his brother André was a participant. Poincaré was successful in wresting policy from Berthelot's hand. The deputy director was increasingly ignored when it came to the formulation of Asian policy.[50]

Poincaré's relations with specific ambassadors were equally as bad. There seems to have been something to the view that the foreign minister initially envisaged a wholesale change in the ambassadorial corps. However, only Crozier and Gérard were recalled while Poincaré

[47] Keiger, *France and the Origins*, pp. 47, 65.

[48] Ibid. 50–1; P. Cambon to J. Cambon, 19 Jan. 1912, AE J. Cambon MSS, 25.

[49] Auffray, *De Margerie* p. 244; 'Notes journalières', 7 Jan. 1914, BN (NAF 16026), Poincaré MSS.

[50] See G. Kurgan van Hentenryk, 'Philippe Berthelot et les Intérêts Ferroviaires Franco-Belges en Chine, 1912–1914', *Revue d'histoire moderne et contemporaine*, 22 (1975), pp. 272–92.

was foreign minister. Further changes did not take place because it was almost impossible to touch the 'political ambassadors'. Lindenlaub stressed this point in attempting to explain to Gérard why he had been sacrificed: 'M. Poincaré ne serait pas désireux de se jeter dans le buisson d'épines que serait le remaniement ou le renouvellement des grandes ambassades d'Europe. Première grosse difficulté, la solidarité des Dioscures de Londres et Berlin.'[51] Furthermore, Poincaré, who was also premier, found himself increasingly preoccupied with internal and Balkan affairs. Sweeping personnel changes would have been ill advised during such a troubled period, and, although Poincaré was successful in stopping Jules Cambon's dialogue with Berlin and in making Barrère take a harder line with Italy, he could not remove them. So drastic a measure became increasingly unlikely as Poincaré became preoccupied with the presidency of the Republic.

Poincaré's collaboration with Paul Cambon was rather more complex. Poincaré fully supported Cambon's determination to strengthen France's links with London. He agreed with Cambon's assessment that Britain would come to the party when needed even though she had refused to sign a treaty of alliance. Consequently, Cambon's impact on Franco-British relations remained basically unaltered.[52] In fact, with the onset of the Balkan crisis in the autumn of 1912 and with the meeting of an ambassadorial conference in London in December 1912, Cambon was able to wrest much of the initiative from Poincaré. Poincaré's comments on the Conference of Ambassadors and on Cambon's role were indicative of the extent to which the latter had reasserted his influence: 'Il est visible qu'elle [the Conference] est l'œuvre spontanée de M[onsieur] P. Cambon et que toutes les observations attribuées à Sir E. Grey ont été préparées en réunion des ambassadeurs sans instruction du gouvernement Français.'[53]

There was nothing unique about Poincaré's foreign policy objectives. They were thoroughly Delcassian. He wanted a reinforcement of the Triple *Entente*, the preservation of a European balance of power, and the strengthening of French defences. He displayed a remarkable determination to retain these principles in spite of repeated criticism from his ambassadors. Undoubtedly his firmness owed much to Germany's

[51] Lindenlaub to Gérard, 14 Nov. 1911, 27 July, 3 Dec. 1912, AN 329 AP 20 Gérard MSS.
[52] Doulcet notes, Aug. 1914, AE Doulcet MSS, 23. For a thorough examination of their relationship see Keiger, *France and the Origins*, pp. 104–5.
[53] 'Notes journalières', BN (NAF 16024), Poincaré MSS.

occupation of his native Lorraine.[54] Yet Poincaré was no *revanchiste*. He made it clear in his diary that his actions as foreign minister were primarily a response to German intimidation.[55] He equated war with the illegality and destruction of the German occupation. The idea of employing bellicosity for domestic or even foreign purposes was consonant with neither his legalism nor his idealism.[56]

In the main, Poincaré's reluctance to open a meaningful dialogue with Germany was due to his deep-seated suspicion of her. He could not forget the occupation of Lorraine and, given the emphasis he placed on legality, it is reasonable to suppose that he viewed the Germans, and especially the Prussians, as lawless barbarians. He saw the Potsdam talks of 1910, the Agadir crisis, and proposals for Franco-German *détente* as manœuvres to isolate France from her friends. The 1912 Anglo-German Haldane talks merely confirmed his analysis of events. Germany must be left to flounder with her unsatisfactory alliances, which were the best means of keeping her reasonably weak.[57] If France was sufficiently strong both diplomatically and militarily, then Germany would be kept in line and no war would arise. His insistence on strengthening France's relations with Great Britain and Russia and on not attempting to dissolve the Triple Alliance was a reflection of two concerns: to be prepared on the one hand for all eventualities and, on the other, to do nothing which could be construed as a desire to attack Germany.[58]

Such a policy was admirable in theory, but hardly worked in practice. To suppose that one could encourage a nationalist revival at home while rejecting constructive conversations with a nation whose *amour propre* was easily wounded was both naïve and downright dangerous. Delcassé, as he had come to recognize by 1911, had paid a heavy price for following such a course.[59] None the less, Poincaré, on principle, was reluctant to pursue a dialogue or even to enter into conversations with Germany unless the past was totally transformed in France's favour. Moreover, he was restrained by public opinion and the press, and he was never one to take risks. Thus he sat dangerously on the fence, doing nothing actively to bring on a war or the recovery of the lost provinces but equally refusing to take steps which would dispel the envenomed atmosphere which plagued Franco-German relations.[60]

[54] Miquel, *Poincaré*, p. 34.
[55] 'Notes journalières', 11 Mar. 1913, BN (NAF 16024), Poincaré MSS.
[56] Keiger, *France and the Origins*, pp. 44–8.
[57] H. Cambon to J. Cambon, 31 Oct. 1912, Louis Cambon MSS.
[58] Ibid.   [59] J. Cambon to Delcassé, 4, 15, 30 Oct. 1911, AE J. Cambon MSS, 14.
[60] P. Cambon to J. Cambon, 4, 5, 20 Nov., 1, 4 Dec. 1912, AE J. Cambon MSS, 25.

Though Poincaré may have contributed to the coming of the First World War, the myth that he consciously conspired for or desired the war needs to be dismissed. As Lloyd George once remarked, the notion of the outbreak of war as the conscious clash of wills is too simplistic. Rather, it was Poincaré's inexperience in foreign affairs along with his idealism and rigidity which had such unfortunate effects. In addition, Poincaré did not think through the consequences of his policy. As Jules Cambon succinctly remarked, the danger lay not in any one particular diplomatic incident but rather in the atmosphere in which such an incident might arise. Nationalism at home, military sabre-rattling, and lack of dialogue abroad maintained a level of tension with Germany which had to be broken in one way or another.

Poincaré thought dividing Italy from other members of the Triple Alliance would only intensify Germany's fear of encirclement.[61] At the same time, one of the reasons underlying Britain's participation in the *Entente*, the preservation of a continental balance of power, would be undermined. On both points, Poincaré found himself in fundamental disagreement with Barrère. Consequently a running battle ensued between the two for control over Franco-Italian policy. Poincaré immediately struck by taking a hard line over the *Carthage–Manouba* incident, which involved the Italian seizure of two French vessels allegedly hiding Turkish soldiers, and by sacking Legrand. Within a month of coming to power Poincaré was severely criticizing the personnel of the Rome Embassy with the idea of diminishing Barrère himself. He lectured the Ambassador sternly: 'le personnel de votre ambassade n'était pas loin de partager le sentiment du gouvernement royal.'[62] The foreign minister relied increasingly on the *cabinet noir* as a basic source of information.

The *Carthage–Manouba* incident was only the first round. The next was the proposed Anglo-French-Italian Mediterranean agreement which Barrère had pursued for a number of years. Poincaré was able to oppose this project with the support of a number of ambassadors, notably Bompard and Geoffray. The agreement was eventually scuttled by a timely leak to the press and by a refusal to recognize Italy's conquest of Tripoli until the last minute.[63]

[61] Ibid., P. Cambon to J. Cambon, 4, 5, 20 Nov., 1, 4 Dec. 1912.

[62] J. Laroche, *Quinze ans à Rome avec Camille Barrère (1898–1913)* (Paris, 1948), p. 261; Poincaré to Barrère, 25 Jan. 1912, AE NS 'Italie', 216.

[63] Bompard to de Selves, 28 Dec. 1911, *DDF* (2), iii. 400; P. Cambon to Poincaré, 25 Jan. 1912, AE NS 'Italie', 11; J. Cambon to Poincaré, 18 July 1912, AE J. Cambon MSS, 13; see also de Margerie's approval of Legrand's role, AE NS 'Italie', 23.

Undoubtedly Poincaré had won some early rounds, but he was incapable in one short year of undoing what Barrère had achieved over the previous fourteen: the partial detachment of Italy from the Triple Alliance and the promise of her military support under certain circumstances. Barrère, moreover, was not prepared to submit to Poincaré's policies. He personally took it upon himself to soften the hard line that the foreign minister was applying. He appealed to men such as Delcassé to support him, and he was successful in postponing the appointment of Legrand's successor until after Poincaré's term. In fact, Barrère was able to employ Pichon, Delcassé, and Clemenceau, all his friends, as powerful counterweights to Poincaré.[64] Despite Poincaré's order to cease unofficial overtures to the Vatican, Barrère continued and even multiplied them.[65] A year later Poincaré had come to approve of the ambassador's policy. Barrère duly ceased to complain that he had become a big bird in a small cage.[66]

Poincaré's attitude towards Austria-Hungary was hardly less severe, and here he was far more successful in implementing policy. He regarded Crozier's belief that Austria-Hungary could be detached from the Triple Alliance as thoroughly unrealistic.[67] Austria would use the money from any French loan to improve her armaments and thereby pose a greater military threat than before. Six weeks after Poincaré took office, Crozier had been replaced by one of Poincaré's men, Alfred Dumaine.[68]

Poincaré's policy towards the Balkans and the Ottoman Empire was complex and beset by 'conflicting interests', as Keiger has aptly commented.[69] His official position was one of political disinterest. For various reasons, not least of which was the possibility of a major outbreak of a European conflagration, Poincaré had to maintain a semblance of the status quo, despite having some sympathy for the Balkan states. But Russia could not be alienated. Equally, if the Ottoman Empire collapsed, France's interests in the Lebanon and Syria would be jeopardized from a number of quarters.[70]

Poincaré's policy towards Russia was complex. He was certainly

---

[64] P. Cambon to Poincaré, 25 July 1912, Poincaré to Barrère, 18 Oct. 1912, AE NS 'Italie', 12, 23; Barrère to Poincaré, AE NS 'Turquie', 216.

[65] Barrère to Delcassé, AE Delcassé MSS, 1; Laroche, *Quinze ans*, p. 261.

[66] Poincaré to Barrère, 18 Mar. 1912, AE NS 'Vatican', 25; in Apr. 1913, Barrère was still discussing the religious protectorate; Barrère to Pichon, 29 Apr. 1912, AE NS 'Vatican', 25.

[67] Barrère to Pichon, 20 June 1912, Inst. de Fr. Pichon MSS, 1.

[68] Note by Poincaré, 18 Mar. 1912, AE NS 'Autriche-Hongrie', 28.

[69] Keiger, *France and the Origins*, p. 122.   [70] Ibid., pp. 121–3.

mindful of St Petersburg's failings and would much have preferred an alliance with Britain.[71] Within limits, he tried to restrain Russia, and he was determined that France should not be dragged into a general conflagration in which she had no direct interest. He was particularly suspicious of Russia's dealings with Italy in the Balkans.[72] However, it was difficult to restrain Russia in view of the existing state of the alliance, one in which Russia was blaming France for her humiliation during the Balkan crisis of 1908.

As the Balkan wars drew nearer, Poincaré undertook something of a balancing act. As Henri Cambon explained to his uncle Jules, Poincaré's policy towards Russia was to 'se cramponner à elle, car c'est l'unique moyen de la maintenir dans les limites de la raison ou de l'empêcher d'opérer son règlement avec d'autres'.[73] At the same time, Poincaré was determined not to antagonise her. He reminded Isvolsky in the middle of November 1912: 'Il [the French government] n'a en attendant, rien dit, ni rien laissé supposer qui puisse impliquer de sa part une défaillance de concours.'[74] Although not actively encouraging Russia, Poincaré was letting it be known that France might support St Petersburg if she were previously consulted. Isvolsky's analysis of French foreign policy, while certainly a bit crude, was not without insight: 'En somme, ajouta M. Poincaré, tout cela revient à dire que si la Russie fait la guerre, la France la fera aussi.'[75] Poincaré's policy, then, was deliberately equivocal. He wanted to discourage Russia from going to war without encouraging her to desert the Dual Alliance.

He was certainly no warmonger, but his policy during the Balkan crises of 1912–13 showed the extent of his concern to maintain solidarity with Russia. Undoubtedly his Balkan proposals of August 1912 were designed to put a lid on events in the Near East. Nevertheless, when Russia rejected this programme, he refused to entertain even genuine proposals from other powers. He curtly rejected German foreign minister Kiderlen-Wächter's call for the collaboration of all the Great Powers. At a time of crisis Poincaré was obviously reluctant to take any step which might offend Russia.[76]

[71] Miquel, *Poincaré*, p. 268.
[72] Poincaré to Louis, Apr. 1912, AE NS 'Russie', 41.
[73] Henri Cambon to J. Cambon, 31 Oct. 1912, Louis Cambon MSS.
[74] *DDF* (3), iv. 468.
[75] Isvolsky to Sazonov, 17 Nov. 1912, *LN* ii. 345–6.
[76] P. Cambon to J. Cambon, 2, 5, 20 Nov., 1 Dec. 1912, AE J. Cambon MSS, 25. The Aug. proposals included a statement of political disinterest in the Near East by Russia and France. No political questions were to be discussed without France, and there was to be prior agreement by the Triple Entente on the Italo-Turkish war.

Towards Austria his attitude was extremely intransigent. Paul Cambon had advised him to accept an Austrian annexation of the Sanjak of
Novi Bazaar in the case of absolute necessity. Poincaré's refusal to entertain such an idea, even though it might be the only way to stave off a
general conflagration, was a clear indication of his commitment to the
Dual Alliance. He argued in addition that Vienna had not made war,
that she had no right to acquire territory in defiance of French public
opinion, and that, above all, her seizure of the Sanjak would constitute
'un échec pour la triple entente'.[77] Apart from these considerations,
there was something personal about Poincaré's intransigence. He was
obviously peeved that his programme had been rejected while Kiderlen-
Wächter's was being seriously considered. A successful external initiative would have helped his campaign for the presidency of the Republic.
As it was, he employed Tardieu to proclaim his hostility to Austria-
Hungary's policies mindful that such publicity would enhance his
electoral prospects.[78]

Though Poincaré had some success in dominating the Quai d'Orsay,
the same could not be said for his immediate successors. When he
became president of the Republic, he was determined to appoint weak
foreign ministers responsive to his influence. To some extent he realized
this aim, but in doing so he allowed the Centrale and the ambassadorial
élite to re-establish their authority. This was the case with Senator
Jonnart, former governor-general of Algeria, who was foreign minister
between January and March 1913.[79]

Jonnart gained his portfolio as the result of a joint decision taken by
Briand and Poincaré.[80] Both before and during his ministry he was very
much under Poincaré's influence.[81] In domestic politics he shared the
same basic views as the newly elected president. Indeed, during the
Dreyfus affair he had appealed to Poincaré to rally the forces of the
Republic against the radical Right and the reactionary clericals.
Throughout his career he had had strong anti-clerical views and per-

[77] Ibid.   [78] Ibid.

[79] Jonnart had combined the posts of senator and governor-general.

[80] Keiger, *France and the Origins*, pp. 119–21. In fact, Jonnart's appointment was a
reward for supporting Poincaré during the presidential elections. See P. Cambon to J.
Cambon, 21 Jan. 1913, Louis Cambon MSS.

[81] Jonnart to Poincaré, 9 Feb. 1899, 11 Jan. 1900, 21 Mar. 1903; undated 1912, 20, 26 Jan.
1913, 'Notes journalières', BN (NAF 16005, 16024), Poincaré MSS.

ceived himself as the defender of a Republic 'de justice, de liberté et d'humanité, qui est sa force et sa raison d'être'.[82]

The minister did not take an active interest in his job. Such in-difference was surprising in view of the fact that his knowledge of foreign affairs was more than considerable. As well as being governor-general of Algeria for a number of years, he had been president of the Comité de l'Afrique Française and patron of the Comité de l'Orient. In collabor-ation with men such as Étienne and Lyautey, he had pursued an expan-sionist Moroccan policy that had been resisted by Delcassé, Pichon and the Cambons.[83] He was thus no newcomer to the diplomatic stage, and was quite familiar with some of the leading officials of the Foreign ministry. Even so, he was particularly useless in the Balkan crisis. Poin-caré noted in his diary that Jonnart made no effort to learn about Balkan cities or Balkan statesmen. He passed his time dreaming and arranging flowers on his desk at the Quai d'Orsay.[84]

To add to his lethargy, Jonnart suffered from a nervous disorder. His ignorance of and disinterest in the issues made him an easy prey for Paléologue and for his *chef du cabinet* Aynard, who was also his brother-in-law.[85] Relations between the political director and the new foreign minister were excellent. Paléologue found Jonnart 'très sympathique personnellement' obviously because Paléologue could manipulate the minister. Nevertheless, Paléologue described Jonnart's initiation into foreign affairs as laborious. The foreign minister appears never to have gone beyond asking questions of a very vague nature. It was left to Paléologue to draft the majority of telegrams, a task he relished after Poincaré's detailed attention to affairs.[86]

Jonnart's foreign policy was almost identical to that of his predecessor. The new foreign minister advocated a strong alliance with Russia, the strengthening of links with Britain, a country he deeply admired, and the building up of France's military strength. Although the idea of the Three Year Law did not originate with him, he was pleased by the successful fashion in which Étienne, as minister of war, gained parlia-mentary acceptance of the measure. Jonnart, like Poincaré, was suspi-

---

[82] Jonnart to Poincaré, 9 Feb. 1899; undated letter 1912, BN (NAF 16005), Poincaré MSS.

[83] Bertie to Foreign Office, 22 Jan. 1913, FO 371/1641; P. Cambon to H. Cambon, 8 Oct. 1904, Louis Cambon MSS; Delcassé to Étienne, 16 Aug. 1904, BN (NAF 24237), Étienne MSS; J. Cambon to P. Cambon, 18 May 1908, AE J. Cambon MSS, 19.

[84] 'Notes journalières', 26 Jan. 1913, BN (NAF 16024), Poincaré MSS.

[85] Ibid.; P. Cambon to J. Cambon, 8 Feb. 1913, Louis Cambon MSS.

[86] M. Paléologue, *Au Quai d'Orsay à la veille de la tourmente* (Paris, 1947), pp. 15, 20, 42.

cious of Germany and fully agreed with Poincaré's policy of firmness towards the Triple Alliance.[87]

Pichon, Jonnart's successor, was foreign minister between March and December 1913. He was far more experienced than Jonnart, but no more enthusiastic.[88] As had been the case during his previous term, his policy was largely the work of the ambassadorial triumvirate of Barrère and the Cambons. Hence, under Pichon, there was a partial reversal of Poincaré's policies. *Détente* was pursued with Germany and Italy, and Pichon adopted a far more disinterested approach towards the Balkans. Poincaré's influence, while not eradicated, was therefore diminished.

Pichon's choice as *chef du cabinet* was Berthelot, who immediately became involved in a rivalry with Paléologue. Pichon, for his part, was determined to reduce the authority of his political director. The ensuing conflict between the two men, though in part a matter of personality, turned primarily about policy issues, in particular Franco-Russian and Franco-German relations. A test of strength soon developed between them when France was asked to participate in the proposed naval demonstration of the Great Powers at Scutari during the First Balkan War. Pichon's victory sent Paléologue's fortunes into decline within the Centrale.[89]

Although Paléologue's power was waning, that of the ambassadorial élite and their allies in the Centrale was not. Pichon identified closely with the ambassadorial triumvirate and worked intimately with Berthelot in Paris. The results were a less intransigent attitude towards Germany and a harsher approach to Russian involvement in the Balkans. Doulcet, the first secretary in St Petersburg, was not far from the mark in labelling Pichon's policies as those of transaction, conciliation, compromise, and concession.[90] Under pressure from Jules Cambon, Pichon sought not only to improve relations between Germany and France, but to reach agreement over Asia Minor.[91] Yet he had become less accommodating since his first stay in office, and his pesssimism was considerable, especially after the famous disclosure, in November 1913, of secret talks between the Belgian and German monarchs. The Kaiser appeared

---

[87] Archives Départementales, Pas de Calais, Jonnart MSS, *sous-série* 26J. These papers contain very little on Jonnart's brief period as foreign minister. Among them are documents relating to the Franco-Spanish convention of 2 Mar. 1913 and to the Three Year Law.

[88] P. Cambon to H. Cambon, 7 Dec. 1913, Louis Cambon MSS.

[89] J. Halfond, 'Maurice Paléologue' (Temple University, 1974), pp. 213–15.

[90] Doulcet to Geoffray, 7 June 1913, AE Doulcet MSS, 21.

[91] Ibid.; Pichon to J. Cambon, 1 Apr. 1913, AE J. Cambon MSS, 16; Paléologue, *Au Quai d'Orsay*, 10 Nov. 1913, p. 228.

to be adopting a belligerent stance under heavy pressure from the German military. By the end of the year Pichon thought that Berlin's policies were alarming.[92]

There was a shift in policy in the Balkans as well. Pichon had always been highly critical of Russian activities in the Balkans. This mistrust remained strong throughout 1913. In specific incidents such as the Scutari affair Pichon worked against Russia. In general, he followed the policy of disinterest suggested by the Cambons, and was unwilling to support the Russians as strongly as Poincaré would have liked. Moerover, Pichon insisted on maintaining the Ottoman Empire, an outlook which ran contrary to Russia's wishes.[93]

Pichon's second stay at the Quai d'Orsay allowed the influence of Barrère and the Cambon brothers to revive. Paul Cambon, in particular, greatly enhanced his authority, and French foreign policy in 1913 and 1914 largely reflected his views. However, the power of the bureaux did not increase along with that of the ambassadorial élite. Despite an effort to exercise greater influence, their star waned with Pichon's arrival. Not only was the ambassadorial team strengthened, but the top echelon of the Centrale (men such as Berthelot and de Margerie) were loath to allow the bureaux much initiative. Berthelot constantly supervised Gout's work, which primarily concerned the Near East, while de Margerie severely curtailed the powers of the Bureau du Maroc. Both offices were kept occupied with tasks of a more technical nature, and policy formulation was left to the top strata.

The collapse of the Barthou government in December 1913 left Poincaré with serious political difficulties. His own influence was steadily waning. Moreover, there was a growing polarization between Left and Right, especially over the Three Year Law. Doumergue was appointed as prime minister and foreign minister only after Deschanel, Ribot, and Dupuy had rejected the posts.[94] Nevertheless, Poincaré's fears were soon allayed. Doumergue was certainly a Radical who championed reforms such as the graduated income tax, but in the realm of external affairs he proved to be as nationalist as Poincaré. He had not found it difficult, moreover, to accept Poincaré's condition of office, namely, that the

[92] Ibid., 25 Nov. 1913, pp. 238–9; Pichon to J. Cambon, 20 Dec. 1919, AE J. Cambon MSS, 16; Pichon to Barrère, 19 Sept. 1911, AE Barrère MSS, 4.
[93] J. Cambon to Pichon, 28 Apr. 1913, AE J. Cambon MSS, 16; 'Notes journalières', 26 Jan. 1914, BN (NAF 16026), Poincaré MSS.
[94] 'Notes journalières', 6 Dec. 1913, BN (NAF 16025), Poincaré MSS; D. Sumler, 'Polarisation in French Politics 1909–1914', Ph.D. thesis (Princeton University, 1969); G. W. Chapman, 'The Decision for War' (Princeton University, 1971), p. 125.

Three Year Law be accepted until a more suitable alternative was found.

Almost immediately Doumergue won over the personnel of the Quai d'Orsay. His courtesy towards subordinates and his penchant for hard work were welcomed.[95] Although he had been a former colonial minister and was thus reasonably well informed, especially about African and Near Eastern affairs, he fully recognized the necessity for sound advice from his officials and relied heavily on Paléologue and, later, on de Margerie and Berthelot. Writing to his brother shortly after Doumergue took office, Paul Cambon breathed a sigh of relief: 'il n'a pas la prétention de traiter, sans les connaître, les affaires de son départment. Il s'est bien entouré et il écoute les conseils des gens auxquels il reconnaît du jugement.'[96] This was a far cry, however, from abdicating responsibility, something he did not fear. He made it plain to Parliament and to the President of the Republic that it was he, supported by his officials ,who would handle foreign affairs.[97]

Doumergue's working habits were in keeping with such energetic pronouncements. He arrived early at the Quai and perused the most important newspaper cuttings, which had been specially selected by an official named Eric Labonne. Decisions were made after consultation with both de Margerie and Berthelot.[98] Doumergue appreciated the steady judgement of both. He decided to make de Margerie both political director and *chef du cabinet* despite the danger of a hostile reaction on the part of the Radicals.[99] He seems to have had a good working relationship with Berthelot, especially when dealing with Near Eastern questions. The increased emphasis placed upon maintaining and strengthening the Triple *Entente* was in large part derived from the influence of de Margerie and Berthelot.

In questions relating to Albania, the Liman von Sanders affair, the elaboration of Armenian reforms, the strengthening of the Russian military effort, and the expansion of Russian strategic railways, he showed himself to be a staunch supporter of Russia. It was Doumergue rather than Poincaré who jumped at the chance of paying a visit to St

[95] J. Aumale, *Voix de l'Orient: Souvenirs d'un diplomate* (Montreal, 1945) p. 39; Paléologue, *Au Quai d'Orsay*, 9 Dec. 1913, p. 252; R. Poincaré, *My Memoirs* (London, 1928), ii. 88.

[96] P. Cambon to J. Cambon, 28 Dec. 1913, *Paul Cambon: Correspondance* (Paris, 1940–6), iii. 57; Chapman, 'Decision for War', p. 183.

[97] 'Notes journalières', 16, 29 Jan., 4 Feb. 1914, BN (NAF 16026), Poincaré MSS.

[98] Paléologue, *Au Quai d'Orsay*, 24 Dec. 1913, pp. 259–60; d'Aumale, *Voix de l'Orient*, p. 39.

[99] 'Notes journalières', 6, 7 Jan., 10 Mar. 1914, BN (NAF 16026), Poincaré MSS.

Petersburg in the summer of 1914.[100] On the other hand, counselled by de Margerie and Berthelot, Doumergue refused to sacrifice French interests in Asia Minor, and he was unwilling to support unnecessary Russian meddling in the Balkans.

If the Franco-Russian alliance was to be strengthened, it followed that links with London should be made more secure and that France's defences should be strengthened. The Radicals' reputation for bad relations with Great Britain was improved, and Doumergue's policy during the Anglo-Portuguese colonial negotiations was so pro-British as to be considered soft by many in his party. Moreoever, he was instrumental in furthering Anglo-Russian naval talks with an eye towards tightening links between France, Britain and Russia. At home, he upheld the Three Year Law and sought to add to France's military capacity.[101]

Doumergue's concern to strengthen the Triple *Entente* and to reaffirm France's military commitments stemmed from several considerations. To begin with, he agreed with his permanent officials that the future was worrisome. According to Paléologue, Doumergue was convinced that Germany was prepared to fight a war in the near future.[102] The foreign minister was suspicious of Germany's diplomatic manœuvres at Constantinople and of the manner in which she was attempting to lure St Petersburg away from the Triple *Entente*.[103] He was hardly less wary of Vienna and Rome. Their handling of the Albanian question showed no concern for the concert of Europe.[104] The Triple Alliance wished to create a 'situation prépondérante' in the Mediterranean. He was determined to discourage such ambitions. Doumergue, then, was fully cognizant of the necessity of a united Triple *Entente*. He was, however, a moderate and peaceful man who was apprehensive of the future conflicts that were likely to arise in the Near East.

[100] Doumergue to Delcassé, 22 Jan. 1914, AE Delcassé MSS, 4; 'Notes journalières', 2, 12, 13 Jan. 1914, BN (NAF 16026), Poincaré MSS.

[101] Marginal note by Doumergue on despatch from P. Cambon to Doumergue, 1 Apr. 1914, AE NS 'Russie', 45; conversations between Grey and Doumergue, 24, 25 Apr. 1914, AE Gout MSS, 10. On a thorough examination of the Three Year Law, see G. Krumeich, 'Aufrustung und Innenpolitik in Frankreich vor dem Ersten Weltkrieg: Die Einführung der Dreijahrigen Dienstpflicht, 1913–1914', Ph.D. thesis (Wiesbaden, 1980). Also his published work, *Armaments and Politics in France on the Eve of the First World War* (Leamington Spa, 1984).

[102] G. Doumergue to M. Reboul, 1934, in G. Doumergue, *Mes causeries avec le peuple de France* (Paris, 1934), pp. 1–10; Paléologue, *Au Quai d'Orsay*, 7 Jan. 1914.

[103] P. Cambon to Doumergue, 1 Apr. 1914, AE NS 'Russie', 45.

[104] Conversations with Grey, 24, 25 Apr. 1914, AE Gout MSS, 10.

Much of the stability which was established in the Centrale before the First World War was in large measure due to the political directors and *directeurs adjoints* between 1912 and 1914. The three officials (Berthelot, de Margerie, and Paléologue) were able to enhance their authority during the period 1912–14. The ambassadors, while keeping the upper hand, viewed de Margerie, Berthelot and Paléologue with considerable respect.

Paléologue played a significant role in re-establishing the power of the political director. Despite the fact that both his subordinates in the Centrale and diplomats abroad often viewed him with suspicion and sometimes with hatred and contempt, Paléologue had a strong sense of duty which he imparted to the Foreign Ministry.[105] Indeed, as de Robien, his attaché in Russia, noted, Paléologue went so far as to demand a high standard of dress from his subordinates.[106] Although Paléologue himself tended to be lazy—having a horror of dispatch writing and a natural love of Parisian social life—he ensured that his underlings drafted telegrams and dispatches in the most impeccable manner. A drafter would have to recopy an entire dispatch if there was a single error.[107] Paléologue was largely successful in putting a stop to the indiscretions of his permanent officials. His penchant for secrecy is supposed to have led to the following admonition: 'Silence indoors, silence out of doors, and bear in mind that in a ministry of foreign affairs it is only published treaties that should not be kept a secret.'[108]

Paléologue's relations with his colleagues were variable. He and de Margerie found each other compatible at work and socially. It was Paléologue who offered the latter both the post of *directeur adjoint* and his lodgings in the Quai d'Orsay.[109] The Cambons, though suspicious of Paléologue, found him to be an agent of considerable talent.[110] They viewed him as a sound, if pessimistic, administrator. Often they preferred to communicate with him rather than with Poincaré, knowing full well that Paléologue would relay essential information to the Minister.[111]

Paléologue's attempts to fortify his position, especially against the

[105] P. Cambon to de Margerie, 15 Dec. 1913, AE de Margerie MSS.

[106] 'Notes concernant le Quai d'Orsay, 1930–44, Paléologue', AN de Robien MSS.

[107] Ibid., 'Souvenirs: Russie, ancien régime', p. 16.

[108] *Washington Post*, 17 Feb. 1920 (cutting in AE Jusserand MSS, 37).

[109] See Auffray, *De Margerie*, p. 231. The two men had developed a friendship after meeting in Madrid at the time of Alfonso XII's marriage.

[110] P. Cambon to de Margerie, 16 Jan. 1914, 15 Dec. 1915, AE de Margerie MSS.

[111] Letters from J. Cambon to Paléologue, 1912–13, AE J. Cambon MSS, 13.

private ministerial cabinet, made him some influential enemies. Within four days of his appointment, he had re-attached the deciphering section to the political division. The result was a battle with Daeschner which lasted throughout 1912 and damaged communication between the two services.[112] Berthelot, Pichon's *chef du cabinet*, proved even more intransigent, and refused to supply Paléologue with a steady flow of information.[113] Berthelot's dislike for his colleague was such that he persistently sought to have him removed.[114]

Paléologue's influence was especially significant in the areas of Franco-German relations and Near Eastern policy. In both, he was characteristically pessimistic about what France could achieve. Indeed, his pessimism was so pronounced that Jules Cambon brought it to the attention of Pichon.[115] Paléologue's suspicion of Germany had not abated since his stay in Bulgaria, his previous post. Though he recognized that Germany was desirous of maintaining peace during the Balkan crisis, he was convinced that she had adopted this attitude only because of the incompleteness of the German military laws of June 1912.[116] This assessment of Germany inevitably led to the notion that a general conflagration was imminent and that France could do little apart from reassuring her allies and friends and from building up her military capacity. He fully shared Poincaré's belief in the futility of *détente* with Germany and about the need for firmness on the part of a united and powerful Triple *Entente*.[117]

The political director's part in the making of France's Balkan policy was very substantial and explains why Poincaré went much further in supporting Russia than he had originally intended. Paléologue considered himself as something of an expert in Balkan affairs. The annexation of Bosnia-Hercegovina in 1908 led him to doubt that St Petersburg and Vienna would reach an agreement over the Balkans.[118] More seriously, his preoccupation with German and Austrian designs blinded him to the deficiencies of Russia's Near Eastern policies.

Poincaré's peace proposal of mid-1912 was the work of Paléologue.[119] The political director, though *au courant* of most of the intrigues under

[112] P. Cambon to J. Cambon, 22 May 1912, P. Cambon to H. Cambon, 20 May 1912, Louis Cambon MSS.

[113] H. Cambon to P. Cambon, 5, 29 Apr. 1913, Louis Cambon MSS.

[114] 'Notes concernant le Quai d'Orsay', p. 27, AN de Robien MSS.

[115] J. Cambon to Pichon, 9 June 1913, AE J. Cambon MSS.

[116] Paléologue, *Au Quai d'Orsay*, pp. 41, 162.

[117] Halfond, 'Paléologue', p. 209.

[118] Hans Madol, 'Qui a voulu la guerre?', *Vu*, no. 261, (15 Mar. 1933).

[119] P. Cambon to Jules Cambon, 24 Sept. 1912, AE J. Cambon MSS, 25.

way in the Balkans, doubted until the last minute that a Balkan war would break out, and his misjudgement partly explains the confusion in France's Near Eastern policy.[120] Paléologue was not perturbed, however, when war came. He concluded that the conflict would be an excellent opportunity to restore St Petersburg's authority in the Balkans. There was also something rather personal about the manner in which he rejoiced over Bulgaria's demise. Although Paléologue advocated utilization of the machinery of the concert of Europe to solve the Balkan imbroglio, he was more interested in tightening the links between Paris, London, and St Petersburg.[121]

Paléologue had an ambivalent attitude towards Great Britain. Like Paul Cambon, he was confident that Britain would render assistance in time of war.[122] Nevertheless, he thought that Britain should adopt a less equivocal stance and provide France with more substantial diplomatic assistance. He doubted whether the British contribution in time of war would be sufficient. Finally, he was often irritated by the moralism of British governments and by what he regarded as their anti-Russian policy in Persia.[123]

His attitude towards Italy was equally ambivalent. He was considered to be responsible for a rather farcical scheme to overthrow the Italian monarchy by means of a republican revolution. This was perhaps not as far-fetched as it sounded, because he had always been intrigued by the machiavellian schemes of the Italian statesman, Cavour. By 1913 he was desirous of enticing Italy away from the Triple Alliance. Though mindful of Italy's foibles in the Balkans and the Mediterranean, he differed with Poincaré over the utility of detaching her.[124]

By the end of 1913 Paléologue's position in the Centrale was precarious. Both de Margerie and Berthelot wanted to have him replaced, and Delcassé's decision to return from St Petersburg provided the perfect opportunity. The political director was not the first choice to succeed Delcassé. St Petersburg was originally offered to de Margerie, who declined for family and material reasons. Only after this refusal did

[120] Lindenlaub to Gérard, 14 Nov. 1912, AN 329 AP 20 Gérard MSS; Bax-Ironside to Nicolson, 28 Nov. 1912, PRO, FO 800/61, Nicolson MSS.

[121] Bertie to Grey, 20 Sept. 1913, PRO, FO 800/54, Grey MSS.

[122] Paléologue, *Au Quai d'Orsay*, 1, 10 Feb. 1913.

[123] Conversations with Doulcet, Feb. 1914, AE Doulcet MSS, 23; Bertie to Grey, 20 Sept. 1913, PRO, FO 800/54, Grey MSS; Paléologue to Doumergue, 21 May 1914, AE Paléologue MSS, 1.

[124] Newspaper article, Jan. 1914, AE Doulcet MSS, 20 *bis*; M. Paléologue, *Three Critical Years, 1904–1906* (New York, 1957), pp. 15, 73.

Poincaré, at Doumergue's express insistence, persuade Paléologue to accept the job.[125]

De Margerie, who became Paléologue's successor in January 1914, represented much that was traditional in the 'career'. An aristocrat of Catholic and royalist views, he had entered the Quai d'Orsay with the support of Francis Charmes in 1883.[126] His ancestors had a record of public service which went back several centuries. He served successively in Copenhagen, in Constantinople under Montebello and Paul Cambon, in Madrid, and in Washington under Jules Cambon. Throughout his career he was protected and promoted by the Cambons and by the influential moderate Republican Joseph Reinach, but even their powerful intervention was useless when the Radicals set out to purge 'reactionary diplomats' in 1906–7. It was not until Poincaré's time that he returned to favour and received the newly created post of *directeur adjoint.*[127]

Although he was a royalist and actually believed in the possibility of a restoration, both his Catholicism and his royalism were moderate. He showed himself to be thoroughly professional by displaying discretion and by defending the Republic abroad.[128] Moreover, his attitudes were evolving in a liberal direction. While not believing in the republican form of government, he considered it to be no worse in its practical functioning than any other government in Europe at the time. In addition, he found it admirable that the rising bourgeoisie was placing increased emphasis on eduation and taking an intelligent interest in French foreign affairs. Although perturbed by the socialist movement of the late nineteenth and early twentieth centuries,[129] his abiding belief in moderation, justice, and the possibility of compromise did not make him unduly pessimistic. If critical of the Left, he was no less hostile towards the movements of the extreme Right, in particular the *Action française.* During the Dreyfus affair he had sided with the Dreyfusards.[130]

Moderation pervaded his attitude to politics and to the world alike. This was not, however, the only quality which made him an admirable

[125] Auffray, *De Margerie*, p. 243–4; 'Notes journalières', 6, 7 Jan. 1914, BN (NAF 16026), Poincaré MSS.

[126] AE *dossier personnel*, de Margerie; Auffray, *De Margerie*, pp. 17–20.

[127] Reinach to de Margerie, 13 Aug. 1911, 4 June 1912, BN (NAF 13534), Reinach MSS; P. Cambon to Quai d'Orsay, 9 Mar. 1893; J. Cambon to de Margerie, 26 Aug. 1910, P. Cambon to de Margerie, 13 Dec. 1913, AE de Margerie MSS; P. Cambon to Pichon, 13 July 1910, Inst. de Fr. Pichon MSS, 2.

[128] Auffray, *De Margerie*, pp. 28, 46, 48, 57, 253, 274.

[129] De Margerie to Jusserand, 20 June 1899, AE Jusserand MSS, 22.

[130] Auffray, *De Margerie*, p. 255.

diplomat. De Margerie was not a highly original thinker, but he was a good synthesizer of other people's ideas. His great strengths, whether abroad or at the Centrale, were his capacity for compromise, his administrative expertise and his skill in presenting sound rational policies based on diplomatic realities. As his various superiors constantly noted, his sang-froid, his excellent education, his affability, his passion for work, and his extreme courtesy made him ideal for the highest positions.[131] The very fact that he had been posted to various parts of Asia, Europe, and America meant that he was highly experienced and knowledgeable. He was not, however, unlike many members of the Centrale in that he was highly ambitious. Indeed, his collaborators and superiors were fully conscious of his determination to reach the top.[132]

De Margerie enjoyed the respect of Paléologue, which did much to provide the Centrale immediately before the war with stability and a harmonious working environment. De Margerie tried to moderate Paléologue's pessimism and vivid imagination, though in general the two men had similar policy aims. They had a mutual interest, moreover, in Parisian salons, in pretty women, and in the artistic productions of the *belle epoque*.[133] De Margerie's relationship with Berthelot was less cordial. To some extent, a friendship between the two men was inhibited by their different political and religious ideals, their divergent taste in art and music, and their intense ambition. Nevertheless, they had the highest respect for each other's professionalism, intelligence, and capacity for work. De Margerie asked for Berthelot's appointment as his deputy in 1914, while Berthelot had no hesitation about recommending de Margerie as *chef du cabinet* when he wished to relinquish the post after Pichon's term.[134] Because of his affability, he was well liked by his subordinates, and he was able to create a cohesion which hitherto had been lacking. He succeeded to a large extent in reconciling factions and in instilling a badly needed discipline.[135]

De Margerie had very definite and sound ideas about reforming the Centrale. To him the main problem was one of personnel and resulted from a series of unfortunate appointments over the previous decade.

---

[131] AE *dossier personnel*, de Margerie.
[132] J. Cambon to Revoil, 1 Dec. 1905, AE Revoil MSS, 2; note by Berthelot, 10 Sept. 1906, AE *dossier personnel*, de Margerie; de Margerie to de Billy, 23, 29 Nov. 1905, AE de Billy MSS, 63; Geoffray to Doulcet, 27 Sept. 1913, AE Doulcet MSS, 21.
[133] Auffray, *De Margerie*, p. 232.
[134] Ibid., pp. 168, 250, 253; note by Berthelot, 10 Sept. 1906, AE *dossier personnel*, de Margerie.
[135] 'Notes concernant le Quai d'Orsay', AN de Robien MSS.

Only a wholesale purge would be sufficient to create greater objectivity in the Centrale. Not only was the Centrale's preoccupation with Moroccan affairs and its Germanophobia alarming, but the rift between the central administration and the ambassadorial élite threatened to paralyse the decision-making process. In view of this division, de Margerie wanted the appointment of a secretary-general or, barring that, a much strengthened political director. But he had to be content with a moderation of the North African services' expansionist tendencies and a relaxation of the Centrale's rigid anti-German sentiment.[136]

De Margerie, like Poincaré, wanted a powerful Triple *Entente* and a strengthening of the French army and navy.[137] However, he differed to a considerable extent from Paléologue and Poincaré in wanting to conduct conversations with Germany, and it was in this area especially that the Cambon's optimism made its mark. De Margerie had no illusion whatsoever about Germany's capacity for duplicity and intimidation, having experienced these tactics at first hand during the Algéçiras Conference in 1906.[138] Nevertheless, he did not see Germany as a thoroughly sinister power. He recognized that many of the problems which had arisen between the two nations derived as much from France's bungling as from aggressive intentions on the part of Berlin. Although de Margerie appears to have been unwilling to go as far as Jules Cambon in seeking *détente*, he fully realized that to ignore Berlin would be dangerous. A policy of frankness and courtesy combined with practical agreements of a limited nature would help to dispel the envenomed atmosphere that had long surrounded Franco-German relations. Towards this end, he supported and even encouraged talks with Germany over the future of Asia Minor. On the other hand he foresaw arrangements which would be largely devoid of political significance.[139]

In the case of Russia, as well as Germany, de Margerie's attitudes owed a good deal to the Cambons. He championed the Dual Alliance, and he was generally *persona grata* with the Russians themselves. Apart from having a natural sympathy with the royalist idea and entertaining intimate relations with high-ranking Russian aristocrats, he saw the

[136] De Margerie to Reinach, 25, 26 Jan. 1912, BN (NAF 13547), Reinach MSS.

[137] Chapman, 'Decision for War', p. 183; Auffray, *De Margerie*, p. 248; de Margerie to Reinach, 26 July 1909, 26 Jan., 25 Feb. 1912, BN (NAF 13547), Reinach MSS.

[138] De Margerie to J. Cambon, 17, 26 Jan., 3, 19, 26 Feb., 3, 12, 14, 19 Mar., AE J. Cambon MSS, II; de Margerie to de Billy, 1, 23 Nov. 1905, 30 June 1906, AE de Billy MSS, 63.

[139] De Margerie to J. Cambon, 23 Nov. 1912, AE J. Cambon MSS, 16.

strategic value of an alliance which partially encircled Germany.[140] Doumergue's stronger commitment to Russia in 1914 came about largely as a result of de Margerie's prodding. This commitment did not preclude criticism of St Petersburg. In fact de Margerie was wary of the manner in which Russia tried to employ the alliance in the Balkans and the Ottoman Empire.[141]

Having experienced the Armenian massacres under Paul Cambon in Constantinople, de Margerie was extremely reserved about France's participation in the affairs of the Near East. To him, the Great Powers rarely profited or came out unscathed after intervening in Balkan affairs. As *directeur adjoint* he had opposed the aggressively pro-Balkan attitudes of the Centrale with little success. He was equally unsuccessful in warning the Balkan powers in September 1912 that France would not support their aspirations. With the coming of the First Balkan War, however, his power increased. As the president of the French delegation to the Commission financière internationale des affaires balkaniques, he pursued a policy of firmness and moderation. With Pichon's accession to office, his views increasingly held sway and France took a more disinterested stance.[142]

De Margerie's view of Great Britain differed little from Paul Cambon's. The Conference of Algéçiras had confirmed his belief in Britain's loyalty towards her friends and, despite some apprehension over Anglo-German *détente*, especially the 1912 talks, his position remained basically the same.[143] It was with a sense of relief that Paul Cambon and the British government learned of his accession to the post of political director. De Margerie obliged by facilitating his former superior's work in London.

De Margerie was highly critical of the Porte, an attitude derived from a long period of service at Constantinople. He was appalled at the way in which the Ottoman government dodged its responsibility to reform. The accession of the Young Turks in 1908 had done little to modify his hostility. Nevertheless, despite talk of parcelling out Asiatic Turkey and taking Syria for France, de Margerie opposed the dismemberment of the Ottoman Empire. Indeed, he saw economic and political benefits in her

[140] Doumergue to Delcassé, 8 Jan. 1914, AE Delcassé MSS, 4; de Margerie to J. Cambon, 19 Feb., 5 Mar. 1906, AE J. Cambon MSS, 11.

[141] Isvolsky to Sazonov, 12 Mar. 1914, *LN* ii. 245.

[142] De Margerie to Doulcet, 15 Jan. 1896, AE Doulcet MSS, 17; de Margerie to Reinach, 25 Feb. 1912, BN (NAF 13547), Reinach MSS; Auffray, *De Margerie*, p. 233.

[143] De Margerie to P. Cambon, 3, 19 Feb. 1906, 19 Mar. 1906, AE J. Cambon MSS, 11; de Margerie to Reinach, 25 Feb. 1912, BN (NAF 13547), Reinach MSS.

maintenance. Not only did France's religious protectorate ensure a certain moral ascendancy, but the defence of her economic interests could best be carried out if the territorial integrity of the Ottoman state was preserved.[144] This stance brought him into conflict with St Petersburg, and he found himself in the unenviable position of trying to strengthen links with Russia on the one hand while keeping the 'big bear' out of Asiatic Turkey on the other. It also led him to throw his considerable weight behind the agreement of 1914, which he saw as a means of strengthening the Turkish Empire and of tying her more closely to France's purse strings.

Though de Margerie's views carried great weight with Poincaré and Doumergue, and though his relationship with French ambassadors was excellent, his position at the Centrale remained precarious and largely dependent on the goodwill of his *directeur adjoint* Philippe Berthelot. Unlike de Margerie, Berthelot had refused to entertain the idea of serving in foreign posts, and he successfully built up a power base in Paris through internal patronage and through the cultivation of influential politicians. His friendship with men such as Briand was typical of the good relations he maintained with important parliamentarians. Pichon's second term as foreign minister had strengthened Berthelot's position. The two men were friends, and Pichon chose Berthelot as his *chef du cabinet*. Apart from the fact that Pichon was able to employ him as a counterweight to Paléologue, Berthelot was extremely hard-working and able to carry out the functions of foreign minister. Moreover, he was able to use the *chef du cabinet's* power of appointment to further his personal ambitions. Although he relinquished the post to de Margerie in December 1913 out of consideration for Pichon, whose objectivity and foresight he highly appreciated, his authority was increased when he was appointed *directeur politique adjoint*. De Margerie became increasingly preoccupied by his position as *chef du cabinet* and almost all dispatches emanating from the Centrale were the work of Berthelot.[145]

The new *directeur adjoint* applied himself in a vigorous and methodical way. The de Margerie–Berthelot combination worked well before the war, despite subsequent rivalries. De Margerie counselled Doumergue on broader issues and attended to the general administration of the

---

[144] 'Note pour le Ministre', 11 Sept. and 'Note pour le Conseil des ministres', 20 Sept. 1913, AE Doumergue MSS, 1; C. M. Andrew and A. S. Kanya-Forstner, *France Overseas* (London, 1981), p. 66.

[145] Berthelot to Revoil, 21 Sept. 1913, AE Revoil MSS, 6; de Robien, 'Souvenirs: Russie, ancien régime', p. 27, AN de Robien MSS; conversations with Paléologue, 27 Feb. 1914, Daeschner to Doulcet, 13 Mar. 1913, AE Doulcet MSS, 20.

Centrale while Berthelot occupied himself with the political division. Dispatches at this time showed a marked improvement in their objectivity and clarity.[146] The Sciences-po grouping, despite a certain revival in 1913, was kept under close scrutiny by Berthelot. He took charge of important work and delegated matters of minor interest to his *sous-directeurs*, Gout, Piccioni, Chevalley, and Peretti de la Rocca. By 1914, Berthelot had emerged as the most powerful man in the Centrale.

Under Pichon, Berthelot, as *chef du cabinet* and as head of the Sous-direction d'Asie, which now included the Levant, took a more active interest in the Balkans. His policy was in conformity with the Centrale's inclination to favour the Balkan nationalities at the expense of Austria-Hungary. The notion of a fledgeling nation striving for independence appealed to him. Moreover, he developed an intense dislike for Austria-Hungary, believing her to be moribund and blaming her for most of Europe's woes in the Near East.[147] Despite such strong feelings, he believed, however, that France's vital interests were not in jeopardy in the Balkans. Consequently he encouraged Pichon to adopt a more neutral attitude.

Surprisingly, Berthelot judged Russia almost as severely as he did Austria-Hungary. He was naturally hostile towards the autocratic empire and more importantly, he regarded Russia's policies as egotistical. Through her constant adventures in Asia she had drastically weakened the Triple *Entente* in Europe.[148] When she had developed a renewed interest in the European continent, she pursued a reckless policy of *revanche* in the Balkans, which resulted in the crippling legacy of the 1908–9 Bosnian crisis. As Berthelot complained to Gérard in November 1912:

La situation extérieure inquiète beaucoup le président du conseil … il est très pessimiste de nature … le directeur politique l'est également; cependant, on peut difficilement croire que le pays se laisserait entraîner, dans une guerre où se jouerait sa destinée, uniquement pour suivre les fantaisies slaves de la Russie et la revanche d'amour propre qu'elle poursuit de son échec diplomatique du temps d'Aehrenthal.[149]

Berthelot's attitude towards Britain was ambivalent. On the one hand, he admired her political institutions, her fidelity, and her respect for the given word.[150] He would much have preferred to make the London–Paris

---

[146] Manneville to Doulcet, 23 Jan. 1914, AE Doulcet MSS, 21.

[147] 'Notes concernant le Quai d'Orsay' p. 73, AN de Robien MSS.

[148] Note, AE NS 'Russie', 42; Berthelot to Gérard, 1 June 1912, AN 329 AP 20 Gérard MSS.

[149] Berthelot to Gérard, 26 Nov. 1912, AN 329 AP 20 Gérard MSS.

[150] Claudel, 'Philippe Berthelot', *Bulletin de la Société Paul Claudel*, 28 (1967), p. 51.

link the basis of French foreign policy rather than the Franco-Russian alliance. He endeavoured to strengthen Franco-British links where mutual interest existed. On the other hand, he often demonstrated violent hostility to London. Britain was a competitor with France in the Near East and Asia. A note by Gregory, a permanent official of the British Foreign Office, attributed his animosity to the affair of the Banque industrielle de Chine in which, during 1911, his brother and he had opposed the consortium of French, British, German, and American banks in China. Whatever his motive, Berthelot defended his attitude to Great Britain on the grounds that Britain was not doing enough for the Triple *Entente* and was leaving an open field to the Triple Alliance.[151]

Not much is known about his attitude towards Germany immediately prior to the war. During the First Moroccan Crisis he had advised Rouvier and Bourgeois to take a hard line. His mistrust of Germany during subsequent years appears to have grown rather than diminished. By 1914, he was clearly apprehensive of Germany's intentions and, although prepared to accept Franco-German *pourparlers* over Turkey in 1913, was keen to empty them of political significance.

Jean Gout, who succeeded Defrance as *sous-directeur du Levant* in May 1909 and who became *sous-directeur d'Asie* in March 1914, was one of a growing number of officials who had entered the political division after service in the consular corps. Along with Berthelot and Ristelhueber, head of the Commission des affaires syriennes at the Quai, Gout was important in the debate over France's conflicting Near Eastern policy prior to the First World War.[152] He was the exponent of an aggressive economic expansionism, which often led him to be critical of the British government. Britain, he thought, was determined not only to obstruct the workings of France's religious protectorate in the Ottoman Empire but to carve out an economic and territorial empire.[153] While Germany was France's major competitor in Turkey, Britain ran a close second. Thus Gout argued that French interests should not be sacrificed on the altar of *Entente* solidarity.[154] However, although less devoted to the status quo than Bompard or Delcassé, he was not in favour of any

[151] J. F. V. Keiger, 'Raymond Poincaré and French Foreign Policy, 1912–1914' (Cambridge University, 1980), p. 68; Bertie to Grey, 14 Feb. 1916, PRO, FO 800/168, Bertie MSS; note by Gregory, 25 Mar. 1916, FO 800/96, Grey MSS; Manneville to Doulcet, 21 Mar. 1914, AE Doulcet MSS, 21; A. Bréal, *Philippe Berthelot* (Paris, 1937), pp. 72, 73.

[152] Andrew and Kanya-Forstner, *France Overseas*, p. 50.

[153] P. Cambon to de Margerie, 15 Dec. 1913, AE de Margerie MSS; note by Gout, undated, AE Gout MSS, 6.

[154] Note, June 1910, Gout to Rustem Bey, 18 Apr. 1911, AE Gout MSS, 6.

immediate partition of Asia Minor. The Franco-Turkish loan agreement of 1914 reflected his views by providing for reforms, increased
economic concessions, and maintenance of the Ottoman Empire.

Poincaré's favour did not extend to Jules Cambon. The Ambassador
had viewed the November 1911 Franco-German treaty as the beginning
of a sincere *détente*. Throughout the period of 1912–14 the memories of
Ems and Fashoda remained imprinted on his mind. Almost immediately
after Poincaré's arrival in office, Cambon bombarded him with suggestions for *détente*. The Ambassador emphasized the pacific nature of
men such as Wilhelm II and Bethmann-Hollweg, the chancellor, and
attributed signs of aggression to the pressure of internal politics.[155]

Poincaré, on the other hand, considered any further improvement of
Franco-German relations to be dangerous. By the end of 1912 Cambon
and Poincaré were thoroughly hostile to each other. The Berlin Ambassador supported a proposal by Kiderlen-Wächter for Franco-German
mediation in the Balkan wars. His suggestion was summarily dismissed
by the foreign minister.[156] Cambon nevertheless refused to abandon the
mediation proposal and widened it to embrace the concert of Europe.[157]
Far from inciting disorder in the Balkans, Germany, he argued, was
pulled unwillingly along by Rome and Vienna.[158] His views fell on deaf
ears, and he was reduced to voicing his complaints to his brother and
Paléologue.

Pichon's sudden arrival in office in March made possible a certain
revival in Jules Cambon's influence. He certainly contributed to Pichon's more disinterested position and to his desire to settle the Balkan
crisis by using the European concert. Moreover, Cambon was instrumental in having the Three Year Law adopted.[159] He was in close
contact with Étienne, the minister for war. He urged Poincaré and
Pichon to have the bill passed. Such advice, coming from an ambassador
who was considered too pacific and too 'soft' by some members of the
Centrale and Parliament, had all the more effect. Furthermore, while
the initial proposals were the work of General Joffre, newly appointed
chief of the general staff, Cambon's arguments were used to seek public

[155] J. Cambon to Poincaré, 3, 27, 31 Mar., 29 Apr., AE J. Cambon MSS, 16.

[156] Ibid. 19, P. Cambon to J. Cambon, 4 Nov. 1912.

[157] Ibid. 16, J. Cambon to Poincaré, 28 Oct. 1912.

[158] Ibid. 19, J. Cambon to Poincaré, 14, 26, 28 Oct., 14, 27 Nov., 9 Dec. 1912; J. Cambon
to P. Cambon, 27 Nov., 14, 16 Dec., 1912.

[159] Ibid. 16, J. Cambon to Poincaré, 23 Mar. 1912; J. Cambon to Pichon, 30 Mar., 6 May
1913, Inst. de Fr. Pichon MSS, 2.

approval. His efforts were not motivated by any wish for a conflict with Berlin. On the contrary, he considered the Three Year Law as the best guarantee of peace. Germany only respected strength. A defenceless France had always had the concomitant effect of tempting Berlin to wage war. He saw the key to German intentions in her overwhelming desire for economic and colonial expansion. By applying to Berlin Bismarck's policy of imperial distraction, Cambon hoped to ease within the foreseeable future any prospect of a conflagration. Not only did he initiate Franco-German *pourparlers* over Asia Minor, but he did his best to bring them to a successful conclusion.[160]

None the less, the Ambassador was apprehensive about several German officials who were coming to the fore in 1914, and was carefully scrutinizing developments, but he left it to pessimists such as Paléologue to make dire predictions. As Cambon had done throughout his career, he applied himself in the months preceding the war to easing tensions. In April 1914 he quoted approvingly a statement made by Jagow, the new German foreign minister, to the effect that agreements in Africa would preserve peace and provide Germany with an 'almost limitless field of activity'.[161]

On the whole, the period 1912–14 was a disappointing one for Jules Cambon. Poincaré squashed any talk of Franco-German *rapprochement* and maintained tight control over his actions. The Centrale, too, enjoyed some success in its efforts to sabotage *détente*. Though Cambon's authority in Berlin and Paris revived somewhat during Pichon's term, it never fully recovered from the Poincaré period. Consequently rumours of his replacement or retirement were widespread.

Paul Cambon, like his brother, had differences with the Centrale in the years 1912–14, but he was far more capable of maintaining and even augmenting his influence. He was the natural leader of the older ambassadorial team. He was not the target of the Centrale's Germanophobic sentiments. Hardly anyone differed with his assessment of Franco-British relations. Moreover, while he was prepared to hold talks with Germany and even to admit that she was not responsible for all Europe's

---

[160] J. Cambon to Pichon, 28 May, 8 July 1913, AE, J. Cambon MSS, 16; J. Cambon to P. Cambon, 12 Dec. 1913, Louis Cambon MSS; J. Cambon to de Margerie, 29 Dec. 1913, 23 Jan., 16 Feb. 1914, undated, 1914, AE de Margerie MSS.

[161] J. Cambon to Pichon, 10, 24 Nov. 1913, AE J. Cambon MSS, 16; J. Cambon to de Margerie, 2 Feb., 13 Apr. 1914, AE de Margerie MSS; J. Cambon to Doumergue, 15, 19 Jan. 1914, 16 Feb. 1914, AE NS 'Allemagne', 52, G. Tabouis, *Jules Cambon par l'un des siens* (Paris, 1938), pp. 232, 239, 242, 397; Auffray, *De Margerie*, pp. 66–7; A. Thierry, *L'Angleterre au temps de Paul Cambon* (Paris, 1961), p. 110.

problems, he was still suspicious of her and mindful of the dangers of a deterioration in Franco-Russian relations.

Paul Cambon's confidence in Great Britain remained unchanged during the period 1912–14. He was not alarmed by British Minister Haldane's talks of 1912, which he regarded as the corollary of Franco-German *détente*. Nor did he worry much about the influence of the pro-German Tyrell over Grey, the pacific bent of British Radicals, or the pro-German leanings of the City. In his opinion, it was Grey, supported by Prime Minister Asquith, who determined foreign policy. The British Foreign Secretary had given no indication of disloyalty. If Cambon tended to overestimate the speed with which Britain would enter a war, he was correct in thinking that her vital interests corresponded with France's.[162]

He thought that an Anglo-French alliance was impossible because British opinion would never sanction such a pact.[163] However, agreements of a technical nature could be obtained and would offer the advantage of restricting the alternatives open to London. Spurred on by his success in negotiating the Anglo-French naval agreements, he initiated a series of *pourparlers* which resulted in the Grey–Cambon letters of November 1912. He saw this as as an important step towards committing Britain militarily to the Franco-Russian alliance.[164]

Though Cambon was left largely with a free hand in Franco-British relations, this was not the case in other areas. Poincaré's refusal to inform Cambon of the secret agreements between the Balkan states until the last moment reflected serious policy differences.[165] Whereas both men were intent on strengthening the Triple *Entente*, Cambon was far more critical of St Petersburg's actions in the Balkans.[166] Nor was he as severe on Vienna as Poincaré. In fact, despite a certain suspicion of Austria, he felt that she had limited ambitions because of her internal problems. Nevertheless, Poincaré's more intransigent line triumphed,[167]

---

[162] Keiger, *France and the Origins*, pp. 102–16; P. E. Prestwich, 'French Attitudes towards Britain, 1911–1914', Ph.D. thesis (Stanford University, 1973), pp. 239–45.

[163] P. Cambon to Pichon, 23, 24 Nov. 1906, Inst. de Fr. Pichon MSS, 2; P. Cambon to Delcassé, 25 Mar. 1903, AE Delcassé MSS, 3; P. Cambon to J. Cambon, 4 Dec. 1912, AE J. Cambon MSS, 25.

[164] Z. Steiner, *The Foreign Office, and Foreign Policy, 1898–1914* (Cambridge, 1969), p. 104; *DDF* (3), ii. 363; draft of a letter to Poincaré from the French Ambassador, Oct. 1912, AE P. Cambon MSS, 12.

[165] Poincaré to P. Cambon, 15 Oct. 1912, AE P. Cambon MSS, 12.

[166] K. Eubank, *Paul Cambon* (Norman, Okla., 1960), pp. 156, 161; P. Cambon to Pichon, 12 Mar., 26 July, 12 Aug. 1913, Inst. de Fr. Pichon MSS, 2.

[167] P. Cambon to J. Cambon, 5, 20 Nov. 1912, AE J. Cambon MSS, 25.

and Cambon was unsuccessful in trying to reduce France's involvement in the Balkans.

With the advent of Pichon and Doumergue, the London Ambassador's authority was restored. On the former, he was able to impress the necessity for a limited role in the Near East.[168] For all his determination to resolve the Balkan impasse peaceably, however, he was unwilling to do anything which would jeopardize the Franco-Russian alliance.[169] The maintenance of a powerful, unified Triple *Entente*, he thought, was the best guarantee of peace.

While at times the Cambons and Barrère were severely criticized between 1912 and 1914, they survived. The same could not be said of Georges Louis, ambassador to St Petersburg in the years 1909 to 1913, who failed to do his job to the satisfaction of Poincaré. In Pichon's first ministry Louis had been solidly established, but his career ended abruptly when he was recalled under humiliating circumstances in 1913.

Louis's conflict with Poincaré was more the result of personal factors than of policy differences. The Ambassador often recognized that he was no longer equal to his task. He suffered from bronchitis, dreaded the Russian winter, and was going blind.[170] His wife had not followed him to St Petersburg, he refused to entertain or to mix with Russian high society, and was therefore incapable of informing Paris on a whole range of issues. He was oblivious to the storm brewing in the Balkans in the summer of 1912. Indeed the purpose of Poincaré's trip to St Petersburg at that time was as much to discover Russia's views as to strengthen a rather shaky alliance.[171]

The belief that Louis disagreed with Poincaré's policies needs to be re-evaluated. To begin with Louis was impressed with Poincaré's sense of order, his discretion, and the care with which he handled important issues.[172] Moreover, like Poincaré, Louis did not believe that Russian policy was unduly bellicose. He thought Sazonov, the Russian foreign

---

[168] Ibid.; P. Cambon to Pichon, 26 July 1913, 25 Nov. 1913, Inst. de Fr. Pichon MSS, 2.

[169] Poincaré to P. Cambon, 15 Oct. 1912, AE P. Cambon MSS, 5.

[170] Louis to P. Loüys, 28 Nov. 1911, AE Louis MSS, 3; report by German Ambassador, 27 Apr. 1910, Bonn, F. 108, vol. 18. Paul Cambon wrote to F. Charmes on 30 Jan. 1911: 'Louis, homme d'intelligence de sens et d'expérience mais qui n'offre que des qualités d'un éminent bureaucrate et qui n'a pas de riposte.' In the following year, he stated that 'Louis, là nous n'avons personne, nous ne savons rien, en un pareil moment c'est lamentable' (Louis Cambon MSS).

[171] J. Cambon to P. Cambon, Feb. 1913, Louis Cambon MSS; see also Briand interview, 13 Feb. 1913, published by *L'Éclair* of 13 Feb. 1913 (press cutting in AN F7 13959, 'Police générale'); and Paléologue, *Au Quai d'Orsay*, p. 21.

[172] Louis to P. Loüys, 30 Jan. 1913, AE Louis MSS, 3.

minister, was unwilling to pursue an adventurous policy in the Balkans and desirous of maintaining the status quo.[173] He incurred Poincaré's disfavour only because he had clearly failed to provide adequate information about events in the Near East.

Ironically, Théophile Delcassé, who nominated Louis to the position of political director in 1904, replaced him as ambassador to St Petersburg in the early months of 1913. Despite his overthrow in 1905, he had returned to office as minister of the marine by 1911. After the November 1911 treaty he had become increasingly hostile towards Germany. His mission as Ambassador to St Petersburg was to reaffirm the solidarity of the Franco-Russian alliance.[174]

As a former foreign minister of considerable eminence, he was to exercise a very substantial influence in the Russian capital. Though later commentators were confused by the brevity of his ambassadorship, Delcassé had made it quite plain to Poincaré and to his friends that he would stay in St Petersburg only until the elections of 1914 were held.[175] He clearly entertained the idea that he could then become premier or, at least, foreign minister. A short but determined effort to shore up the sagging Dual Alliance was undoubtedly what he had in mind.

It seems highly likely that Delcassé was suffering from a mental disorder by the time he replaced Louis and that this disequilibrium seriously impaired his judgement. His Germanophobia was such that when he stopped in Berlin to meet Jules Cambon he refused to alight from his train and touch German soil. In St Petersburg he fostered the notion that Austria-Hungary was to blame for all problems in the Near East, and he seems to have hoped that her dissolution would soon occur.[176]

Delcassé performed a great disservice to European peace by supporting and pushing to the forefront Russian aspirations in the Balkans and at the Straits.[177] Poincaré himself found this policy quite unjustifiable. Indeed, so disturbed was the President about Delcassé's influence over the Russian court that his request to return to Paris was hastily agreed to.[178] Delcassé seemed incapable of making the distinction between a

[173] Louis to Pichon, 16 Oct. 1909, Inst. de Fr. Pichon MSS, 3.

[174] Paléologue, *Au Quai d'Orsay*, p. 33; Doulcet to Geoffray, 7 June 1913, AE Doulcet MSS, 20.

[175] Daeschner to Doulcet, 23 Mar. 1913, AE Doulcet MSS, 20; Kreis, 'Frankreichs Großmachtpolitik', p. 107, n. 310.

[176] Paléologue, *Au Quai d'Orsay*, p. 256; G. Buchanan, *My Mission to Russia* (London, 1923), p. 186; J. Cambon to Pichon, 28 Sept. 1913, AE J. Cambon MSS, 16.

[177] 'Notes journalières', 26, 29 Jan. 1914, BN (NAF 16026), Poincaré MSS.

[178] Keiger, *France and the Origins*, p. 138.

legitimate defence of Franco-Russian interests and subservience to Russian adventurism. Nevertheless, despite his early departure from St Petersburg, he became foreign minister in August 1914.

Maurice Bompard's term as ambassador to the Porte was considerably more successful than his embassy to Russia. He believed that the preservation of the territorial integrity of the Ottoman Empire was a necessity for peace in the Near East and for the maintenance of French influence. He was hostile to those who envisaged a French Syria, and, to the chagrin of the French Colonial party, advocated the construction of a French railway network in the vicinity of the Black Sea. He was highly suspicious of Russian intrigues in the Turkish Empire, and became increasingly critical of Britain, whom he thought was undermining France's influence at Constantinople.[179]

Between 1909 and 1911 Bompard had encountered considerable opposition from the anti-Turkish and pro-Slavic Sciences-po grouping in the Centrale. However, with the advent of Poincaré, government policy conformed largely to Bompard's desires. Revoil, who was on intimate terms with Poincaré, and who was also newly appointed director of the Banque ottomane, strongly supported Bompard's policies. Admittedly, by 1913 Bompard had somewhat modified his views. He supported a railway agreement with Germany which effectively divided Turkey into spheres of influence. While desirous of preserving the Ottoman Empire as long as possible, he wanted to ensure that France would not be excluded from a later territorial partition. With de Margerie and Jules Cambon he was instrumental in preparing the Franco-Turkish and Franco-German accords of 1914.[180]

On the whole, the power of the Quai d'Orsay between 1912 and 1914 increased. Poincaré was without doubt a powerful figure, but his inexperience forced him to turn to an inner cabinet consisting of Paléologue and, to a lesser extent, of Daeschner and de Margerie. With Poincaré's election to the presidency of the Republic and his replacement by two inexperienced men, Jonnart and Doumergue, and by the obliging Pichon, who identified closely with his permanent officials, the Quai d'Orsay's star shone as brightly as ever. Even the Centrale, which had disgraced itself in 1911, regained some of its authority despite the tight

[179] Bompard to P. Cambon, 7 Apr. 1911, AE P. Cambon MSS, 11; Revoil to Poincaré, 3 Jan. 1911, BN (NAF 16015), Poincaré MSS; undated note by Bompard, AE Revoil MSS, 6; Pichon to Louis, 27 August 1909, AE Louis MSS, 2.

[180] Note by Poincaré, 20 January 1914, 'Notes journalières', BN (NAF 16026), Poincaré MSS; Bompard to Revoil, 5 May 1913, AE Revoil MSS, 4.

control of Berthelot. This resurgence of the career diplomats was made possible by the absence of reform. It was facilitated by the rapid turnover of foreign ministers and by the inexperience of Poincaré, Jonnart, and Doumergue, who were forced to rely rather heavily on the advice of Foreign Ministry officials. With the continuation of ministerial instability in 1914, the diplomats and bureaucrats were left largely in control of the decision-making process.

This situation could have been extremely dangerous in view of the Centrale's tradition of aggressive Germanophobia. However, though the rift between the Centrale and the ambassadorial élite still existed, the Sciences-po grouping was successfully disciplined by Berthelot and de Margerie. As a result, Paul Cambon's authority was at its zenith. He used his stature to create a stability rarely seen in the department and to moderate the Centrale's Germanophobia. Nevertheless, the First World War began at a time when those diplomats most desirous of peace dominated the Foreign Ministry. This was a war, moreover, for which France bore some responsibility. The paradox can best be explained by the failure of reformers to create a powerful secretary-general. The absence of such an official meant that French diplomatic agents, unlike the diplomatic agents of Britain and Germany, could still initiate personal policies. Ambassador Paléologue was able to do so, with disastrous consequences, in 1914.

II

The Quai d'Orsay and the July Crisis of 1914

With the assassination of the Austrian Archduke Franz Ferdinand on 28 June 1914, the Quai d'Orsay was soon confronted by a crisis which entered an acute phase on 23 July, when Austria-Hungary issued a severe ultimatum to Serbia. Mindful of 1911, the Foreign Ministry sought to formulate a collective policy in response to the events. As in 1905-6 and 1911 the government came to rely heavily on the advice of the Quai d'Orsay. The new Viviani government which had taken power only in early June, was overwhelmingly preoccupied with internal issues.[1] The cabinet had made no decision about how the crisis should be handled. Moreover, while the crisis was unfolding, Viviani and President Poincaré were virtually incapable of influencing the course of events. Between 23 and 29 July, they were stranded at sea on board the *France*. Bienvenu-Martin, the acting prime minister and acting foreign minister, had little knowledge of foreign affairs and was dependent on Berthelot, the *directeur adjoint*, whose views were largely translated into policy. After the 29th de Margerie, the political director, became highly influential when both Viviani and Poincaré listened carefully to his advice.[2]

While de Margerie and Berthelot were successful in formulating an official policy, they were unable, to an important extent, to ensure that it was put into effect. Their efforts, and those of the Quai d'Orsay as a whole, to preserve peace were sabotaged by Maurice Paléologue, who had established an 'ambassadorial dictatorship' at St Petersburg. Paléologue was in a powerful position to influence events, and he was also able, like many ambassadors prior to 1914, to act in a remarkably independent way. Because of his personal diplomacy, Paris was either misinformed or kept uninformed during vital periods of the July crisis. Without the consent of his government, Paléologue extended explicit support to Sazonov, the Russian foreign minister. His assurances actively encouraged the Russians to adopt a bellicose attitude, and

---

[1] Deschanel, 'Notes sur la guerre, crise de Juin 1914', AN 151 AP 46 Deschanel MSS.
[2] For the most recent and most thorough analysis of the origins of the First World War, see J. Joll, *The Origins of the First World War* (London, 1984).

thereby made an important contribution to the outbreak of a general war. It is difficult to envisage St Petersburg risking such a conflict without the support of Paléologue, who claimed to be acting in the name of France.

Paléologue's responsibility for the outbreak of war has been extended to the French military by historian L. C. F. Turner. This view seems untenable. The War Minister, Messimy, rightly complained in 1914 of the manner in which Berthelot kept the initiative in his hands, relaying information hours and even days late. Messimy himself was reluctant to implement the military measures envisaged by the French general staff. He made a point of submitting the requests of the chief of staff, Joffre, to his fellow cabinet members. Moreover, while he made it clear to the Russian general staff that France wanted Russia to attack Germany as quickly as possible if war occurred, he did not encourage the Russian general staff to attempt a military solution of the July crisis.[3]

L. C. F. Turner's assertion that Paléologue's position was considerably strengthened by French military leaders is largely unfounded. Paléologue may have have reflected the general staff's confidence, but he was working on his own. In fact, there is evidence to suggest that there was a rift between Paléologue and his military attaché General de Laguiche, who evidently realized the lengths to which the Ambassador was pushing St Petersburg.[4] In Paris, Joffre was clearly of the opinion that the government alone was responsible for determining French policy during the crisis.[5]

Though there were differences of detail, the Quai d'Orsay in July 1914 was united in its deepening suspicion of Germany which, in consequence, led to the placing of increased emphasis upon the need to support Russia whatever the cost. Warnings before July 1914 about the nature of the German armament programme as well as about the increasingly favourable position of the militarists in Germany were unequivocal. Reports from the Ministry of the Interior informed the Quai d'Orsay that the preliminary economic measures requested for German mobilization (movements of oil and money) were being taken.[6] Jules Cambon's reports of Wilhelm II's virtual abdication of power in the face of militarist pressure were reinforced by dispatches emanating from the

[3] 'Origines de la guerre et la responsabilité', AN Messimy MSS, 1, 5; L. C. F. Turner, *The Origins of the First World War* (London, 1976), pp. 89, 104.

[4] De Robien, 'Souvenirs: Russie, ancien régime' p. 32, AN de Robien MSS; Turner, *Origins*, pp. 89, 104.

[5] Joffre to Messimy, 28 July 1914, AN Messimy MSS, 2.

[6] See reports of 28 Feb., 2 Mar. 1914, AE NS 'Allemagne', 52.

French legation in Brussels. Moreover, even before July, a series of minor issues had envenomed Franco-German relations.[7]

Undoubtedly evidence of belligerent thinking can be found in the Quai d'Orsay. What characterized it, however, was an underlying suspicion of Germany which filled the upper echelons with a deep-seated pessimism about the future.[8] In 1914, with the exception of Paléologue (and perhaps Barrère), most of the Foreign Ministry's leading officials were profoundly pacific, well endowed with moderation and good sense, and little impressed by militaristic arguments. Their attitude was in part a reaction to what was going on in Berlin.[9] Their understanding of events in Germany, coupled with their pessimism and suspicion, made them ready to accept a general European conflagration if the German government threw down the gauntlet. Their readiness was the greater because of a general consensus both inside and outside the Quai d'Orsay that the Russian and French armies were adequately prepared for war.[10] Moreover, few, if any, French officials envisaged prolonged trench warfare with its subsequent economic, political, social, and emotional upheaval.[11] A belief in brevity and limited consequences of a general war encouraged the Quai d'Orsay to contemplate warfare as the ultimate diplomatic weapon. Such an outlook was reinforced by the belief that no general strike would be called to paralyse initial military manœuvres.[12]

For all its pessimism, the Quai d'Orsay envisaged armed conflict with Germany only in some hardly foreseeable future. The Sarajevo assassination was not expected to lead to an immediate diplomatic crisis. As the Bavarian Minister in Paris commented, 'L'absence de tous les dirigeants de la politique française, y compris M. de Margerie suffit à prouver

[7] Ibid., de Fontarce to Doumergue, 3 Mar. 1914, and Manneville to Doumergue, 4 June 1914. On the policy of pinpricks pursued by both sides see AE NS 'Allemagne', 52, May, June 1914.

[8] J. Laroche, *Au Quai d'Orsay avec Briand et Poincaré* (Paris, 1957), p. 19; note by A. Ferry, 27 July, AE Ferry MSS; d'Aumale, *Voix de l'Orient: Souvenirs d'un diplomate* (Montreal, 1945), p. 39; notes by Reinach, BN (NAF 15558), Reinach MSS.

[9] For a discussion of French militarism see E. Weber, *The Nationalist Revival in France, 1905–1914* (Los Angeles, 1968), p. 108.

[10] See 'L'Accélération de l'offensive russe en août 1914', AN Messimy MSS, 1; notes by Louis de Robien, 'Voyage de Poincaré' pp. 59, 83, AN de Robien MSS; Paléologue to Doumergue, 21 May 1914, AE Paléologue MSS, 1.

[11] See the following newspaper reports: *Le Gaulois*, 31 July 1914; *L'Intransigeant*, 29 July 1914; *Le Figaro*, 1 Aug. 1914. See also *La Revue des deux mondes*, 15 Aug. 1914, for the official viewpoint. See Bertie to Grey, 3 Aug. 1914, PRO, FO 800/116, Bertie MSS.

[12] A general strike called for 16 Dec. 1912 by the CGT had failed dismally, and foreign policy experts believed that any future strikes would be limited and would not critically restrict the government's action. (AN F7 12934, Report No. M/95: 38, 1 Aug. 1914.)

combien la crise a surpris tout le monde.'[13] Certainly no one dismissed
the crisis, but the Quai tended to view it as a continuation of recurrent
Balkan problems which would be resolved without igniting the powder
keg. The agenda of discussions drafted on 12 or 13 July by de Margerie
for Viviani's and Poincaré's use during the forthcoming trip to St
Petersburg indicated how lightly the Austro-Serbian dispute was taken
by the Quai d'Orsay.[14]

The actual visit to St Petersburg was further proof that the crisis was
far from uppermost in the minds of French officials and politicians. The
journey had been arranged in January for July despite the objections of
Poincaré, who would have preferred a later date.[15] Its objective was
threefold: to discuss Russo-British relations, especially in Persia; to hasten the construction of Russian strategic railways; and to put an end to
intrigues associated with Count Witte's idea of a Russo-German-
French alliance.[16] During the three-day visit, the Austro-Serbian dispute was placed higher on the list of discussions. Indeed, de Margerie
and Poincaré were worried that Austria-Hungary was preparing a *coup
de théâtre*. However, their concern resulted simply in a vague statement to
the effect that firmness was the best means of safeguarding peace.[17]
Russia was not encouraged to adopt a bellicose attitude towards the
Central Powers. In the end, most of the Franco-Russian *pourparlers* concerned economic and commercial questions and a Russo-British naval
plan. Poincaré seemed most interested in the establishment of better
Russo-British relations, which were suffering rather acute difficulties in
the Near East.[18]

One of the main reasons why, prior to 25 July, the Quai was rather
undisturbed by the crisis was the fact that it was not receiving any

[13] B. Auffray, *Pierre de Margerie (1861–1942) et la vie diplomatique de son temps* (Paris, 1976), p. 278.

[14] It was placed well down the list at no. 14. (P. Renouvin, 'La Politique française en juillet 1914 d'après les Documents diplomatiques français', *Revue d'histoire de la Guerre mondiale* (Jan. 1937), p. 7.

[15] That the visit was hardly the occasion for a 'war council' is shown by J. J. Becker, *Comment les Français sont entrés dans la guerre 1914* (Paris, 1977), p. 140. See also *Notes Journalières*, 1 Jan. 1914, BN (NAF 16026), Poincaré MSS; Auffray, *De Margerie*, p. 278.

[16] Poincaré noted: 'Si les renseignements de Paléologue sont exacts, il va falloir cher-cher immédiatement à dénouer ces intrigues. Le voyage en France et mon voyage en Russie me permettront d'agir.' 'Notes journalières', 26 Mar. 1914, BN (NAF 16027), Poincaré MSS; Auffray, *De Margerie*, p. 279; P. Cambon to Doumergue, 1 Apr. 1914, AE NS 'Russie', 45.

[17] Notes by de Robien, 'Voyage de Poincaré', p. 54, AN de Robien MSS.

[18] 'Notes journalières' 21, 22, 23 July, BN (NAF 16027), Poincaré MSS.

information from its legation in Belgrade. Descos, the French minister there, was ill. No dispatch or telegram of any description arrived from the Belgrade legation between 14 and 25 July.[19] The Centrale was thus largely ignorant of the conditions of the assassination and of the contents of the ultimatum until Boppe arrived in Belgrade on the 25th.[20] Combined with this misfortune was the poor quality of information being transmitted from the Paléologue embassy in St Petersburg. Both Russian moderation and German intransigence were exaggerated. On 27 July the Centrale was sent three different versions of the preliminary measures taken by Russia on the 25th.[21] On occasion, telegrams which were originally composed hours after the event reached the Quai d'Orsay only after considerable delay.

Newspaper and private reports reaching the Centrale from Berlin also lacked accuracy and exaggerated German belligerence. No better example of this can be seen than in the events of 30 and 31 July, when a constant flow of reports, all false or distorted, spoke of German general mobilization.[22] The Centrale, like its foreign agents, was incapable of differentiating between the technical terms *Kriegsgefahrzustand* and *Kriegszustand*. Berthelot himself seems to have made this error.[23] As a result, the Foreign Ministry became increasingly fearful and suspicious of Germany.[24]

This deepening apprehension was further reinforced by the Quai's lack of confidence in the new Premier and foreign minister, René Viviani.

[19] Berthelot wrote: 'Aucune dépêche, aucun télégramme n'ont été expédiés de la légation de France à Belgrade entre le 14 et le 25 Juillet' on Bienvenu-Martin to Dumaine, 24 July, AE NS 'Autriche', 32.
[20] Renouvin, 'La Politique française en Juillet 1914', p. 3.
[21] See Paléologue to Bienvenu-Martin, 25 July 1914; De Laguiche to Bienvenu-Martin, 26 July 1914, annotation by Berthelot on Bompard to Bienvenu-Martin, 27 July 1914, AE NS 'Autriche', 32, 33.
[22] Notes by Abel Ferry during a cabinet meeting, 31 July: 'Le Président Poincaré ouvre en demandant la mobilisation immédiate. Messimy l'appuie. La mobilisation a lieu en Allemagne sous le couvert du secret ... Nous sommes en retard de deux jours,' AE Ferry MSS; Viviani to P. Cambon, 12.30 p.m. 31 July 1914, Prefect of Police (Paris) to Viviani, 30 July, J. Cambon to Viviani, 1.30 a.m. 31 July, Mollard to Viviani, 4.11 p.m., unnumbered telegram, 31 July, AE NS 'Autriche', 34, 35.
[23] It was a case of error upon error. Mollard's telegram had announced the launching of general German mobilization, when it was only a matter of *Kriegsgefahrzustand*. When Mollard came to correct it at 5.21 p.m. he made another mistake by placing *en état de guerre (Kriegszustand)* instead of *en état de danger de guerre (Kriegsgefahrzustand)*.
[24] J. F. V. Keiger, 'Raymond Poincaré and French Foreign Policy, 1912–1914' (Cambridge University, 1980), p. 348; also by the same author *France and the Origins of the First World War* (London, 1983), pp. 161–2.

An anti-clerical Socialist, Viviani was a brilliant orator but an extremely excitable man whose habit of uttering the wrong phrase at the wrong time severely embarrassed Poincaré and hampered French diplomacy during the July crisis. As a liaison between the Quai d'Orsay and the new parliamentary majority, he was perfect. As Paléologue noted in his journal, Poincaré appreciated Viviani's patriotism and the richness of his oratory while at the same time realizing that he was *persona grata* with the Radicals. However, Viviani's usefulness was distinctly limited. He was totally incapable of understanding the most basic diplomatic conventions, let alone the wider implications of France's foreign policy. This 'ignorance noire des choses de la politique extérieure', as Poincaré observed, manifested itself in the most rudimentary errors during July 1914. The President of the Republic noted that 'Il [Viviani] n'a pas pu, une seule fois, en lisant un télégramme de Vienne parler de Ballplatz sans dire le Bol-platz ou le Baliplatz.'[25] Moreover, Viviani often lost his dossiers, and hurled inane abuse at officials in a fit of nervousness or rage.[26]

The Quai d'Orsay feared that Viviani might do damage to the Franco-Russian alliance.[27] Admittedly he was determined to uphold the Three Year Law for the foreseeable future.[28] At first, however, he was not convinced that a German attack was likely. Moreover, he was critical of what he considered to be pessimistic and bellicose elements in the Quai d'Orsay.[29] In the important debate with Paléologue over the form of the toasts which were to be exchanged between heads of state during the St Petersburg trip, he was particularly determined to moderate what was said, so as not to provoke a reaction among the Central Powers.[30] He took a similar initiative in forcing Paléologue to tone down the *communiqué* to be issued after the visit. According to de Robien, the French attaché at the embassy in St Petersburg, Viviani was

---

[25] M. Paléologue, *Au Quai d'Orsay á la veille de la tourmente* (Paris, 1947), 13 June 1914, p. 302; Auffray, *De Margerie*, p. 257; 'Notes journalières', 27 July 1914, BN (NAF 16027), Poincaré MSS; Keiger, *France and the Origins*, p. 162.

[26] D'Aumale, *Voix de l'Orient*, p. 39.   [27] See Auffray, *De Margerie*, pp. 256–8.

[28] 'Les Semaines qui ont précédé la mobilisation: L'État des esprits en juillet 1914', p. 4, AN Messimy MSS, carton 5; Weber, *Nationalist Revival*, p. 140. For a recent discussion see G. Krumeich, 'Aufrustung und Innenpolitik in Frankreich vor dem Ersten Weltkrieg' (Wiesbaden, 1980), pp. 240–60.

[29] Paléologue, *Au Quai d'Orsay*, 18 June 1914, p. 311; notes by de Robien, 'Voyage de Poincaré', p. 62, de Robien MSS; M. Paléologue, *La Russie des tsars* (Paris, 1922), pp. 15–17; note by Viviani, 3 Jan. 1923, AE Paléologue MSS, 5.

[30] See the exchange of telegrams between Paléologue and Viviani between 10 and 12 July 1914, AE Paléologue MSS, 1.

reluctant to issue a note which could in any way be construed as encouragement to Russia:

> Viviani, qui paraissait véritablement excédé par toutes ces manifestations de l'esprit militaire et qui était en réaction très nette contre elles, s'y opposa et ne consentit qu'à regret à constater dans la note pour la presse la communauté des vues des deux pays en ce qui concerne les divers problèmes que le souci de paix générale et de l'équilibre européen pose devant les puissances notamment en orient.[31]

It is obvious that Viviani was suspicious of Russia's Balkan policy and reluctant to commit France to the Serbian cause.[32]

Viviani's caution and his concern to maintain peace were reflected in his response to the Austrian ultimatum. In his telegrams to London and St Petersburg on 24 July he requested an extension of the time limit and the setting up of an international inquiry. More importantly, he advised acceptance of as many of the Austrian conditions as could be reconciled with national dignity.[33] During the next few days he attempted to apply pressure on Russia. His telegram to Paléologue on 27 July affirmed the solidarity of Franco-Russian interests in the search for peace. On 30 July he repeated this declaration and emphasized that Russia should do nothing to offer Germany a pretext for partial or general mobilization.[34] This action seems to have been determined largely by German Ambassador Pourtalès's *démarche* in St Petersburg on the previous day. The German ambassador had warned Sazonov of German general mobilization, if Russia's former military preparations were not immediately ceased. Viviani clearly realized the exact implications of any Russian mobilization.[35]

Between 30 July and 1 August, information being transmitted from all major posts stressed Germany's aggressive stance, and Viviani appears to have been largely won over to the Quai d'Orsay's analysis of the situation.[36] Nevertheless the foreign minister held out almost against hope during the last days, especially when Schön, the German Ambas-

---

[31] AN de Robien MSS.　　[32] Ibid., Paléologue, *La Russie des tsars*, p. 17.

[33] 'Notes journalières', 24 July 1914, BN (NAF 16027), Poincaré MSS.

[34] Poincaré, *Au service de la France* (Paris, 1926–33), ii. 221, 229; P. Renouvin, *The Immediate Origins of the War* (London, 1928), p. 205; P. Miquel, *Raymond Poincaré* (Paris, 1961), p. 338.

[35] P. Cambon to Viviani, 24 July 1914, J. Cambon to Viviani, 25 July 1914, AE NS 'Autriche', 32.

[36] Note by Abel Ferry, 31 July 1914, AE Ferry MSS; See also A. Ferry, *Les Carnets secrets d'Abel Ferry* (Paris, 1957), p. 27.

sador in Paris, did not ask for his passports during their meeting of 1
August.[37]

Throughout the July crisis Viviani's attitude was characterized by
moderation and by a desire for peace. He was perhaps the only French
politician who could substantially have altered the course of events. He
failed to do so for several reasons. He was preoccupied with the internal
situation in France, and was especially apprehensive of what would
transpire during the Caillaux trial, a result of the murder of the journalist Calmette by Madame Caillaux. There was a possibility that secret
documents relating to the Second Moroccan Crisis would be published
in order to embarrass the government. De Robien noted during the visit
to St Petersburg that 'Viviani était très nerveux et réclamant sans cesse
des nouvelles des pièces qui seules semblent l'intéresser, car le sort de son
cabinet pouvait en dépendre. Les affaires de Serbie jusqu'à ce moment
étaient tout-à-fait au second plan.'[38] Combined with this overwhelming
interest in domestic affairs was the sincere belief that the assassination at
Sarajevo would not lead to a major diplomatic crisis.[39] Viviani's ignorance of events between 23 and 29 July encouraged him to think that the
crisis arising from the Austrian ultimatum would eventually be solved.
Nothing would be gained by unduly hurrying back to Paris.[40]

However, even if Viviani had realized the urgency of the situation, it is
doubtful that he would have followed a successful or consistent policy.
He had had little time in which to become acquainted with his portfolio
or to formulate clear ideas.[41] For the most part, therefore, he was forced
to rely on Berthelot, de Margerie, and Poincaré. Given Viviani's
shortcomings and preoccupations, the President of the Republic had
been able to retain considerable authority in the area of foreign affairs.
During the St Petersburg visit it was he rather than Viviani who took
charge of most discussions.[42] On 29 July Poincaré candidly wrote in his
diary: 'Je tiens à assumer moi-même l'action de Viviani. Je crains qu'il
ne soit hésitant et pusillanime.'[43]

Undoubtedly, Viviani's inability to assert his authority over Poincaré
was in part a function of Poincaré's powerful personality, but fundamentally it was due to the weaknesses of his own character and to the fact

---

[37] 'Notes journalières', 31 July, 1 Aug. 1914, BN (NAF 16027), Poincaré MSS.
[38] Ferry, *Carnets*, p. 19; 'Voyage de Poincaré', p. 53, AN de Robien MSS.
[39] D'Aumale, *Voix de L'Orient*, p. 39; AN Messimy MSS, 5.
[40] 'Notes journalières', 26 July 1914, BN (NAF 16027), Poincaré MSS.
[41] 'Notes sur la guerre, crise de juin 1914', AN 151 AP 46 Deschanel MSS.
[42] 'Voyage de Poincaré', p. 63, AN de Robien MSS.
[43] *Notes journalières*, 29 July 1914, BN (NAF 16027), Poincaré MSS.

that he had some awareness of his limitations. On crucial occasions, moreover, the *président du conseil* was simply incapable of conducting himself properly. On 22 July, during an inspection of Russian regiments, Viviani was subject to a nervous attack. Poincaré noted: 'Viviani attend, debout sur le terrain, près de la tente impériale et d'après ce que m'ont rapporté Paléologue et Martin, il maugrée, bougonne, jure au point de se faire remarquer par tout le monde. Paléologue essaie de le calmer ... lui persuade qu'il a une crise de foie et demande le Docteur Cresson.'[44]

After he arrived in France on 29 July he recognized that the situation was more serious than he had previously realized, but he seemed incapable of behaving with calm and resolution. He became increasingly agitated, and oscillated between moods of pessimism and incredible optimism.[45] Nevertheless, it would be a mistake to suppose that Viviani became involved in a major confrontation with the Quai d'Orsay or Poincaré. Though prepared to urge moderation on Russia for most of the crisis, he was strongly committed to the Franco-Russian alliance. Few if any French statesmen would have been willing to adopt a more conciliatory approach.[46] As James Joll has aptly commented, throughout all of Europe politicians' freedom to choose was restricted by many interlocking factors.[47] Viviani was no exception.

The authority of Bienvenu-Martin, the acting foreign minister, was decidedly limited. Messimy described him as a modest and cultivated lawyer.[48] Though certainly ill suited to the position of foreign minister and almost totally ignorant of foreign affairs, he never lost his sang-froid or shirked the burden of responsibility, especially during his interviews with Schön.[49] He excelled at calming his colleagues Ferry and Messimy, who tended to be carried away by the situation.[50] Nevertheless, his influence upon the diplomatic course of events was minimal. Despite spending considerable time daily during the crisis at the Quai d'Orsay, he worked 'avec assez d'indifférence'.[51] This indifference was largely due to his belief that there were no darkening clouds on the horizon. Indeed, Viviani had left him 'aucune instruction par-

[44] Ibid. 22 July 1914; Keiger, *France and the Origins*, p. 152.
[45] 'Notes journalières', 27, 31 July 1914, BN (NAF 16027), Poincaré MSS.
[46] Letter from a historian, Liveo Zencovich, to Paléologue, 15 May 1937, AE Paléologue MSS, 5.
[47] J. Joll, 'Politicians and the Freedom to Choose: The Case of July 1914', in A. Ryan (ed.), *The Idea of Freedom: Essays in Honour of Isaiah Berlin* (Oxford, 1979), pp. 99–114.
[48] 'Les Semaines qui ont précédé la mobilisation', p. 26, AN Messimy MSS, 5.
[49] Ibid.; Ferry, *Carnets*, p. 22.
[50] Ferry, *Carnets*, p. 21. [51] Ibid. p. 20.

ticulière'.[52] After the Austrian ultimatum was delivered, Bienvenu-Martin became increasingly aware of the gravity of the crisis, and even less willing to take an initiative because he was a mere caretaker. Throughout the days following the ultimatum he increasingly looked to Berthelot for advice and unashamedly declared in later years that Berthelot had dominated decision-making in Paris during the July crisis.[53]

Poincaré's fears that Bienvenu-Martin might dislocate the Triple *Entente* in his search for peace were not without foundation.[54] That he was willing to envisage a localization of the Austro-Serbian conflict, which the Germans proposed on the 24th and 25th, was apparent by the fact that both the German and Austrian foreign offices were led to believe that 'Austria could devour Serbia without involving either Russia, Germany or France'.[55] As Szecsen, the Austrian ambassador to Paris, reported to Vienna, the acting foreign minister made every attempt to avoid defending Serbia and hoped that the dispute would be settled in accordance with Vienna's wishes.[56] The corollary of this attitude was to apply strong pressure on the Russian government as well, as it was unlikely that Russia would otherwise distance herself from Serbia. Bienvenu-Martin in fact entertained this idea, and suggested to Schön on 26 July that a mediation in Vienna and St Petersburg could be undertaken by the four powers least interested in the dispute.[57]

The fact that Bienvenu-Martin subsequently dropped both positions was largely due to the advice of Berthelot, who 'harboured the French career diplomat's deep distrust of German intentions' and did not see any justification for intervening in St Petersburg.[58] To some extent, however, Bienvenu-Martin came of his own accord to agree with Berthelot. The rapid succession of visits in which, on 24 July, German and Austrian ambassadors requested French support for a localization

[52] J. B. Bienvenu-Martin, 'Mon intérim de chef du gouvernement, 15–29 juillet 1914', *La Revue de France* (15 Aug. 1933), p. 439.

[53] Immediately after the ultimatum, Bienvenu-Martin turned to Berthelot for advice: 'Je savais que ce haut fonctionnaire avait une grande expérience des affaires extérieures et je dois reconnaître que ses avis éclairés m'aidèrent beaucoup' (ibid. p. 441).

[54] 'Notes journalières', 27 July 1914, BN (NAF 16027), Poincaré MSS.

[55] K. Eubank, *Paul Cambon* (Norman, Okla., 1960), p. 171: Cambon rushed over from London on 25 July in an attempt to shore up Bienvenu-Martin. See L. Albertini, *The Origins of the War of 1914*, trans. and ed. I. M. Massey (London, 1952–7) ii. 322.

[56] F. L. Schuman, *War and Diplomacy in the French Republic* (New York, 1931), p. 216; B.E. Schmitt, *The Coming of War, 1914*, (New York, 1930), p. 488; Bienvenu-Martin's apologia for his attitude commenced in 'Mon intérim', pp. 442–3.

[57] Bienvenu-Martin to all posts, 8.20 p.m., 26 July, AE NS 'Autriche', 32.

[58] G. W. Chapman, 'The Decision for War' (Princeton University, 1971), p. 207.

of the Austro-Serbian conflict had led him to suspect that they were acting in concert.[59] As the diplomatic conflict developed he began to suspect that he was being tricked. Noulens, a cabinet minister, was told by Bienvenu-Martin just before the outbreak of war that he was being conditioned daily by Schön for the prospect of eventual German mobilization.[60] By the time of Viviani's return on 29 July, Bienvenu-Martin had clearly fallen into line with the more suspicious attitude of Berthelot.

Ultimately, Berthelot's point of view prevailed. In the crisis of 1911 the Centrale had barely functioned for want of strong leadership. In July 1914, however, this quality was supplied by Berthelot. He not only assisted Bienvenu-Martin at meetings with diplomats but even corrected the acting foreign minister's written versions of what had transpired.[61] Furthermore, almost every telegram or dispatch was written in Berthelot's hand, often without the signature of Bienvenu-Martin. To these communications he imparted a precision of thought and a thoroughness which kept all posts fully *au courant* and carefully instructed.[62] Nevertheless, as often happens in bureaucratic systems which depend on the imposition of discipline from the top, there is evidence to suggest that at crucial moments on 29, 30, and 31 July a substantial portion of the immense influx of telegrams was being scanned rather than read carefully.

From the outset, Berthelot was suspicious of Austro-Hungarian and German intentions. Even before the Sarajevo assassination he had been deeply worried about the future. The way events evolved convinced him that, although the Central Powers did not desire a general war at any price, they were prepared, under certain circumstances, to begin such a conflict. In contrast to 1905 and 1911, he believed, Germany was unwilling to accept failure and, barring a great diplomatic victory, would go to war. Moreover, war had only been avoided in the past because France

---

[59] Bienvenu-Martin, 'Mon intérim', p. 441.

[60] Noulens to Ribot, 26 Aug. 1917, AE Doulcet MSS, 25.

[61] Messimy notes, AN Messimy MSS; C. Corbin, 'Berthelot en 1914', *Bulletin de la Société Paul Claudel* (1967), p. 45. For Berthelot's correction of Bienvenu-Martin, see Bienvenu-Martin's note of 29 July 1914, AE NS 'Autriche', 33.

[62] I. Halfond, 'Maurice Paléologue' (Temple University, 1974), p. 270. That the Quai d'Orsay was functioning smoothly while Berthelot was *directeur adjoint* was widely recognized. As Manneville told Doulcet: 'Je suis de reste frappé par la netteté des télégrammes du département en ce moment. C'est beaucoup mieux que sous le règne précédent' (AE Doulcet MSS, 21).

and her allies had made substantial concessions, and there was a limit to the extent to which both security and honour could be compromised.[63]

What most aroused Berthelot's suspicion was the manner in which the ultimatum to Serbia had been communicated to the French government. Like Bienvenu-Martin, he thought the successive visits of Szecsen and Schön decidedly suspect, especially since the latter fully approved of the Austrian note and called for intervention in St Petersburg. Berthelot refused to believe that Jagow, the German foreign minister, was ignorant of the terms of the note and considered that Germany was acting in concert with Austria-Hungary.[64] In the following days he thought Austria more accommodating than Germany,[65] and took the view that Germany was trying to compromise France in the eyes of the Russian government.[66] Thus, when Schön solicited France's support on 27 July for mediation between St Petersburg and Vienna, an act which would not have interfered with Austria's claims, Berthelot replied that such a step was possible but added that its counterpart would be German intervention in Vienna, a step he thought highly unlikely.[67] Though he informed Paléologue of the German *démarche*, he did not send the original communication but rather a very brief résumé.[68]

Berthelot's suspicion that Germany was attempting to dislocate the

[63] Laroche, *Au Quai d'Orsay*, p. 19; Ferry note, 27 July 1914, AE Ferry MSS; d'Aumale, *Voix de l'Orient*, p. 38; Corbin, 'Berthelot en 1914', p. 45; Chapman, 'Decision for War', p. 208; A. Bréal, *Philippe Berthelot* (Paris, 1937), p. 115. Albertini's assertion that the Quai d'Orsay was animated by 'strongly Austrophile sentiments', especially on 24 and 25 July, is incorrect. Berthelot was a known Austrophobe and eagerly championed Balkan nationalism. He was supported by many members of the Sciences-po Balkan group. Bienvenu-Martin alone showed himself favourable to Austria-Hungary, and he withdrew his support at an early stage under pressure from Paul Cambon and Berthelot. See Albertini, *Origins*, ii. 323, 327.

[64] Note by Berthelot for Bienvenu-Martin, 26 July 1914; Berthlot to all major posts, 4.30 p.m., 26 July AE NS 'Autriche', 32; Bréal, *Berthelot*, p. 116; Corbin, 'Berthelot en 1914', p. 45; J. Cambon to Bienvenu-Martin, tel. 185, 1.15 p.m. 25 July 1914, AE NS 'Autriche' 32. Berthelot noted where Jagow supported Austria's energetic note. J. Cambon to Bienvenu-Martin, disp. 434, 24 July 1914. Berthelot also noted the section where Cambon disputed Jagow's claim that he did not know the contents of the note before its transmission. For Berthelot's surprise over the nature of the dual *démarche*, see Berthelot to all major posts, 11.55 a.m., 12.30 p.m., 1.15 p.m., 1.40 p.m., 2. p.m., 25 July, AE NS 'Autriche', 32.

[65] Berthelot to all major posts, 4.30 p.m. 26 July, note by Berthelot on J. Cambon to Bienvenu-Martin, tel. 207, 28 July, AE NS 'Autriche', 32.

[66] Corbin, 'Berthelot en 1914', p. 45.

[67] Bienvenu-Martin to all major posts, 26 July 1914, AE NS 'Autriche', 32 (in Berthelot's hand).

[68] See footnote to *DDF* (3), xi, 151.

Franco-Russian alliance resulted in three specific measures.[69] First, he persuaded Bienvenu-Martin to drop his initial support for a localization of the Austro-Serbian conflict. Secondly, he consigned to a rubbish bin Schön's Franco-German communiqué of 27 July, which spoke of a solidarity and concordance of views, by altering the original beyond recognition.[70] The final version was thoroughly innocuous. Thirdly, he was careful to brief Bienvenu-Martin before meetings which he attended with the idea of stiffening the foreign minister's resolution.[71]

Berthelot was no less desirous of peace than Bienvenu-Martin. Schuman's assertion that the *directeur adjoint* was interested primarily in preserving the peace, though not at the cost of *Entente* solidarity, is correct.[72] His tactic was both logical and simple. He would give Germany and Austria-Hungary full opportunity to reveal their true designs. Germany would be forced to choose between accommodation and intransigence.[73]

However, Berthelot was not prepared to bring pressure to bear on St Petersburg. Apart from the fact that he was *en principe* unwilling to jeopardize the alliance, he thought that Russia had done nothing to warrant a caution.[74] As he noted on 29 July in a telegram sent to most posts: 'Pétersbourg a donné depuis le début les plus grandes preuves de sa modération, en particulier en s'associant aux puissances pour donner à la Serbie le conseil de céder aux exigences de la note autrichienne.'[75]

This attitude clearly owed much to the way in which Paléologue had distorted, omitted, and delayed the transmission of essential information about Russian affairs. The classic example of this procedure concerned the three conflicting versions of the military measures which Russia took on 25 July. In the end, Paléologue's version, which was dismissive of Russian preparations and did not mention the mobilization of the Warsaw, Vilna, and St Petersburg divisions against Germany, became the basis of Berthelot's evaluation. Whereas the more accurate version of de Laguiche, French military attaché in St Petersburg, was communi-

---

[69] According to Ferry, Berthelot thought the *démarche* 'éffroyable'. See note, 27 July 1914, AE Ferry MSS.

[70] Berthelot's revised note, 26 July 1914, AE NS 'Autriche', 32; Bréal, *Berthelot*, p. 118.

[71] Corbin, 'Berthelot en 1914' p. 45; Bréal, *Berthelot*, p. 115; Chapman, 'Decision for War', p. 208.

[72] Schuman, *War and Diplomacy*, p. 231.

[73] Renouvin, 'La Politique française en juillet 1914', p. 5; Bréal, *Berthelot*, p. 117; Berthelot to Thiébaut, 24 July 1914, AE NS 'Autriche', 32.

[74] Bienvenu-Martin to all major posts, 1.30 and 1.50 p.m. 29 July 1914, AE NS 'Autriche', 33.

[75] Ibid.

cated to the Ministry of War, Paléologue's was communicated to Viviani, de Margerie, and Poincaré.[76] Given Berthelot's ignorance of Russian military measures, he could not but continue to believe in Russia's peaceful intentions. Moreover, Paléologue strengthened this belief by forcefully depicting Sazonov as someone of irreproachable conduct who desired direct Austro-Russian negotiations.[77]

Consequently, the distorted picture being transmitted, often belatedly, from Russia, the speed with which events were becoming known in Germany, and Berthelot's logical mind made him judge Germany more harshly than was perhaps warranted. As the crisis unfolded, his suspicions were heightened, and he became more than ever convinced that it was Berlin and not St Petersburg which held the key. Germany, therefore, should act decisively in Vienna, whose refusal to accept the almost total submission of Serbia and the mediation of the powers was as inexplicable as its hasty declaration of war on 28 July. Although Germany had renounced her initial demand for localization and accepted in principle the common action of the four powers, she had rejected 'l'idée d'une conférence sans suggérer aucun autre moyen et en refusant d'agir positivement à Vienne'.[78]

By the morning of 30 July Berthelot was a little more optimistic. Germany had taken direct action on the 29th in Vienna, despite her menacing attitude towards Russia. Berthelot associated this 'temps d'arrêt', if not 'un commencement de détente', with the firmness and disapproval which the three *Entente* capitals had manifested the day before. Berthelot's strategy for the maintenance of peace reflected his adherence to the policy of firmness 'à la Poincaré':

une attitude ferme, sans être intransigeante, de la Russie, une déclaration nette à Berlin de l'Angleterre (dont la réserve persistante risque d'encourager les espérances de l'Allemagne et de Rome), de la maintenir, dans une neutralité

---

[76] Paléologue's telegram of 25 July spoke of a Russian partial mobilization aimed at Austria-Hungary, which was to become effective and public only if Austria-Hungary declared war on Serbia (AE Paléologue MSS, 1). De Laguiche's telegram stated that 4 army corps were mobilized: 'Les circonscriptions militaires de Varsovie, Vilna et St Pétersbourg prennent des dispositions secrètes.' It added that Moscow and St Petersburg were in a state of siege (Laguiche to Messimy, 26 July 1911, AE NS 'Autriche', 32). On 27 July 1914 Isvolsky proffered a third version. 'Même si l'Autriche occupe Belgrade, la Russie ne considère pas qu'elle doit mobiliser les corps de la frontière Autrichienne. Rien n'a été décidé sur ce qui provoquerait cette décision ... elle est laissée au ministre des Affaires Étrangères qui informerait en temps voulu la Guerre.' See the annotation by Berthelot on Bompard to Bienvenu-Martin, 27 July 1914, AE NS 'Autriche', 33.

[77] Ibid.

[78] Bienvenu-Martin to all major posts, 29 July 1914, AE NS 'Autriche' 33, (in Berthelot's hand).

balancée par celle de l'Italie, seraient les meilleurs, et probablement les seules garanties d'un dénouement pacifique.[79]

Berthelot was unhappy about the attitude of Great Britain. By 30 July he appears to have become more suspicious of Russia and of Paléologue's reports,[80] but he believed that it was necessary to act in London rather than in St Petersburg. On this point he seems to have differed with de Margerie, who shared the Cambons' more jaundiced view of Russia and who was more conscious of the need to moderate St Petersburg.[81] Berthelot had been critical of Britain before 1914 believing that she had not supported France actively enough. In July of 1914, he thought that Britain's 'réserve persistante' had increased the danger of war and been of little benefit in resolving the crisis.

Whatever hope Berthelot seems to have had diminished on the afternoon of 31 July and vanished entirely before the day ended. Throughout the 31st the Quai had been receiving reports from the Berlin Embassy which spoke of German mobilization and of the imminent prospect of war. Since he was not informed of Russian mobilization by Paléologue until late on 31 July, the *directeur adjoint* could see no justification for Germany's action. She had displayed a 'duplicity' which, in Berthelot's opinion, extended to the Austrians. He did not believe the Austrian Ambassador when he claimed, on the night of the 31st, that the Serbian question could still be settled with the assistance of a neutral friendly power. Berthelot thought that this *démarche* was designed to make Austria seem less bellicose and Russia the sole troublemaker. Berthelot's response reflected both the suspicion which had characterized his attitude during the crisis and the sense of despair aroused in him by the rapid passage of events. He replied '*à titre tout à fait privé* [underlined by

[79] Here again Berthelot's attitude appears to have been conditioned by what Paléologue was transmitting to him. Pourtalès, the German ambassador to St Petersburg, had warned Sazonov on 29 July that further Russian partial mobilization would lead to German general mobilization. Since Paléologue had continually depicted Pourtlès's tactics as intimidatory and since Berthelot was ignorant of the extent to which Russian military measures had threatened Germany, he drew the only logical conclusion. See Viviani (in Berthelot's hand) to all major posts, 31 July 1914, AE NS 'Autriche', 35. At the same time, Berthelot wanted Grey to urge Rennel Rodd, British ambassador to Rome and Jagow's friend, to take a consistently firm stand in his discussions with San Giuliano, the Italian foreign minister. Laroche to de Fleuriau, *lettre particulière*, 31 July 1914, AE NS 'Autriche', 35.

[80] Well before the crisis Berthelot was suspicious of Paléologue, and in fact detested him ('Souvenirs: Russie, ancien régime', p. 27, AN de Robien MSS).

[81] Note by Berthelot, 1.15 p.m. 31 July, AE NS 'Autriche', 35. Berthelot nevertheless telegraphed the news of this interview to Rome, St Petersburg, and Vienna. See 'Un regard sur le passé', *Le Matin*, 20 Dec. 1920, in AE NS 'Russie', 42. fol. 284.

Berthelot himself] qu'il parassait bien tard et qu'on était gagné par les événements.'

The role of de Margerie, the political director, is somewhat harder to follow than that of Berthelot, though his desire for peace was no less marked. Relatively few notes, telegrams, or dispatches were drafted in his hand, and between 24 and 29 July he was on board the *France*, cut off from the main flow of information. On his return, Berthelot continued to control the machinery of the Quai d'Orsay, though this was a situation of which de Margerie approved.[82]

During the visit to St Petersburg de Margerie's role was rather minor.[83] By his own admission, the political director was not present at any of the talks held between heads of state and foreign ministers between the 20th and the 23rd. He neither made nor saw any report relating to the conversations.[84] Basically this was the result of a certain Russian snobbery, an unwillingness on the part of responsible Russian ministers and high society to deal with a mere official assisting the *président de conseil*. That de Margerie himself was irked by this attitude and displeased with the trip was apparent.[85] Nevertheless, his influence over Viviani cannot be underestimated. The Premier was highly appreciative of his director's skill, tact, and plain good sense. On the other hand, de Margerie was concerned about Viviani's nervous disposition and his attitudes. While the political director was not apprehensive about their personal relations (even though de Margerie's uncle Jules Auffray had defeated Viviani in parliamentary elections in 1902), he was fearful that the Premier would lose his mental and nervous equilibrium during the crisis and that he might be vulnerable to German intimidation. De Margerie's strategy was therefore to provide as much guidance as possible. During the sea voyage he wrote all of Viviani's telegrams, and on their return attended all of his meetings.[86] He also made a point of holding personal interviews with foreign ambassadors and of handling as much work as possible.[87]

[82] Auffray, *De Margerie*, pp. 253, 283.
[83] Renouvin, 'La Politique française en juillet 1914' p. 6.
[84] De Robien, though mentioning Poincaré, Viviani, and Paléologue on many occasions, makes only one reference to de Margerie. See 'Voyage de Poincaré', AN de Robien MSS.
[85] 'Notes concernant le Quai d'Orsay, 1930–44' (Dossier on de Margerie), p. 127, AN de Robien, MSS. See also Auffray, *De Margerie*, p. 279.
[86] Auffray, *De Margerie*, pp. 1, 257, 258, 284–9; 'Notes journalières', 3 Aug. 1914, BN (NAF 16027), Poincaré MSS.
[87] 'Notes du 23 Juillet au 4 août', p. 25, AN Messimy MSS, 5.

De Margerie had been responsible for planning the official trip to Russia. He established a series of notes on the most important questions, such as Russian high society, ministers and political parties, the problem of a Russian delegate on the Commission of the Ottoman Debt, negotiations between Russia and Britain over a naval accord, and Austro-Russian relations. It is evident that he was more than quietly worried by this last issue, and he considered an amelioration of relations very unlikely in the near future. On the one hand, Austria was fomenting trouble in the Balkans by urging Bulgaria to revise the Treaty of Bucharest. On the other, Russia was encouraging Serbia to retake 'sa Bosnie et son Herzégovine'. At the same time, however, de Margerie's proposed agenda of 12 or 13 July suggests that he did not foresee major complications arising out of the Sarajevo assassination.[88]

During the St Petersburg visit de Margerie appears to have been highly critical of Russia, an outlook which owed much to the influence of the Cambon brothers. According to de Robien, de Margerie 'passait son temps à tout critiquer aux fêtes des Czars. Il préférait peut-être les réceptions bourgeoises de la République.'[89] Similarly, de Margerie's impression of Russian espionage and intrigue was 'pénible' to say the least.[90] Like Viviani, he appears to have been annoyed by the pervasive military spirit. This 'mauvaise impression' persisted throughout the July crisis and made him suspicious of Russia's actions.

If there was one word which characterized his position during the crisis, it was moderation. From the outset he placed a premium on reasonable firmness and peace with dignity. It was he who redrafted the communiqué at the end of the St Petersburg visit and who was careful to include the words of general peace which Paléologue had not even mentioned. The communiqué underlined 'la communauté de vue des deux gouvernements sur les divers problèmes que le souci de la paix générale et de l'équilibre européen pose devant les Puissances, notament en Orient'. Whereas Paléologue's version could be interpreted as giving French support to Russia's Balkan policy, de Margerie's referred to the maintenance of peace and general equilibrium without making specific reference to Serbia and without creating problems of interpretation.[91]

During the return voyage the political director had difficulty in

[88] Auffray, *De Margerie*, pp. 279, 280; d'Aumale, *Voix de l'Orient*, p. 38.

[89] 'Notes concernant le Quai d'Orsay, 1930–44', dossier 2, personnel, p. 127, and 'Voyage de Poincaré', pp. 55–9, AN de Robien MSS.

[90] Auffray, *De Margerie*, p. 280.

[91] 'Voyage de Poincaré', p. 62, AN de Robien MSS; 'Notes journalières', 23 July 1914, BN (NAF 16027), Poincaré MSS.

following events. In fact, on the 24th, when the Austrian ultimatum had been sent, there was a virtual communications blackout. On learning of the ultimatum the next day he drafted a telegram which stressed the need to give Austria-Hungary full satisfaction if her case was proven. He suggested an international inquiry which would ensure that justice was done. His main consideration was the maintenance of peace through concertation with Russia and Britain: 'Nous devons examiner dès à présent avec la Russie et l'Angleterre les moyens de prévenir un conflit dans lequel les autres Puissances pourraient se trouver rapidement engagés.'[92]

By 27 July the situation had visibly worsened. The sudden return of the Kaiser from his cruise in the Baltic coupled with the likely declaration of war by Austria on Serbia made it necessary for the *France* to return. In view of these circumstances de Margerie was concerned to strengthen *Entente* solidarity, especially with Russia. The original draft of the telegram that was eventually transmitted to St Petersburg and the additions he made to the final version suggest his preoccupation with a peaceful settlement of the crisis. The original read, '[France], appréciant comme la Russie la haute intérêt qu'ont les deux pays à ne négliger aucun effort en vue de la solution du conflit, est prête à seconder entièrement l'action du gouvernement impérial.' De Margerie strengthened the pacific character of this draft considerably by revising the final clause to read: 'est préte à seconder entièrement *dans l'intérêt de la paix générale* l'action du gouvernement impérial'.[93]

Thus, the seconding of St Petersburg was linked to the need to neglect no effort to maintain peace. De Margerie appears not as yet to have been suspicious of Russia's actions. After all, it was Paléologue's 'toned-down' version of Russian military measures that was transmitted to him. This lack of suspicion and ignorance was evident on the 28th when he sent a telegram to Bienvenu-Martin. He stated that 'il est inadmissible qu'on exige de nous des conseils de modération à la Russie, qui n'est pas responsable du conflit actuel et n'a encore procédé à aucune mesure quelconque pouvant éveiller le moindre soupçon'. Any *démarche* in St Petersburg was dependent upon Germany giving 'avis écoutés' in Vienna. The political director also pressed for the acceptance of a meeting of the four less-interested powers (Germany, France, Italy, and Britain) in London.

[92] Viviani to Bienvenu-Martin, 4.05 p.m. 25 July 1914, AE NS 'Autriche', 32. This dispatch was written and signed by de Margerie.
[93] Viviani to Paléologue, 27 July 1914, AE NS 'Autriche', 33.

In support of this proposal he told Bienvenu-Martin that 'il est essentiel que l'on sache à Berlin et à Vienne que notre plein concours est acquis'. Despite his refusal to intervene in St Petersburg (although all the telegrams he sent there showed his desire for moderation and the maintenance of the peace), he did envisage joint pressure on Serbia. Not only would this action contain the problem within the confines of an Austro-Serbian dispute, but it would lessen German intransigence.[94]

Upon his return to Paris on the afternoon of 29 July de Margerie was able to play a far more active role. He opposed the more pessimistic views of his colleagues and tried, along with Berthelot, to bar the route to war.[95] By 30 July, he was increasingly suspicious of Russia and disturbed about the influence of Paléologue.[96] On the night of 29/30 July de Margerie had received news from Isvolsky, whom he thoroughly distrusted, that Russia considered it necessary to accelerate her military preparations. Isvolsky's activity was a response to Pourtalès's *démarche* in St Petersburg on 29 July, which had warned of general German mobilization unless Russian partial mobilization ceased. Russia, according to Isvolsky, counted on France militarily. He wrote to de Margerie as follows: 'Il ne nous reste qu'à hâter nos armaments et à envisager l'imminence de la guerre.' The political director found these words highly alarming. He was well aware that Russian mobilization would entail German general mobilization. As if this information was not worrying enough, Isvolsky also expressed in the same note Russia's gratitude for the assurances of French support which she had received from Paléologue.[97]

De Margerie reacted immediately. He woke Viviani up in the early morning and proceeded to draft a terse telegram which was sent to Paléologue early in the morning of the 30th. This telegram needs to be quoted at length since it subsequently caused undue controversy during the 1920s. Despite its assurance that France was resolved to fulfil all the obligations of the Franco-Russian alliance, it was unequivocal in its effort to restrain Russia. It began as follows: 'Le gouvernement de la République est décidé à ne négliger aucun effort en vue de la solution du

[94] Viviani to Bienvenu-Martin, tel. 16, 1.40 p.m. 28 July 1914, AE NS 'Autriche', 33 (written by de Margerie).

[95] D'Aumale, *Voix de l'Orient*, p. 41.

[96] See Viviani to Paléologue, tel. 470, 30 July 1914, AE NS 'Autriche', 34. This telegram was written by Berthelot and signed by de Margerie.

[97] Note from Russian Embassy to de Margerie, 3 a.m. 30 July 1914, AE NS 'Autriche', 34.

conflit et à seconder l'action du gouvernement impérial dans l'intérêt de
la paix générale. La France est, d'autre part, résolue à remplir toutes les
obligations de l'alliance.' After issuing the assurance of France's loyalty
in the final instance, de Margerie concluded with a clear statement of
restraint:

Mais, dans l'intérêt même de la paix générale et étant donné qu'une conversation est engagée entre les puissances moins intéressés, je crois qu'il serait oppor-
tun que dans les mesures de précaution et de défense auxquelles la Russie croit
devoir procéder, elle ne prît immédiatement aucune disposition qui offrît à
l'Allemagne un prétexte pour une mobilisation totale ou partielle.[98]

The Quai was thoroughly convinced that Russian mobilization meant
war. That de Margerie's telegram was designed to restrain Russia was
evident by what Isvolsky transmitted to St Petersburg, by what Poincaré
noted in his diary, and, most importantly, by what Paléologue wrote in
reply to it. The Ambassador had no doubts about its nature or about its
veiled criticism of his actions. He replied in the afternoon that 'ce matin
même, j'ai recommandé à M. Sazanoff d'éviter toute mesure militaire
qui pourrait [donner] à l'Allemagne un prétexte à la mobilization
générale'.[99]

De Margerie's specific sentiments were also reflected in his continued
support for Grey's four-power mediation (slightly revised as the 'Halt in
Belgrade plan') and for Sazonov's promise to halt Russian military preparations if Austria eliminated from her ultimatum clauses injurious to
Serbian sovereignty. De Margerie insisted that even if Austria refused

---

[98] Viviani to Paléologue, 7 a.m. 30 July 1914, AE NS 'Autriche', 34 (written by de Margerie, signed by Viviani). This telegram is particularly important in assessing de Margerie's thought. Very few telegrams were written by him during the crisis and the urgency with which he woke Viviani and dispatched this communication is revealing.

[99] P. Cambon to Viviani, tels. 132, 133, 24 July 1914, J. Cambon to Viviani, tel. 186, 25 July 1914, AE NS 'Autriche', 32. Isvolsky's telegram to Sazonov, also transmitted to the Quai d'Orsay, was abbreviated in the *DDF* to such an extent that it gives the wrong impression. The full version makes de Margerie's peaceful stand clearer: 'M. de Margerie m'a dit que le gouvernement français sans vouloir intervenir dans nos préparatifs militaires estimerait très désirable, en présence de la continuation des pourparlers ayant pour but le maintien de la paix, que ces préparatifs portent un caractère aussi peu ostensible et aussi peu provoquant que possible' (Note from Isvolsky to Sazonov, 30 July 1914 (sent to de Margerie by Sevastopoulo, 23 Jan. 1915), AE NS 'Autriche', 34). Poincaré's words are also clear: 'Nous faisons savoir à Pétersbourg que, bien entendu, nous remplirons nos obligations d'alliés, mais que nous recommandons au gouvernement impérial de ne rien faire, dans ces préparatifs de défense, qui puisse offrir à l'Allemagne un prétexte à l'agression.' ('Notes journalières', 30 July 1914, BN (NAF 16027), Poincaré MSS.)

this last proposal, Paléologue should urge Sazonov to seek a new formula of accommodation.[100]

By the morning of 1 August de Margerie was rapidly losing hope. Admittedly, Austria appeared more willing to respect Serbia's sovereign rights. In a memorandum prepared for Viviani, who was to meet Schön at 11 a.m. on 1 August, de Margerie noted that Austria 'affirme qu'elle n'a aucune ambition territoriale et notamment qu'elle n'attaquera pas le Sandjak. Elle paraît donc disposée à écarter la querelle et à chercher le résultat.' He differed, therefore, with Berthelot's more sceptical evaluation of Austria-Hungary's intentions and tended to accept Szecsen's words at their face value.

Nevertheless, Germany's attitude had hardened and the only explanation seemed to be that she was determined to make war. Not only had she sent St Petersburg an ultimatum on the afternoon of the 31st, when Russia had shown herself disposed to agree to British mediatory attempts, but, to de Margerie's intense chagrin, Schön had asked for his passport. This measure, according to the political director, proved that Germany wished to provoke a Franco-German conflict.[101] Even so, de Margerie continued to work for a peaceful outcome. Speaking of the possibilities of peace, he stated that 'il ne faut pas les négliger cependant et nous ne devons pas cesser de travailler à un arrangement'.[102]

The declaration of war by Germany on 1 August destroyed all such possibilities, but the fact remains that, throughout the crisis, de Margerie had worked for a peaceful solution. He had supported satisfaction for Austria without injury to Serbian sovereignty, various British proposals for mediation, and even unequivocal restraint of Russia. Though he was an advocate of 'fermeté à la Poincaré' and though he was mindful of the absolute need for *Entente* solidarity, he was less extreme than Berthelot, who was convinced that the assertion of *Entente* solidarity had caused Germany to waver on 29 and 30 July. Whereas Berthelot in his logical way thought that the solution to peace lay primarily in Britain ranging herself behind France and Russia, de Margerie, whose sense of moderation owed much to experience abroad, placed considerable emphasis on transaction and on restraining Russia.

[100] Auffray, *De Margerie*, p. 285; Viviani to all posts, tel. 481, 5 p.m. 31 July 1914, AE NS 'Autriche', 35.

[101] 'Note pour la visite de M. de Schön', drafted before 11 a.m. 1 Aug. 1914, AE NS 'Autriche', 36. See also de Margerie to all major posts, 3 a.m. 1 Aug. 1914, AE NS 'Autriche', 36.

[102] Ibid.

Paul Cambon, the doyen of French ambassadors, shared many of de Margerie's views and was an influential figure during the July crisis. As ambassador to London, he was especially conscious of Germany's efforts to woo Britain. In his opinion, Britain held the key to the situation. A firm stance by Grey would certainly make the Germans 'pull their horns in'.[103] Cambon was probably instrumental in persuading Grey to go further than he would have liked. The Ambassador was an important adviser to Bienvenu-Martin, being present in Paris between 25 and 28 July. As the crisis worsened, Cambon continued to strive for peace, but he came increasingly to agree with his brother's assessment, which was that Germany was bent on war. The last few days saw him place as much emphasis on securing British military assistance as on resolving the diplomatic crisis.

Paul Cambon had been much more optimistic in the immediate aftermath of the Sarajevo assassination. He was so little concerned by it that in the second half of July he continued to plan on a fortnight's vacation. He was inclined to discount suggestions that Austria-Hungary would issue an ultimatum to Serbia. As Eubank says, his attitude was conditioned by reports which he received from the Centrale, which claimed that the military extremists in Austria-Hungary had been curbed.[104] Though he considered Austria difficult to reason with and blamed her for being the chief troublemaker in the Balkans, he was confident that Germany would sensibly restrain her. Consequently, there was a qualitative difference between his evaluation of Germany and that of Berthelot. As Isaac, a French historian, has commented, Cambon's mistrust of Germany was 'moins irréductible'.[105] That his suspicion was not overwhelming was evident in his words to Nicolson and in his telegrams to Bienvenu-Martin immediately after the sending of the Austrian ultimatum. He remarked to Nicolson, a pessimistic British diplomat, that Germany had no interest in causing a general war and that, with some forceful encouragement from Grey, she would be willing to use her influence with Vienna in order to obtain a moderation of the ultimatum. If this effort proved unsuccessful, she would support a mediation of the four non-interested powers.[106]

[103] Eubank, *Paul Cambon*, p. 169; A. Thierry, *L'Angleterre au temps de Paul Cambon* (Paris, 1961), III; P. Cambon to Bienvenu-Martin, 22 July 1914, AE NS 'Autriche', 31.

[104] Eubank, *Cambon*, p. 168.

[105] Ibid. p. 169; Jules Isaac, 'Observations complémentaires sur les Documents français', *Revue d'histoire de la Guerre mondiale* (Jan. 1937), p. 22.

[106] P. Cambon to Bienvenu-Martin, tels. 132, 133, and 154, 24 July 1914, 5.53 p.m. 6.06 p.m. 24 July, AE NS 'Autriche', 32.

Between the 25th and the 28th, Cambon had a considerable impact on French policy-makers. He came to Paris to be present at a baptism, but he stayed because he did not have full confidence in Berthelot. He was also apprehensive of the way in which Bienvenu-Martin had given the Austrian and German foreign offices the impression that Austria could devour Serbia without Russia's, Germany's, or France's consent.[107] Along with Berthelot, he was successful in forcing Bienvenu-Martin to drop any talk of localizing the conflict. He persuaded the acting Minister that Serbia should be advised to solicit British assistance.[108]

Ultimately, Cambon's gaze was fixed on London, whose attitude he regarded as crucial to the outcome of the crisis. His reasoning was that only the British government had sufficient authority to sway the leading powers, especially Germany. For this reason he disliked the idea of direct Austro-Russian *pourparlers*, arguing that the erratic Russians would only aggravate a crisis which the four disinterested nations might be able to end.[109]

In keeping with Cambon's outlook, his influence was not restricted to the Quai d'Orsay, but extended to Grey, the British foreign minister. The idea for four-power mediation appears to have come largely from Cambon.[110] In the course of the July crisis, he continually encouraged Grey in his attempts to bring about a four-power mediation. Nor was he prepared to brook any interference by Russia. As he told Bienvenu-Martin on 28 July:

Il convient d'encourager Sir Edward Grey dans sa tentative de médiation à quatre. A un moment où le moindre retard peut avoir de si fatales conséquences, l'initiative de M. Sazanoff me paraît des plus regrettables. Elle entrave l'action de Sir Edward Grey et procure à l'Autriche un moyen de se dérober à l'intervention amicale des quatre puissances.[111]

By 30 July, Cambon was beginning to take out the insurance he had paid for since 1898. During much of the crisis he had been confident that Britain would fulfil her moral obligations towards France in the event of

---

[107] Eubank, *Cambon*, p. 169, Isaac, 'Observations', p. 22.

[108] Bienvenu-Martin informed all major posts (8.20, 9, 10.15 p.m. 26 July 1914, AE NS 'Autriche', 32), that 'M. Sazonov a conseillé à la Serbie de demander la médiation anglaise, et sur l'avis de M.Paul Cambon j'ai appuyé cette suggestion à Londres'. See also Ferry to de Fleuriau, tel. 329, 26 July 1914, AE NS 'Autriche', 32.

[109] Eubank, *Cambon*, p. 172.

[110] Thierry, *Paul Cambon*, p. 111; P. Cambon to Bienvenu-Martin, tels. 134, 135, 24 July 1914, AE NS 'Autriche', 32.

[111] P. Cambon to Bienvenu-Martin, tels. 150, 151, 28 July 1914, AE NS 'Autriche', 33.

a Franco-German war.[112] Though he was still attempting on the 29th to have Britain put greater pressure on Germany, events had so worsened by the evening of the 30th that he was more interested in seeking British intervention in any future war than in promoting British mediation. He was at last thoroughly convinced that Berlin wanted a conflagration.

It was at precisely this time, however, that his confidence in the availability of British support was shaken. Between 1 and 3 August he was 'dans la plus grande incertitude'. His famous words to Grey asking whether the word honour had been struck from the British vocabulary were far more than just rhetorical acrobatics. He was confident of the support of Grey, Churchill, and Asquith, but believed that the rest of the cabinet, as well as Parliament, the press, and the City, had been influenced by Germany.[113] For all his uncertainty, Cambon continued to believe that Britain ultimately would defend France. He flatly refused to follow Viviani's order to 'transmettre une véritable injonction du gouvernement de la France d'avoir à se décider immédiatement'.[114]

Jules Cambon appears to have been no less influential than his brother during the July crisis. He had been urging a policy of *détente* with Germany for years, a view based on the belief that Germany was not desirous of continually creating pinpricks. He had been a voice crying in the wilderness. Thus, the fact that he had been signalling since November 1913 an increased bellicosity in the highest political circles in Berlin made the Centrale sit up and take notice. He fully agreed with Berthelot and Paul Cambon that only Britain could ensure peace. If London adopted a firm stance, he was convinced Germany would not risk a war.[115]

Before 25 July, however, Cambon appears only vaguely to have perceived the threatening circumstances. Between 5 and 23 July he remained in Paris on holidays. Though he reported that the idea of war was gaining support in the inner circles of government in Germany and that she had taken some preliminary measures, he did not foresee an imminent war.[116] He informed the Centrale that Berlin would support whatever *démarche* Vienna made, and he rejected Jagow's assertion that

[112] P. Cambon, 5.45 p.m. 29 July 1914, AE NS 'Autriche', 33.

[113] P. Cambon to Viviani, 30 July 1914, AE NS 'Autriche', 34.

[114] Thierry, *Paul Cambon*, p. 116.

[115] See R. Recouly, *Les Heures tragiques de l'avant-guerre* (Paris, 1921); G. P. Gooch, *Recent Revelations in European Diplomacy* (London, 1924) p. 146; G. Tabouis, *Jules Cambon par l'un des siens* (Paris, 1938), p. 255; Manneville to Doulcet, 14 Aug. 1914, AE Doulcet MSS, 21.

[116] J. Cambon to Viviani, 13 July 1914, AE NS 'Allemagne', 52; Messimy, '23 Juillet au 4 Août', part 2, p. 9, AN Messimy MSS, 5.

the German government knew nothing of the ultimatum. Nevertheless, he did not regard such a policy as particularly sinister. Germany was supporting Austria, he thought, because of Wilhelm's heightened sense of monarchical solidarity. Cambon was inclined to attribute the ultimatum itself to Austria's desire to repair the mistakes she had made since 1908.[117]

By the end of the 24th, however, Cambon's suspicions were fully aroused. The intransigence in Jagow's tone convinced him that Germany had decided to support Austria militarily if necessary.[118] According to his sources, Germany believed that Britain would keep France and Russia in check. Britain was therefore of importance to the outcome of the crisis. A policy of absolute unity between the members of the Triple *Entente* might succeed in deterring Berlin, though Cambon doubted whether even this concordance would deflect Germany from its warlike course. From 25 July he continually urged necessary military measures 'pour n'être pas surpris par les événements'.[119] As the days went by, his calm advice turned to frenzied warnings. In the event of general war, it was inevitable, because of the Schlieffen Plan, that France would be attacked first. Furthermore, if Russian mobilization reached an advanced stage, Germany would act before an Austro-Russian war began.[120]

Far from plumping for the war, Cambon was still doing all that was possible to arrest the march of events. He noticed that Grey's warning to Lichnowsky on 29 July had produced the desired effect, and he continued to stress the necessity of British diplomatic intervention.[121] Britain needed to harden her attitude even further, since only she could alter the policy of the German government. By the 31st, however, Cambon had clearly lost all hope for a peaceful solution. He now reported that, contrary to what Jagow had asserted, Germany might not even wait for Russian general mobilization before acting. He could do no more than to pack his bags and to participate in a war he had tried to avoid during most of his diplomatic career.[122]

[117] J. Cambon to Bienvenu-Martin, 24 July 1914, AE NS 'Autriche', 32.

[118] AN Messimy MSS, 5.

[119] J. Cambon to Bienvenu-Martin, tels. 186 and 188, 25 July 1914, tel. 193, 26 July 1914, AE NS 'Autriche', 32.

[120] J. Cambon to Bienvenu-Martin, tel. 193, 26 July 1914 and dispatch 436, 27 July 1914, AE NS 'Autriche', 32.

[121] Jules Cambon to Viviani, tels. 211 and 212, 29 July 1914, AE NS 'Autriche', 33.

[122] J. Cambon to Viviani, tels. 231 and 234, 31 July 1914, and tels. 244, 246, 1 Aug. 1914, AE NS 'Autriche', 36.

In a crucial area, that of Franco-Russian relations, France's policy during the July crisis was made not by the Centrale but rather by Maurice Paléologue, the newly appointed ambassador to St Petersburg. He was certainly in a position to influence events. The French government was effectively stranded on the high seas between 24 and 29 July. As the representative of the French government, Russia's only ally, he was the diplomat most closely listened to by St Petersburg. Nevertheless, at no time did he really use his influence to restrain Russia. Instead he encouraged the Russians to challenge Germany, even at the risk of war. In doing so he showed yet again what exceptional authority an ambitious ambassador could wield in pre-war French diplomacy. Unfortunately, while the 'dictatorship' of some ambassadors had made a positive contribution to French policy-making, particularly in times of ministerial instability, that of Paléologue, in the circumstances of July 1914, proved disastrous.

Paléologue was not a natural militarist. What motivated him during the July crisis was the deepest pessimism about relations between the powers and the conclusion that Germany was determined to unleash a major conflagration in the near future.[123] At the same time, he seems genuinely to have believed that, because of the parliamentary crisis which had beset the Viviani ministry, he was entitled to take independent action. His 'great man' theory of history, in particular his admiration for the Italian Cavour, whose initiative at a time of crisis he had much applauded, further emboldened him. Worse, Paléologue was subject to flights of imagination which suggested a certain mental disequilibrium.[124]

Several other factors help to explain Paléologue's conduct. He possessed precise knowledge of the Schlieffen Plan. In an age where even the best diplomats or politicians were ignorant of the technicalities raised by mobilization, Paléologue who had for years been in charge of secret files at the Quai d'Orsay, was well aware of how quickly Germany would fall on France before attempting to crush Russia. Given his belief that Germany wanted war, he was anxious to hasten Russian general mobilization as quickly as possible.

Paléologue's unreserved support of Russian objectives can also to some extent be attributed to an eagerness to remove the suspicion with

---

[123] Conversations with Doulcet, Nov. 1913, Feb. 1914, AE Doulcet MSS, 23; Paléologue, *La Russie des tsars*, p. 23; Paléologue, *Au Quai d'Orsay*, p. 25; Notes by de Robien, 'Souvenirs: Russie, ancien régime', AN de Robien, MSS.

[124] Conversations with Doulcet, 14 Aug. 1914, AE Doulcet MSS, 23; Paléologue to Jusserand, 4 July 1921, AE Jusserand MSS, 37. For a good analysis of the connection between Paléologue and his writings, see Halfond, 'Paléologue', p. 104.

which he was viewed by Russian high society and political circles. As Daeschner told Doulcet, one of Paléologue's immediate advisers, Paléologue 'aura été précédé aussi de trop de mauvais rapports pour que la confiance s'établisse'. He was particularly mistrusted by the grand dukes. Paléologue's reply to this attitude was to spread Poincaré's name around and to provide lavish dinners in the hope of impressing his hosts.[125]

His determination to encourage an aggressive policy was also bolstered by the support rendered by his staff, especially Chambrun and Doulcet. They were not perhaps bellicose, but they believed that since war was inevitable it was necessary to prepare for it. Undoubtedly Delcassé had encouraged them to think in this way during his ambassadorship. Doulcet had earlier developed an undying hatred for Austria and a dedication to the principle of Balkan national self-determination. Both Chambrun and Doulcet were strongly sympathetic to the notion of 'fermeté à la Poincaré'.[126]

To all these reasons for a strong stand against Germany must be added Paléologue's conviction that the French and Russian armies were at their peak. He dismissed both Bompard's questioning of Russia's political and military strength and the revolutionary potential of the Russian peasantry.[127]

From the time of his arrival in St Petersburg, Paléologue sought to convince the Russian government that France would support its policy without reserve and wherever it led. From his first interview with the Tsar in February 1914 he emphasized the unqualified nature of French backing. A few days after the Sarajevo assassination he entered into an acrimonious debate with Viviani over the wording of toasts to be made during the forthcoming state visit. He protested openly against Viviani's use of 'ensemble de leurs forces' instead of his own phrase 'en maintenant la plénitude de leurs forces'. The importance which Paléologue attached to this dispute is made clear by the daily notes of his collaborators de Robien and Doulcet. He went so far as to write to Viviani: 'Depuis que l'alliance existe, ce serait la première fois qu'un des deux alliés insisterait pour obtenir dans l'affirmation publique de

---

[125] 'Notes journalières', 4 Feb., 1 Mar. 1914. Contrary to the myths spread about after the war, it was Doumergue and not Poincaré who chose Paléologue for Russia, 7 Jan. 1914, BN (NAF 16026), Poincaré MSS. See also Daeschner to Doulcet, 5 May 1914, and Manneville to Doulcet, 23 Jan. 1914, AE Doulcet MSS, 21.

[126] 'Souvenirs: Russie, ancien régime', AN de Robien MSS.

[127] Bompard to Doumergue, 9 July 1914, and Paléologue to Doumergue, 21 May 1914, AE Paléologue MSS, 1.

leurs obligations réciproques une atténuation d'importance et d'efficacité.'[128]

In keeping with his dislike for governmental direction, especially that of the Viviani government, Paléologue decided to maximize his personal authority and, where possible, to act on his own initiative. Well before July, Buchanan, the British ambassador, had noted this tendency in a dispatch to the Foreign Office.[129] That Paléologue was working under some special mandate from Poincaré needs to be dismissed. While Poincaré supported Paléologue's nomination to St Petersburg, it was Doumergue who made the final decision. Poincaré wrote in his diary on 7 January 1914 that 'il [Doumergue] préfère en tout cas, désigner Paléologue et comme il craint une certaine hésitation de la part de celui-ci, il me prie de chercher à le décider'.[130] It is also clear that Poincaré's policy of firmness was quite different from that embraced by Paléologue. During 1914 Poincaré was critical of France's readiness to second Russia's Balkan policy. Delcassé's resignation had been accepted by Poincaré for this very reason. Despite their friendship, the President was suspicious of Paléologue's diplomacy. His diary entry of 1 March 1914 makes this clear. He wrote that Paléologue 'se laisse un peu circonvenir par la grande duchesse Wladimir, qui n'est pas très bien en cour, et par d'autres personnes, trop entreprenantes, dans l'aristocratie russe. Il a également le tort de répéter partout qu'il est mon ami et me tutoie. Le grand duc [Nicholas Michael] croit qu'il sera bien de la surveiller un peu.'[131]

It was certainly necessary to keep a watchful eye on Paléologue during the crisis. Not only did he often act without authorization, but at critical points he deliberately misled his superiors. In the final days of the July crisis he created an almost total communications blackout. His aim was essentially to keep the French government in the dark about Russian mobilization during 30 and 31 July. He could safely assume that as long as Viviani was unaware of these military preparations, he would make no concerted attempt to restrain Russia.

During the official visit Paléologue appeared overexcited by the occasion and revelled in the military pomp and circumstance. In a

---

[128] Ibid., Paléologue to Viviani, 12 July 1914; 'Souvenirs: Russie, ancien régime', AN de Robien MSS; AE Doulcet MSS, 24.

[129] G. Buchanan, *My Mission to Russia* (London, 1923), pp. 186–200.

[130] *Notes Journalières*, 7 Mar. 1914, BN (NAF 16026), Poincaré MSS.

[131] The commonly held view that Paléologue was following Poincaré's policy during the July crisis is unfounded. For an example of this thesis, see Turner, *Origins*, p. 89. For the opposing view, see Keiger, *France and the Origins*, p. 160.

communiqué which he was charged with drafting at the end, he distorted Poincaré's words to such an extent that no mention of peace was made. According to de Robien, he wished to commit France fully to Russia's Balkan policy: 'L'ambassadeur qui lui-même était surexcité par ces journées prétendit souligner encore tout ce qu'avait de menaçant les paroles de P [Poincaré] en faisant dans le communiqué officiel une allusion directe à la Serbie.'[132]

When foreign minister Sazonov learned of the Austrian ultimatum on 24 July he invited Buchanan and Paléologue to lunch to discuss the situation. Undoubtedly, Sazonov wished to pick up the gauntlet that the Austrians had thrown down. It appears to have been Paléologue, however, who took the lead by arguing that the Triple *Entente* should stand up to the Central powers.[133] Basing himself on the toasts recently exchanged (despite the fact that Poincaré had toned down his speech so as not to make it provocative), on the reciprocal declarations of the two ministers of Foreign Affairs (though Viviani had shown himself to be hostile to bellicose thinking), and finally on the communiqué of 24 July (which was redrafted by de Margerie out of a concern for peace) Paléologue proffered Sazonov unequivocal French support. According to de Robien: 'A ce déjeuner néfaste ils se sont excités les uns et les autres. Paléologue a dû être particulièrement véhément en se targuant des conversations qu'il avait eues avec Poincaré, qui avait quitté la Russie la nuit précédente à bord de la France.'[134] Buchanan, for his part, observed

---

[132] 'Voyage de Poincaré', p. 61, AN de Robien MSS.

[133] On Paléologue's continued initiatives in St Petersburg after the outbreak of war, and on his misrepresentation, even fabrication of Russian war aims, see W. A. Renzi, 'Who Composed, "Sazonov's Thirteen Points": A Re-examination of Russia's War Aims of 1914', *American Historical Review*, 88/2 (Apr. 1983), pp. 347–57.

[134] Annotation by de Robien on 'Copie de notes prises par Chambrun du 23 juillet au 3 août 1914', p. 2, AN de Robien MSS. Chambrun's notes, along with other documents, suggest an attempted cover up on the part of Paléologue. Immediately after the outbreak of war, the question of responsibility was posed, and Paléologue was conscious of criticism of his actions by the time of Viviani's telegram of 31 July 1914, informing him that the Quai d'Orsay was 'nullement renseigné' about Russian general mobilization. Apart from repeating his earlier telegram of 31 July, on the subject of Russian mobilization, which was sent at 9.30 a.m. on 1 Aug. 1914, he drafted an explanatory note in which he attempted to cover himself. Interestingly enough, still sensitive to criticism, he remarked to Doulcet in Aug. 1914 that it was necessary to avoid post-mortems: 'une instruction, un ordre, ne se suffisent à lui-même sans qu'on ait besoin de les qualifier de formes impératives' (AE Doulcet MSS, 21). In the middle of Aug. 1914 Paléologue had Chambrun draw up a 'Récapitulation des faits qui se sont produits du 23 juillet au 3 août 1914'. Though Paléologue, in a manuscript note of 5 Feb. 1935 (AE Paléologue MSS, 5), labelled this memo as a simple reminder of events, it looks more like a conscious attempt on his part to make

that Paléologue's appeal to him to join France and Russia could only have one consequence: war. 'I was determined', he wrote in his memoirs, 'not to say one word that could be interpreted as an encouragement to Russia to declare war on Austria. To do so might have diminished any chance of a pacific solution of the question.'[135] Paléologue's desire to give the impression of *Entente* solidarity was not surprising in view of Britain's determination to restrain Russia. He subsequently rejected the proposed 'médiation à quatre' for direct Austro-Russian negotiations, which would have eliminated London's pacific influence.

At the same time as he was giving unqualified support to St Petersburg, Paléologue was sending back to the Centrale distorted reports about what was happening in the Russian capital. He did not inform the Quai d'Orsay of Buchanan's mediation attempts during the 24th or of Sazonov's personal view that mobilization was necessary. Nor did he inform Paris that Russia had issued a communiqué on 25 July stating that she could not remain indifferent to Serbia's fate. The most important negligence was his failure to report the extent of military measures taken by Russia after a cabinet meeting on the 25th. His telegram noted only that 'Russie a décidé en principe de mobiliser les treize corps d'armée qui sont éventuellement destinés à opérer contre l'Autriche. Cette mobilisation ne sera rendu effective et publique que si le gouvernement Austro-Hongrois prétend contraindre la Serbie par armes. Les préparatifs clandestins commencent néanmoins.'[136]

Nothing could have been further from the truth. Not only had he not informed the Quai, as Isvolsky did later, that the decision to mobilize against Austria-Hungary had been left to Sazonov, but he gave the clear impression that despite some secret and unspecified preparations, mobilization would be rendered effective and public only after the beginning of an Austro-Serbian war. In fact, mobilization measures were already under way. According to de Robien, the military districts of Kiev, Odessa, Kazan, and Moscow were put 'en état de mobilisation'

---

sure that the embassy adopted his version of events and that his actions were placed in the best possible light. With this idea in mind, presumably, he made some rather sweeping revisions of Chambrun's notes and then circulated the 'Récapitulation' to embassy staff.

[135] Buchanan, *My Mission*, pp. 186–200. See also his report to London: 'The French Ambassador gave me to understand that France would not only give Russia strong diplomatic support but would, if necessary, fulfil the obligations imposed on her by the alliance.' *BD* 3, xi. 101.

[136] Paléologue to Bienvenu-Martin, tel. 284, 25 July 1914, AE Paléologue MSS, 1; Albertini, *Origins*, ii. 326.

and not simply ordered to take measures 'préliminaires à la mobilis-ation'.[137] Worse, Paléologue failed to transmit the news that secret measures were being undertaken by military districts designed to operate against Germany rather than Austria (Vilna, St Petersburg, and Warsaw) and that St Petersburg and Moscow were in a state of siege.

Throughout the period 25-9 July Paléologue depicted Sazonov as peaceful and open to any reasonable transaction. In contrast, he por-trayed Germany, especially Ambassador Pourtalès, as dangerous and intimidating. Pourtalès's initiative for direct Austro-Russian talks was not communicated to the Centrale. In fact, Paléologue indicated the reverse. Germany and Austria, he said, had let pass 'peace feelers' by Sazonov. Paléologue thought that Austro-Russian talks could be useful, but he had been convinced since 25 July that Germany and Austria were toying with the Triple *Entente* and that Germany's proposal was a measure designed to put Russia in the wrong. In his opinion, the only possible outcome of the July crisis was armed conflict. The assistance he wanted from Britain was military intervention in a war and not diplo-matic mediation for peaceful purposes.

By the 29th, the situation had visibly worsened. Austria had declared war on Serbia and, at 3 p.m., Russia had decreed partial mobilization. During the night this order was converted into general mobilization but rescinded after a telegram arrived from Wilhelm II. Paléologue did not report the partial mobilization decision until shortly before midnight, some nine hours after the decree.[138] More importantly, he did not inform the Centrale that general mobilization had even been con-sidered.[139] Paléologue's omissions were truly remarkable, and years later Viviani justifiably complained about being thoroughly ill informed.[140]

---

[137] 'Voyage de Poincaré', p. 65, AN de Robien MSS.

[138] Paléologue to Viviani, tel. 304, 11.45 p.m. 29 July 1914, AE Paléologue MSS, 1. It is interesting to note that Paléologue removed from the files of the Quai d'Orsay in-criminating telegrams which were sent during this period. The rule *à la rigueur* was that all telegrams were the official property of the French government. Some of Paléologue's telegrams were handed over in 1927 after requests were received by Poincaré and Re-nouvin, the historian. The rest were returned in 1945 by Paléologue's nephew, Pierre Lebon.

[139] Paléologue, *La Russie des tsars*, 29 July 1914, p. 35. There is controversy over whether general mobilization was ever rescinded. Some have alleged that Tsar Nicholas gave the order but that it was not carried out (Renauld to Poincaré, 2 Apr. 1921, AN Messimy MSS, 2). For a thorough coverage of the Sukhomlinoff trial (Mar.–Aug. 1917) in which the former Russian minister of war alleged that the order was not rescinded, see *Le Correspondant*, Feb.–May 1918. De Robien expressed a similar view in his annotation of Chambrun's notes for the period 23 July to 3 Aug. 1914, p. 4, AN de Robien MSS.

[140] Note by R. Viviani, 3 Jan. 1923, AE Paléologue MSS, 5.

The trend continued on 30 and 31 July. Paléologue's aim was to prevent the French government from using any restraining influence it may have been able to exercise in St Petersburg. On the afternoon of 30 July he had received de Margerie's telegram stating that, though France would fulfil all of its obligations, Russia should take absolutely no measure which would result in German general mobilization. Paléologue's reply, drafted while Russian general mobilization was in the process of being decreed, was a classical piece of deception. At this point, sixteen hours after the event, he first mentioned Russia's secret military preparations without adding that general mobilization was imminent. Even then, he referred to these clandestine measures only in passing and emphasized that Russia was fundamentally peaceful. The Russian general staff 'avait précisément fait surseoir à quelques précautions secrètes dont la divulgation avait pu alarmer l'Allemagne'. Furthermore, the chief of the Russian general staff had told the French military attaché that the Russian partial mobilization begun on the morning of the 30th had been exclusively aimed at Austria.[141] The Centrale could be excused for believing that nothing too disturbing had transpired at St Petersburg.[142]

Needless to say, Paléologue was employing similar tactics with the Russians. De Margerie's telegram, a telegram of restraint, was used to strengthen Paléologue's declarations of unequivocal support for Russia. Sazonov's belief that he could be certain of French support clearly indicated that Paléologue had utilized the phrase 'la France est résolue à remplir toutes les obligations' without acknowledging the context in which it had been written.

On 31 July Paléologue continued to keep the French government totally ignorant. According to most accounts, the telegram informing the Centrale of Russian general mobilization was sent between 10 and 11 a.m., eighteen hours after the decree had been issued. This telegram did not reach the Quai until 8.30 p.m.[143] For nearly thirty hours, then, the Centrale had had no reliable report of Russian general mobilization and had been dependent on the German account, which had taken only a couple of hours to reach Berlin. It is not surprising, therefore, that the Quai d'Orsay believed that Berlin was seeking to justify her military preparations by making Russia seem the aggressor. Moreover, there is

[141] Paléologue to Viviani, tel. 311, 3.50 p.m. 30 July 1914, AE Paléologue MSS, 1.

[142] Renouvin, 'La Politique française en juillet 1914', p. 10.

[143] Later Viviani was unsure whether it was at this stage or early the next morning that he eventually received news of general mobilization (note by Viviani, 3 January 1923, AE Paléologue MSS, 5).

evidence that Paléologue's telegram was not transmitted until 5 or 6 p.m. on 31 July. Doulcet noted in his journal under the heading 'dates officielles communiqués par Wehlin' that 'le décret de mobilisation générale a été signalé le 18/31 juillet, le télégramme concernant la mobilisation générale à été envoyé le 18/31 juillet entre 5 et 6 heures du soir'.[144] This delay would explain why the telegram arrived at 8.30 p.m.

During the period 1-3 August, Paléologue appears to have been in the forefront of those who harangued the crowds around the French Embassy.[145] It would, however, be a mistake to see him as a mere warmonger. He was deeply suspicious of Germany and convinced that war was unavoidable. His patriotism was undeniable. Unfortunately, it encouraged him to follow an extreme course which, whatever Germany's motives, did much to prevent a peaceful resolution of the July crisis.

In the final analysis, the July crisis provided a further illustration of the Quai d'Orsay's importance in the formulation of French foreign policy, but also of the authority and independence which could be accumulated by French ambassadors in the pre-1914 Third Republic. That the private initiatives of the ambassadorial team had been salutary in times of diplomatic uncertainty and ministerial instability cannot be denied. Nevertheless, this often unchallenged independence could result in policies that neither the French government nor the Quai d'Orsay as a whole wanted. Without a thorough structural reform of departmental machinery, in particular the creation of a powerful secretary-general to provide added co-ordination and supervision, there was always the possibility that the personal initiatives of individual ambassadors would have disastrous consequences. This is exactly what transpired in July 1914. Despite the firm but pacific sentiments of officials such as Berthelot, de Margerie, and the Cambons, Paléologue successfully sabotaged official policy and may have helped to cause a European conflagration which very few Frenchmen desired.

[144] Note, AE Doulcet MSS, 24. Paléologue's 'explanatory note' (AE Paléologue MSS, 1) does not stand up to scrutiny.
[145] Annotation by Doulcet, AE Doulcet MSS, 24.

Conclusion

Between the years 1898 and 1914 the Quai d'Orsay developed into the most powerful and independent foreign office in Europe. It was unparalleled among such institutions in the extent of its involvement in both the implementation and formulation of policy. It was quite distinct from its British and German counterparts. The Wilhelmstraße developed into a governmental body subservient to the political will of the imperial Kaiser and Chancellor. In London, the Foreign Office evolved from an administrative body into an institution whose members could substantially voice their opinions and contribute to political decisions, but foreign secretaries such as Grey consistently retained ultimate authority. In contrast, during the crises of 1905–6, 1911, and 1914 the Quai d'Orsay had a decisive impact on the French decision-making process.

What factors explain the unique importance of the Quai d'Orsay? The endemic ministerial instability of the Third Republic is part of the answer. A bewildering succession of foreign ministers between 1870 and 1914 had little opportunity to acquaint themselves with their duties, their subordinates, or their dossiers. Nowhere was the impact of ministerial instability more apparent than in the international crises of 1905–6, 1911, and 1914, when French foreign ministers came and went with startling rapidity. In such circumstances, the Quai d'Orsay, or parts of it, was largely able to determine and implement foreign policy.

The outlook and ability of the men who staffed the Quai d'Orsay also help to explain its exceptional influence. They had a highly developed sense of their own importance, which was derived not only from ministerial instability but from an awareness of France's long history as a Great Power. Many of these men were imbued with a belief that the Republic's ineptness and internal divisions forced them to develop a spirit of initiative and independence. Indeed, contempt for the parliamentary regime, combined with a somewhat spiritual notion of France's destiny, encouraged both bureaucrats and diplomats to act in defiance of official policy. On the whole, the men of the Quai d'Orsay displayed exceptional competence in the years 1898–1914. While political instability alone might have produced men of high calibre in the diplomatic corps, it was sheer chance that the likes of the Cambons, Barrère, Jusserand, Constans, de Margerie, Berthelot, and Paléologue graced the diplomatic arena during this period. They were all men of rare talent, whose astuteness and energy enabled them to acquire exceptional stature and, at times, to behave in a remarkably independent way.

The power of the Quai d'Orsay suffered surprisingly little under Delcassé, Pichon, and, to a lesser extent, Poincaré, all of whom were foreign ministers who enjoyed a lengthy stay in office. Delcassé, intent on being master in his own house, gathered around him men who, while not being sycophants, were basically faceless administrators who had little say in the more important matters. Nevertheless, by working and identifying closely with his major ambassadors, he made possible the emergence of an influential ambassadorial élite. Whether the *Entente Cordiale* was Cambon's or Delcassé's work, or whether Franco-Italian *rapprochement* was the achievement of the Foreign Minister or Barrère, are questions which lose much of their significance when viewed against the underlying harmony of aims, views, and policies. Perhaps paradoxically, it was under Delcassé, one of the Third Republic's most famous foreign ministers, that the role of the French ambassador reached its peak. Pichon, a former diplomat with numerous close friends in the Foreign Ministry, was both lazy and, at times, easily influenced. During his years in office the Centrale, dominated by Louis and staffed by exceptional bureaucrats such as Berthelot and Conty, regained the authority it had lost while Delcassé was Foreign Minister. Admittedly, under Poincaré the Quai d'Orsay suffered a brief diminution in prestige. Poincaré ruled both bureaucrats and diplomats with an iron hand. Yet for all Barrère's complaints about being a mere postal service for the Foreign Minister, neither he nor his policies were overturned. Despite the personality clashes between Paul Cambon and Poincaré, the latter adhered to Cambon's policies. Moreover, the Quai d'Orsay's diminution lasted only as long as Poincaré was Foreign Minister. With his accession to the presidency of the Republic, its power reached new heights.

The Quai d'Orsay, of course, did not make foreign policy in a vacuum. Because of the Republic's rather chaotic constitutional framework, inherent ministerial instability, or individual links with the Foreign Ministry, the press, big business, Parliament, and colonial groups were able to shape certain decisions. In fact, the distinction between the outside world and the Foreign Ministry was much less evident in France than in Great Britain, which had a clearer chain of command. The journalist Tardieu and the businessman and politician Étienne were consistently influential during the years 1898–1914. Pressure groups such as the Colonial party and the Comité des forges, and newspapers such as *Le Temps* and *Le Journal des débats*, exercised considerable sway at times. In the final analysis, however, the Quai d'Orsay was usually of decisive importance in the determination of foreign policy, and it often utilized external individuals and groups to achieve its own objectives.

For all the authority of the Quai d'Orsay, it did not always function efficiently. The reforms of 1907 were an attempt to remedy this state of affairs, but they did not result, contrary to P. G. Lauren's contention, in a successful transformation of the organizational structure, the overseas service, and the personnel policies of the Quai d'Orsay.[1] Admittedly, the reforms brought the French Foreign Ministry into the twentieth century. Berthelot's achievement in the area of professional administration was noteworthy. A new breed of diplomats, exemplified by the Sciences-po group, began to replace the older figures. The interconnection of economics and politics was recognized by the establishment of a political and commercial division under a single *directeur*, who was to be assisted by a *sous-directeur d'Europe, d'Afrique et d'Océanie*. Indeed, the establishment of four new subdivisions ('Europe, Afrique, et Océanie, Asie, Levant, and Amérique) was a timely recognition of the redistribution of international power. A valuable attempt was also made to standardize conditions of service.

In several important respects, nevertheless, both the substance and the implementation of the 1907 reforms were decidedly unsatisfactory. In terms of organizational structure, the new political and commercial director remained inferior in rank to the ambassadors and very much dependent on the relationship he enjoyed with the incumbent foreign minister. Only the creation of a powerful secretary-general (not envisaged in the 1907 reforms) could have given the Foreign Ministry the necessary overall control. Furthermore, the new geographical divisions created as many problems as they solved. The previous division of Nord and Midi was clearly outdated. However, the newly created Sous-direction d'Europe, d'Afrique et d'Océanie, while temporarily concealing the European consequences of the Moroccan question, did nothing to elevate Africa and Oceania to the importance they deserved. It did little, moreover, to dispel the idea that the Quai d'Orsay remained traditionalist and Eurocentric. As for the new and unstable subdivisions which

[1] P. G. Lauren, *Diplomats and Bureaucrats* (Stanford, Calif., 1976), pp. 79–80.

emanated from the 1907 reforms, their attributions were not properly defined and therefore led to intense rivalry among ambitious officials. Still more significantly, the 1907 reforms failed to curb the power and independence of the *chef du cabinet*. By 1911 he was increasingly able to interfere with the formulation of policy and to challenge the authority of the political director.

The 1907 reforms, in dealing with overseas services, did little to bring about equality either between the consular and diplomatic corps or between the overseas services and the Paris central administration. Standardization of overseas agents' wages and conditions was not effected as quickly as envisaged. The stature of the consular corps was not augmented. Despite the introduction of a common examination after 1907, the rules of the *concours* were such that only those with high marks were allowed to enter the diplomatic corps. Despite the intentions of the 1907 reforms, interpenetrability of services with equivalence of rank had not been sufficiently achieved by 1914. Furthermore, those with long external careers remained at a considerable disadvantage in comparison to those who pursued their careers largely in the Centrale.

In the area of personnel, the 1907 reforms had clearly provided for a separation of the private ministerial cabinet and the Bureau du personnel. Unfortunately, this proposal was not put into practice. The *chef du cabinet* retained an unwelcome stranglehold over the two divisions. His frequent intrusions into personnel matters seriously limited attempts to arrive at objective criteria for both entry into the service and promotion. The impact of political nepotism on appointments did not decline after 1907.

In explaining the limited significance of the 1907 reforms, it has to be remembered that they came largely from within the Quai d'Orsay and that they were not the product of a strong and durable reform movement. There was little chance that they would be fully implemented once the Radicals, the leading advocates of change, became absorbed by such divisive internal issues as the progressive income tax and labour unrest. Implementation was also inhibited by Foreign Minister Pichon, who, along with Paul Cambon, moderated Clemenceau's reforming zeal. International tension caused by the Near Eastern and Moroccan crises made French governments increasingly reluctant to tamper with the machinery of the Quai d'Orsay. In addition, several reforms were sabotaged and diluted by the resistance of Foreign Ministry officials.

The assertion of an eminent diplomatic historian, Arno Mayer, that the Quai d'Orsay was 'an aristocratic stronghold even after the Dreyfus affair' is incorrect.[2] Until 1877 aristocrats had remained strongly entrenched at the Quai d'Orsay, but between 1877 and 1880, when the Republicans took over the Republic, a period of change began. The cry for a new bourgeois corps was too strong to neglect, and under Jules Herbette in the 1880s an *épuration* of the aristocracy took place. As a result, a bourgeois élite began to conduct the affairs of the Quai d'Orsay. The new bourgeois diplomat was usually a man of the middle or upper middle class and a lawyer with professional or literary interests. He often developed distinctly conservative views, in part a legacy of his aristocratic predecessors. He was generally a practising Catholic, hostile to Jews, Protestants, and the parliamentary system. He viewed himself as an expert entitled to resist and even to reject governmental initiatives when he saw fit.

The bourgeoisification of the Quai d'Orsay intensified as its recruitment became more closely linked to educational qualifications. French diplomats were increasingly graduates of the École libre des sciences politiques. As early as 1898, in fact, this *grande école* began to acquire a decisive role in the training of Foreign Ministry candidates. In 1898 it provided only 5 per cent of the service, but between 1899 and 1936 it supplied 249 of the 284 individuals who were admitted to the diplomatic corps. The emphasis which the Quai d'Orsay placed on education was such as to differentiate it clearly from the British and German foreign offices, where social class remained the most dominant qualification for office.

In many ways the leading figures of the Quai d'Orsay adopted common attitudes towards other countries during the period 1898–1914. They had a decidedly Eurocentric outlook which frequently led them to view in rather patronizing fashion less technically advanced parts of the world. While their hostility to Britain was keen in the late 1890s, this sentiment gradually dissipated, and they became pro-British after 1904. Other shared priorities can be detected. The Franco-Russian alliance was viewed as the cornerstone of French policy. The Mediterranean, while considered to be of less importance, assumed much greater significance after the turn of the century. Apart from periods of crisis, the Balkans, the Near East, and the Far East ranked further down the scale of significance. Only a few far-seeing men such as the Cambons recognized the future of America and the Pacific.

---

[2] A. J. Mayer, *The Persistence of the Old Regime* (New York, 1981), p. 309.

The most important of all the Quai d'Orsay's common attitudes was its hostility to Germany. Quite simply, a pro-German lobby did not exist in the Foreign Ministry. Almost all French diplomats, apart from a few notable exceptions such as Jules Cambon, were thoroughly anti-German. Even he could not fully overcome the pervasive influence of the French military defeat in 1870-1 and the subsequent loss of Alsace-Lorraine. The impact of the Franco-Prussian war was even more marked in the cases of Barrère, Paul Cambon, Pichon, Delcassé, and Paléologue. Moreover, the influence of Gambetta upon those who staffed or headed the Foreign Ministry cannot be sufficiently emphasized. In spite of his moderation in later years, he never viewed Germany as a natural partner for France. According to his latest biographer, his long-term objective remained 'the recovery of the lost provinces which he never forgot'.[3] Jules Cambon, clearly echoed the sentiments of Gambettists such as Barrère, Delcassé, Paul Cambon and Pichon when he lauded Gambetta in a reception speech delivered to the Académie française: 'Comment ne pas subir la séduction de cet homme éloquent et généreux, dont l'âme était ardente et qui portait en lui un sentiment si vif de la grandeur de la France?'[4]

Certain myths about the July crisis which arose in the 1920s as a result of the polemical *Kriegschuldfrage* need to be dispelled. Luigi Albertini's assertion that the Foreign Ministry was 'totally unequal to dealing with the situation' during the days immediately after the Austrian ultimatum is erroneous.[5] Indeed, in spite of the absence of Viviani, Poincaré, and de Margerie, the Quai d'Orsay for the most part functioned in a highly effective way under the intelligent supervision of Philippe Berthelot. Besides, Jules and Paul Cambon were both in Paris for much of this crucial period. Equally fallacious is Albertini's contention that the Quai d'Orsay was 'as in the crisis of 1908-9, animated by strongly Austrophile sentiments'.[6] The sympathy which Bienvenu-Martin initially felt for Austria-Hungary was rapidly ovecome by the chiefs of the Centrale. In addition, the French Embassy in St Petersburg was strongly anti-Austrian and pro-Balkan, a legacy in part of Delcassé's days as foreign minister and as ambassador.

During the July crisis both the French government and the Foreign Ministry in general were resolutely pacific. President Poincaré's atti-

[3] J. P. T. Bury, *Gambetta's Final Years* (London, 1982), p. 357.
[4] G. Tabouis, *Jules Cambon par l'un des siens* (Paris, 1938)
[5] L. Albertini, *The Origins of the War of 1914* (London, 1952-7), ii. 322.   [6] Ibid.

tudes and actions need to be dissociated from those of Paléologue.[7] Furthermore, the visit by high-ranking officials and politicians to St Petersburg between 20 and 23 July was not the occasion for either a *Kriegsrat* or an assurance of explicit French diplomatic support.[8] Finally, there seems to be little justification for the emphasis placed by L. C. F. Turner on the influence of the French military.[9]

In the course of the July crisis, the role of Paléologue was highly significant and surely contributed to the coming of the war. In the most recent study of France and the origins of the First World War, J.F.V. Keiger has viewed Paléologue's responsibility as something altogether personal. He argues, in fact, that Paléologue's independence, 'contrary to orders from Paris, shows by the same token that France was not to blame'.[10] However, the independent course followed by Paléologue in July 1914 was by no means an isolated phenomenon. It was but a further example of the manner in which French diplomats, in the absence of a secretary-general, were able to initiate important policies and to disregard governmental prerogatives. Ultimately, therefore, Paléologue's responsibility for the outbreak of the war can be extended to the French government, which had failed to overcome what, in the circumstances of July 1914, was a serious structural defect in the Quai d'Orsay.[11]

---

[7] Ibid. ii. 197; L. C. F. Turner, *The Origins of the First World War* (London, 1976), pp. 89, 90; G. Krumeich, 'Aufrustung und Innenpolitik in Frankreich vor dem Ersten Weltkrieg' (Wiesbaden, 1980), pp. 340–6; J. F. V. Keiger, *France and the Origins of the First World War* (London, 1983), p. 160.

[8] Albertini, *The Origins of the War of 1914*, ii. 196–7; Turner, *Origins*, p. 90.

[9] Turner, *Origins*, pp. 89, 104.

[10] Keiger, *France and the Origins*, p. 160.

[11] For the impact of a malfunction of governmental structures on German foreign policy, see J. C. G. Röhl, *Germany without Bismarck* (London, 1967).

BIBLIOGRAPHY

Primary Sources: Archival Material

FRANCE

Ministry of Foreign Affairs, Paris

Private Papers

Alphand MSS.
d'Aunay MSS.
Barrère MSS.
Beau MSS.
Beaucaire MSS.
Berthelot MSS.
Bihourd MSS.
Billot MSS.
de Billy MSS.
Bonin MSS.
Bourgeois MSS.
Cambon, J., MSS.
Cambon, P., MSS.
Charles-Roux MSS.
Chaudordy MSS.
Chevandrier de Valdrome
  MSS.

Collin de Plancy MSS.
Constans MSS.
Dard MSS.
Delcassé MSS.
Doulcet MSS.
Doumergue MSS.
Dutasta MSS.
Ferry MSS.
de Fleuriau MSS.
de Freycinet MSS.
Gérard MSS.
Gout MSS.
Hanotaux MSS.
Hansen MSS.
Hermite MSS.

Jusserand MSS.
Louis MSS.
de Margerie MSS.
de Mouy MSS.
Nisard MSS.
d'Ormesson MSS.
Paléologue MSS.
Pean MSS.
Revoil MSS.
Ribot MSS.
Ring MSS.
Rouvier MSS.
Saint-René-Taillandier
  MSS.
Thiébaut MSS.
Valfrey MSS.

Personal Dossiers

Bapst.
Beau.
Beaucaire.
Berthelot.
Bompard.
Chevalley.
Cogordan.
Conty.

Daeschner.
Defrance.
Delavaud.
Dutasta.
Gavarry.
Herbette (Maurice).
Louis.

de Margerie.
Paléologue.
Piccioni.
Raindre.
Revoil.
Saint-René-Taillandier.
Soulange-Bodin.

Diplomatic Archives, New Series: Political and Commercial Correspondence

'Allemagne' 26, 34, 35, 36, 37, 38, 39, 40, 52.
'Autriche' 32, 33, 34, 35, 36.

'Espagne' 41.
'Grande Bretagne' 12.
'Maroc' 172, 5, 211, 212, 213.
'Russie' 42, 42 *bis*, 45, 641.

Divisions des archives

'Papiers du cabinet' (card file).
'Décrets concernant l'organisation du Ministère des affaires étrangères, 1870–1947'.
'Mémoires et documents', France 31.
'Organisation et réglements du Ministère', 1547–1806.

Other Documents

Séries: Comptabilité: 'Décrets et décisions ministerielles', cartons 44 (1900), 50 (1906), 51 (1907), 53 (1907), 58 (1910), 59 (1910), 61 (1911), 62 (1912), 63 (1912), 64 (1913).
Série: Personnel: 'Lois, ordonnances, décrets et arrêtés', carton 29 (1907).

Direction du personnel

'Affaires étrangères: Textes et projets de réforme antérieurs à 1912', carton 85.
'Commission de réorganisation de la comptabilité et de l'architecture, 1911', carton 86.
'Organisation du Ministère: Décrets, arrêtés, rapports, ordonnances, circulaires, notes, etc., 1860–1896', carton 27.
'Projet de la Réorganization de l'administration centrale, 1899–1900', carton 28.

Archives nationales, Paris

Berteaux MSS.
Deschanel MSS.
Gérard MSS.
Messimy MSS.
de Robien MSS.
Tardieu MSS.
F7: Police général: Interior.
Ministère du commerce et de l'industrie, carton F12, 9288, 'Office national du commerce extérieur'.

Bibliothèque nationale, Paris

Caillaux MSS.
Étienne MSS.
Lavisse MSS.
Millerand MSS.
Poincaré MSS.
Reinach MSS.

Institut de France, Paris

Pichon MSS.
Waldeck-Rousseau MSS.

Archives départementales de la Marne

Bourgeois MSS.

Pas de Calais: Archives départementales

Jonnart MSS.

Aigues-Vives: Maison natale

Doumergue MSS.

Papers in Private Possession

Louis Cambon MSS.
Félix Faure MSS, Fonds Berge.
Millerand MSS.
Notes: Geneviève Tabouis.

UNITED KINGDOM

Private Papers

Bertie MSS, Public Record Office, London.
Chamberlain MSS, University of Birmingham.
Crowe MSS, Public Record Office, London.
Grey MSS, Public Record Office, London.
Hardinge MSS, Cambridge University Library.
Lansdowne MSS, Public Record Office, London.
Nicolson MSS, Public Record Office, London.
Rosebery MSS, National Library of Scotland.
Salisbury MSS, Christ Church Library, Oxford; Hatfield House.

Foreign Office Correspondence: Public Record Office, Kew

FO 99 (Morocco).
FO 368 (commercial correspondence).
FO 369 (consular correspondence).
FO 371 (political correspondence).
FO 425 (confidential print).

GERMANY

Foreign Office, Bonn

'Aktengruppe: Abteilung 1A'.
F. 105 n. 1.
'Französische Staatsmänner', vols. 24, 25, 26, 27, 28, 29, 30.
F. 108.
'Die diplomatische Vertretung Frankreichs im Auslande', vols. 10, 11, 12, 13, 14, 15, 16, 17, 18, 19, 20, 21.

Primary Sources: Published Material

Almanach impérial (Paris, 1805).
Annuaire diplomatique et consulaire (1871–1914).
Archives diplomatiques: Recueil mensuel d'histoire diplomatique et de droit international: Series 1–4 (1861–1914).
GOOCH, G. P., and TEMPERLEY, H. V. (eds.), *British Documents on the Origins of the War, 1898–1914* (London, 1926–38).
Journal officiel, Chambre.
Journal officiel, Sénat.
LEPSIUS, J., MENDELSSOHN BARTHOLDY, A., and THIMME, F. (eds.), *Die Große Politik der europäischen Kabinette, 1871–1914* (Berlin, 1922–7).
MARCHAND, R. (ed.), *Un livre noir: Diplomatie d'advant guerre d'après les documents russes: Novembre* 1910-juillet 1914, 2 vols. (Paris, 1922–2).
Ministère des affaires étrangères (ed.), *Documents diplomatiques français, 1871–1914* (Paris, 1930–53).
State Papers (Britain).

Primary Sources: Newspapers

Le Correspondant.
L'Écho de Paris.
Le Figaro.
Le Gaulois.
L'Intransigeant.
Le Journal.
Le Journal des débats.
La Justice.
Manchester Guardian.

Le Matin.
Le National.
La Petite République.
La Quinzaine coloniale.
La Révolution française.
La Revue des deux mondes.
The Times.
Vu.
Washington Post.

Primary Sources: Memoirs and Autobiographies

AUMALE, J. D', *Voix de l'Orient: Souvenirs d'un diplomate* (Montreal, 1945).
BENOIST, C.,*Souvenirs* (Paris, 1932).
BLUNT, W. S., *My Diaries* (London, 1919).
BOMPARD, M., *Mon ambassade en Russie* (Paris, 1937).
BUCHANAN, G., *My Mission to Russia* (London, 1923).
CAILLAUX, J., *Agadir* (Paris, 1919). *Mes mémoires*, 3 vols. (Paris, 1942–7).
CAMBON, J., *Le Gouvernement-général de l'Algérie, 1891–1897* (Paris, 1918).
CAMBON, P., *Paul Cambon: Correspondance, 1870–1924,* ed. H. Cambon (Paris, 1940–6).
CHAMBRUN, C. DE, *L'Esprit de la diplomatie* (Paris, 1944).
CHARLES-ROUX, F., *Souvenirs diplomatiques d'un age révolu* (Paris, 1956).
DOUMERGUE, G., *Mes causeries avec le peuple de France* (Paris, 1934).
DUMAINE, A., *La Dernière Ambassade de France en Autriche* (Paris, 1921).
——Choses d'Allemagne (Paris, 1925).
——Quelques oubliés de l'autre siècle (Paris, 1931).
EINSTEIN, L., *A Diplomat Looks Back* (New York, 1968).
FARAMOND, Captain, *Souvenirs d'un attaché en Allemagne et Autriche, 1910–1914* (Paris, 1932).
FERRY, A., *Les Carnets secrets d'Abel Ferry* (Paris, 1957).
GÉRARD, A., *Mémoires d'Auguste Gérard* (Paris, 1928).
HOMBERG, O., *Les Coulisses de l'histoire: Souvenirs, 1898–1928* (Paris, 1938).
JUSSERAND, J. J., *What Me Befell* (New York, 1933).
LAROCHE, J., *Quinze ans à Rome avec Camille Barrère (1898–1913)* (Paris, 1948).
——Au Quai d'Orsay avec Briand et Poincaré (Paris, 1957).
LOUIS, G., *Les Carnets de Georges Louis* (Paris, 1926).
PALÉOLOGUE, M., *La Russie des tsars* (Paris, 1922).
——Au Quai d'Orsay à la veille de la tourmente: Journal 1913–1914 (Paris, 1947).
——Three Critical Years, 1904–1906 (New York, 1957).
——My Secret Diary of the Dreyfus Case (1894–1899 (London, 1957).
POINCARÉ, R., *My Memoirs*, 2 vols. (London, 1928).

——*Au service de la France*, 10 vols (Paris, 1926–33).

RANC, A., *Souvenirs: Correspondance* (Paris, 1913).

RODD, R., *Social and Diplomatic Memories* (London, 1923).

SAINTE-AULAIRE, Comte DE, *Confessions d'un vieux diplomate* (Paris, 1953).

Secondary Sources: Books

AGREVAL, B. D', *Les Diplomates français sous Napoléon III* (Paris, 1872).

ALBERTINI, L., *The Origins of the War of 1914*, trans. and ed. I. M. Massey, 3 vols. (London, 1952–7).

ALLAIN, J. C., *Agadir* (Paris, 1978).

——*Joseph Caillaux: Le Défi victorieux* (Paris, 1978).

ANDERSON, E. N., *The First Moroccan Crisis* (Urbana, Ill., 1930).

ANDERSON, M., *Conservative Politics in France* (Oxford, 1974).

ANDERSON, R. D., *France, 1870–1914: Politics and Society* (London, 1977).

ANDREW, C. M., *Théophile Delcassé and the Making of the Entente Cordiale* (London, 1968).

——and KANYA-FORSTNER, A. S. *France Overseas* (London, 1981).

AUFFRAY, B., *Pierre de Margerie, (1861–1942) et la vie diplomatique de son temps* (Paris, 1976)

BAILLOU, J. (ed.), *Les Affaires étrangères et le corps diplomatique*, 2 vols. (Paris, 1984).

BARIÉTY, J., and POIDEVIN, R., *Les Relations franco-allemandes, 1815–1975* (Paris, 1972).

BARTHÉLEMY, J., *Démocratie et politique étrangère* (Paris, 1917).

BECKER, J. J., *Comment les Français sont entrés dans la guerre 1914* (Paris, 1977).

BELLANGER, C., GODECHOT, J., GUIRRAL, P., and TERROU, F., *Histoire générale de la presse française*, iii: *1871–1940* (Paris, 1972).

BERGHAHN, V. R., *Germany and the Approach of War in 1914* (London, 1973).

BLAISDELL, D. C., *European Financial Control in the Ottoman Empire* (New York, 1929).

BLANC, E., *La Jeunesse de Delcassé* (Paris, 1934).

BOURGEOIS, L., *Solidarité* (Paris, 1896).

——*La Société des nations* (Paris, 1911).

BRÉAL, A., *Philippe Berthelot* (Paris, 1937).

BREDIN, J. D., *Joseph Caillaux* (Paris, 1980).

BROGLIE, Duc DE, *Histoire et diplomatie* (Paris, 1888).

BROWN, R. G., *Fashoda Reconsidered: The Impact of Domestic Politics on French Policy in Africa, 1893–1898* (London, 1969).

BRUNSCHWIG, H., *French Colonialism, 1871–1914: Myths and Realities* (London, 1966).

BURKE, E., *Prelude to Protest in Morocco* (Chicago, 1976).

BURY, J. P. T., *Gambetta's Final Years* (London, 1982).

BUSK, D., *The Craft of Diplomacy* (London, 1967).

CAMBON J., *The Diplomatist* (London, 1931).

CAMERON, R. E., *France and the Economic Development of Europe, 1800–1914* (Princeton, NJ, 1961).

CANDELA, R., *The Military Cipher of Commandant Bazeries* (New York, 1938).

CARR, E. H., *Propaganda and International Politics* (New York, 1939).

CARROLL, E. M., *French Public Opinion and Foreign Affairs, 1870–1914* (New York, 1931).

CARTON, E. DE WIART, *Léopold II: Souvenirs des dernières années, 1901–1909* (Brussels, 1944).

CECIL, L., *The German Diplomatic Service, 1871–1914* (Princeton, NJ, 1976).

CHARLE, C., *Les Hauts Fonctionnaires en France au xix siècle* (Paris, 1979).

CHARTON, G., *Guide pour le choix d'un état* (Paris, 1842).

CIPOLLA, C. (ed.), *The Fontana Economic History of Europe* (London, 1973).

COHEN, W. B., *Rulers of Empire* (Stanford, Calif., 1971).

CONTAMINE, H., *La Revanche, 1871–1914* (Paris, 1957).

——*Diplomates et diplomatie sous la Restauration, 1814–1830* (Paris, 1970).

COOKE, J. J., *New French Imperialism, 1880–1910: The Third Republic and Colonial Expansion* (Hamden, Conn., 1973).

CORCE, P. M., DE LA, *The French Army* (London, 1963).

CRAIG, G.A., and GILBERT, F., *The Diplomats* (New York, 1972).

DELAISE, F., *La Guerre qui vient* (Paris, 1911).

DOLLOT, R., *Les Introducteurs des ambassadeurs, 1585–1900* (Paris, 1901).

DUPEUX, G., *La Société française, 1789–1960* (Paris, 1964).

EUBANK, K., *Paul Cambon: Master Diplomatist* (Norman, Okla., 1960).

FAY, S. B., *The Origins of the World War*, 2 vols. (Toronto, 1966).

FEIS, H., *Europe: The World's Banker, 1870–1914* (New Haven, Conn., 1930).

FISCHER, F., *Griff nach der Weltmacht* (Dusseldorf, 1961).

——*Krieg der Illusionen* (Dusseldorf, 1969).

GANIAGE, J., *L'Expansion coloniale de la France sous la Troisième République, 1871–1914* (Paris, 1968).

GIRARDET, R., *L'Idée coloniale en France de 1871 à 1962* (Paris, 1972).

GIRAULT, R., *Emprunts russes et investissements français en Russie, 1887–1914* (Paris, 1973).

GOGUEL, F., *Les Politiques des partis sous la Troisième République, 1906–1914* (Paris, 1946).

GOOCH, G. P., *Recent Revelations in European Diplomacy* (London, 1924).

GRENVILLE, J. A. S., *Lord Salisbury and English Foreign Policy* (London, 1964).

GRIOLET, H., *Le Ministère des affaires étrangères* (Paris, 1900).

GUILLEN, P., *L'Allemagne et le Maroc, 1870–1905* (Paris, 1969).

—— *Les Emprunts marocains, 1902–1904* (Paris, 1974).

HALÉVY, D., *La République des comités* (Paris, 1934).

HALLGARTEN, W., *Imperialismus vor 1914 (Munich, 1951).*

HAMILTON, K., *Bertie of Thame: Edwardian Ambassador* (Woodbridge, 1990).

HANOTAUX, G., *Histoire de la France Contemporaine*, vols. i–iv (Paris, 1898).

HINSLEY, F. (ed.), *British Foreign Policy under Sir Edward Grey* (Cambridge, 1977).

HOHENBERG, P., *A Primer on the Economic History of Europe* (New York, 1968).

HOWARD, J., *Parliament and Foreign Policy in France* (London, 1948).

IIAMS, T. M., *Dreyfus: Diplomatists and the Dual Alliance* (Paris, 1962).

JERROLD, L., *The Real France* (London, 1911).

JOLL, J., *The Origins of the First World War* (London, 1984).

KEIGER, J. F. V., *France and the Origins of the First World War* (London, 1983).

KEMP, T., *Industrialisation in Nineteenth Century Europe* (London, 1968).

—— *The French Economy, 1913–1939* (London, 1972).

KRUMEICH, G., *Armaments and Politics in France on the Eve of the First World War: The Introduction of the Three Year Conscription* (Leamington Spa, 1984).

LANGER, W. G., *The Diplomacy of Imperialism* (New York, 1960).

LAUREN, P. G., *Diplomats and Bureaucrats* (Stanford, Calif., 1976).

LEBOVICS, H., *The Alliance of Iron and Wheat in the Third French Republic, 1860–1914: Origins of the New Conservatism* (London, 1988).

LEGENDRE, P., *Origines et histoire des cabinets de ministres en France* (Geneva, 1975).

LEYRET, H., *Le Président de la République* (Paris, 1973).

LISSAGARAY, P., *Histoire de la Commune de 1871* (Paris, 1896).

LOPPIN, P., *Léon Bourgeois* (Paris, 1964).

MARTET, J., *Clemenceau* (Paris, 1930).

MAYER, A. J., *The Persistence of the Old Regime* (New York, 1981).

MIQUEL, P., *Raymond Poincaré* (Paris, 1961).

MILWARD, A., and SAUL, S. B., *The Economic Development of Continental Europe, 1780–1870* (London, 1973).

MONTEIL, E., *L'Administration de la République* (Paris, 1893).

NÉTON, A., *Delcassé (1852–1923)* (Paris, 1952).

NEWTON, Lord, *Lord Lansdowne* (London, 1929).

NICOLSON, H., *Sir Arthur Nicolson Bart, First Lord Carnock: A Study in the Old Diplomacy* (London, 1948).

NOËL, L., *Camille Barrère* (Bourges, 1948).

OSBORNE, T. R., *A Grande École for the Grands Corps* (Boulder, Col., 1983).

OUTREY, A., *L'Administration française des affaires étrangères* (Paris, 1954).

PARSONS, F. V., *The Origins of the Morocco Question, 1880–1900* (London, 1976).

PICCIONI, C., *Les Premiers Commis des affaires étrangères* (Paris, 1929).

POGNON, H., *Lettre à Monsieur Doumergue au sujet d'une réforme de la Ministère des affaires étrangères* (Paris, 1914).

POIDEVIN, R., *Finance et relations internationales, 1887–1914* (Paris, 1970).

—— *Les Relations économiques et financières entre la France et l'Allemagne de 1898 à 1914* (Paris, 1969).

—— *Histoire générale de l'Europe* (Paris, 1980).

PORCH, D., *The March to the Marne 1871–1914* (Cambridge, 1981).

PORTER, C. W., *The Career of Théophile Delcassé* (Philadelphia, 1936).

RALSTON, D. B., *The Army of the Republic* (Cambridge, Mass., 1967).

REBÉRIOUX, M., *La République radicale: 1899–1914* (Paris, 1975).

RECOULY, R., *Les Heures tragiques de l'avant-guerre* (Paris, 1921).

RENOUVIN, P., *The Immediate Origins of the War* (London, 1928).

RÖHL, J. C. G., *Germany without Bismarck* (London, 1967).

ROLO, P. J. V., *Entente Cordiale* (London, 1969).

SAINT-RENÉ-TAILLANDIER, Madame GEORGE, *Silhouettes d'ambassadeurs* (Paris, 1953).

SCHMITT, B. E., *The Coming of War, 1914*, 2 vols. (New York, 1930).

SCHUMAN, F. L., *War and Diplomacy in the French Republic* (New York, 1931).

SERRES, J., *Manuel pratique de protocole à l'usage des postes diplomatiques et consulaires de France à l'étranger* (Paris, 1950).

—— and WOOD, J. R., *Diplomatic Ceremonial and Protocol* (New York, 1970).

SHARP, W. R. (ed.), *Civil Service Abroad* (New York, 1935).

SIWEK-POUYDESSEAU, J., *Le Corps préfectoral sous la Troisième et la Quatrième République* (Paris, 1969).

SORLIN, P., *La Société française*, i: *1840–1914* (Paris, 1969).

SOULIER, A., *L'Instabilité ministérielle sous la Troisième République* (Paris, 1959).

STEINER, Z., *The Foreign Office and Foreign Policy, 1898–1914* (Cambridge, 1969).

—— *Great Britain and the Origins of the First World War* (London, 1977).

SUAREZ, G., *Aristide Briand* (Paris, 1938).

TABOUIS, G., *Jules Cambon par l'un des siens* (Paris, 1938).

TARDIEU, A., *Le Mystère d'Agadir* (Paris, 1912).

—— *La Conférence d'Algéçiras* (Paris, 1907).

THIERRY, A., *L'Angleterre au temps de Paul Cambon* (Paris, 1961).

THOMSON, D., *Democracy in France since 1870* (Oxford, 1969).

TURNER, L. C. F., *The Origins of the First World War* (London, 1976).

VACHEROT, E., *La Politique extérieure de la République* (Paris, 1881).

VAILLÉ, E., *Le Cabinet noir* (Paris, 1950).

WEBER, E., *The Nationalist Revival in France, 1905–1914* (Los Angeles, 1968).

WILKINSON, R. (ed.), *Governing Elites: Studies in Training and Selection* (New York, 1969).

WILLIAMSON, S. R., *The Politics of Grand Strategy: Britain and France Prepare for War, 1904–1914* (Cambridge, Mass., 1968).

WRIGHT, G., *Raymond Poincaré and the French Presidency* (Los Angeles, 1942).

ZELDIN, T., *France, 1848–1945*, i–iii (Oxford, 1973).

Secondary Sources: Articles

ABRAMS, L. and MILLER D. J., 'Who were the French Colonialists: A Reassessment of the "Parti colonial", 1890–1914', *Historical Journal*, 19 (1976).

ANDREW, C. M., 'Déchiffrement et diplomatie: Le Cabinet noir du Quai d'Orsay sous la Troisième République', *Relations internationales*, 5 (1976).

—— 'German World Policy and the Reshaping of the Dual Alliance', *Journal of Contemporary History*, 1/3 (1960).

—— and Kanya-Forstner, A. S., 'French Business and the French Colonialists', *Historical Journal*, 19 (1974).

—— ——'The French "Colonial party": Its Composition, Aims and Influence, 1885–1914', *Historical Journal*, 14 (1971).

Barrére, C., 'La Chute de Delcassé', *La Revue des deux mondes* (Aug. 1932, Jan. 1933).

Bienvenu-Martin, J. B., 'Mon intérim de chef du gouvernement, 15–29 juillet 1914', *La Revue de France* (15 Aug. 1933).

Cairns, J. C., 'Politics and Foreign Policy: The French Parliament, 1911–1914', *Canadian Historical Review*, 34 (1953).

—— 'International Politics and the Military Mind: The Case of the French Republic', *Journal of Modern History* (Sept. 1953).

Castellan, G., 'Les États balkaniques, 1895–1914', *Revue Historique*, 152 (1926).

Charles-Roux, E., 'L'Oeuvre diplomatique de Camille Barrère', *La Revue des deux mondes* (1941).

Clarétie, J., 'Journal', *La Revue des deux mondes* (Nov. 1949).

Claudel, P., 'Phillipe Berthelot', *Bulletin de la Société Paul Claudel*, 28 (1967).

Cooper, M.B., 'British Policy in the Balkans 1908–9', *Historical Journal*, 7 (1964–5).

Corbin, C., 'Berthelot en 1914', *Bulletin de la Société Paul Claudel*, 28 (1967).

Edwards, E. W., 'The Franco-German Agreement on Morocco, 1909', *English Historical Review*, 81 (1963).

Fulton, L. B., 'France and the End of the Ottoman Empire', in M. Kent (ed.), *The Great Powers and the End of the Ottoman Empire* (London, 1984).

Girault, R., 'Pour un portrait nouveau de l'homme d'affaires français vers 1914', *Revue d'histoire moderne*, 16 (1969).

Gordon, M. R., 'Domestic Conflict and the Origins of the First World War: The British and German Cases', *Journal of Modern History*, 46 (1974).

Guillen, P., 'Les Questions coloniales dans les relations Franco-Allemandes à la veille de la Première Guerre mondiale', *Revue historique*, 248 (1972).

—— 'Les Emprunts marocains, 1902–1904', *Revue historique* (1963).

—— 'Les Accords coloniaux franco-anglais de 1904 et la naissance de l'Entente cordiale', *Revue d'histoire diplomatique* (Oct.-Dec. 1968).

Hamilton, K. A., 'An Attempt to Form an Anglo-French "Industrial Entente"', *Middle Eastern Studies*, 11 (1975).

—— 'The Air in Entente Diplomacy: Great Britain and the International Aerial Navigation Conference of 1910', *International History Review*, 3/2 (Apr. 1981).

—— 'Great Britain, France, and the Origins of the Mediterranean Agreements of 16 May 1907', in B. J. C. McKercher and D. J. Moss (eds.), *Shadow and Substance in British Foreign Policy, 1895–1929: Memorial Essays Honouring C. J. Lowe* (Edmonton, 1984).

—— 'The "Wild Talk" of Joseph Caillaux: A Sequel to the Agadir Crisis', *International History Review*, 9/2 (May 1987).

Hayne, M. B., 'The Quai d'Orsay and Influences on the Formulation of French

Foreign Policy, 1898–1914', *French History*, 2/4 (1988).

—— 'Great Britain, the Albanian Question and the Concert of Europe, 1911–14', *Balkan Studies*, 28/2 (1987).

—— 'The Quai d'Orsay and the Formation of French Foreign Policy in Historical Context', in R. Aldrich, and J. Connell, J. (eds.), *France in World Politics* (London 1989).

—— 'Change and Continuity in the Structure and Practices of the Quai d'Orsay 1871–1898', *Australian Journal of Politics and History*, 37/1 (1991).

ISAAC, J., 'Observations complémentaires sur les Documents français', *Revue d'histoire de la Guerre mondiale* (Jan. 1937).

JEANNENEY, J. N., 'Finances, presse and politique: L'Affaire de la Banque industrielle de Chine, 1921–1923', *Revue historique*, 251 (1975).

JOLL, J., 'Politicians and the Freedom to Choose: The Case of July 1914', in A. Ryan (ed.), *The Idea of Freedom: Essays in Honour of Isaiah Berlin* (Oxford, 1979).

KURGAN-VAN-HENTENRYK, G., 'Philippe Berthelot et les intérêts ferroviaires franco-belges en Chine, 1912–1914', *Revue d'histoire moderne et contemporaine*, 22 (1975).

LANGLOIS-BERTHELOT, D., 'Philippe Berthelot, 1886–1934', *La Revue de deux mondes* (June 1976).

LEAMAN, B. R., 'The Influence of Domestic Policy on Foreign Affairs in France, 1898–1905', *Journal of Modern History*, 14 (1942).

MADOL, H., 'Qui a voulu la guerre?', *Vu*, 261 (15 Mar. 1933).

MITCHELL, A., 'A Situation of Inferiority: France's Military Organisation after the Defeat of 1870', *American Historical Review*, 86 (1981).

NEWELL, W., 'The Agricultural Revolution in Nineteenth Century France', *Journal of Economic History*, 33/4 (1973).

OUTREY, A., 'L'Histoire et principes de l'administration française des affaires étrangères', *Revue française de science politique*, (1953).

PERSELL, S. M., 'Joseph Chailley-Bert and the Importance of the Union coloniale-française', *Historical Journal*, 17 (1974).

PHELPS, D., 'La France et la Crise Liman von Sanders', *Revue d'histoire de la Guerre mondiale* (Jan. 1937).

RENOUVIN, P., 'La Politique française en juillet 1914 d'après les Documents diplomatiques français', *Revue d'histoire de la Guerre mondiale* (Jan. 1937).

—— 'Les Relations franco-allemandes de 1871 à 1914: Esquisse d'un programme de recherches', in A. O. Sarkissian (ed.), *Studies in Diplomatic History* (London, 1961).

RENZI, W. A., 'Who Composed "Sazonov's Thirteen Points": A Re-examination of Russia's War Aims of 1914', *American Historical Review*, 88/2 (Apr. 1983).

SAINT-RENÉ-TAILLANDIER, Madame, 'Avant le sacerdoce: Le Vicomte Chaptal diplomate', *La Revue des deux mondes* (1943).

SCHMITT, B., 'The Relation of Public Opinion and Foreign Affairs before and during the First World War', in A. O. Sarkissian (ed.), *Studies in Diplomatic History* (London, 1961).

SMITH, E. G., 'An Ambassador of the Republic of Letters', *Blackwood's Edinburgh Magazine*, 176 (1904).

SUMLER, D. E., 'Domestic Influences on the Nationalist Revival in France, 1909–1914', *French Historical Studies*, 6/4 (1969).

THOBIE, J., 'Finance et politique: Le Refus en France de l'emprunt ottoman 1910', *Revue historique*, 235 (1966).

TITTONI, T., 'Visiti ad ambasciatori', *Nuova antologia*, 108/4 (1903).

WATSON, D.R., 'The Making of French Foreign Policy during the First Clemenceau Ministry, 1906–9', *English Historical Review*, 86 (1971).

Secondary Sources: Unpublished Theses

ABRAMS, L., 'French Economic Penetration of Morocco, 1906–1914: The Economic Bases of Imperialist Expansion' (Columbia University, 1977).

CHAPMAN, G. W., 'The Decision for War: The Domestic Political Context of French Diplomacy, 1911–1914' (Princeton University, 1971).

DONNELLY, A. L., 'France and the Society of Nations' (Trinity College, 1980).

HALFOND, I., 'Maurice Paléologue: the Diplomatist, The Writer, the Man' (Temple University, 1974).

HAUSE, S. C., 'Théophile Delcassé's First Years at the Quai d'Orsay: French Diplomacy between Britain and Germany, 1898–1901', (Washington University, 1969).

KEIGER, J. F. V., 'Raymond Poincaré and French Foreign Policy, 1912–1914', (Cambridge University, 1980).

KREIS, G., 'Frankreichs republikanische Großmachtpolitik, 1870–1914', (Basle University, 1980).

KRUMEICH, G., 'Aufrustung und Innenpolitik in Frankreich vor dem Ersten Weltkrieg: Die Einführung der Dreijahrigen Dienstpflicht, 1913–1914' (Wiesbaden, 1980).

MACDONALD, J. F., 'Camille Barrère and the Conduct of Delcassian Diplomacy, 1898–1902' (University of California, 1969).

MILLER, D. J., 'Stephen Pichon and the Making of French Foreign Policy' (Cambridge University, 1976).

OSBORNE, T. R., 'The Recruitment of the Administrative Elite in the Third French Republic, 1870–1905' (Connecticut University, 1974).

PRESTWICH, P. E., 'French Attitudes towards Britain, 1911–1914' (Stanford University, 1973).

RUST, M. J., 'Business and Politics in the Third Republic: The Comité des forges and the French Steel Industry, 1896–1914', (Princeton University, 1973).

SUMLER, D., 'Polarisation in French Politics, 1909–1914' (Princeton University, 1969).

WALKER, J. R., 'The Comité de l'Afrique française, 1890–1895: A French Colonial Pressure Group' (University of California, 1977).

WEINER, R. I., 'Paul Cambon and the Making of the Entente Cordiale' (Rutgers University, 1973).

WILEY, E. V., 'Jean Jules Jusserand and the First Moroccan Crisis, 1903–1906' (University of Pennsylvania, 1959).

INDEX

DATE DUE

2014 -12- 0 6			